THE
DISORDER
OF THINGS

THE
DISORDER
OF THINGS

A Foucauldian Approach to the Work of Nuruddin Farah

JOHN MASTERSON

WITS UNIVERSITY PRESS

Published in South Africa by:

Wits University Press
1 Jan Smuts Avenue
Johannesburg

www.witspress.co.za

Copyright © John Masterson 2013

First published 2013

ISBN 978-1-86814-570-6 (print)
ISBN 978-1-86814-587-4 (digital)

Cover images:
Portrait of Nuruddin Farah (Photograph by George Hallett)
Portrait of French philosopher Michel Foucault in Paris, France in February 1977.
(Photo by Francoise VIARD/Gamma-Rapho via Getty Images)
Cover design by Hothouse South Africa
Design and typesetting by Orchard Publishing
Edited by Louise Banks
Printed and bound by Creda Communications

For my mother, Liz,
and in memory of my father, Eddie

Contents

Acknowledgements

*T*HE *DISORDER OF THINGS* BUILDS ON WORK CARRIED OUT FOR A PHD AT the University of Essex. I would not have been able to undertake this without the funding support of The States of Jersey's Department of Education, Sport and Culture. I remain grateful to them for allowing me to extend my studies and hope that future generations of students will continue to benefit from such investment. I would like to thank Angela Smith, who was an inspirational mentor to me during an MPhil year at the University of Stirling. Angela introduced me to Farah's work. As such, she played a decisive role at a formative stage of this project. In the years that have followed, Angela has continued to be a source of great support. I must thank my colleagues and friends in the Department of Literature, Film and Theatre Studies at the University of Essex. The late Joe Allard, Sanja Bahun, Emily Barker, James Canton, Clare Finburgh, Maria Cristina Fumagalli, Esther Kober, Wendy McMahon, the late David Musselwhite, Ildiko Olah, Owen Robinson, Phil Terry, Jane Thorp, Jonathan White and Penny Woollard, in particular, offered me great personal and professional guidance. I reserve special thanks for my supervisor, Peter Hulme. My decision to return to Essex was, in large part, motivated by the desire to work with Peter. Throughout my studies, he always provided considered advice whilst allowing me to pursue my own research interests. The working relationship between any student and their supervisor is critical and I am fortunate to have enjoyed such a productive one with Peter.

As I discuss throughout the book, *The Disorder of Things* was galvanised by my relocation to South Africa in 2010. I owe a particular debt of gratitude to colleagues in the Department of English at the University of the Witwatersrand, Johannesburg. Michelle Adler, Gerald Gaylard, Victor Houliston, Sofia Kostelac, Kirby Mania, Robert Muponde, Denise Newfield, the late Arlene Oseman, Chris Thurman, Tim Trengove-Jones and Merle Williams have all been incredibly supportive. I feel the benefits of their collegiality, professionalism and friendship on a daily basis. Michael Titlestad has been much more than a 'line manager' and I owe him a particular debt of gratitude. He allowed me to buy-out some of my teaching in 2012 so that I could complete this book project. On a personal and professional level, I thank him warmly. Antonette Gouws, Libby Meintjes, Moipone Ndala and Delia Rossouw of the School of Literature, Language and Media have also been very supportive.

At Wits University Press, Roshan Cader, Veronica Klipp, Tsitsi Makina and Tshepo Neito have been thoroughly patient and professional. Louise Banks has offered wonderful editorial advice and I remain extremely grateful to her. Special thanks also go to Julie Miller. Julie believed in this project when few others did. I applaud and appreciate her persistence. I am also grateful for the insights offered by anonymous peer-reviewers. *The Disorder of Things* is much richer for their comments. I must offer particular thanks to my friend and colleague Ashlee Neser. Ashlee read sections of the manuscript in the lead-up to publication, offering always considered and constructive feedback. I have no doubt the book is stronger because of this. I am grateful to Cambridge Scholars Publishing and Rodopi for granting me permission to feature versions of chapters that originally appeared in their publications. The previous incarnations of what is now Chapter 7, 'Bringing It All Back Home: Theorising Diaspora and War in *Yesterday, Tomorrow* and *Links*', were published as 'Borders Immaterial? Recent Developments in the Work of Nuruddin Farah,' in Baker, C. & Norridge, Z. (Eds.). 2007. *Crossing Places: New Research in African Studies* (Newcastle: Cambridge Scholars Press, 2007), pp. 88–100 and 'A Post-mortem on the Postmodern? Conflict and Corporeality in Nuruddin Farah's *Links*' in Makokha, JKS. & Wawrzinek, J. (Eds). *Negotiating Afropolitanism: Essays on Borders and Spaces in Contemporary African Literature and Folklore* (Amsterdam: Rodopi, 2011), pp. 141–162.

My friends and family have and continue to put up with the good, the bad and the ugly from me. Whilst words fall short, this book would simply not have been possible were they not the people they are. It is my privilege to count Lee and Natalie Tatum amongst my best friends. I do not think I could ever repay the kindness and care they have shown me. As this book came into being, so too did Esme and Zac Tatum. They bring great joy into my life and, whilst thousands of miles separate us, they have and will always have a special place in my heart. For their support and compassion through it all, I must also thank Alan and Jill Clarke as well as Brian and Mandy Masheter. For reminding me what friendship is all about, my appreciation goes out to Robert Ball, Andrew Cook, Neil Corbel, Declan Cullinan, Anmol Kalsi, Joel Martins, Paul Martins, David McLoughlin, Ian Simpson, Simon Suleman and David Wooton, amongst many others. To the Sanchez and Italian crews in South Africa, thank you for making me feel at home away from home.

Anna Masheter was a source of great support and strength throughout the initial stages of this project. Whilst the thank you comes late, I remain truly grateful to her. Similarly, Kate Powis was incredibly positive about this study from the moment we first discussed it. I thank her for her care and compassion. I must also take this opportunity to express my gratitude to Alan Jones and Michael Wood. Whilst it took me years to call him by his first name, Alan is largely responsible for putting me on this literary path. For good or ill, *The Disorder of Things* is the result. Michael is a dear friend as well as being a source of musical inspiration. To him as well as Isobel, Gerald and Philip Wood, I owe particular thanks.

Lastly, my love and gratitude go to my family. To Kathleen Masterson, Stuart and Marlyn Somers, Graham and Dorothy Somers, Archie and Nan Somers: you have helped and inspired me in so many ways. Thank you for being you.

My father, Eddie, passed away before this book found its way into the world. I dedicate *The Disorder of Things* to him. To my mother, Liz, I offer it as a token of my love and appreciation.

The Principal Works of Nuruddin Farah as Referred to in *The Disorder of Things*

A Naked Needle. 1976. London: Heinemann African Writers Series.

From a Crooked Rib. 1970. London: Heinemann African Writers Series.

Sweet and Sour Milk (*S&SM*). 1992 [1979]. Minnesota: Graywolf Press.

Sardines (*S*). 1982 [1981]. Oxford: Heinemann African Writers Series.

Close Sesame (*CS*). 1992 [1983]. Minnesota: Graywolf Press.

Maps (*M*). 1986. New York & London: Penguin.

Gifts (*G*). 1992. New York & London: Penguin.

Secrets (*Sec*). 1998. New York & London: Penguin.

Yesterday, Tomorrow: Voices from the Somali Diaspora (*YT*). London & New York: Cassell.

Links (*L*). 2004. New York: Riverhead Books.

Knots (*K*). 2007. New York: Riverhead Books.

Crossbones. 2011. New York: Riverhead Books.

1

Taking On Foucault and Fleshing Out Farah: Opportunities for Dialogue and Reflections on Method

For myself, I prefer to utilise the writers I like. The only valid tribute to thought such as Nietzsche's is precisely to use it, to deform it, to make it groan and protest.

(Michel Foucault – 'Prison Talk', 1980: 53–54)

I wrote *The Offering* for the University of Essex, for my M.A. thesis … on the day I was to submit it I had a conflict, an open, theatrical clash with one of my lecturers, and I used bad language, or she used bad language. And then I walked out and never went back to collect the degree.

(Nuruddin Farah – 'How Can We Talk of Democracy?', 2002a: 40)

University libraries are like madhouses, full of people pursuing wraiths, hunches, obsessions. The person with whom you spend most of your time is the person you're writing about. Some people write about schools, groups of artists, historical trends or political tendencies … but usually one central figure emerges.

(Patricia Duncker – Hallucinating Foucault, 1997: 4–5)

O N RARE OCCASIONS, YOU STUMBLE ACROSS A TEXT THAT MAKES YOU smile and wince at the same time. Such was my experience with Patricia Duncker's debut novel. Her anonymous student protagonist obsesses over and finally locates errant author Paul Michel in a provincial French asylum. He subsequently helps him escape, sleeps with him and, various twists of fate later, attends his funeral. Beyond its intrigues of plot and character, Duncker's novel succeeds in representing the problematic, because human, aspect of research. Before his meeting with Paul Michel, her protagonist has only a tepid passion for academic investigation. It is only when researcher and researched collide that he feels his work truly begins to 'mean' anything. When the scholar uncovers previously confidential correspondence between his author and namesake Michel Foucault, the analogy between university library and madhouse appears even starker: 'Paul Michel was a novelist and Foucault was a philosopher, but there were uncanny links between them' (Duncker 1997: 6). In the final reckoning, Paul Michel explains how the young scholar might achieve a healthier balance in life, within the university and beyond: 'I make the same demands of people and fictional texts, petit – that they should be open-ended, carry within them the possibility of being and of changing whoever it is they encounter' (Duncker 1997: 111).

In my case, the truth has not been quite as strange as fiction. The long shadow cast by Foucault throughout Duncker's novel has, however, had a similarly profound effect on my writing and thinking. Without much by way of gentle introduction, the first lecture I attended as an undergraduate at the University of Essex began with a reading of the striking description that opens *Discipline and Punish*. Forced to imagine Damiens' dismembered body, as I also struggled to deal with novice nerves, induced a queasiness I took to be synonymous with university life. Whilst I cannot recall the rest of the lecture, this graphic depiction had a marked impact. Years later, and in a different academic setting, a similar feeling set in after reading visceral descriptions of menstruation, as well as sexual and political violence in Nuruddin Farah's *Maps*. From this experience, an interest in forging the 'uncanny links' identified by Duncker's narrator was born. I began hallucinating Foucault once more and, on discovering the Somali author had spent a period as a graduate student at my old institution, an eerie inevitability began to charge the dialogic impulse behind this book. With a view to pushing beyond the personal, however, this introduction indicates how I intend to avoid the maddening pitfalls of Duncker's imagined reader.

Whilst the remainder of this chapter provides a discursive foundation for the study as a whole, particularly in terms of why I believe Foucault's work offers an enabling lens through which to view Farah's, I begin by introducing the Somali writer. This also allows me to establish what this book is not. In no sense is *The Disorder of Things* a literary biography. Whilst Farah is a subject worthy of such an endeavour, I make no claims to it here. In establishing a platform for what follows, however, I suggest that the peculiarities of Farah's own narrative, particularly the manner in which he has negotiated his own exile from Somalia as well as a series of transnational wanderings, necessarily informs his oeuvre.

Locating Farah

Born on 24 November 1945 in Baidoa, a southern Somali city then under Italian control, Nuruddin Farah's story was entangled with the contested national narrative from a young age. In 1947, his family moved to Kallafo in the Ogaden region, soon to be ceded to Ethiopia by the British. As I discuss below, Farah's most critically and commercially acclaimed novel, *Maps* (1986), is set against the backdrop of the Ogaden War (1977–1978) between Somalia and Ethiopia. Following an earlier conflict in the region after Independence in 1960, Farah's family was compelled to move to the capital, Mogadiscio[1]. To a significant degree, therefore, the constant dislocations and relocations that defined this formative period have had a profound impact on his literary vision. As I argue throughout this book, Farah's obsession with disputed borders, whether cartographic or conceptual, derives from intimately personal and intensely political contexts. Similarly, whilst adept in various genres and languages, it is arguably the complex notion of being 'at home' that casts the longest shadow over Farah's own story and, by extension, his fictional and non-fictional work. After receiving his BA in Literature and Philosophy from Punjab University, India in 1969, Farah returned to his native Somalia following the military coup that brought Siyad Barre to power. It was during his time teaching at the National University of Somalia, as well as in some of Mogadiscio's secondary schools, that Farah published his first novel, *From a Crooked Rib* (1970). Focusing on the trials and tribulations of a stoic female protagonist Ebla, who moves from rural village to the metropolis, the text establishes some of the enduring political and ethical concerns that have preoccupied Farah throughout his career of more than forty years. If this initiated his attempt to speak the truth to power, in the Saidian sense, his literary activities in the mid – to late seventies would see him fall foul of Barre's regime and its censors.

Following the suspension of his Somali-language novel *Tallow Waa Telee Ma*, which was serialised in a national newspaper in 1973, Farah was awarded a UNESCO grant to pursue his postgraduate studies. He left for England the following year, establishing a temporary intellectual home at Essex. His departure from Somalia would prove pivotal in more ways than one. In 1976, Farah published his second English language novel, *A Naked Needle*. A satirical, if sobering portrait of an increasingly authoritarian society, the book inevitably met with the disapproval of Barre's regime. Following a fortuitous phone call home to his brother, who warned him of the controversy stirred by *A Naked Needle*, Farah avoided a return to incarceration or worse. That this conversation took place whilst he was in Rome, en route to Somalia, is significant. Farah would effectively remain in transit for much of his life, not returning to Somalia until 1996. Whilst Farah has frequently reflected on the personal toll exacted by such a separation, he has also suggested that this distance allows him to be more productive as well as refining his writerly and political vision. In 'A Country in Exile', for instance, he maintains that '[a]lthough one often links a person in exile to a faraway locality, the fact is I felt more joined to my writing than to any country with a specific territoriality' (Farah 1992: 5). It is therefore notable that, whilst his novels regularly feature protagonists whose routes take in former colonial centres, whether British or Italian, or neo-colonial hubs such as the United States or Canada, his fictions remain rooted, however precariously, in Somalia's contested soil. Farah's oft-cited comment to this effect ('I have tried to keep my country alive by writing about it') is once more resonant in both intimately personal and intensely political terms, particularly when considered in relation to Somalia's turbulent postcolonial narrative. A fascination with the ways in which this personal/political dialectic is negotiated throughout Farah's writing informs much of what follows.

The eighties saw Farah living and working in locations as diverse as Los Angeles and Khartoum, Bayreuth and Kampala. It was also a time of great literary productivity. Following an appointment as Visiting Reader at the University of Jos, Nigeria, Farah continued his itinerant journey across Africa, moving to Gambia in 1984 and then to Sudan following the publication of *Maps*. In the early nineties, during a spell teaching at Makerere University in Uganda, Farah once again fell foul of the political powers-that-be. After the Swedish-language publication of *Gavor* (*Gifts*) in 1990, Farah resigned his position following criticism by President Museveni. If this got the decade off to a rather inauspicious start, 1991 was a year of watershed moments. Whilst Farah collected the Tucholsky Literary Award in Stockholm, it was

Siyad Barre's fall from power that had the most significant impact on his life and work. In the post-Barre power vacuum, uncertainty about Somalia's political future mounted, culminating in the failed U.S.-led intervention Operation Restore Hope. America's military misadventures in the Horn of Africa would provide the backdrop for Farah's first, post-9/11 novel, *Links* (2004). As helicopters burned and bodies were beaten in Mogadiscio, Farah found comparative stability in Nigeria following the birth of a daughter and a son. After spells in other parts of the continent and beyond, one of his next journeys would prove particularly decisive. Following Barre's death in Abuja in 1995, Farah returned to Somalia after 22 years in exile. An emotional homecoming, the 1996 trip allowed him to witness firsthand how much his country had changed and its people had suffered since his own departure in the seventies. These experiences fed into the writing and publication of *Secrets*, the final instalment of the *Blood in the Sun* trilogy that began with *Maps*. After years of uprooting, Farah and his family settled in Cape Town in 1999.

Whilst my own journeys have been freely willed and much more modest in comparison with Farah's, I use the concluding section of this study to reflect on how a meeting with him in Cape Town in 2011 galvanised this project anew. Following my relocation to South Africa in 2010, questions of home, roots and routes have assumed particular burdens of significance, both personally and professionally. In its own, necessarily 'unhomely' way, Farah's work continues to have a resonant power. What I will argue throughout this book, however, is that it is the manner in which he marries the intimately personal with the intensely political that distinguishes his finest writing. If this can be seen to both pass comment on and reflect the various ruptures that have defined his own narrative as well as that of Somalia, I explore how and why it is underpinned by an enduring set of ethical and political convictions. Having offered a contextual overview of Farah's own narrative, marked as it has been by locations, dislocations and relocations, the remainder of this introduction explores why a discursive marriage between his work and that of Michel Foucault is so enabling.

Why Farah? Why Foucault? Why Now?

Throughout this contrapuntal study, I explore how Foucault's reflections on power, body, resistance, disciplinary institutions and biopower might be seen in productive conjunction with some of the most urgent concerns of Farah's oeuvre. These preoccupations have endured since *From a Crooked Rib* to *Crossbones*, a text that appeared in South Africa in 2012. Whilst my analytical approach builds on the idea that there are a series of 'uncanny links' between their respective projects, it is important to foreground the book's commitment to investigating sites of potential convergence and divergence. In what follows, therefore, I focus on some of the key theoretical coordinates of the study as a whole. I consider how pioneers working in predominantly postcolonial and feminist fields have readily accepted the challenge to salvage rather than savage Foucault for their own ends. The lessons taken from their work are salutary, inspiring me too to make Foucault groan and protest in what, at first sight, may seem unfamiliar settings. As I claim throughout this book, many of the 'open-ended' qualities that characterise Foucault's speculations are analogous with Farah's work. Whilst the latter has been the subject of fine single-author studies and critical compendiums, *The Disorder of Things* strives for something different. For a writer who is often spoken about in the same breath as Chinua Achebe, Gabriel García Márquez and Salman Rushdie, Farah warrants the same theoretically substantive engagement afforded to them. My contention, therefore, is that the at-once ethical and political imperatives underpinning Farah's writing, fictional and non-fictional, invite his readers to situate it within more interdisciplinary, Foucauldian-inflected frameworks.

As such, my approach, here and throughout *The Disorder of Things*, takes its lead from Sam Binkley's sense of multiple Foucaults: '[h]ave changing times required that we discard our old Foucaults and invent new ones, or are there parts we can save, parts we should revise, or previously neglected parts we should draw to the fore and emphasize?' (Binkley 2010: xi). Building on this, I argue that both Farah's fictive and Foucault's discursive concerns morph and evolve as they shift from one key text to another. As such, Foucault's more identifiably 'literary' concerns, such as the 'death of the author', are less significant for the purposes of this study than his privileging of particular sites, spaces and discourses concerning discipline and power. Whilst, particularly when it comes to engaging with Farah's *Blood in the Sun* trilogy (comprising *Maps*, *Gifts* and *Secrets*), I consider contentious issues of authorship, its premature or otherwise demise and readerly responsibility, the analyses that follow are inspired by Foucault in a broader sense. This is the figure whose interventions and legacy have proved critical catalysts for writers and thinkers as diverse as Edward Said and Ann Laura Stoler, V.Y. Mudimbe and Alexander Butchart, to name only a few of those who inform this discussion. My primary interest, therefore, lies in exploring the extent to which the comparative reader can map certain key developments within Farah's oeuvre in relation to similarly key negotiations in Foucault's thinking and writing. When it comes to examining Farah's first trilogy, *Variations on the Theme of an African Dictatorship* (1979–1983), for instance, I suggest how its claustrophobic, quasi-Orwellian portrait of life under autocratic rule can usefully be read in light of early Foucauldian interventions. In drawing on *Discipline and Punish* and *Madness and Civilization* in particular, I argue that an awareness of Farah and Foucault's respective concerns with the use and abuse of power within what can be seen as carceral societies need not result in an airbrushing of contextual or other crucial differences. As my engagement with a range of secondary sources suggests, the manifest blind spots that, for many, blight Foucault's vision have not prevented succeeding generations of scholars, in fields as diverse as anthropology and the medical humanities, from engaging with and taking his work in provocative new directions. At the outset, therefore, I suggest the success, or otherwise, of this book can be judged by how effectively it operates in such a discursive spirit.

If carceral concerns haunt Farah's first trilogy, I consider the ways in which a reading of his second might be enlivened by reflecting on the shift away from predominantly spatial and disciplinary preoccupations in Foucault's early work to those of biopolitics and normalisation. I maintain that similar negotiations, away from the carceral and towards the bio-political, take place as readers cross from Farah's *Variations* to his *Blood in the Sun* cycles. The in-depth discussion of opening instalment *Maps* provides a case in point. Whilst the novel's dramatic action centres on what will become Somalia's defeat in the Ogaden War with Ethiopia over disputed geo-political boundaries, it is just as preoccupied with the ways in which the conflict is both conceived and fought in terms of an equally contentious series of bio-political lines. Accordingly, I draw on Foucault's *The History of Sexuality* as well as his provocative lecture series '*Society Must Be Defended*'. I use them to argue that this shift away from a concern with the use and abuse of sovereign power as well as its protection to a position where the governing dictum for Foucault 'consists in making live and letting die' provides a compelling way to approach *Maps* as well as to consider the key reorientations, in terms of thematic and political focus, that take place between Farah's first and second trilogies (Foucault 2003: 247). My analyses of *Gifts* (1992) and *Secrets* (1998) are also filtered through bio-political prisms.

In *Gifts*, omnipertinent debates concerning the complexities and complicities of international aid are set against a backdrop of famine. Accordingly, I explore how and why a host of Foucauldian speculations, from those taxonomies of individual and collective bodies upon which international fiscal and other policies are based, to discourses of normalisation and the treatment of those designated as 'bare life' within certain humanitarian situations, have inspired scholars working in fields such as development and post-development studies. Moving on from the novelistic exploration of war, its escalation and fallout in *Maps*, to that of famine, international aid and cycles of dependency in *Gifts*, *Secrets* provides a fitting conclusion to *Blood in the Sun* for the comparative reader. At one of its many narrative levels, *Secrets* functions as a continuation as well as an intensification of what has taken place in the two earlier instalments. Once again, it focuses on those scars that mark the Somali body politic as the demise of Barre's regime precepitates a brutal civil war. Whilst this in itself invites a bio-political reading, it is Farah's decision to pursue a transnational AIDS narrative alongside that of domestic atrophy that is most intriguing. I argue that a more substantial engagement with the novel can result from considering Foucault's later work and the ways its legacy has been employed by others. One of the central thrusts of this book, therefore, is that the opening up and out of Farah's preoccupations, from what at times appears to be a hermetically sealed Somali narrative to a position where this very national thread is viewed in terms of a much more entangled, confused and often confusing (dis)order of things, finds a discursive counterpart in Foucault's work as well as the ways in which it has been negotiated.

Building on this, the final section of *The Disorder of Things* considers how and why the notion of 'entanglement' is increasingly useful when it comes to engaging with Farah's more recent work. This includes his journalistic study, *Yesterday, Tomorrow: Voices from the Somali Diaspora* (2000) as well as the recently completed *Past Imperfect* trilogy, comprising the aptly titled *Links* (2004), *Knots* (2007) and *Crossbones* (2012). In this section, I am more concerned with showing how and why Foucault's work has been put to use in a globalised context, framed by everything from an ongoing 'War on Terror' to the global credit crunch. If the following survey and analyses of earlier novels draws from figures such as Edward Said, Jana Sawicki and Ann Laura Stoler, all of whom rise to the Foucauldian challenge of revisioning his work for their own ends, these later chapters refer to the critical interventions of Giorgio Agamben, Judith Butler and Slavoj Zizek, amongst others, to explore how and why they too carry Foucault's legacy into our twenty-first century. It is an era in which debates concerning national sovereignty, patterns of transnational migration, networks of international terrorism and the processes by which they are monitored have emerged as the defining issues of our time. Whether it be his study of Somali refugees, his fictional exploration of Operation Restore Hope and its aftermath or his counter-hegemonic representation of piracy, Farah provides alternative narratives in order to promote alternative perspectives.

In light of the above, I suggest that Farah's work in the roughly ten-year period from *Yesterday, Tomorrow* to *Crossbones* synthesises many of the preoccupations of the *Variations* and *Blood in the Sun* trilogies. Whether in journalistic or novelistic form, Farah offers a sustained exploration of the significant ways in which carceral and bio-political paradigms and practices have fused. It is on this globalised stage that the (dis)order of things plays itself out. As some of the most pioneering, Foucauldian-inspired scholarship has demonstrated, a concern with the various intersections of sovereign power and disciplinary societies, as well as bio-political discourses and norms, frames the agendas and practices of everyone from politicians to media providers. These and associated preoccupations cast a significant shadow over Farah's latest work. They also correspond with something that has motivated his authorial career from the outset. This is the sense that that which appears specific to one geo-political space is in fact entangled in much more complex, often complicit and confusing, networks of power, genealogy and vested interests. As Farah emphasises at strategic points throughout his fiction, if this was the case during Somalia's peculiarly intense experience of colonisation, so it remains in the globalised present.

As I illustrate in the remainder of this introduction, the almost all-engrossing Eurocentrism of Foucault's work has been singled out and seized upon by a host of commentators. Yet, staying true to the generosity of discursive spirit that imbues many of his own pronouncements on his thought and its potential legacy, these critical voices have transposed its significance onto much broader geo-political and epistemological maps. This same impulse, I argue, has informed and continues to inform much of Farah's most stimulating writing. My closing speculations, therefore, imagine what directions his work might take next. This in turn provides a final opportunity to consider how and why more substantial engagements with Farah's oeuvre might be inspired by the kind of rich, endlessly stimulating discourse that has grown up around Foucault and of which *The Disorder of Things* is a direct product. It is to the 'uncanny links' between them that I now turn.

Spectres of Foucault: To Savage or Salvage?

If Foucault has captivated the imagination of innumerable scholars, Nietzsche had a similar effect on him. As James Miller maintains in *The Passion of Michel Foucault*, the 'will to know' impulse was to prove formative in Foucault's intellectual development:

> Philosophers, Nietzsche had written ... 'must no longer accept concepts as a gift, not merely purify and polish them, but first make and create them, present them and make them convincing. Hitherto one has generally trusted one's concepts as if they were a wonderful dowry from some sort of wonderland.' But this trust must be replaced by mistrust: 'What is needed above all ... is an absolute skepticism toward all concepts.' Hence 'critique'. (Miller 2000: 303)

As my opening epigraph suggests, the highest tribute that can be paid to any 'founder of discursivity' is to listen to how and why their thought comes down to us through time, bidding us to make it groan and protest so that it might echo anew. Similarly provocative, in terms of the contrapuntal motivations behind *The Disorder of Things*, is an interview in which Foucault invites us to carry on and contest his interventions long after he is gone:

> A book is made to serve ends not defined by the one who wrote it ... All my books ... are, if you like, little tool boxes. If people want to open them, use a particular sentence, idea or analysis like a screwdriver or wrench in order to short-circuit, disqualify or break up systems of power, including the very ones from which my books have issued... well, all the better! (Foucault 1996: 149)

It is in such a deconstructive spirit that Laura Ann Stoler has taken up her predecessor's challenge. Her work thus enables a wider reflection on how Foucault has been reformed and reapplied within areas of postcolonial and/or feminist study, as evidenced by Jana Sawicki's *Disciplining Foucault: Feminism, Power and the Body* (1991), amongst many others. A closer consideration of it establishes the theoretical foundation from which I speculate how Farah's work might be added to what Said, supplementing Antonio Gramsci, has termed a critical 'inventory'. In *Race and the Education of Desire*, Stoler offers a contrapuntal reading of *The History of Sexuality* against what were then only fragments of the lectures that would become '*Society Must Be Defended*'. She declares the revisionist aims of her study, specifically the desire to transpose certain Foucauldian templates, recasting them in the colonial context of the East Indies. Stoler maintains that 'in outlining some of the genealogical shifts eclipsed in Foucault's tunnel vision of the West, I focus on certain specific domains in which a discourse of sexuality articulated with the politics of race' (Stoler 1995: 11). In an appeal echoing Miller's, she calls for 'students of colonialism to work out Foucault's genealogies on a broader imperial map' (1995: 19).[2] She sets about constructing a critique of the absences and aporias resulting from the Eurocentric focus of his work. Stoler also argues that the seemingly more radical impulses behind Foucault's discussions of state racism, in light of Nazi eugenics and Stalinism, were somewhat compromised by an inability and/or unwillingness to make more extensive geo-political linkages.

Stoler's approach provides a provocative test case for the purposes of this book. In many respects, her study follows Foucault's own interrogative agenda, sharing with him the conviction that discursive dogma is akin to death. In its earliest stages, Stoler situates her investigation within a broader intellectual context where Foucault strains to be heard amidst a host of competing voices and claims. She states that '[our] ethnographic sensibilities have pushed us to challenge the limits of Foucault's discursive emphasis and his diffuse conceptions of power, to flesh out the localized, quotidian practices of people who authorized and resisted European authority, to expose the tensions of that project and its inherent vulnerabilities' (Stoler 1995: 2). It is revealing that Stoler relies on such embodied rhetoric to capture this critical motivation. Her sense that there is something approaching a visceral need to respond to Foucault's work, drawing on the same fleshy terms in which it is authored, informs *The Disorder of Things* as a whole.

Stoler attends to Foucault's pivotal series in a chapter entitled 'Towards a Genealogy of Racisms: The 1976 Lectures at the Collège de France'. As she maintains in her later study, *Carnal Knowledge and Imperial Power: Race and the Intimate in Colonial Rule* (2002), it offers an alluring supplement, allowing her to launch her contrapuntal reading in earnest. 'I am more interested in the productive tensions between *The History of Sexuality* and this subsequent project [the lectures] and in the ways they converge and precipitously diverge in linking biopower and race … I am interested in what we might glean from his insights and where we might take them' (Stoler 1995: 59). It seems safe to assume that the conviction with which Stoler approaches Foucault's work against the grain would have earned his approval. The close of the third chapter provides an effective summary of many of the qualities and quandaries inherent in Foucault's writing and thought. As my emphases suggest, Stoler deliberately employs a series of terms that in themselves have become associated with the original discourse:

> In contemporary perspective, Foucault's analysis has an almost **eerie** quality.
> It speaks to, and even seems to anticipate, the conditions for 'ethnic cleansing'
> in Eastern Europe's fractured states. If these lectures did not work as effective
> history, it is because Foucault did not try. As a history of the present, the lectures
> are **disturbingly relevant** today, and given the questions raised by those in
> the Collège de France audience, they were **disturbing** at the time. His attack
> on socialism certainly caught the attention of those who attended, but **no one
> took up** his more pessimistic indictment; namely that racism was intrinsic to the
> nature of all modern, normalizing states and their biopolitical technologies. Nor
> was he **called upon to account for** those varying intensities of racist practice
> ranging from social exclusion to mass murder. The state looms so large in his
> account, but the critical differences between state formations that discursively
> *threaten* expulsion and extermination as opposed to those that *carry it out* went
> **unaddressed**. On this **unsettling** note, he ended an extraordinary seminar.
> (Stoler 1995: 88)

The more ghostly and/or quasi-prophetic overtones of Foucault's speculations that enchant Duncker's reader, galvanise Miller's critique and underpin this analysis are captured by 'eerie'. If frustration over his shortcomings is inevitable, it precipitates the kind of discursive wrangling practiced by Stoler.

Similarly, Stoler's disdain for the audience's unwillingness to prod and probe chimes with Foucault's own comments on the limitations of the lecture format. Cited in the foreword to '*Society Must Be Defended*', Gérard Petitjean recounts how:

> Foucault stops. The students rush to his desk. Not to talk to him, but to
> switch off their tape recorders. No questions. Foucault is alone in the crush.
> Foucault comments: 'We ought to be able to discuss what I have put forward.
> Sometimes, when the lecture has not been good, it would not take a lot, a
> question, to put everything right. But the question never comes. In France, the
> group effect makes all real discussion impossible. And as there is no feedback
> channel, the lecture becomes a sort of theatrical performance. I relate to the
> people who are there as though I were an actor or an acrobat. And when I have
> finished speaking, there's this feeling of total solitude.' (Foucault 2003: xi)

The despair that Foucault-as-tutor and Stoler-as-student identify is somewhat eased, as the latter grapples with the former's porous investigations. As Homi Bhabha's explanation of the supplement in *The Location of Culture* maintains, the very fact that it comes later allows it to pose those uncompromising questions elided first time round:

> Coming 'after' the original, or in 'addition to' it, gives the supplementary question the advantage of introducing a sense of 'secondariness' or belatedness into the structure of the original demand. The supplementary strategy suggests that adding 'to' need not 'add up' but may disturb the calculation. As Gasche has distinctly suggested 'supplements … are pluses that compensate for a minus in the origin.' (Bhabha 1994: 155)

Foucault's 'tunnel vision of the West' does not foreclose the possibility that his meditations might be put to productive use elsewhere. Stoler identifies his work's prophetic power as viewed from the then contemporary perspective of the mid-nineties, when ethnic cleansing in the Balkans remained fresh in the political consciousness. As Mark Kelly maintains, the tentative prising open of a vast Pandora's toolbox of reflections on state racism, biopower and blood that Foucault begins here becomes all the more unsettling, eerie and urgent in the historical present of the twenty-first century: 'the "war on terror" is a bio-political war … it operates according to the logic of a bio-political drive to defend the national population, justified by a stripped-down state racism in which one is either with America (good) or against America (evil)' (Kelly 2004: 58). Whilst, building on this, I gesture towards the potential application of Foucault's work to the Somali situation in particular, it is necessary to sharpen the focus on power in postcolonial Africa. This is an overarching concern throughout Farah's work.

If Stoler's objective is to expand Foucault's territorial and discursive horizons, her own fleeting reference to the prophetic force of his analyses also serves as an interventionist invitation. Whilst she is preoccupied with colonial anthropology, her Eastern European aside has an altogether more pressing appeal for postcolonial scholars. In *The Black Man's Burden*, Basil Davidson draws timely parallels between the Balkanisation of the African continent and the experience of its peoples:

> The circumstances of Africa, it may be objected, differ in many ways from those of Eastern Europe. I am far from sure of this, but in any case the circumstances here relate to speeds of change, notably of ideological change. Europe has needed two centuries to go through its experience of nation-statism from its formative beginnings … to the unfolding thought that nation-statism has come

near the end of its useful life. But it seems that Africa has covered this ground in just half a century. (Davidson 1992: 288)

Published during the Balkans conflict, *The Black Man's Burden* shares the same contrapuntal convictions as Stoler's study. Davidson, too, rails against the prevalence of what he terms 'the culturally compartmentalizing power of imperialism', designed to limit possibilities for more interesting dialogue (Davidson 1992: 160). Typically, Edward Said works against this reductive grain. As such, he provides a useful bridge to Farah's work.

Edward Said: Speaking the Truth to Foucault

Whilst Stoler makes Foucault groan in an ethnographic context, Said enlists him for the kind of literary purposes that have more recognisable links to this book. In two essays ('Michel Foucault, 1927–1984' and 'Foucault and the Imagination of Power'), Said adopts a similar approach to Stoler's, both heralding the possibilities and probing the limitations of Foucault's work. Joining axiomatic figures such as Adorno, Gramsci, Vico and Williams, Foucault becomes a discursive touchstone for Said. The essays focus on the enigmatic qualities that speak to the recuperative spirit of *Reassessing Foucault*, amongst many other collections. 'Even after [Foucault's] biological death … those who work within his shadow prefer to use his writings as a springboard … rather than fall back on pious repetition and incantation' (Jones & Porter 1994: 12–13). Like Jones and Porter, Said's objectives are dialectical; taking account of Foucault's 'tunnel vision of the West', he also extols the philosopher's 'transnational vocation' (Said 2001: 197). This suggests how Foucault's work, beyond its focus on microsites and microphysics of power, functions as an extensive meditation on the nature as well as the necessity of self-reflexive methodologies. As noted, Foucault used the fissures in his work to extend invitations to future writers and thinkers: 'they were like an outline for something. It's up to you to go on with them or give them a different configuration' (Foucault 2003: 4).

Once again, it is perhaps the more personal and personable tone of Said's reflections that suggests Foucault's haunting influence, within and beyond the academy. As above, he shows how the opening of *Discipline and Punish* captures the visceral force of Foucault's destabilising analyses:

There is no such thing as being at home in his writing, neither for reader nor for writer. Dislocations, a dizzying and physically powerful prose (for example, the description of torture that opens *Discipline and Punish* …), the uncanny ability to invent whole fields of investigation: these come from Foucault's everlasting effort to formulate otherness and heterodoxy without domesticating them or turning them into doctrine. (Said 2001: 191–192)

As with Foucault's own description of getting to grips with Nietzsche, Said employs deliberately robust rhetoric. Once the labyrinth has been entered, if not fully fathomed, it becomes clear that, in a suitably literary sense, Foucault is at his striking best when grounding his critiques and investigations at the level of contested corporeality. This is one uncanny link I pursue throughout this book, arguing that, from his earliest novel to his most recent, the poetics and politics of Farah's oeuvre are anchored by fleshy materiality.

Like Stoler, Said suggests that Foucault's blind spots are both highly revealing and in more urgent need of interrogation than ever before. He too mounts a critique against both a discursive provider and public who fail to differentiate rigorously between theories and practices of power. This has prompted Neil Lazarus, amongst others, to bemoan Foucault's 'talismanic' status (Lazarus 1999: 11). It is when such speculations are situated in a specifically postcolonial context, where the use and abuse of this power assumes greater immediacy, that Said's oppositional stance comes to the fore:

[Foucault] showed no real interest in the relationships his work had with feminist or postcolonial writers facing problems of exclusion, confinement, and domination. Indeed, his Eurocentrism was almost total, as if 'history' itself took place only among a group of French and German thinkers … But whether Foucault is read and benefited from as a philosopher or as a superb intelligence riskily deploying language and learning to various, often contradictory ends, his work will retain its unsettling, antiutopian influence for generations to come. (Said 2001: 196)

It appears no coincidence that the same phrase recurs in two distinct contexts to capture Foucault's anxiety of influence. For both Said and Stoler, the key term remains 'unsettling'. It is for the identification and illumination of such antiutopian impulses that Foucault retains a peculiar place on the inventory of this study. This Gramscian notion remains critical.

The title of the series to which *Reflections on Exile* belongs is significant. 'Convergences – Inventories of the Present' should elicit nods of recognition from those even casually acquainted with *Orientalism*. As Said's critical project developed, the term would only assume greater burdens of significance. In the introduction's third section, 'The personal dimension', Said shows how something of crucial importance was previously lost in translation:

> In the *Prison Notebooks* Gramsci says: 'The starting-point of critical elaboration is the consciousness of what one really is, and is "knowing thyself" as a product of the historical process to date, which has deposited in you an infinity of traces, without leaving an inventory.' The only available English translation inexplicably leaves Gramsci's comment at that, whereas in fact Gramsci's Italian text concludes by adding, 'therefore it is imperative at the outset to compile such an inventory.' (Said 2003: 25)

If Foucault would later become preoccupied with the project of 'knowing thyself' of greatest interest here is how Said begins to construct an inventory of sorts to flesh out his critique of the French philosopher (Foucault 2005: 12–19). He takes him on, in the most explicitly postcolonial sense, in 'Foucault and The Imagination of Power', adopting the same contrapuntal approach as Stoler:

> Many of the people who admire and have learned from Foucault, including myself, have commented on the undifferentiated power he seemed to ascribe to modern society. With this profoundly pessimistic view went also a singular lack of interest in the force of effective resistance to it, in choosing particular sites of intensity, choices which, we see from evidence on all sides, always exist and are often successful in impeding, if not actually stopping, the progress of tyrannical power. (Said 2001: 241)

Charges against Foucault's all-engrossing pessimism are familiar. This intervention, however, prefigures the essay's rhetorical crescendo. Like Stoler, Said pays the greatest of tributes by identifying and making the case for the 'but' that is pivotal, because stubbornly resistant. He continues, '... there is no doubt at all that Foucault is nevertheless extraordinarily brilliant as a visionary of power who calls forth in his reader a whole gamut of responses testifying not so much to the rightness of Foucault's reports but to alternative visions of power not entirely suppressed or obliterated by his work, but stimulated and enlivened by it' (Said 2001: 242–243).

Critically, the stimulating supplement derives not only from the oppositional, if still Eurocentric, discourse of Williams and Gramsci, but also from a more worldly literary grouping. After juxtaposing Foucault with a notable entrant on his own inventory (Ibn Khaldun), Said somewhat inevitably turns to Frantz Fanon. He is a fitting adversary: charged with dragging Foucault groaning and protesting into an anti-colonial/postcolonial context where power and the myriad strategies set in opposition to it take on more embodied immediacy. As the essay moves towards its denouement, Said unfurls an eclectic lineup to reinforce his critique:

> Fanon himself, Sayed Atlas, Abdallah Laroui, Panikkar, Shariati, Mazrui, novelists like Ngugi and Rushdie – all these as well as the enormously powerful adversarial work of feminists and minority cultures in the West and the Third World amply record the continuing attraction to libertarian struggle, for which I have gathered Foucault and others in his camp felt either resignation or spectatorial indifference after the Iranian Revolution. (Said 2001: 244)[3]

The inventory is impressive. Yet, with its necessarily fleeting survey of figures all but canonised in postcolonial studies, it provides an invitation as compelling as Foucault's own. Like Stoler's cursory reference to contemporaneous biopolitics in Eastern Europe and, via Davidson's intervention, a Balkanised Africa, Said leaves the discursive door ajar. In what follows, I explore how Nuruddin Farah, with intense personal and political investments in Foucauldian matters such as biopower, body politics and the nation, might be added to Said's list.

Both Foucault's and Said's work serve as provocative catalysts for others. It is the candour with which the former admits this that has enabled it to be revised, reconfigured and in places 'unlearnt' with such provocative results. As discussed in *The Hermeneutics of the Subject*, for instance, for Foucault, '[to] 'unlearn' (*dediscere*) is an important task of the culture of the self' (Foucault 2005: 495). In a postcolonial context, of course, the idea of 'unlearning' is central to the work of Gayatri Spivak, amongst many others (Spivak 1999: 118–125). Said is typically lucid when assessing these qualities:

> The great invigoration of [Foucault's] work, in its extremism and its constant savaging of limits and reifications, is its disquieting recollection of what, sometimes explicitly but often implicitly, it leaves out, neglects, circumvents, or displaces … But nowhere is this engagement more gripping than in the conflict between Foucault's archaeologies and social change itself, which it must remain for his students … to expose and if possible resolve. (Said 2001: 245)

Terms such as 'disquieting' and 'displaces' recur throughout a critical survey of those who have reflected on their various Foucauldian encounters. It is the notion of a 'constant savaging of limits', however, that I find particularly valuable.

It is at this juncture that Foucault's comments on heterogeneous power begin to chime with his notion of expedient and self-reflexive thought. In the second Collège lecture, he considers problems relating to totalising conceptions of power. Whilst I discuss the significance of such analytics in relation to Farah's critical project, a semantic transplant might be useful here. By substituting 'power' for 'Foucault's discourse', the warning he delivers becomes even more salutary:

> Do not regard power as a phenomenon of mass and homogenous domination … keep it clearly in mind that unless we are looking at it from a great height and from a very great distance, power is not something divided between those who have it and hold it exclusively, and those who do not have it and are subject to it. Power must, I think, be analyzed as something that circulates, or rather as something that only functions as part of a chain … Power functions. Power is exercised through networks, and individuals do not simply circulate in those networks; they are in a position to both submit to and exercise this power. They are never inert or consenting targets of power; they are always its relays. In other words, power passes through individuals. It is not applied to them. (Foucault 2003: 29)

This simple act of substitution illuminates the key knowledge/power dialectic at the core of Foucault's thinking. It is one in which the chain is not rhetorically employed to link master and slave and/or tutor and student in unbreakable bonds of domination. Indeed, for many, replacing 'power' with 'Foucault's discourse' may make what is being said here a little more palatable. As Stoler, Said and Sawicki rigorously maintain from their own strategic positions, there is an urgent need to distinguish between theories and threats to exercise repressive power and their ever more practical applications. Once again, therefore, Foucault's own words have an eerie prescience:

> I think that you are completely free to do what you like with what I am saying. These are suggestions for research, ideas, schemata, outlines, instruments … Ultimately, what you do with them both concerns me and is none of my business … it does concern me to the extent that, one way or another, what you do with it is connected, related to what I am doing. (Foucault 2003: 2)

Foucault in/and Africa

James Miller includes witness accounts of Foucault adopting full revolutionary garb during a pitched battle with police at the Vincennes campus on 23
January 1969 and how 'he exulted in the moment, gleefully lobbing stones
– although he was careful not to dirty his beautiful black velour suit' (Miller
2000: 179). Of greater interest, in terms of a book concerned with various locations, dislocations and relocations, however, is the way in which Foucault's
subversive sabbatical in Tunisia, between 1966 and the end of 1968, proved
definitive in terms of his intellectual and transnational vocations. Beyond his
cloistered study, the visceral explosion of revolutionary energy made flesh
in student uprisings at the University of Tunis had a profound impact upon
him. In light of the issues outlined above, this geo-political shift is highly
significant. Before and beyond the events of Paris later that year, Foucault
experienced a powerful jolt to his views concerning Marxism, direct action
and effective strategies of resistance. As Alessandro Fontana and Mauro Bertani maintain in 'Situating the Lectures', 'against this backdrop of war, of the
wars, struggles and rebellions of those years when, as the saying went, "there
was red in the air", *Society Must be Defended*" might be described as the
meeting point, the hinge or the point of articulation of the political problem
of power and the historical question of race' (Foucault 2003: 286). The image
of the celebrated *enfant terrible* of French letters temporarily trading lectern
and lectures for roof top and rocks holds a peculiar attraction for those concerned with challenging certain caricatures of Foucault. As Robert Young
has persuasively argued, that these actions took place on streets far from the
European centres that dominate his writing and thought is of crucial importance (Young 2001: 395–410). Pre-empting his more problematic association
with the Iranian Revolution, Foucault encountered the peculiar immediacy
of his speculations regarding power and disciplinary mechanisms outside
the metropolitan, colonial centre. This in turn suggests that the answer to
Stoler's question, as posed in *Carnal Knowledge*, is 'yes': '[w]as it significant
that [Foucault] had spent 1966 through spring 1968 in Tunisia – a former
French colony – where he wrote *The Archaeology of Knowledge*, wrote friends
about anti-Semitism, and had his work repeatedly interrupted by student
strikes against the governing policies of a newly empowered state?' (Stoler
2002: 143).

Once again, the '*Society*' lectures occupy an intriguing position here.
Delivered some years after the embryonic revolts in Tunisia and Paris, and
before events in Iran, they are distinguished by a peculiar rhetoric espousing

the need to recuperate fragmented, contingent and subjugated knowledges. It therefore seems no coincidence that, throughout this period, Foucault attended to the dissolution of much that previously appeared stable: 'I would say: for the last ten or fifteen years, the immense and proliferating criticizability of things, institutions, practices, and discourses; a sort of general feeling that the ground was crumbling beneath our feet, especially in places where it seemed most familiar, most solid, and closest to us, to our bodies, to our everyday gestures' (Foucault 2003: 6). It is impossible to divorce this simultaneous attraction to doubt and fear of change from Foucault's own experiences against a broader socio-historical and geo-political backdrop. With the anti-colonial insurrections in Indochina and Algeria never far from French political consciousness, and with the 'distant roar of battle' still echoing from Tunisian Kasbah to Parisian streets, Foucault's lectures reflect a deeper need for pause, hesitation and reassessment (Foucault 2003: 273). It is the collision between a strategic grappling with doubt alongside a shift to consider more contemporaneously urgent forms of biopower that gives the 'Society' lectures their piquancy. They inform large swathes of *The Disorder of Things*.

Disturbing Postcolonial Studies: Foucault-style

By way of focusing on more particular links between the discursive projects of Foucault and Farah, I offer a comparison between the former's doubtful formulations and Salman Rushdie, a more recognisably postcolonial entrant on Said's inventory:

> Doubt, it seems to me, is the central condition of a human being in the 20th century. One of the things that has happened to us in the 20th century as a human race is to learn how certainty crumbles in your hand. We cannot any longer have a fixed view of anything – the table that we're sitting next to, the ground beneath our feet, the laws of science are all full of doubt now. Everything we know is pervaded by doubt and not by certainty. (White 1993: 235)

Whilst Rushdie is describing the eruption of modernist sensibilities during the early twentieth century, it is striking that he chooses to articulate such doubt in terms so similar to Foucault. Fissures emerge, certainty crumbles and for both it is, to borrow from Rushdie's eponymous novel, 'the ground beneath our feet' that begins to subside, threatening instability at the most embodied of levels. Besides a shared rhetorical register, both articulate sentiments that cannot be divorced from specific socio-historical periods. In the aftermath of World War Two, with the advent of Partition and the eruption of anti-colonial resistance, Rushdie speaks with peculiar poignancy about both the desirability and the inevitability of more intense cultural-political doubt. It is in this spirit of strategic scepticism, re-evaluation and rupture that Foucault's own critique, cited by Miller, can be seen to correspond with many of the central preoccupations of postcolonial studies: 'my project is precisely to bring it about that they "no longer know what to do", so that the acts, gestures, discourses that up until then had seemed to go without saying become problematic, difficult, dangerous' (Miller 2000: 235). As the editors of the 'Society' lectures suggest, this can be seen as a counter-hegemonic principle that not only informed his working practices, but also underpinned his discursive and political project: 'it is typical of Foucault's approach that until the end of his life, he constantly "reread", resituated, and reinterpreted his early work in the light of his later work and, so to speak, constantly updated it' (Foucault 2003: 275).

In various attempts to explore one of the key tenets of his thesis (the Clauswitzean inversion that war might be considered 'the continuation of politics by other means'), Foucault calls for various acts of recuperation (Foucault 2003: 267). He wants to refresh the blood that has dried on antique parchments and laws. He seeks to amplify the distant roar of battle. A spirit of reanimation prevails. As Said maintains, this focus upon the remnants of historico-political/juridical discourse is indicative of the overarching objective of Foucault's work to open up spaces from which to analyse the marginalised and transgressive components of society. Taken onto a more transnational level, this recuperative impulse resonates with some of the key negotiations that have taken place in postcolonial studies over the past decade or so. In *Postcolonial Moves: Medieval through Modern*, for instance, Patricia Ingham and Michelle Warren argue that 'medievalists working explicitly with postcolonial theories have been analyzing the ways in which "the medieval" may be said to haunt the field' (Ingham and Warren 2003: 6). Here and elsewhere, the pivotal, Foucauldian-inflected relationship concerns power and discourse:

> But alongside this crumbling and the astonishing efficacy of discontinuous, particular, and local critiques, the facts were also revealing something that could not, perhaps, have been foreseen from the outset: what might be called the inhibiting effect specific to totalitarian theories, or at least … all-encompassing

> and global theories. Not that all-encompassing and global theories haven't, in
> fairly consistent fashion, provided – and don't continue to provide – tools that
> can be used at a local level; Marxism and psychoanalysis are living proof that they
> can. But they have, I think, provided tools that can be used at the local level only
> when, and this is the real point, the theoretical unity of their discourse is, so to
> speak, suspended, or at least cut up, ripped up, torn to shreds, turned inside out,
> displaced, caricatured, dramatized, theatricalized, and so on. (Foucault 2003: 6)

The rhetoric is typically robust. Buoyed by the residual energy of a period
still marked by the events of 1968, Foucault conceives of the pressing need
to interrogate totalising schemes. Indeed, for the purposes of this book, it
is the very eclectic nature of his toolkit that makes it both functional and
inspirational. By highlighting the possible limitations of global discourses,
Foucault demonstrates a willingness, however tentative, to engage in work
that might pave the way towards more transnational dialogue. There is a call
to attend to the mediation between the macrological and the micrological
or, in other words, a reconsideration of more embodied and local relays of
power, discipline and the possibility of resistance. Finally, it is this act of
blurring theoretical boundaries, separating speculations on discourse and
methodology and the analysis of 'body politics' that is most productive for
my purposes. Such 'translation' has a peculiar relevance when considered
both in the context of postcolonial Africa and in relation to the critical preoccupations of Farah's work.

Whilst I look at specific reconfigurations of Foucauldian thought in relation to colonial and postcolonial power in Africa throughout this book, a
brief overview is instructive here. In their respective contexts, both Ngũgĩ wa
Thiong'o and V.Y. Mudimbe have extended some of Foucault's most penetrating observations on 'carceral space', discourse and colonial anthropology. For
Mudimbe, in *The Invention of Africa*, it is precisely the disruptive quality of
Foucault's thought, alongside that of Levi-Strauss, that most appeals:

> Although most Western anthropologists have continued up to now to argue
> about the best models to account for primitive societies, Levi-Strauss, Foucault,
> and, since the 1960s, Africans have been destroying the classical frame of
> anthropology. By emphasizing the importance of the unconscious and
> questioning the validity of a universal subject as the center of signification,
> they simultaneously demand a new understanding of the strange object of
> the human sciences and a redefinition of at least three fields, anthropology,
> history, and psychoanalysis, as leading disciplines of self-criticism. Foucault

dreamed of the prestige of an anthropology that will 'seek its object in the area
of the unconscious processes that characterize the system of a given culture'
and 'would bring the relation of historicity, which is constitutive of all ethnology
in general, into play within the dimension in which psychoanalysis has always
been deployed'. (Mudimbe 1988: 37–38)

Similarly, in her exacting study of the use and abuse of biopower in colonial Africa, *Curing Their Ills*, Megan Vaughan has drawn extensively from
The History of Sexuality to provide a critique of some of Foucault's essen-
tialist speculations. Likewise, Alexander Butchart's *The Anatomy of Power*
seeks to apply 'some of the theoretical tools developed by Michel Foucault
to the problem of the African body as it exists to western socio-medical science' (Butchart 1998: ix). In a chapter entitled 'The Aesthetics of Vulgarity',
Achille Mbembe provides a striking juxtaposition between descriptions of
two Cameroonian 'malefactors' and the opening evocation of Damiens' dismemberment in *Discipline and Punish*. It haunts *On the Postcolony*, as it does
so many other texts: 'the postcolony is a particularly revealing, and rather
dramatic, stage on which are played out the wider problems of subjections
and its corollary, discipline ... [the] fact is that power, in the postcolony,
is carnivorous' (Mbembe 2001: 102–103). In this spirit, innumerable collections have focused on the practical and variously punitive applications
of some Foucauldian meditations on discipline. In his essay 'Torture and
the Decolonization of French Algeria', included in *Colonial and Postcolonial Incarceration*, James D. Le Sueur makes strategic references to Foucault,
variously taking him to task for what he perceives to be his dangerous Eurocentrism (Le Sueur 2001: 161–175). Similarly, he emerges as a prominent if
problematic referent throughout the rich collection *A History of Prison and
Confinement in Africa* (2003). Whilst selective, this initial survey suggests
that the Foucault/Africa discursive marriage is neither as incongruous nor
as speculative as it might appear to some.

Farah and Foucault: Reflections on Beginnings

For Said in *Orientalism*, 'the act of beginning, necessarily involves an act
of delimitation by which something is cut out of a great mass of material,
separated from the mass, and made to stand for, as well as be, a starting
point, a beginning' (2003: 16). Whilst *The Disorder of Things* aims to offer
a comprehensive analysis of Farah's work to date, it necessarily involves its

own acts of delimitation. Significant as both *From a Crooked Rib* and *A Naked Needle* are to an appreciation of Farah's oeuvre, I refer to them only in passing throughout what follows. My principal concern lies with the three trilogies (*Variations on the Theme of an African Dictatorship*, *Blood in the Sun* and *Past Imperfect*) as well as the documentary study *Yesterday, Tomorrow*, all of which I consider in chronological sequence. As this book was going to press, Farah released *Crossbones*, the final instalment of his *Past Imperfect* cycle, in the United Kingdom and the United States. As such, I touch on it only briefly in a conclusion that is unapologetically open-ended. This is in keeping with what I take to be the interrogative spirit of both Foucault and Farah's respective projects.

To return to the beginning, however, I suggest that, beyond the 'uncanny links' that join their varied preoccupations with biopolitics, power and resistance as well as their experiences of transnational uprooting, more fundamental connections exist between Michel Foucault and Nuruddin Farah. In their respective contexts and throughout their alternative discourses, their peculiarly intense focus on body politics might be seen to stem, in part at least, from formative moments in admittedly very different childhoods. For Foucault, the experience of having his place at the top of the Saint-Stanislas class jeopardised by an influx of Parisian refugees in the 1940s had a profound impact:

> Foucault recalled how, during this period [in occupied France], his 'private life was really threatened' … school had been 'an environment protected from exterior menaces' – but with the coming of war, there was no safe haven. 'Maybe that is the reason why I am fascinated by history and the relationship between personal experience and those events of which we are a part,' he later speculated: 'I think this is the nucleus of my theoretical desire.' (Miller 2000: 369)

Some twenty years after the end of the war and on a different continent, Farah found himself confronted with a more immediate menace. In 'Why I Write', he recalls how his soon-to-be-published 'longish short story' 'Why Dead So Soon?' was conceived 'when in hospital, in pain and certain I would not survive the operation I was to undergo … I might have written the first story because I was afraid of dying' (Farah 2002b: 5). At the core of these anecdotes is a fundamental concern with moving from the micro to the macro, the personal to the political. Just as such negotiations can be seen to characterise both projects, they have, in turn, influenced my own approach in the opening and closing sections of this book. As *The Disorder of Things* begins with a personal aside, so it ends with a reflection on how and why my relocation to South Africa from the United Kingdom gave fresh impetus to this comparative study.

At the sentient level of fear and threat, both incidents appear to have had a simultaneously haunting and compelling influence on Foucault and Farah's work. Reading these formative narratives alongside one another gives a sense of the contrapuntal approach I adopt throughout what follows. Similarly, when Farah conceives of the slippery concept of and incessant need to critique holistic truths, his argument is purposively fleshy:

> The body politic whose sinewed muscles, strong as pillars, embodied the collective strength to which every member of the community contributed: in Africa that was sadly lacking … The 'truth' that matters, indeed! What if I argue that truth must be 'spoken' whether in the privacy of one's chambers or in the presence of others? What if I argue that it must be given a body, a physical existence, that truth must be clothed in the bodied concepts of words, of motions – so that others may share it, challenge it or accept it? (Farah 2002b: 10–12)

The anxious period in an Ogaden hospital bed proved the initial catalyst for Farah as a writer. As I argue throughout this book, preoccupations with body politics shift from the intimately personal to the intensely political throughout his work, continuing to characterise it to this day. A similarly fleshy vision seems to have driven Foucault's own discursive investigations. With due acknowledgement of the elliptical quality of memory, Miller recounts Foucault's own childhood tale of how his doctor father forced him to witness an amputation. The uncanny scene operates in conjunction with some of the discursive touchstones that resurface throughout Foucault's work:

> The image … has all the ingredients of a recurrent nightmare: the sadistic father, the impotent child, the knife slicing into flesh, the body cut to the bone, the demand to acknowledge the sovereign power of the patriarch … Like debris from a shipwreck, fragments of the scene keep bobbing up and down throughout Foucault's life and work … One is reminded … of the strange link the philosopher makes in *The Birth of the Clinic* between sadism and the scientific foundations of modern medicine. And then there is the truly terrible diorama that opens *Discipline and Punish*. In this passage, the philosopher forces us to watch as the regicide Damiens has his legs and arms carved up and pulled off by a team of six horses. (Miller 2000: 366–367)

The groans and protests become audible once more as the spectres of 'strange links' hang heavy. With these in mind, my opening chapter builds upon the theoretical foundations I have laid throughout this introduction. In it, I offer an analysis of Farah's *Sweet and Sour Milk* (1979) in light of Foucauldian concerns with carceral power.

References

Bhabha, H. 1994. *The Location of Culture*. London: Routledge.

Binkley, S. 2010. 'Introduction'. In S. Binkley & J. Capetillo-Ponce (Eds). *A Foucault for the 21st Century: Governmentality, Biopolitics and Discipline in the New Millenium*. Cambridge Scholars Publishing: Newcastle.

Butchart, A. 1998. *The Anatomy of Power: European Constructions of the African Body*. London: Zed Books.

Davidson, B. 1992. *The Black Man's Burden – Africa and the Curse of the Nation-State*. New York: Times Books.

Duncker, P. 1997. *Hallucinating Foucault*. London: Picador.

Farah, N. 1992. 'A Country in Exile'. *Transition*, Issue 57.

Farah, N. 2002a. 'How Can we Talk of Democracy? An Interview with Nuruddin Farah by Patricia Alden and Louis Tremaine'. In D. Wright (Ed.). *Emerging Perspectives on Nuruddin Farah*. New Jersey: Africa World Press.

Farah, N. 2002b. 'Why I Write'. In D. Wright (Ed.). *Emerging Perspectives on Nuruddin Farah*. New Jersey: Africa World Press.

Foucault, M. 1980. 'Prison Talk'. In C. Gordon (Ed.). *Power/Knowledge – Selected Interviews and Other Writings*. Harlow: Pearson Education Ltd.

Foucault, M. 1996. 'From Torture to Cellblock'. In S. Lotringer (Ed.). (L. Hochroth & J. Johnston, Trans.). *Foucault Live – Michel Foucault, Collected Interviews, 1961–1984*. New York: Semiotext(e).

Foucault, M. 2003. *'Society Must Be Defended' – Lectures at the Collège de France 1975–1976*. Bertani, M. & Fontana, A. (Eds). (D. Macey, Trans.). New York: Picador.

Foucault, M. 2005. *The Hermeneutics of the Subject: Lectures at the Collège de France, 1981–1982*. Gros, F. (Ed.). (G. Burchell, Trans.). New York: Palgrave Macmillan.

Jones, C. & Porter, R. 1994. 'Introduction'. In C. Jones & R. Porter (Eds). *Reassessing Foucault – Power, Medicine and the Body*. London: Routledge.

Kelly, M. 2004. 'Racism, Nationalism and Biopolitics: Foucault's *Society Must Be Defended*, 2003.' *Contretemps* 4.

Lazarus, N. 1999. *Nationalism and Cultural Practice in the Postcolonial World*. Cambridge: Cambridge University Press.

Le Sueur, J.D. 2001. 'Torture and the Decolonization of French Algeria: Nationalism, 'Race' and Violence during Colonial Incarceration'. In G. Harper (Ed.). 2001. *Colonial and Postcolonial Incarceration*. London: Continuum.

Mbembe, A. 2001. *On the Postcolony*. Berkeley: University of California Press.

Miller, J. 2000. *The Passion of Michel Foucault*. Cambridge, Mass.: Harvard University Press.

Mudimbe, V.Y. 1988. *The Invention of Africa – Gnosis, Philosophy and the Order of Knowledge*. Bloomington: Indiana University Press.

Said, E. 2001. 'Michel Foucault, 1927–1984'. In E. Said. *Reflections on Exile and Other Literary and Cultural Essays*. London: Granta.

Said, E. 2003. *Orientalism*. London: Penguin.

Spivak, G. 1999. *A Critique of Postcolonial Reason: Toward a History of the Vanishing Present*. Cambridge, Mass.: Harvard University Press.

Stoler, A. 1995. *Race and the Education of Desire – Foucault's History of Sexuality and the Colonial Order of Things*. Durham and London: Duke University Press.

Stoler, A. 2002. *Carnal Knowledge and Imperial Power: Race and The Intimate in Colonial Rule.* Berkeley: University of California Press.

White, J. 1993. 'Politics and the Individual in the Modernist Historical Novel: Gordimer and Rushdie'. In J. White (Ed.). *Recasting the World: Writing after Colonialism.* Baltimore and London: John Hopkins University Press.

Young, R. 2001. *Postcolonialism – An Historical Introduction.* Oxford: Blackwell Publishers.

Endnotes

1   I use this spelling throughout, as does Farah in his novels. Whilst he uses 'Mogadishu' in 'The City in My Mind,' I retain 'Mogadiscio'.

2   See also Cooper, F. 2005. *Colonialism in Question: Theory, Knowledge, History.* Berkeley: University of California Press, pp. 48–49 and Cooper, F. and Stoler, A. (Eds). 1997. *Tensions of Empire:* Colonial *Cultures in a Bourgeois World.* Berkeley: University of California Press.

3   For further speculations on Foucault and the Iranian Revolution, see El-Din Aysha, E. 2006. 'Foucault's Iran and Islamic Identity Politics Beyond Civilizational Clashes, External and Internal.' *International Studies Perspectives,* Vol. 7, No. 4, pp. 377–394.

2

Quivering at the Heart of the *Variations* Cycle: Labyrinths of Loss in *Sweet and Sour Milk*

In every epoch, writers have grasped the possibility of forming out of words a labyrinth in which to hide. That a maze of language could also hold the reader 'captive', because 'captivated', was a possibility Foucault had learned from Robbe-Grillet, Roussel, and also Jorge Louis Borges ... The appeal of the labyrinth to the writer's imagination was therefore doubtless manifold ... a place where a person might come to 'think differently', it facilitated, as a literary device, self-effacement and self-expression simultaneously.

(James Miller – The Passion of Michel Foucault, 2000: 147)

A writer's imagination is always intensely fascinated by relationships – between objects and events in time and space. Certain symbolic, or seemingly symbolic, parallels, convergences, divergences, circles are irresistible to the imagination.

(Ngũgĩ wa Thiong'o – Detained, 1981: 121)

FOUCAULT'S EXAMINERS RAISED A NUMBER OF RESERVATIONS DURING THE defence of his original thesis, with the Sorbonne historian Henri Gouhier expressing his profound unease with this student who 'thought in allegories' (Miller 2000: 104). For the purposes of this analysis, I am grateful Foucault refused to alter his approach. The following chapters consider Farah's first trilogy, *Variations on the Theme of an African Dictatorship*, exploring it in relation to those carceral concerns and tropes that litter Foucault's early work. Alongside them, what Michael Senellart refers to as Foucault's 'taste for the labyrinth' in *Security, Territory, Population* also captures the imagination (Foucault 2007: 380). Whilst the labyrinth has various allegorical meanings, the above marriage between power as design and literature as obfuscation is particularly enabling. It corresponds with the murky world of *Variations* where, as D.R. Ewen suggests, 'a weird cognitive fog envelops even simple facts', leaving identities fragmented, disappearances routine and bodies either broken or obliterated (Ewen 1984: 201). Farah's preoccupation with the insurgent, if ultimately misplaced energies of the Group of 10 (a group of young intellectuals opposed to the General's rule in *Variations*) has provoked fierce debate. Whilst his created 'priviligentsia' resembles a quasi-clan, focusing on them allows Farah to shed revealing light on the ways in which, to borrow from Eyal Chowers' provocative study, *The Modern Self in the Labyrinth: Politics and the Entrapment Imagination*, 'the individual is enmeshed within a web of power' (Chowers 2004: 168). Debates concerning webs of affiliation, the entanglements of history and outlets for potential resistance all cluster around the Group. The result is a necessarily claustrophobic portrait of authoritarian society. As I come to illustrate, a key difference between the *Variations* and *Blood in the Sun* trilogies is that, whilst a certain uncertainty distinguishes both plot and protagonist in the former, the target of Farah's critique remains the autocratic regime. With *Maps'* exploration of the fallout from defeat in the Ogaden War, the national narrative has begun to unravel, causing Farah's focus to shift accordingly.

In *Discipline and Punish*, Foucault maintains that:

> there is no risk … that the increase of power created by the panoptic machine may degenerate into tyranny; the disciplinary mechanism will be democratically controlled, since it will be constantly accessible 'to the great tribunal committee of the world' … The seeing machine was once a sort of dark room into which individuals spied; it has become a transparent building in which the exercise of power may be supervised by society as a whole. (Foucault 1991: 207)

The carceral environs of the *Variations* series demonstrate how and why Farah is equally preoccupied with circuitous, surveying systems of power. The individual novels, however, return the reader to this very 'dark room', suggesting that tyranny can flourish when panoptic and labyrinthine disciplinary schemes fuse. To initiate the oftentimes compelling dialogue between

Foucault's discourse and Farah's fiction, I have found the work of Latin American scholars similarly concerned with manifestations of power particularly enabling.[1] For both Claudio Lomnitz-Adler and Gerald Martin, for instance, the labyrinth has more than figurative significance. Focusing on myriad tensions within Mexico in *Exits from the Labyrinth: Culture and Ideology in the Mexican National Space*, the former maintains:

> the political importance of national culture and the difficulty in describing [it] in any terms other than the terms of nationalism has generated a circular dialectic, a vicious cycle that is built on the tensions that occur between the maze of social relations that exist within the national space and the ideologies regarding a common identity, a shared sense of the past, and a unified gaze towards the future. I call this complex of issues the labyrinth. (Lomnitz-Adler 1992: 3)

This complex of issues can be seen to correspond with the specifically Somali concerns of Farah's work. Tensions between the competing claims of individual clans cutting against appeals to pan-Somali nationalism, for instance, have and continue to define the (dis)order of things. Lomnitz-Adler argues that many anthropologists and social historians experience 'literature envy', finding that novels, for example, explore the labyrinthine construction and dissemination of power in unusually productive ways (Lomnitz-Adler 1992: 8). Building on this in relation to the *Variations* series, I suggest that paying greater attention to the relationship between the texts' form and content illustrates how and why they allow us to engage more critically with processes and technologies of power. To supplement Martin's intervention in *Journeys through the Labyrinth: Latin American Fiction in the 20th Century*, I maintain that it is the richness of the labyrinth-as-motif that is most appealing when it comes to considering Farah's work:

> The labyrinth is everywhere … The twentieth century has rediscovered this metaphor with a vengeance, and for contemporary Derrideans and Foucauldians textuality, with its decentring and its difference and its gaze into the abyss, has been repeatedly likened to a web, a forest or, above all, a labyrinth … it has its own entirely concrete basis in a continent at once unitary and diverse, where identity is never given, and where history and culture themselves have always seemed to be a question of opting between different, already existing choices and alternative forking paths. (Martin 1989: 360)

Whilst this final, Borgesian image has been used to describe *Maps*, I argue that Farah's entire oeuvre is preoccupied with 'decentering' and 'difference', at levels both micrological and macrological as well as in terms of plot and polity. This resonates with the author's claim that his primary objective, in these and other novels, is not to launch a conventional polemic against the abuse of power by despotic leaders. Farah is rather more concerned with exploring the complex underlying conditions of family, kin and blood that allow autocrats to maintain and misuse power in the first place, as discussed in I.M. Lewis' *Blood and Bone: The Call of Kinship in Somali Society* (1994). When the critique is opened out in such a way, issues of hegemony and oppression are shown to be much more intertwined. The onus is placed on individuals to negotiate these structures and, where necessary, define themselves against rather than in terms of various groups.

The *Variations* trilogy has a necessarily nightmarish quality, as it presents us with an autocratic General imagined to have panoptical power. When *Sweet and Sour Milk's* Soyaan refers to father Keynaan as 'a miniature creature in a flat world dominated by a God-figure high and huge as any mountain anyone has seen' (*S&SM*: 83), it is not clear whether he is referring to Allah, the General or both. The slippage is crucial. Once in this position, the General is able to survey all beneath him, watching his intellectual adversaries lose themselves in mazes of both his and, more peculiarly, their own making. As Felix Mnthali suggests in 'Autocracy and the Limits of Identity: A Reading of the Novels of Nuruddin Farah':

> the remote and shadowy figure of the General is in everything and in everyone's life and yet the immediate impression is that of clans fighting amongst themselves while the real culprit remains detached from it all. He resuscitates clan animosities by seeming to give power to the clans while closely monitoring their discussions and making sure that his secret police plants the right amount of fear in everyone's mind. (Mnthali 2002: 178)

The result is that the reader is given a penetrating insight into repressive systems, dependent upon suitably Foucauldian relays for their very existence. Alongside this, an enduring fascination with the relationship between individual body politics and the collective body politic lies at the heart of Farah's fictional labyrinth. I suggest this can be seen in relation to Diane Nelson's study, *A Finger in the Wound: Body Politics in Quincentennial Guatemala*:

> [because] there is a body in the metaphor, but a body that is deeply
> contradictory – scarred and wounded by violence – I think the metaphor is
> useful for describing the body politic of the Guatemalan nation. Guatemala
> is emerging from a civil war that displaced one-eighth of the population and
> left some one hundred and twenty thousand people dead or disappeared: the
> wounded body politic is thus also terribly material. (Nelson 1999: 2)

Whilst analogies with the situation in contemporary Somalia are striking, it
is Nelson's attention to the fleshy materiality of 'the wounded body politic'
that informs this analysis of *Sweet and Sour Milk*, as it does the book as a
whole. Inevitably, Nelson makes Foucault groan and protest in a Guatamalan
context (Nelson 1999: 5). Like her, I again find that *Discipline and Punish*
usefully captures the body/power dialectic I flesh out in this section:

> Power in the hierarchized surveillance of the disciplines is not possessed as
> a thing, or transferred as a property; it functions like a piece of machinery.
> And, although it is true that its pyramidal organization gives it a 'head', it is the
> apparatus as a whole that produces 'power' and distributes individuals in this
> permanent and continuous field … Thanks to the techniques of surveillance,
> the 'physics' of power, the hold over the body, operate according to the laws
> of optics and mechanics, according to a whole play of spaces, lines, screens,
> beams, degrees and without recourse, in principle at least, to excess, force or
> violence. It is a power that seems all the less 'corporal' in that it is more subtly
> 'physical'. (Foucault 1991: 172)

For Farah, as for Foucault, processes and techniques of control never operate in monolithic, unilateral ways. As such, if not dismantled at a structural
level, they remain in place long after the removal of power's 'head'. Events
in post-Barre Somalia have provided sombre support to this effect. As the
above passage suggests, it is precisely at this rhetorical level that Foucault
captures the imagination. Throughout his work, as evidenced in *The History
of Sexuality, An Introduction*, references abound to 'perpetual spirals', 'circular incitements' and 'relays' of power (Foucault 1990: 46–47). As Ali Jimale
Ahmed points out in *Daybreak is Near*, this concept of power has a peculiar
resonance when viewed within a Somali context: 'herein lies the importance
of hegemony in understanding the seemingly confusing dialectics of power
in Somali society: power is not amorphous' (Ahmed 1996: 40). Whilst staging
a contrapuntal dialogue between Farah and Foucault, I am equally concerned
with sites of critical divergence. Whereas Foucault's Francocentrism leads

him to conceive of power in terms of a politics of entrapment, Farah suggests that an escape from the disciplinary design may be achieved through renegotiating the terms of the social contract between the body politic and more intimate body politics. Once again, therefore, I turn to Said as a critical intermediary. Comparing Foucault and Fanon, Said suggests that the former 'moved from what appeared to be insurrectionary scholarship to the kind of scholarship that confronted the problem of power from the position of someone who believed that ultimately very little resistance was possible to the controls of a disciplinary or carceral society' (Said 2002a: 53). Whilst there are pronounced similarities between Farah and Foucault's insistence on the individual microphysics of struggle and the 'agonism' that defines relationships between power and resistance, the former's Orwellian cycle explores the kind of oppositionality that, for Said, is precluded by the latter. In attempting to capture the simultaneously exhilarating and exasperating qualities of these *Variations* novels, both Derek Wright and Ali Jimale Ahmed invoke the term 'labyrinthine'.[2] In what follows, I consider how and why the image assumes different burdens of significance.

Negotiating the Labyrinth: Texts and Contexts

> But why would something so blindly experienced be revealed today with no detours, no sidestepping, no desire for a labyrinth?
>
> *(Assia Djebar – So Vast the Prison, 2001: 54)*

Sweet and Sour Milk, Sardines and *Close Sesame* all demonstrate how the dialectical relationship between form and content operates in Farah's work. If, as Ahmed has argued, faith in the ideals of the Somali Revolution of 1969 has withered by this stage in his socio-political evolution, the shadow of earlier text *A Naked Needle*, originally conceived as the first instalment of *Variations*, still hangs heavy over *Sweet and Sour Milk* (Ahmed 1996: 75–99). Yet, in the spirit of exploring Ngũgĩ wa Thiong'o's circular patterns, there is an alternative route into the series. At the outset of the novel, the reader is confronted with Soyaan who, described as having 'disturbed features', does not have long to live. Before the prologue is over, the reader sees him 'hiccup his last'. The pervasive sense of disintegration is amplified following the discovery that Soyaan was a key architect of the Group of 10, charged with usurping the General and reclaiming the betrayed ideals of the Revolution. After this perishing prologue, we follow the search of twin brother Loyaan to identify the guilty parties and gain justice in the name of his sibling. Along the way, Loyaan stumbles into the inner sanctum of power struggles familial, group and governmental. Ministerial doors creak open, allowing him to engage in subversive bouts of shadow play with representatives of the regime, only to be slammed in his face when his questioning becomes too threatening. As he battles to prevent the co-option of his brother's militant legacy by the regime, he clashes with his authoritarian father Keynaan, a ruthless if largely incompetent ex-stooge of the General.

As such, the majority of the text concerns this 'fight over the dead soul of Soyaan' (*S&SM*: 75). For Ewen:

> the only order [in *Sweet and Sour Milk*] is a bizarre form of institutionalized disorder. The novelist, writing with lizard-like agility in a collage of dissolving styles, presents a hideously convincing, and an uncomfortably hypnotic, study of a situation that bears the same relation to any reasonably sane society as Milton's Hell does to Heaven: a post-colonial Pandemonium. (Ewen 1984: 200)

In essence, *Sweet and Sour Milk* is a brooding experiment in quasi-detective fiction. The reader accompanies bewildered sleuth Loyaan deeper into the heart of the state apparatus, where walls have eyes and, most crucially within the largely oral-cultural context of Somalia, ears. The disciplinary labyrinth metamorphoses into a distorted echo chamber, designed to monitor and neutralise dissent. By the novel's close, the reader is left, like Loyaan, with a series of unanswered questions concerning complicity and culpability. If both protagonist and reader struggle to piece together the puzzle of meaning, it is the very process of this struggle that suggests Farah's incremental critique of the use and misuse of power. Fittingly, therefore, one of the richest terms in *Sweet and Sour Milk* is 'complications'. When the shadowy Dr. Ahmed-Wellie attempts to uncover the reason for Soyaan's death, he is told it resulted from 'blood complications' (*S&SM*: 42). Playing with this idea, Alden and Tremaine suggest, 'if it is true, as we are led to believe, that Soyaan was murdered in some way, what caused him to be killed was the complications of his own multiple involvements and commitments and the complicating of truth by its appropriation for political purposes' (Alden & Tremaine 1999: 52). Whilst these are precursors to the later identity interrogations of Askar in *Maps* and Kalaman in *Secrets*, they are here invoked to intensify the determined indeterminacy that haunts both novel and its protagonists. Mother Qumman may well cling to the Koran as a harbinger of certainty ('[it] is all we know that cures without complications', *S&SM*: 5). Yet, in a socio-political situation where the General has ordained an unlikely marriage between Marx and Mohammed, even the rules of this metaphysical game are confused: 'in one hand, the Blue Book of the General and Lenin's writings in improvised translations; in the other, the Holy Koran' (*S&SM*: 133). For Soyaan, the General is adept at providing 'cocktails of contradictions' (*S&SM*: 14).

As demonstrated most vividly in *Close Sesame*, Farah's exploration of links between colonial and neo-colonial regimes is a significant feature of his work. The comparative reader will note the rhetoric he employs in different contexts when conceiving of power as a system under the Italians. The following, for instance, is taken from *Yesterday, Tomorrow*: 'Italy's colonialism is full of disasters … a tragic history ending in colonial cul-de-sacs … it shared in the carving up of Africa into spheres of future disorders' (*YT*: 62). Similarly, in *Sweet and Sour Milk*, the foundations upon which such social structures are built are recast at the level of narrative. Mazes become figurative and functioning and, by the close, Loyaan's admission that 'there are a hundred questions I haven't had answers for' (*S&SM*: 203), speaks to the novel as a whole. Similarly, the internal monologue Farah employs to trace Loyaan's exasperated search mirrors that of his reader: '*Am I too tired to catch the significance of all this?*' (*S&SM*: 213). Approach this opacity from another angle, however, and it has a direct correspondence with the nature of its target. Considered in this way, the Foucauldian overtones are pronounced. As Hubert Dreyfus and Paul Rabinow suggest in *Michel Foucault, Beyond Strucuralism and Hermeneutics*, '[there] are areas of unclearness and sketchiness which can be read either as confusion or, more sympathetically, as problems [Foucault] has opened up for further exploration, either by his subsequent work or by others' (Dreyfus & Rabinow 1983: 126). As Ian Adam similarly argues in 'The Murder of Soyaan Keynaan', if Farah seems to delight in confounding his reader, his opaque narratives are not simply the result of authorial indulgence:

> In the classical detective story … the labyrinth is mapped, signs direct you away from the wrong turn and blocked exit … from multiple possibilities, polygraphy of meaning, emerges meaning single and definitive … it seems clear that *Sweet and Sour Milk* departs radically from the classic genre in this pattern of closure … one senses the relative lack of closure to derive less from epistemological scepticism than from an ethical principle which looks with mistrust at the egocentric tyrannies of the General's or Keynaan's 'I am'. The notion of a single superb deductive intelligence implied in the figure of the traditional detective

> ... comes rather too close to the belief in one leader, one rescuer, that the novel
> opposes. (Adam 2002: 342–343)

Expectations are critically complicated, with few easy answers given to despots or readers alike. What may appear stylistic solipsism to the latter is ideological anathema to the former. Whilst Ngũgĩ writes in an alternative context, his thoughts enable us to see how Farah's choice of genre corresponds to some more longstanding convictions. In *Penpoints, Gunpoints, and Dreams*, he maintains that:

> Art has more questions than it has answers. Art starts with a position of
> not knowing and it seeks to know ... There may be answers implied in the
> questions. But they are often hints, open-ended possibilities, and not certitudes
> ... The state, on the other hand, has plenty of answers and hardly any questions.
> The more absolutist the state, the less it is likely to ask questions of itself or
> entertain questioning by others. (Ngũgĩ 1998: 15)

As Jacqueline Bardolph maintains, the complexities and frustrations of Loyaan's quest compel the reader to become an active producer of textual meaning: '[Farah] does not underestimate our capacity to react and think as free moral agents. The tale is a riddle ... [he] risks losing us at times ... but we come back for more, because the enigmas he entertains us with are of the kind that aim at transforming our vision' (Bardolph 2000: 121). The transformative, arguably ethical imperatives bubbling beneath the surface of *Sweet and Sour Milk* are integral to its success. Accordingly, it is crucial that Farah portrays an unwilling and, at times, unwitting protagonist. The circular dialectic and architecture of power that both Foucault and Ahmed allude to in their respective fields is realised in Loyaan's maddening search: '[he] took several possible roads but came upon a cul-de-sac as before. Questions and questions. Whys and no wherefores' (*S&SM*: 58).

Whilst Farah presents Loyaan's quest as a reflection of the General's obfuscatory order, the maze is a puzzle predicated on the existence, however cryptic, of an exit. In 'Wild Orchids and Trotsky', Said suggests that '[Foucault] is like a scribe of a kind of irresistible, ineluctable power', with his totalising vision of power consigning us, as subjects, to indefinite wandering in a labyrinth of repression (Said 2002b: 170). Whilst Farah's protagonists may struggle, the process itself enables them to explore alternative 'truths' within autocratic society. Returning to a more foundational micropolitics of the body becomes the catalyst for more systemic resistance. To this effect, the concluding tableau of *Close Sesame* and, therefore, the trilogy as a whole centres on a 'scattering of limbs' and the dismembered corpse of elderly martyr Deeriye. As with Soyaan's mysterious liquidation, the reader is confronted with conflicting reports of Deeriye's death and the triptych concludes as it commenced; under a cloud of certain uncertainty. Whilst the aptly titled *Variations* series is buttressed by two deaths, carried out on the General's orders, both representations are, to varying degrees, preoccupied with reclaiming the bodies and identities of their respective victims. Whilst they mark literal and figurative dead ends, they frame explorations of familiarly Foucauldian themes; incarceration, madness, dissidence and illness amongst them. Numerous commentators have identified confinement and containment as Farah's major concerns in the *Variations* series. In the remainder of this analysis, I suggest how and why this should be supplemented by exploring his commitment to more urgent relationships between bodies and power.

The State as Stage: Torture and Performance in *Sweet and Sour Milk*

> Everything is happening on centre stage and in broad daylight. But let us not forget about the events taking place offstage, in dark labyrinths and deep tunnels where you see nothing, hear nothing, where terror's powerful pincers grab you by the throat, and where that desperate, superhuman cry that might save your soul while you offer up your body is pulled back into your gut.
> (*Mouloud Feraoun – Journal, 1995–1962: Reflections on the French-Algerian War*, 2000: 240)

Feraoun's chilling journal entry corresponds with a recurrent analogy throughout Farah's work. Whilst metaphors tend towards the overdetermined in some of his writing, the image of the theatre as a disciplinary, if shadowy, arena is both enduring and effective. Towards the inconclusive close of *Sweet and Sour Milk*, Loyaan conceives of his search, and Somalia itself, in darkly dramatic terms: 'this read like a badly-written play, with stage-directions almost non-existent, the stage dark and hardly lit, the actors and actresses unbriefed, and the dialogue unrehearsed' (*S&SM*: 203). Whilst the reader also cries out for direction, this is an almost literal transcription of Farah's own comments on the Barre regime. In 'Why I Write', he states, 'Somalia was a badly written play … and Siyad Barre was its author … he was also the play's main actor … he was its stage-designer and light-technician, as well as the audience. You can imagine how Siyad-Barre-as-subject oppressed and obsessed me' (Farah 2002: 10). Similarly, in *Close Sesame*, Deeriye describes Somalia as 'a stage where the Grandest Actor performs in front of an applauding audience that should be booing him' (*CS*: 214). To build from this, a theoretical and figurative marriage between Ngũgĩ on postcolonial Africa and Foucault on disciplinary designs proves instructive. The former's depiction of neo-colonial authoritarianism as extending the architecture(s) of oppressive power has been referred to. *Discipline and Punish* emerges as a particularly enabling intertext, however, due to its series of imagistic juxtapositions: light and shade, performance and punitive techniques and consequently the stage and prison panopticon.

In *Penpoints, Gunpoints, and Dreams*, Ngũgĩ suggests, 'the prison yard is like a stage where everything, including movement, is directed and choreographed by the state. The *mise-en-scène*, the play of light and shadows, the timing and regulation of actions … are directed by armed stage-hands they call prison warders' (Ngũgĩ 1998: 56). It is significant that Farah's imagined General is described, primarily in Soyaan's pronouncements, as the 'Grand Warder' of a Gulag-style society in which he manipulates the bonds of kith and kin to secure his dominance (*S&SM*: 10). The description is strikingly similar to accounts by detainees of Barre's regime. In *The Cost of Dictatorship – The Somali Experience*, Jama Mohamed Ghalib includes 'Inside Labaatan Jirow Secret Maximum Security Prison', an abridged report by Mohamed Barood Ali, a political prisoner. Alongside accounts of torture, Ali includes a diagram of the prison compound, describing how its design served as a concrete reflection of the divide-and-rule policies of Barre's regime (Ghalib 1995: 231–256). Considered in this light, the 'imaginary intensity' identified by Foucault also crackles throughout Farah's work: 'the panopticon functions as a kind of laboratory of power … a cruel, ingenious cage. The fact that it should have given rise, even in our own time, to so many variations, projected or realized, is evidence of the imaginary intensity that it has possessed for almost two hundred years' (Foucault 1991: 205). This, in turn, has a chilling correspondence with Wole Soyinka's carceral account, *The Man Died*. It is a text that, like *Discipline and Punish*, casts a lengthy shadow over the entire *Variations* cycle: 'interlocking cages, they appear to the uninitiated as mazes designed by mad scientists for testing the intelligence of mice … From mice to men is one easy intelligent step, cages and mazes to disorientate the mind' (Soyinka 1972: 124). In Farah's early work, the labyrinth emerges as the variation on this Foucauldian mechanism of power.

One playful technique established in *Sweet and Sour Milk* that comes to dominate Farah's fictional landscape is that of doubling or mirroring, both in terms of events and characters. Here, the comparisons and contrasts are intensified by situating them within the familial sphere. The twin brother juxtaposition comes early, concludes with a typical allusion to openness and is shot through with a dash of self-reflexive irony:

> Soyaan: a man of intrigue, rhetoric, polemic and politics. Loyaan: a man of melodramatic scenes, mundanities and lost tempers. Loyaan would insist, for instance, in removing all inverted commas from phrases like 'revolution in Africa', 'socialism in Africa', 'radical governments', whereas Soyaan was fond of dressing them with these and other punctuational accessories; he was fond of opening a parenthesis he had no intention of closing. (*S&SM*: 14)

Farah uses inverted commas to interrogate constructs such as 'nation' and 'postcolonial identity', as he does throughout his work. Similarly, it is entirely appropriate that, in a text primarily concerned with deciphering cryptic codes, the narrative should conclude with an incomplete parenthesis: 'doors untried had begun to open: the hinges of these doors creaked as they opened' (*S&SM*: 241). Whilst these motifs represent the tentative interpretative strategies of protagonist and reader alike, Farah pushes against moral doors that, in normal circumstances, have to remain sealed. As such, he engages in an 'unsettling, antiutopian' and thus suitably Foucauldian critique in which the seemingly rigid dichotomy between ruler and ruled is problematised. As Foucault states in *The History of Sexuality*, '[there] is no binary and all-encompassing opposition between rulers and ruled at the root of power relations, and serving as a general matrix' (Foucault 1990: 94). This relational conception of power is critical for the purposes of this study as a whole. In *Sweet and Sour Milk*, it is only by exploring the contested matrix between ruler and ruled that the reader comes to appreciate the necessity of employing protagonists who belong to a 'priviligentsia'.

Fittingly, therefore, one of the novel's principle mazes is that of morality, designed to present protagonists and readers alike with a series of navigational challenges. The contours of this moral maze are illuminated when Loyaan meets one of the General's ministers in an attempt to piece together some clues regarding his brother's death. Effectively, it marks his transition from bumbling sleuth to strategic interrogator. He comes tantalisingly close to penetrating the General's disciplinary labyrinth by scrutinising one of its stooges. It is crucial that Loyaan, like Khaliif in *Close Sesame*, focuses on the regime's reliance on torture to deal with opponents committed to speaking out against power. This resonates with a key assertion from *The History of Sexuality*: 'since the Middle Ages, torture has accompanied [confession] like a shadow, and supported it when it could go no further: the dark twins' (Foucault 1990: 59). In a Somali context, it also intersects with testimony from victims of the Barre regime: '[s]ometimes our tormentors concentrated on routinely sensitive parts of the body; on other occasions there were brutal and indiscriminate beatings of the whole body … The [National Security Service] officers often took part in the torture and seemed to enjoy it' (Ghalib 1995: 232). In *Sweet and Sour Milk*, Loyaan speculates that Il Siciliano's secretary, Mulki, has been dragged into the state's punitive machinery, only to be subjected to the kind of prolonged intimidation detailed in *The Cost of Dictatorship*. It also foreshadows the comparably carceral concerns of *Close Sesame*, which amplifies the Kafka-esque tones of this first *Variations* novel: '[p]eople had strange ways of disappearing into the prison-bowels of the Somali security system; and those who tried to find the missing at times disappeared into another hole just as black' (*CS*: 119). The introduction of torture in *Sweet and Sour Milk* provides Farah with a platform from which to launch a more nuanced critique of relays and networks of power. If Loyaan's investigative breakthrough sheds more light on the badly written play performed on the General's dimly lit stage, it also crucially obliges him to turn the spotlight on himself. This forces him to confront his own role as complicit 'extra':

> Perversely, Loyaan was enjoying himself now … He believed he would see … the Minister just fade away … He saw himself as the torturer, as the powerful pervert who puts the needle between the flesh of the thumb and the nail, screws it in harder, deeper, further and further, until it draws blood … Drill it in, harder, deeper … turn the ailing soul's cry into the scream of the tortured. (*S&SM*: 182)

The penetrating imagery is necessarily visceral. It allows the comparative reader to consider it in the same bloody company as depictions of rape and infibulation in *Sardines*, mutilation and menstruation in *Maps* or, with its chilling reference to 'enjoyment', Ali's testimony about his treatment at the hands of National Security Service officers.

As was the case in *Discipline and Punish*, I find it revealing that Farah relies on motifs of light and shade, revelation and concealment. It deepens the sense that the narrative action is shrouded in a veil of indeterminacy. The reader thus enters a moral labyrinth, in which the distinction between those carrying the oppositional light of truth against the General's obfuscations becomes less than clear. To build on this, I find Foucault's notion of 'agonism', as discussed by Chowers, particularly enabling: '[agonism] demands the acceptance of this fragmentary nature of power, as well as the lack of easy, nameable targets' (Chowers 2004: 169). Whilst Farah names his target (the General), the terms in which he does so are deliberately vague, just as the sadistic allure of power in the above passage creates an agonistic ambivalence between those associated with state repression and those seeking to resist it. This is a transposition of the 'complications' that characterise Soyaan's death and, I suggest, serve as a password for the entire text (*S&SM*: 31). It can also be seen in relation to Chowers' riposte to those who would charge Foucault's work with overwhelming quietism and pessimism: 'perhaps by insisting upon the anonymity of power Foucault seeks to convey another idea: that power is in me as well as in you, that it is internal as well as external, that I am responsible for its operation as well as you are' (Chowers 2004: 170). This informs what I take to be Farah's more compelling critique of power, as well as his interest in considering how it might be more effectively resisted. In the above tableau, for instance, Loyaan is represented as having access to the authoritarian regime of power as well as the capacity to oppose or mimic this regime. Typically, the onus is placed on the individual, as moral agent, to take responsibility for such negotiations with power. For Alden and Tremaine, it is the inherent tensions of Farah's protagonists, invariably situated between rulers and ruled, that make them both convincing and unsettling (Alden & Tremaine 1999: 45). For me, his focus on this vanguard class concentrates rather than dilutes his critique of power. It allows him to explore various ambivalent spaces in something like the disruptive fashion described by Said in *Representations of the Intellectual*: 'real intellectual analysis forbids calling one side innocent, the other evil. Indeed the notion of a side is ... highly problematic ... [and not] all either good or evil' (Said 1996: 119). In *Sweet and Sour Milk*, complications abound because caricatures of good and evil are unpacked. The result is that existential burdens are placed on individuals situated within complex processes.

In light of the above, Farah's preoccupation with power throughout the *Variations* sequence can be seen in the titular terms of two much later novels, *Links* (2004) and *Knots* (2007). By this, I mean that his critique is intensified by gesturing towards those invariably entangled complicities, complications and connections between characters and, by extension, a wider audience. By their very nature, these are often as profound as they are unpalatable. Yet, exploding reductive standards and narrowing the distances between oppressive and oppositional forces does not lead to a conflation of the two. Farah uses his fiction to explore how and why the contestatory degrees of difference between the spheres of despotic regime and its opponents might hold out the promise of genuine change. The most telling signposts, therefore, are in the trilogy's title. Whilst the overarching concern is dictatorship, it is the variations on this theme that give the critique of power real substance. In the typically elaborate terms of many of Farah's interior narratives, Loyaan imagines himself 'challenged like a torturer who couldn't make the tortured confess after the umpteenth piercing of the needle' (*S&SM*: 182). The simile is pivotal here. Likewise, when Deeriye playfully describes daughter Zeinab as a dictator, it obliges reader and protagonist to step back and re-evaluate the construction of comfortable moral distances at a more immediate level: '"[y]ou would be a dictator, you act like one, you are a prisoner of your own obstinacy, insisting on being right all the time. Which is what dictators do," he said teasingly' (*CS*: 93). As in *Sardines*, it is the inherent agonism of, rather than the chasm between, such differences that is vital. This once more corresponds with Foucault's more relational and therefore more refined conceptualisation of power. He sets this out in 'The Confession of the Flesh': 'in so far as power relations are an unequal and relatively stable relation of forces, it's clear that this implies an above and a below, a difference of potentials' (Foucault 1980a: 200–201).

For Alden and Tremaine, 'it is ... precisely [the elite's] education and wide experience that make them so attentive to the issue of individual autonomy, that loosen the hold of imposed identities on their consciousnesses, and that place them thereby in a position to recognize and to disclose the lies by which dictators gain and hold power' (Alden & Tremaine 1999: 84). By foregrounding the activities of his privileged group, Farah knocks power from its pedestal, making it susceptible to challenge rather than capitulating before it. For Barbara Turfan, however, his presentation of the 'Group of 10' is inherently troubling:

> The reader gets the impression that most of these elite neither know nor care about their fellow countrymen ... it is not clear in these novels whether [Farah] is not interested or whether it is his characters that are so. This is an imbalance ... [and] this weakness ... remains, I think, a very real one ... He cannot be putting over his message sufficiently clearly if the reader remains uncertain as to what that message actually is. (Turfan 2002: 278–280)

I would counter this by once again reiterating that Loyaan's bumbling quest in *Sweet and Sour Milk* is presented as an exploration of, rather than an arrival at, certain solutions. The very uncertainty of the process, therefore, becomes its critical feature. As Mnthali suggests in relation to *Maps*, perhaps some of the unease caused by Farah's ambivalent portraits comes from a dubious desire to have 'Africans' conform to dominant archetypes: 'we Africans should be excused the exasperation we often feel at not being considered "ordinary" unless we are poor and live in rural areas, a classification which has its roots in colonial anthropology' (Mnthali 2002: 191). Alden and Tremaine also take up this vital issue:

> In Farah's writing, unlike that of [his] contemporaries, we find no peasants forced from their land, no workers brutalized through rapid industrialization … Those who resist are drawn from a privileged class … often educated abroad, widely travelled, multilingual, and materially comfortable. For some readers this choice of protagonists undermines Farah's political analysis … Part of the distinctive importance of Farah's work is that he draws the attention of many non-African readers, by his choice of characters, to a complexity of social experience in Africa that such stereotypes have trained them to think does not exist or is not 'really African'. (Alden & Tremaine 1999: 83)

Some of the most enthralling and disquieting features of these novels concern the turbulent development and subsequent dissolution of an intellectual cadre. When the prospect of overhaul starts to crumble, the priviligentsia's program of resistance is reconfigured, brought back home to start again from concrete, local, often domestic sites and struggles. Consciousness on a suitably liberating scale is awakened as they come to see how and why their fellow countrymen are also engaged in pyramidal power relations. Whilst having a head, these cannot be effectively resisted until work has begun on dismantling the structure and system itself. If we are to accept Ngũgĩ's postcolonial state/penitentiary comparison, as discussed above, I suggest something akin to Foucault's response to an interviewer's question in 'The Eye of Power' chimes with Farah's broader aims in *Variations* and beyond: Perrot – 'And there's no point for the prisoners in taking over the central tower?' Foucault – 'Oh yes, provided that isn't the final purpose of the operation. Do you think it would be much better to have the prisoners operating the Panoptic apparatus and sitting in the central tower, instead of the guards?' (Foucault 1980b: 164–165). Transposed in an anti-colonial context, this is strikingly similar to Said's description of Fanon's resistant ideology in *The End of the Peace Process*: 'Fanon was right when he said to Algerians in 1960 that to substitute an Algerian policeman for a French one is not the goal of liberation: a change in consciousness is' (Said 2002c: xxvii).

It is therefore critical that Farah represents the Group's failure to mount a coherent challenge in terms of factional bad faith. As with the motif of disintegration introduced by spluttering Soyaan at the outset, the reader learns (through Ahmed-Wellie) how the intellectuals separated into two camps:

> 'Three meetings at most, and we split. One group was headed by Medina and the other by Soyaan. Medina held on to the belief that the General was the Master of Grand Irrelevances and Irreverences … and that no intellectual in his senses should take him seriously … Soyaan and I were of a different opinion. We held the view that there is a pattern studyable, that there is a logic behind almost all the General has done.' (*S&SM*: 140)

The key term here is 'pattern' precisely because, as Nonno tells Kalaman in *Secrets*, 'things look more complex than they seem when you study patterns' (*Sec*: 111). In order to speak out against power effectively, its labyrinthine mechanisms must be identified before they can be challenged and, ultimately, changed. Ahmed-Wellie alludes to the Group's ideological schism in terms of their divided thoughts about the ordered disorder manipulated by the General to retain his grip on power. In unwittingly accepting it as anarchic, and therefore unworthy of their resistant energies, key members appear to evade their resistant responsibilities.

The torture motif also links certain characters, enabling Farah to extend his meditations on the intellectuals' functions in order to foreground the relativity of their world views. Into Loyaan's already shaken world walks the mysterious Margaritta clutching her son Marco. Complications intensify following the revelation that Marco is Soyaan's son. Margaritta holds one key to unlocking *Sweet and Sour Milk's* cryptic labyrinth as she has a copy of the memorandum composed by her lover against the regime. In order to reclaim his brother's legacy, Loyaan must reaffirm his oppositional stance. As such, the document assumes particular importance. Farah tells how Margaritta 'had a decent and very well-paid job. In addition to that, she had recently inherited her (Italian) father's wealth … She was registered as an external student at the University of Rome, registered for a degree in law, and had recently begun to research for her thesis' (*S&SM*: 68). Coming from this privileged background, Margaritta considers herself qualified to hold forth on the colonial and neo-colonial woes of Africa's body politic. She does so in typically visceral terms:

> 'Africa, for nearly a century, was governed with the iron hand of European colonial economic interests: these ran Africa as though it were a torture-chamber. Africa has known the iron-rod, the whiplash, thumb-screwing and removing of testicles: Africa has been humiliated one way or another … Came the seventies. Army coups. Barefaced dictatorships. We see Africa 'taken back' to an era she had lived through before, the era of European dictatorship, concentration-camps. Africa is again a torture-chamber.' (*S&SM*: 124)

This final image corresponds with much of the most exhilarating work that has been done on the carceral realities of many colonial and postcolonial situations, as evidenced in the impressive *A History of Prison and Confinement in Africa*, amongst others.

Whilst the essence of her argument may be correct, Margaritta indulges in what Foucault, in 'Power and Strategies', calls 'scare-quote' logic, suggesting how and why it compromises the Group's effectiveness, both individually and collectively (Foucault 1980c: 135–136). Typically, she is less willing to acknowledge the culpability and complicity of the elite she belongs to. Alongside this, the discursive space between the internal evocation of torture to depict Loyaan's struggle with the vagaries of power and this image of Africa as sprawling torture-chamber captures those micrological/macrological negotiations that define Farah's work. The reader learns that Soyaan once described his brother as 'a man less mature politically, less conscious of social and political pressures' (*S&SM*: 115). It is again critical to emphasise, however, that this very political unpreparedness makes him an ideal guide. The text is refracted through Loyaan's quest to crack codes, resist official claims to his brother's name and navigate a path through the labyrinth of power. Accompanying him, the reader comes closest to deciphering 'the personal in the political' dialectic identified by Medina in *Sardines*. Margaritta's academic training at once endows and burdens her with a capacity for theoretical extrapolation. Whilst allowing her to forge productive links between despotic states, it means she also runs the risk of eliding the micrological in favour of the macrological. Genuine critique, the text seems to suggest, can only come from analysing their reciprocal relations. For Farah, it is the interrogation of these interconnections, alongside privileging the fleshy materiality of the body itself, that remains crucial.

Shall I Be Released?

In *Daybreak is Near*, Ahmed focuses on the 'complexity of metaphorical language'. He cites Adonis who suggests, 'metaphor does not allow a final and definitive answer, because it is in itself a battleground of semantic contradictions. It remains a begetter of questions, an agent of disruption, in contrast to the type of knowledge which aspires to certainty' (Ahmed 1996: 5). If this notion of disruption is akin to Kwame Appiah's statement on the academic function in *In My Father's House*, it also corresponds with the figurative fecundity of shifting body politics throughout *Sweet and Sour Milk* (Appiah 1992: 290). With Soyaan dead, the remaining family members argue over the post-mortem. This not only allows the reader to explore the supposed schisms between traditional and modern medical practices (Qumman refuses to have her son's body carved up in accordance with her belief in the Koran's 'uncomplicated' edicts), but also establishes the prevailing aura of confinement. In a revealing early aside, Loyaan establishes the dialectic between Soyaan's corpse and the polymorphous nature of narrative by demanding his deceased brother yield up his secrets: 'would a post-mortem examination have told us something you wouldn't want us told? … What if we had you cut up and restitched … would that reveal an untoward secret?' (*S&SM*: 20). If Ahmed's invocation of Adonis is reconfigured in corporeal terms, it becomes clear how some of the most prescient aspects of Farah's critique are refracted through this bodily prism.

For commentators such as I.M. Lewis and Alice Hashim, corporeal motifs are irresistible when it comes to describing the Somali (dis)order of things. In *A Modern History of the Somali*, for instance, Lewis states that 'Somalis sometimes speak about their diminished nationalism … in a way that recalls patients whose limbs have been amputated but still "feel" intact. Theirs is a phantom-limb view of their dismembered body politic' (Lewis 2002: ix). Similarly, for Hashim in *The Fallen State – Dissonance, Dictatorship and Death in Somalia*, '[predatory] rule in Somalia was the last resort of a failed state … [it] represented a terminally ill condition for the State was in the throes of a struggle for survival' (Hashim 1997: 4). In *Sweet and Sour Milk*, Soyaan also frames his critique of the General's gulag-esque state in fleshy terms: 'if we cannot totally remove the hernia of inefficiency … we might as well try to make the pimples of the body-politic bleed' (*S&SM*: 81). This reliance on body imagery sees Farah tread a tightrope between his own and/or his protagonists' imagistic indulgence (Amin and Gaddafi are represented with entrails garlanding their necks, *S&SM*: 90), whilst allowing him to suggest how it offers the regenerative promise of escape from the labyrinth. Wright's attention to the counter-hegemonic significance of these fleshy metaphors is critical:

> Recurring images of wombs, fertilizing sperm, foetuses and eggs are not merely symbolic of the aborted hopes of the 1969 Revolution or of the faith in the future which is pinned to the creative energies of Somalia's women. They also appear to represent the private bodily and sexual realities over which the state has no claim of ownership, that tender pragmatism of the flesh which becomes the only touchstone, the only tangible thing individuals have to hold onto in the enveloping malaise. (Wright 1994: 65)

As with all of Farah's touchstones, however, the desiring and disciplined body is locked in a fraught relationship with power. Soyaan's fatal poisoning may be the catalyst in a corporeal continuum that unfurls across this first trilogy and throughout Farah's oeuvre. Yet, as with Loyaan's investigative search, it is the very nature of this unravelling process that is significant. If Marco and baby Soyaan (son of Keynaan's young second wife Beydan) embody the regenerative hope of delivering Somalia anew, as do Ubax in *Sardines*, Samawade in *Close Sesame* and, perhaps more problematically, Askar in *Maps*, Farah is eager to juxtapose them with figures, often grandparents, who represent the sacrifices of and for history. As Adam maintains, 'new generations will bury the old, the Soyaans the Keynaans … The establishment of a new order will not give any one person the responsibility for final solutions, and indeed will preclude such absoluteness in favour of the endless provisionality of group agreement' (Adam 2002: 343). A key figure in this respect is Qumman. A focus on her besieged body allows Farah to present his centrifugal critique of power, something that intensifies across successive novels. It is also signalled, in two very different but mutually enabling contexts, by Chowers and Hashim. For Chowers, 'if discourse is the centripetal mode of our language, literature is the centrifugal one' (Chowers 2004: 159). For Hashim, 'the centrifugal aspect of Somaliness prevailed over the centripetal' (Hashim 1997: 4). I build on these interventions to show how relationships between bodies, designs and the shaping of world views in Farah's fiction are influenced by these centrifugal forces.

Mother to the twins and their younger sister Ladan, Qumann allows Farah to reflect on the embodied and enduring suffering of women. In so doing, he introduces the reader to evermore chilling features of the Grand Patriarch's hegemony: 'it was as if different parts of her had been dismantled at puberty and reassembled, in a rush, at old age. Also, today, she had bruises. Her forehead had bled and dried. There was a scar a night old on her head as well' (*S&SM*: 23). The source of this beating, meted out the night of Soyaan's death, is Keynaan. As becomes clear, it is one episode in a disturbingly long line:

> Whenever some superior officer humiliated him, he came and was aggressive to the twins and his wife. He would flog them, he would beat them – big, and powerful that he was, the Grand Patriarch whose authority drenched his powerless victims with the blood of his lashes. She would wait until the twins grew up, she confided to a neighbour. She would wait … Society, on top of it, required women to be tolerant, to be receptive, to be receiving – and forgiving … Keynaan and his generation have never known women … Soyaan would argue. (*S&SM*: 84)

With a loaded reference to being 'on top of it', Farah renders the patriarchal society Keynaan represents to be as sexually aggressive as it is overbearing. As Ahmed maintains, Farah's preoccupations with the sovereignty of the female body and the punitive relationship between authoritarian power and patriarchy have endured since *From a Crooked Rib* (Ahmed 1996: 78).

Whilst the embodied focus is unequivocal here, commentators have been less eager to explore the attendant ambivalences that distinguish portraits of figures such as Qumman. In turn, the nuances of Farah's critique of individual and collective responsibility, and its correspondence to his overarching concern with power, have not been afforded the attention they deserve. It is ironic that Qumman should alert Loyaan to the shadowy figure of Ahmed-Wellie and his tribal affiliations with the General ('Cousins only twice removed, that man's father and the General', *S&SM*: 79), as it is Ahmed-Wellie in turn who dismisses her world view:

> 'Qumman is simply a woman who feels threatened by Beydan and Margaritta; Beydan … being the wife Keynaan prefers and also because Soyaan supposedly ate poisoned food at her place; Margaritta because she represents the type of woman Qumman's generation detests' … Qumman detested young, educated, 'liberated women, the Margarittas, the Medinas.' Well, that simplified things, thought he. (*S&SM*: 164)

Loyaan's final comment is deliberately deceptive. What at first appears an oasis of order in the midst of textual chaos is in fact the primary target of Farah's critique. Once again, complications abound at the narrative and national levels because little is simple. The order of things can only be challenged once this reductive view has been dismissed. Elsewhere, it is revealed how Qumman despises Beydan for being a woman of 'inferior tribal breeding' (*S&SM*: 56) when she comes to pay her respects following Soyaan's death.

Complications define relationships in generational and clan terms alike. The essential point is that ways of being and seeing govern the world at both individual and societal levels. Turfan's critique of the Group as unconcerned with the plight of their fellow countrymen becomes more problematic when taking into account their impassioned discussions of competing ideologies within various domestic settings. From Farah's perspective, the Machiavellian General derives power simply by replicating the disciplinary designs found within the homes of figures such as Qumman. Once again, therefore, Foucault's comments in 'The Confession of the Flesh' have a certain resonance:

> I heard someone talking about power the other day … He observed that the famous 'absolute' monarchy in reality had nothing absolute about it. In fact it consisted of a number of islands of dispersed power, some of them functioning as geographical spaces, others as pyramids, others as bodies, or through the influence of familial systems, kinship networks and so forth. (Foucault 1980a: 207)

Transposing this in relation to Farah's work, we might substitute 'absolute monarchy' for 'absolute dictatorship'. Divide-and-rule tactics at the macrological level are seen as distorting the logic behind social organisation in a clan-based society where power is conceived in all its pyramidal complexity. This preoccupation with world views and/as disciplinary designs is similarly explored through the figure of Keynaan.

Described as if he were a Foucauldian delinquent, Keynaan is perhaps the most morally reprehensible figure in *Variations*: 'a former police inspector, a man forced to retire because of scandalous inconveniences he had created for the regime … An informer, a daily gatherer of spoken indiscretions, an 'ear-servant' of the National Security Service since he was semi-literate' (*S&SM*: 9). Commentators have written extensively on the oppressive dialectics of family and state in Farah's work. It is, however, a critique that benefits from the kind of Foucauldian supplement offered by Dubravka Juraga: '[Farah's] view of the function of the family as a tool of official oppression closely parallels Foucault's description of the bourgeois family of Victorian England as a focal point for power relations in a society' (Juraga 2002: 294). Before Soyaan dabbled in subversive memorandums, it was the abuse suffered by his mother that ignited his Oedipal/political conviction to usurp his father and all he could be seen to represent. Whilst body politics provide the unequivocal, if besieged, base of Farah's novels, they are also a gateway into considering the broader interplay of ideas that preoccupy him. As Alden and Tremaine suggest, 'to enter into [the Group of 10's] world as a reader … is to enter into a discourse of ideas imagined as flesh and blood, a lived debate, one that goes on both among and within characters' (Alden & Tremaine 1999: 45). This conceptual contest is exemplified in an exchange between Keynaan and Loyaan.

Like Idil in *Sardines*, Keynaan offers a scathing critique of the intelligentsia's incompetence: 'no young man of your age that I know has ever appeared as 'dangerous priority' on the list drawn up by the Security … You have no common ideology for which you fight. You have no organised protest … you are no threat … The General fears tribal chieftains or men of his age. Not you, nor Soyaan, nor anyone of your Generation' (*S&SM*: 91). It is revealing that this episode emerges immediately before the end of Part One, with Part Two being introduced by the pivotal Wilhelm Reich epigraph: 'in the figure of the father the authoritarian state has its representative in every family, so that the family becomes its most important instrument of power' (*S&SM*: 95). Keynaan's indictment strikes a dispiriting blow to the Group's insurgent aspirations. Whilst lacking the wisdom of Deeriye in *Close Sesame* or the compassion of Nonno in *Secrets*, Keynaan does display an awareness of 'power as a system', in turn showing how he and the General play their patriarchal parts in it. As such, his accusation that the Group effectively represents an ideological void against the General's manipulation of existing social structures and affiliations is pertinent. The spectre of total despair, however, is in turn challenged by this portrait of counter-hegemonic fallibility, with Farah keeping his focus firmly on the incremental processes of resistance.

Farah places this confrontation at the close of Part One. If this suggests his critical convictions, it also indicates the centrality of designs within the trilogy as a whole. Having argued about Keynaan's role in Soyaan's death and the subsequent reappropriation of his legacy, Loyaan identifies a familiarly savage glint in his father's eye. It reminds Loyaan of an incident in the twins' childhood, when Keynaan slashed the ball the boys were playing with. This memory, which is presented early and recurs throughout the text, recalls Soyaan's promise that 'I will kill him. When I am old enough to use a knife. I will' (*S&SM*: 94), before returning to the narrative present in which Keynaan announces to brotherless Loyaan, 'I am the father. It is my prerogative to give life and death as I find fit. I've chosen to breathe life into Soyaan. And remember one thing, Loyaan: if I decide to cut you in two, I can. The law of this land invests in men of my age the power. I am the Grand Patriarch' (*S&SM*: 94). With this flourish, Keynaan departs, leaving the reader in little doubt as to the despotic comparisons between domestic and national patriarchs. As Adam maintains, '[Keynaan's] attitude to women (always a touchstone for enlightenment in Farah) parallels that of the General to his subjects: it is tyrannous, dismissive of their capacities and proprietorial of their role' (Adam 2002: 340). Elsewhere, Fanon has drawn attention to this patriarchy/power dynamic. In *The Invention of Somalia*, Ahmed, amongst others, considers how Fanonian thought might be transposed within a Somali context (Ahmed 1995: 149). In *Black Skin, White Masks*, Fanon declares that 'there are close connections between the structure of the family and the structure of the nation. Militarization and the centralization of authority in a country automatically entail a resurgence of the authority of the father' (Fanon 1967: 141–142). To maintain a Foucauldian perspective, it is necessary to note a key divergence, as discussed in *The History of Sexuality*: 'the father in the family is not the "representative" of the sovereign or the state; and the latter are not projections of the father on a different scale. The family does not duplicate society, just as society does not imitate the family' (Foucault 1990: 100). If Farah's position exists somewhere between these two statements, his most compelling critique comes from what appear to be the textual margins.

When Keynaan bursts his sons' ball, it heralds 'the age of challenge. The age of growth' (*S&SM*: 94). It is a statement applicable to both protagonists within this text and the Group's general socio-political development. The dialectical progress of history rests on struggle and it is this process that fascinates author and reader throughout *Variations*. Accordingly, Patricia Alden's *Sardines* note can be applied to the trilogy as a whole: 'with Medina the positive and negative perspectives are located within history: the unresolved questions involve evaluating the efficacy of her actions in history, and this efficacy cannot be established' (Alden 2002: 379). The destructive intent with which Keynaan wields the knife recalls the painful infibulation undergone by Somali women. The connections between patriarchal power at both micro and macro levels of governance are pronounced. Indeed, the novel implies that it is Keynaan's dismissal of body politics as a touchstone for the Group that might eventually constitute his undoing and that of the system itself. When he accuses Loyaan's young generation of having no coherent ideology, he omits mention of the embodied political concepts upon which their loftier insurgent aspirations are based: the right of corporeal sovereignty and respect for individual liberties. As Juraga suggests, this familial conflict allows Loyaan to gain a clearer insight into power as system. Foucauldian parallels remain striking:

> Farah suggests that the authoritarian structure of the Somali family makes Somali society inherently susceptible to political oppression. In that he parallels Foucault, who points out that in bourgeois Europe the family organization is used to support other 'maneuvers' of the larger alliances of power in the society. In a sense, the family acts as a 'back-up' to other strategies of power by enacting the power hierarchy already existing in the society. (Juraga 2002: 289)

Keynaan destroys the ball the twins used to imagine their universe in an apocalyptic precursor to Askar's vision of a globe without boundaries in *Maps*. Whilst this symbol is self-explanatory, it captures the central relationship between micrological and macrological designs of and on power. Ideologies are oftentimes conceived in geometric terms in *Variations*, and it is Loyaan's recollection of the words his brother used to articulate the divergent world views of father and twins that will come to haunt the trilogy. They also express the fundamental imperatives of Farah's critique of power: 'not so much generational as they are qualitative – the differences between us twins and our father. My father grew up with the idea that the universe is flat; we, that it is round … We believe that his are exclusive, that they are flat (and therefore uninteresting) as the universe his insularities tie him to' (*S&SM*: 83). Such degrees of difference or 'potential', to borrow from Foucault once more, remain critical. Effectively, Keynaan's conceptual failure lies in his refusal to acknowledge the presence of alternative geometries. He thus replicates the General's propagandistic power. Loyaan internalises his brother's sentiments. His description of appeals to a lofty figure eradicating complications and answering all questions offers a portrait of despotic deity crossed with omniscient detective and omnipotent prison warder aloft his watchtower:

> 'My father sees himself as a miniature creature in a flat world dominated by a God-figure high and huge as any mountain anyone has ever seen … When you confront him with a question of universal character, his answer is tailor-made, he will say: 'Only Allah knows, only Allah.' A miniature creature dependent upon his creator to answer his questions. Suddenly, however, he behaves as if he were

the most powerful of men, the biggest. Suddenly, he is, as Soyaan called him, the Grand Patriarch.'(*S&SM*: 83)

The image of detached, surveying power conjures up spectres of Foucault. As such, it informs the remainder of this analysis.

Architectures of Power and Resistance

Power has its principle not so much in a person as in a certain concerted distribution of bodies, surfaces, lights, gazes; in an arrangement whose internal mechanisms produce the relations in which individuals are caught up.

(Michel Foucault – Discipline and Punish, 1991: 202)

Summarising *Variations*, Alden and Tremaine compare the more overt subversion of *Sardines* and the outright violence of *Close Sesame* with *Sweet and Sour Milk's* preoccupation with 'research, documentation and disclosure' (Alden & Tremaine 1999: 58). Whilst this resonates with a Foucauldian obsession with discourse and its normalising impulses, a supplementary interpretation might consider Soyaan's original memorandum as a meditation on the technology of power itself. Soyaan's collaborator, Ibrahim Musse, explains the relevance of its title, 'Dionysius's Ear', to an inquisitive Loyaan:

'The Syracusan tyrant had a cave built in the shape of a human ear which echoed to him in polysyllables whatever the prisoners whispered secretly to one another. Soyaan and I saw a similarity between this and the method the General has used so far. The Security Services in this country recruit their main corps from illiterates, men and women who belong to an oral tradition, and who neither read nor write but report daily, report what they hear as they hear it … Everything is done verbally … We say in our Memo that the General (with the assistance of the Soviets) has had an ear-service of tyranny constructed.' (*S&SM*: 136–137)

With the emphasis placed on relays, networks and constructed surveillance systems, the above description places individuals akin to Foucault's delinquents within a specifically Somali context. As Perrot maintains in relation to the Panopticon's archetypal design in 'The Eye of Power', 'at the same time one is very struck by the techniques of power used within the Panopticon. Essentially it's the gaze; but also speech, because he has

those famous 'tin tubes', that extraordinary invention, connecting the chief
inspector with each of the cells, in which Bentham tells us that not just a single
prisoner, but small groups of prisoners are confined' (Foucault 1980b: 154).
Once again, this works in an intriguingly contrapuntal manner with Ali's
testimony in *The Cost of Dictatorship*. In it, he details how inmates devised
their own, ingenious method of communication:

> our knocking on the cell walls developed secretly into a fine art. We devised
> an alphabet from the two distinct sounds available to us – a loud note made
> with the knuckles of the middle fingers and a low drumming note … I cannot
> overestimate the value of our alphabet because it was the only method of
> human contact left to us. The guards could not see us and never made the
> mental leap of deducing that we were able to understand each other by
> 'touching the walls'. (Ghalib 1995: 245)

If this provides a discursive framework in which to read some of *Sweet and
Sour Milk's* carceral concerns, Ibrahim's depiction of dystopian design once
again confounds Medina's dismissal of the General as unworthy adversary.
The 'politically immature' Loyaan illustrates the extent of his development
by couching his critique in relation to his fallen brother, even acknowledging
the power wielded over posthumous reputations: 'the Master of Grand
Irrelevances? No, Medina is wrong. The man kills. The man has designs on
our lives. The man can eliminate a person and then take possession of his
soul and have him discredited in the eyes of his friends' (*S&SM*: 142).

As with Ahmed-Wellie's attention to patterns, it is this focus on design
and the architecture(s) of power that elevates this opening instalment. It also
obliges the reader to consider links between it and the body-politics motif
that runs throughout Farah's oeuvre. The labyrinthine, quasi-detective quest
Loyaan is engaged in is ominously reflected in the authoritarian society's
disciplinary designs. He both operates within and is ultimately charged with
deciphering and opposing them. Read in this way, Foucault's notion of getting
'caught up' assumes greater significance. Here, the labyrinth is characterised
by reverberation, rumour and reiteration, with whispers and echoes amplified
to such an extent that they come to sound like 'truths'. Farah offers something
akin to an Orwellian dystopia, in which the entanglements of power relations
are such that family members occupying the same space clash with one
another. The buffer zone between despotic regime and counter-hegemonic
intelligentsia is most obviously represented by Keynaan. As such, Farah can
be seen as playing with Foucault's notion of the relationship between secrecy

and the mechanisms of power. In *The History of Sexuality*, he states that '[p]ower is tolerable only on condition that it mask a substantial part of itself … secrecy is not in the nature of an abuse; it is indispensable to its operation' (Foucault 1990: 86). In the General's Somalia, webs of political affiliation are an open secret; the fundamentally cellular nature of power is veiled by the façade of socialist advancement. What makes the situation even more ominous is that, accepting Ngũgĩ's concept of the tyrannical neo-colonial African state as penitentiary, the agents of resistance are hampered by the axial invisibility and limited communication depicted by Foucault. Chowers explains it in the following terms: 'atomized individuals find it difficult to assemble the knowledge and develop the cognitive understanding needed to truly and comprehensively fathom their predicament; moreover, even if such an understanding could be attained, detached individuals lack the mutual trust and social practices necessary for ameliorative collective action' (Chowers 2004: 190–191). In Farah's fiction, the oppositional hope manifest in the 'touching of walls' described in Ali's testimony is constantly under threat.

In *Discipline and Punish*, Foucault refers to 'a microphysics of what might be called a "cellular" power' (Foucault 1991: 149). He maintains that 'discipline organizes an analytical space … Even if the compartments it assigns become purely ideal, the disciplinary space is always, basically, cellular' (Foucault 1991: 143). With awareness of the alternative contexts in which these concepts are employed, I find something like these notions of cellular power and disciplinary/analytical space at play throughout the *Variations* cycle. In place of the authoritarian gaze that will come to dominate proceedings in *Sardines*, *Sweet and Sour Milk* is concerned with oral resonance within a society where 'rumour rules' (*S&SM*: 116). In the regime's disciplinary design, it is the peculiar conjunction of surveillance eyes and ears that guarantees the order of things. Soyaan's 'Dionysius's Ear' document circumvents the channels of oral communication and attacks power on paper. Whilst this largely constitutes the radical threat that must be neutralised, in the guise of its author, it is also its major flaw. In a society more reliant on speech than writing, the transcription of subversive material to print can only ever have a limited reach. Simply put, the 'captive' and/ or 'entrapped' Group fails to spread its oppositional message. The strength of Farah's critique of power lies in demonstrating how the Syracusan tyrant utilises the essentially cellular base of power in Somalia, manipulating its oral networks and distorting clan logic in order to retain control. As the Barre and post-Barre national narratives attest, the trajectories of fiction and fact run conspicuously parallel.

Beyond this, however, Farah displays the all-too-human fallibilities of his imagined intelligentsia by illustrating how they succumb to cellular power struggles. The multiple meanings of the term 'cell', therefore, are of particular significance. To extend the penitentiary metaphor further, Farah's Group can be seen in terms of the greater prison of the Grand Warder's Somalia. As in the fractured relationship between Qumman and Beydan, their descent into factional squabbles provides sobering evidence of the success of his divide-and-rule policies. When rumour triumphs, trust evaporates and political allegiances are strained to breaking point. The autocrat sits aloft in his privileged tower surveying the ordered disorder that solidifies his power base. Individual compartments in the imagistic prison of the surveillance state are replicated in the composition of political 'cells'. Both are defined by paradoxically porous walls; they allow information to leak into the sphere of the General's control whilst preventing the kind of intercommunication needed to mount a coherent program of resistance. Whilst resonating with Ngũgĩ's postcolonial state/penitentiary association, Farah's portrait of the intelligentsia and its failings is also uncannily close to Foucault's notion of 'lateral invisibility', as set out in *Discipline and Punish*:

> Each individual, in his place, is securely confined to a cell from which he is seen from the front by the supervisor; but the side walls prevent him from coming into contact with his companions. He is seen, but he does not see; he is the object of information, never a subject in communication. The arrangement of his room, opposite the central tower, imposes on him an axial visibility; but the divisions of the ring, those separated cells, imply a lateral invisibility. And this invisibility is a guarantee of order. (Foucault 1991: 200)

The sinister designs Loyaan identifies as the General's are replicated in the social structure and architecture of power on the ground. The specificities of this cellular authority are first considered in an earlier work.

Whilst *A Naked Needle* functions as a conceptual laboratory for Farah, an intriguing and lengthy episode shows protagonist Koschin acting as a guide for his foreign girlfriend, Nancy. Escorting her round Mogadiscio, he identifies the General's growing personality cult in those incessant reminders of his dominance. For Ahmed, 'Koschin treats the city both as a backdrop and as a political space both to attack Barre's regime and to rewrite Somali historiography' (Ahmed 1996: 92). By the more ominous time of *Sweet and Sour Milk*, the propagandistic banners and murals remain. His omniscient power is, however, really represented by Orientation centres attended by citizens so that they can be 'educated' in the goals of the faux-revolutionary regime. In an Orwellian pastiche, these centres are effectively surveillance cells operating to monitor and, where necessary, neutralise dissent. Loyaan's evocation of the confined, cellular cityscape and Soyaan's description of the Grand Warder with the master keys again has eerie associations with Foucault:

> '[Mogadiscio] is broken into thirteen cells, of which all but one is of manageable size.[3] The security deems it necessary to break this sandy city into these, have each house numbered, the residents counted ... The General has the master key to all cells, whether numbered or unnumbered. He is the Grand Warder ... Thrice weekly, civil servants should report themselves to the Centres at which they are registered ... If any person is found missing on two counts of six, he or she loses his or her job.' (*S&SM*: 87)

The notion of punitive and political cells is again reconfigured as Farah seems preoccupied with the dialectic of disciplinary apparatus and space. When grafted onto the already complex divisions of Somali society, Foucault's meditations on the authoritarian gaze and the surveillance relationship between (Orientation) centre and periphery can be translated effectively: 'the perfect disciplinary apparatus would make it possible for a single gaze to see everything constantly ... a perfect eye that nothing would escape and a centre towards which all gazes would be turned' (Foucault 1991: 173). Like the Syracusan tyrant, the General employs parts of the perfect ear that hears all.

The concern with confinement, enclosure and entrapment in *Variations* is established in both private and public spheres. Mnthali has made a persuasive comparison between such elements in Farah's work and Sembene Ousmane's *Xala*. In both, the transgressive threat represented by beggars must be purged for the benefit of visiting leaders: 'before any head of state visited a town, the Local Government and the Security swept away these ugly sights and kept them at bay for the whole period the foreign dignitaries were in the country' (*S&SM*: 145). If the presence of these itinerant figures shatters the illusion of socialist harmony, it also embodies a challenge to the cellular power and containment procedures relied upon by the regime. Like Khaliif in *Close Sesame*, the beggars are audience members witnessing the General's badly written play. Their negligible position means they are under no pressure to keep up appearances. The result is that they emerge as disruptive, and therefore potentially dangerous, hecklers:

> They were among the ugly sights of poverty, the bad conscience of the
> Revolution, beggars who reminded one of the grave situation of the national
> economy despite the statistics published in government bulletins. One of them
> started to sing the General's praises and choked on them. Another tried to lift
> the refrain from where the other had left it but couldn't continue … It was like
> a theatre audience not agreed on whether to clap: the solitary applause died at
> the immature stage of ridiculousness. (*S&SM*: 235)

As in *Xala*, beggars blur the boundaries of state authority, oftentimes evading
the surveillance gaze. As such, they pose a series of 'complications'. They
have a comparably disquieting function to the lepers in Foucault's discursive
imagining. In effect, they are disorder made flesh. It is only through their
definitive removal that the disciplinary apparatus can re-establish the
normative and cellular division of the wider body politic. Reappropriating
Adonis' notion of the inherent instability of metaphorical language, however,
Farah does entertain the possibility of regenerative and resistant hope. An
analysis of power and resistance that privileges the microphysics of struggle
provides one such outlet. A supplementary, suitably Foucauldian outlet
in Farah's imagining sees a return to the unstable sphere of personal and
biological cells.

Ahmed's project concerns 'how literature captures in an inchoate form the
incremental process: the accretions that caused the original cell (containing
the replicating Somali mitochondria) to become dangerously turgid; the
fraying at the seams that led to the cataclysmic disintegration of the abode
that had hitherto housed the "Somali character"' (Ahmed 1996: 34). Similarly,
Farah's texts are preoccupied with incremental processes at micrological
and macrological levels. Central to both his fictional labyrinth, as well as
the disciplinary designs of the regime, is the body. As such, Farah's work
traces the oscillations between body and polity, and how the realisation
of these ongoing interconnections offers the most enduring prospect of
escape. Whilst writing in a South African context, this is something touched
on by Paul Gready in *Writing as Resistance*: '[i]nternal space (the body)
and external space (the cell, the prison, and beyond) can be mobilized to
transgress the repressive spatial design and its central components: isolation,
immobilization, and surveillance' (Gready 2003: 86). In *Sweet and Sour Milk*,
this point is illustrated through the twins' sister, Ladan, to whom they offer
the gift of reading the world differently:

(It was here that Loyaan's memory swam away back to days when Ladan was barely two … How the twins had protected her from those murderous looks of Keynaan and the – at times – indifferent attitudes of Qumman to a girl. They would invest in Ladan their hopes, they would trust their future with her. They used to take turns telling her fables from faraway lands, the sagas of Iceland and Norway, the Nights of Arabia, the stories of Tagore, the tales of Ukraine and those of China. They fed her small brain on figures round, complete and open-ended. They trained her young mind with the aid of circles, squares and trigonometry. She was like them – except she was a girl. *The world is an egg and it awaits your breaking it. Clear the mistiness of the white off your eyes and the yolk is yours – yellow and sick, yes, but yours for the asking*). (*S&SM*: 108)

Revealingly framed in parentheses, this incident is distinguished in Loyaan's memory as belonging to a brighter, more integrated past set aside from the determined indeterminacy of the present. It is essential that, whilst the text ends with an open parenthesis, this memory is complete. Whilst the playful presentation lends it an almost throw-away quality, it strikes me as an attempt to catch the reader off-guard, capturing as it does so many of Farah's major preoccupations. The regenerative hope invested in Marco and baby Soyaan is given a longer historical perspective within the (potentially oppositional) domestic sphere. The cosmopolitan influences of this first post-Independence group are typically on display. It is the emphasis on design and trigonometry, however, that appears most crucial in relation to concerns with narrative, the construction of various labyrinths and the possibility of release. The gifts bestowed by the twins are both the imagined howl of Saul Bellow's dog ('For God's sake, open the universe a little more!') and the confidence to construct alternative ways of engaging that world (Rushdie 1992: 21). That these seeds of autonomy should be planted in a cultural context where a young girl is treated with indifference by her own mother lends the act additional hope. The reader may dismiss Farah's final italicised sentences as indulgent. Yet, considered within *Sweet and Sour Milk's* murky context, they do resonate with the concept of deciphering a code in order to find a way through the labyrinth.

Viewed in this light, the mistiness of the white symbolises the novel's evasiveness, with its yellow yolk constituting the body existing at the core of both disciplinary and emancipatory designs. References to circles and patterns recall the *Detained* epigraph above. The notable allusion to 'figures round, complete and open-ended', however, resonates both with the narrative's unresolved nature and Farah's broader aims. His novels and protagonists have been criticised for their inconclusiveness. Narratives taper off, characters disappear and no coherent plan of revolutionary action is implemented. Yet, in a society where confinement, containment and surveillance are the norm, a little indeterminacy is to be prized, rather than derided under the lazy exegeses of what Idelber Avelar, borrowing an epigraph from Foucault, calls 'self-satisfied postmodernism' (Avelar 1999: 233). Labyrinths can be fathomed when alternative exits are sought. The reclamation of Wright's 'tender pragmatism of the flesh' represents one such outlet. What he cites as the inadequacy of Ladan's portrait might, I suggest, constitute her exceptionalism: 'it is Ladan who, significantly, is left at the end of the book holding the child born out of Beydan's death and who names him Soyaan ... Ladan seems therefore to hold the key to Soyaan's posthumous future. Yet she is, puzzlingly, one of the few characters who fails to reappear or receive any substantial mention in the next two volumes of the trilogy' (Wright 1994: 64).

Ladan is represented as exiting the maze of Farah's dystopian imagining. Individual agents emerge to take charge of their political being and, in the process, begin to dismantle the very foundations upon which despotic power is based. Fittingly, therefore, one of the text's most poignant portraits captures the union between the two young women, Ladan and Beydan. In contrast to her indifferent mother, Ladan breaks a myopic cycle by attending to her less privileged 'sister' during her difficult pregnancy: 'the patternless loom of shades, after a while, answered a known design; all those present, save Ladan and Qumman, turned their eyes away. And from that rubble rose Ladan. She came over and took Beydan's other arm. *Of such gestures are understanding sisters made*, thought he' (*S&SM*: 57). It is one of Farah's more hopeful experiments in doubling, accompanied as it is by the statement that 'the universe is round and not flat. It is oval-shaped like an egg awaiting a hand to break it in half like a rubber ball' (*S&SM*: 101). The imagery evokes memories of Keynaan's despotic worldly designs as well as the faded symbols of the Somali Revolution. The act of breaking, however, signals transformative change, bestowing Ladan with the possibility of resistant agency and the chance to form other bonds, more emancipatory than carceral. Loaded with imagistic as well as ideological significance, Farah gestures towards alternative networks of communication: 'doors untried had begun to open: the hinges of these doors creaked as they opened ... Let creaking doors creak. And use them while you may' (*S&SM*: 241). Mysteries are half-revealed until the very end of *Sweet and Sour Milk*. Crucially, however, some key interpretative doors have been tried and alternative exits from the labyrinth sought. They open onto the associated concerns of *Sardines*, a novel in which questions surrounding the political sovereignty of the female body are dragged centre stage.

References

Adam, I. 2002. 'The Murder of Soyaan Keynaan'. In D. Wright (Ed.). *Emerging Perspectives on Nuruddin Farah*. New Jersey: Africa World Press.

Ahmed, A.J. 1995. '"Daybreak is Near, Won't You Become Sour?" Going Beyond the Current Rhetoric in Somali Studies'. In A.J. Ahmed (Ed.). *The Invention of Somalia*. New Jersey: The Red Sea Press Inc.

Alden, P. 2002. 'New Women and Old Myths: Chinua Achebe's *Anthills of the Savannah* and Nuruddin Farah's *Sardines*'. In D. Wright (Ed.). *Emerging Perspectives on Nuruddin Farah*. New Jersey: Africa World Press.

Alden, P. & Tremaine, L. 1999. *Nuruddin Farah*. New York: Twayne Publishers.

Appiah, K. 1992. *In My Father's House – Africa in the Philosophy of Culture*. London: Methuen.

Avelar, I. 1999. *The Untimely Present – Post-dictatorial Latin American Fiction and the Task of Mourning*. London: Duke University Press.

Bardolph, J. 2000. 'On Nuruddin Farah.' *Research in African Literatures*, Vol.31, No.1.

Chowers, E. 2004. *The Modern Self in the Labyrinth – Politics and the Entrapment Imagination*. Cambridge, Mass.: Harvard University Press.

Djebar, A. 2001. *So Vast the Prison*. (B. Wing, Trans.). New York: Seven Stories Press.

Dreyfus, H. & Rabinow, P. 1983. *Michel Foucault: Beyond Structuralism and Hermeneutics*. (2nd ed.). Chicago: The University of Chicago Press.

Ewen, D.R. 1984. 'Nuruddin Farah'. In G.D. Killam (Ed.). *The Writing of East and Central Africa*. London: Heinemann.

Fanon, F. 1967. *Black Skin, White Masks*. (C. Markmann, Trans.). New York: Grove Press.

Farah, N. 2002. 'Why I Write'. In D. Wright (Ed.). *Emerging Perspectives on Nuruddin Farah*. New Jersey: Africa World Press.

Feraoun, M. 2000. *Journal, 1955–1962: Reflections on the French-Algerian War*. (M. Wolf & C. Fouillade, Trans.). Lincoln: University of Nebraska Press.

Foucault, M. 1980a. 'The Confession of the Flesh'. In C. Gordon (Ed.). *Power/Knowledge – Selected Interviews and Other Writings*. Harlow: Pearson Education Ltd.

Foucault, M. 1980b. 'The Eye of Power'. In C. Gordon (Ed.). *Power/Knowledge – Selected Interviews and Other Writings*. Harlow: Pearson Education Ltd.

Foucault, M. 1980c. 'Power and Strategies'. In C. Gordon (Ed.). *Power/Knowledge – Selected Interviews and Other Writings*. Harlow: Pearson Education Ltd.

Foucault, M. 1990. *The History of Sexuality, An Introduction*. (R. Hurley, Trans.). London: Penguin.

Foucault, M. 1991. *Discipline and Punish – The Birth of the Prison*. (A. Sheridan, Trans.). London: Penguin.

Foucault, M. 2007. *Security, Territory, Population: Lectures at the Collège de France, 1977–1978*. Senellart, M. (Ed.). (G. Burchell, Trans.). New York: Palgrave MacMillan.

Ghalib, J. 1995. *The Cost of Dictatorship – The Somali Experience*. New York: Lilian Barber Press.

Gready, P. 2003. *Writing As Resistance – Life Stories of Imprisonment, Exile, and Homecoming from Apartheid South Africa*. New York: Lexington Books.

Hashim, A. 1997. *The Fallen State – Dissonance, Dictatorship and Death in Somalia*. Maryland: University Press of America.

Juraga, D. 2002. 'Nuruddin Farah's *Variations on the Theme of an African Dictatorship*: Patriarchy, Gender and Political Oppression in Somalia'. In D. Wright (Ed.). *Emerging Perspectives on Nuruddin Farah*. New Jersey: Africa World Press.

Lewis, I.M. 2002. *A Modern History of the Somali*. (4th ed.). Oxford: James Currey.

Lomnitz-Adler, C. 1992. *Exits from the Labyrinth – Culture and Ideology in the Mexican National Space*. Los Angeles: University of California Press.

Martin, G. 1989. *Journeys through the Labyrinth – Latin American Fiction in the 20th Century*. London: Verso.

Miller, J. 2000. *The Passion of Michel Foucault*. Cambridge, Mass.: Harvard University Press.

Mnthali, F. 2002. 'Autocracy and the Limits of Identity: A Reading of the Novels of Nuruddin Farah'. In D. Wright (Ed.). *Emerging Perspectives on Nuruddin Farah*. New Jersey: Africa World Press.

Nelson, D. 1999. *A Finger in the Wound – Body Politics in Quincentennial Guatemala*. Los Angeles: University of California Press.

Ngũgĩ wa Thiong'o. 1981. *Detained: A Writer's Prison Diary*. London: Heinemann.

Ngũgĩ wa Thiong'o. 1998. *Penpoints, Gunpoints, and Dreams: Towards a Critical Theory of the Arts and the State in Africa*. Oxford: Clarendon Press.

Rushdie, S. 1992. *Imaginary Homelands – Essays and Criticism 1981–91*. London: Granta Books.

Said, E. 1996. *Representations of the Intellectual – The 1993 Reith Lectures*. New York: Vintage Books.

Said, E. 2002a. 'Overlapping Territories: The World, The Text, and The Critic'. In G. Viswanathan (Ed.). *Power, Politics, and Culture – Interviews with Edward W. Said*. New York: Vintage Books.

Said, E. 2002b. 'Wild Orchids and Trotsky'. In G. Viswanathan (Ed.). *Power, Politics, and Culture – Interviews with Edward W. Said*. New York: Vintage Books.

Said, E. 2002c. *The End of the Peace Process – Oslo and After*. London: Granta.

Soyinka, W. 1972. *The Man Died: Prison Notes of Wole Soyinka*. London: Rex Collings Ltd.

Turfan, B. 2002. 'Opposing Dictatorship: Nuruddin Farah's *Variations on the Theme of an African Dictatorship*'. In D. Wright (Ed.). *Emerging Perspectives on Nuruddin Farah*. New Jersey: Africa World Press.

Wright, D. 1994. *The Novels of Nuruddin Farah*. Bayreuth: Bayreuth African Studies Series.

Endnotes

1   See also Johnson, L. (Ed.). 2004. *Death, Dismemberment, and Memory: Body Politics in Latin America*. Albuquerque: University of New Mexico Press and Trigo, B. (Ed.). 2001. *Foucault and Latin America: Appropriations and Deployments of Discursive Analysis*. London: Routledge. For an important historical survey, see Fraginals, M. (Ed.). 1984. *Africa in Latin America – Essays on History, Culture, and Socialization*. (L. Blum, Trans.). New York: Holmes and Meier Publishers. Also consider Margaritta's thesis title in *Sweet and Sour Milk*: 'The Burgeoning of the National Security Service as an Institution of Power in Africa and Latin America' (*S&SM*: 68).

2   Ahmed refers to the 'labyrinthine' quality of *A Naked Needle* in *Daybreak is Near*, p. 96, whilst Wright alludes to Loyaan's ignorance of the 'labyrinthine passages of political life' in *The Novels of Nuruddin Farah*, p. 45.

3   Whereas Farah refers to 13 cells, Lewis maintains there were actually 14 in Barre's Mogadiscio. Lewis, IM. 1994. *Blood and Bone – The Call of Kinship in Somali Society*. New Jersey: The Red Sea Press Inc., p. 156. This slippage is akin to the one Hawley identifies between the Group of 10 who are actually 11 in 'Tribalism, Orality, and Postcolonial Ultimate Reality'. Wright, D. (Ed.). *Emerging Perspectives on Nuruddin Farah*. New Jersey: Africa World Press, p. 71.

3

So Vast the Prison: Agonistic Power Relations in *Sardines*

Closed systems have always appealed to writers. This is why so much writing deals with prisons, police forces, hospitals, schools. Is the nation a closed system? In this internationalized moment, can any system remain closed?

(Salman Rushdie – 'Notes on Writing and the Nation', 2002: 67)

This enclosed, segmented space, observed at every point, in which individuals are inserted in a fixed place, in which the slightest movements are supervised, in which all events are recorded … all this constitutes a compact model of the disciplinary mechanism … The plague as a form, at once real and imaginary, of disorder had as its medical and political correlative discipline … The plague-stricken town, traversed throughout with hierarchy, surveillance, observation, writing; the town immobilised by the functioning of an extensive power that bears in a distinct way over all individual bodies – this is the utopia of the perfectly governed city.

(Michel Foucault – Discipline and Punish, 1991: 197–198)

IN *PENPOINTS, GUNPOINTS AND DREAMS*, NGŨGĨ CONCLUDES HIS SURVEY of dissident African writers with a customary flourish: 'prison then is a metaphor for the postcolonial space, for even in a country where there are no military regimes, the vast majority can be condemned to conditions of perpetual physical, social and psychic confinement' (Ngũgĩ 1998: 60). This is the dominant motif of a chapter entitled 'Enactments of Power', in which

Ngũgĩ draws heavily from *Discipline and Punish*. His attempt to forge epistemological connections between modes of power in feudal Europe and those of post/neo-colonial Africa supplements the philosophical inquiries of V.Y. Mudimbe, amongst many others. This chapter builds on the foundations established in the analysis of *Sweet and Sour Milk*, arguing that the central *Variations* novel signals an intensification of Farah's primary concern with the complex interplay between the microphysics of power and resistance. From the Foucauldian perspective of this study, however, *Sardines* stands alone for several reasons. Critical debates have raged over the complex and at times contradictory figure of Medina, the only female member of the 'Group of 10', as well as her wider role within Farah's fictional oeuvre. For Wright, the 'problem remains … that so much of the narrative is presented from the perspective of [her] intransigent idealism and coloured by her priggish self-righteousness' (Wright 1994: 70). In the salvaging rather than savaging spirit I have drawn on thus far, I argue that the peculiarities of Medina's portrait are inevitably bound up with Farah's wider preoccupation with a more nuanced analytics of power and/as process. As such, I continue to find Foucauldian concepts of agonism, coping and differences of potential enabling.

Throughout *Sardines*, the reader is invited to consider the compelling relationship between the punitive General and its central protagonist. Medina is oftentimes shown behaving in the sort of quasi-despotic manner imagined as exclusive to the figure she considers her ideological nemesis. One of Farah's underlying concerns, however, is the agonism rather than the chasm of difference between the two. Whilst the concept has been gestured towards in postcolonial scholarship, it has remained somewhat undertheorised. Chidi Okonkwo, for instance, refers to a 'liberation agonistic' in *Decolonization Agonistics in Postcolonial Fiction*. Whilst he cites 'What is an Author?', a sustained engagement with the term as it appears in Foucault's work is conspicuously absent (Okonkwo 1999: 20–21). For the purposes of this analysis, Foucault's definition in 'The Subject and Power', as cited by Chowers, is particularly appealing: 'rather than speaking of an essential freedom, it would be better to speak of an "agonism" … less face-to-face confrontation [between the individual and power] which paralyzes both sides than a permanent provocation' (Chowers 2004: 164). As I come to illustrate, it is the idea of a 'permanent provocation' that corresponds most suggestively with Farah's depiction of the struggles between Medina and the General's respective order (and ordering) of things.

Sardines is centrally concerned with reclaiming the sovereignty of the contested body as a possible means of resisting and ultimately exiting the disciplinary labyrinth. Medina's defence of daughter Ubax might be interpreted in terms of 'setting the stage for future struggles' and thus stands as one of the more resistant acts of the *Variations* trilogy. Once again, therefore, I find Gready's work immensely enabling. Whilst he was referring to apartheid South Africa, the central thrust of his argument informs my approach to *Sardines*. For Gready, '[t]he core argument put forward in relation to the interaction between oppression and resistance is that the architecture of one contained within it the building blocks of the other' (Gready 2003: 4). A supplement to this, taken from Chowers' appendage to Foucault, reinforces the discursive scaffolding of what follows: 'agonism rather than possession: a person is free only to the extent that she unveils, questions, and refuses a certain configuration of power – and to the extent that she invents, experiments, and elaborates an alternative and self-determined mode of life and selfhood' (Chowers 2004: 164). The use of the feminine pronoun, alongside the notion of unveiling, is critical here, particularly when taking into account those critiques directed at Foucault's predominantly masculinist spheres of reference. This exploration of *Sardines* foregrounds the ways in which various female protagonists, most notably Medina, seek to challenge and resist 'certain configurations of power' and thus 'elaborate an alternative and self-determined mode of life and selfhood'. As such, the chapter's analytical movement reflects the maxim set out by Farah in 'How Can we Talk of Democracy?': 'it's just starting with the small and moving towards the big' (Farah 2002: 31). In a bid to mirror this trajectory, which informs each and every Farah novel, I consider the significance of a seemingly peripheral character.

Writing/Righting Rape

Amina is the closest friend of Sagal, the precocious daughter of long-suffering Ebla of *From a Crooked Rib*. Whilst Sagal drapes Ché Guevara pictures on her walls, zealously declaring her intentions to 'paint the morning' with anti-General polemic, Amina recounts an altogether more intimate and thus more substantial 'political' narrative. As John Coltrane provides the background to Sagal's speculations on poetry, religion and infibulation, Amina's thoughts are underscored by 'a secret' (S: 117). In a manoeuvre reminiscent of acknowledged influences Salman Rushdie and Günter Grass, Farah juxtaposes Amina's slippery misquotation of Hindu mythology with a more exacting and disturbing memory:

> Out of the hole rose the ghosts of the three men who had raped her, although
> in actual fact, whenever she thought about them, their three faces were
> moulded into one … The rest of the sad story is stained with blood, draculared,
> blood on her legs, a knife by her side, and pain, what pain! They took their turn.
> The obscene blood of rape smudged their unzipped trousers, then the smell of
> dawn and nausea. (*S*: 118–119)

The sadistic logic of Amina's attackers permits them to make her suffer for
her father's position within the Government, more particularly his participation in the systematic abuse meted out to their fellow clan members. The
impact of this traumatic revelation is intensified by its position in the narrative. The reader is obliged to place Amina's rape within the corporeal context
of infibulation, a subject Medina muses on just prior to this recollection. It
is an issue that functions as the fleshy pivot around which *Sardines* revolves:
'[i]n Somalia, fifteen percent of [baby girls] wouldn't live to celebrate their
first birthday … And what if they survived? At eight, they are circumcised;
at eighteen or before they are fifteen, they are sold into slavery. Then another barbarously painful re-infibulation awaits them' (*S*: 118). Viewed in this
abject company, Amina is violated as a worthless bridge between her rapists
and her father, both of whom benefit from the patriarchal power structure.

The retelling of this episode at the central point in the trilogy's central text
demonstrates Farah's necessarily graphic attempts to grapple with the political implications of female bodies inscribed with pain. As Ewen argues, such
depictions are 'as savage as they ought to be' (Ewen 1984: 206). Similarly, for
Juraga, this 'politicization of the sexual' intersects with Foucault's work. After
alluding to discursive affiliations with *The History of Sexuality*, she maintains
that for 'Farah, the sexual violence that thoroughly permeates the lives of
Somali women is one of the most important manifestations of violence in
Somalia' (Juraga 2002: 300). Typically, however, Farah obliges his reader to
situate such abuses within a broader framework. Just as it reveals the underlying corporeal scheme of *Sardines*, so it evolves into a cognitive moment
of clarity for Amina. Reflecting on her rape precipitates a probing critique
of the connections between lineage, clan and totalitarian structures as well
as interests operating under the oppressive axes of patriarchal hegemony.
This emerges when she rails against her father for his capitulation before the
General. Like Keynaan, he fears for his position in any bureaucratic reshuffle,
slipping into willed amnesia about his daughter's rape as a consequence. He
attempts to justify this act of forgetting with hollow appeals to the General's faded rhetoric, '[he] would do it for the good name of the Revolution'

(S: 120). The complicities are painfully obvious and inscribed on Amina's body as she maintains 'I want everyone to know that every rape is political; that the powerful rape the weak' (S: 121–122). In a revision of Loyaan's ex-tradition in *Sweet and Sour Milk*, her father is sent to a foreign consulate with the aim of neutralising any threat of reprisal. Amina, however, remains to consult with the community of women headed by Medina. They offer alter-native support and sustenance for her and her newborn child as she moves into her father's house. The reader is invited to read this relocation, loaded with literal and figurative significance, in terms of Amina's 'microphysics of struggle'. As Patricia Alden maintains, 'Amina's story testifies to a woman's ability to assume control, even over the violent rape which caused her to be pregnant, and defy her rapists, her father, and the General, by insisting on bearing her child and raising it in a community of women' (Alden 2002: 376).

To supplement Alden's intervention, I argue that Amina's actions might also be productively interpreted in light of what Chowers sees as Foucault's conception of coping:

> Seeing little grounds for hope on the collective level, entrapment writers insist on placing more weight on individual paths of reclaiming the self. These writers profess that if our collective destiny holds no clear promise of freeing ourselves from the dehumanizing effects of social institutions, then the best we can do is devise personal ways of *coping*. Coping, not rescue; strategies for surviving with dignity, rather than for consummating emancipation and closure … Coping means facing our embeddedness in the dehumanizing circumstances of modernity with a new type of heroism, an ongoing and incomplete assay to recover, integrate, and assert the self. (Chowers 2004: 186)

Whilst this is enabling on a number of levels, the critical caveat in Farah's imagined order of things is that the formation of an alternative female com-munity bolsters rather than compromises Amina's attempts to assert her political self. The potentially resistant presentation of this other, typically open-ended path might thus be read against the grain of what Chowers goes on to define as some of Foucault's more pessimistic prescriptions:

> Foucault … continues the individually-based responses to entrapment advanced by Weber and Freud, sharing with his predecessors a sense of political pessimism, realism, and ambivalence regarding collective action. While he attaches importance to personal measures, local movements, and revolutions

> in resisting contemporary forms of domination, exclusion, categorization, surveillance and so on, he is also sceptical of them. (Chowers 2004: 174)

These qualifications are critical. For my purposes, therefore, Farah's presentation of a relatively autonomous collective might be considered alongside various feminist ripostes to Foucault. Whilst, as I have argued in relation to his portrait of the Group of 10, Farah's stance on 'collective action' is ambivalent at best, this does not eliminate the hope that change might permeate beyond the micrological sphere to shape the macrological.

At both structural and thematic levels, therefore, Amina's recollection captures those negotiations between body politics and the wider body politic that define Farah's work. To borrow from Elaine Scarry's *The Body in Pain: The Making and Unmaking of the World*, this is one of many moments where the reader's face is held steady to confront brutality and blood (Scarry 1985: 65). Whilst there is some conjecture regarding the ability and/or validity of a male writer representing such pointedly gendered experiences, these instances do oblige the reader to anchor the text's loftier, arguably theoretical discourse at a necessarily more embodied level. Such negotiations (between abjection/ambiguity, experience/extrapolation) are represented by the contrasting figures of Amina and Sagal. Farah uses Amina's unambiguous testimony, for instance, to show the disturbing extent of Sagal's rhetorical bluster. As Maggi Phillips argues, therefore, 'in contrast to other issues raised in the novel, infibulation and rape are the two subjects about which the writer admits no equivocations' (Phillips 2002: 387). By occupying this fraught space, Farah deflects Wright's concerns that the urgency of highlighting the barbarity of rape can be substituted for symbolic ends. For Wright, Sagal is the figure most prone to such discomfiting flights of fancy:

> The danger of the intellectual extrapolation of abstract 'significances' from sensitive subjects such as rape and circumcision … is that the metaphoric correlative of the outrage – moral violation, political coercion – is liable to blunt the edge of barbarity itself … by rendering rape purely in political terms the writer may end up presenting it to the reader in much the same way as the assailants present it to their victim – as a merely symbolic act. (Wright 1994: 75)

Wright also justifies his unease by focusing on central protagonist Medina. Her wearying representation of individuals and their attributes ('[Sagal] *is the bridge I crossed yesterday, the muddy and violently wavy river through which I swam*' S: 43) is analogous to Sagal's metaphoric excesses. Inevitably,

however, there comes a point where this ceases, for both author and his protagonists. As such, Wright might be accused of conflating Farah's approach
with those of his characters. For Ewen, this distinction is crucial if the transformative impulses as well as the simmering rage underpinning his writing
are to be brought more starkly into focus: 'Sardines is, like its antecedents, a
novel productive of anger. For all their suavity of style and the appearance
of haphazard poise, Farah's novels are firesetters, urging their readers less to
sedate approval of the way things are going in the Horn of Africa than to a
renewed passion to reform the world' (Ewen 1984: 206).

Tremulous Private and Public Bodies

Whilst Medina imagines Sagal embodying the hopes for an emancipat-
ed future, her protégé remains untutored in the ways of some of the older
women. They have an all-too-painful appreciation of the decisive blows
variously aimed at the body. A forerunner to Askar in *Maps*, Sagal hides behind verbosity, desperately hoping this will protect her from having to take
responsibility for her actions. Caught in the interstices of not-quite child,
not-yet woman, she lacks the sentient learning that distinguishes significant
others in the novel. Ebla is one such figure who, with a mixture of pride and
trepidation, muses how '[Sagal] was never realistic, never walked with her
feet on the ground; never woke to reality when she had dreamed' (S: 40).
This gives a sense of how and why *Sardines* is centrally concerned with the
constant interplay between metaphysical abstractions and all-too-physical
'regroundings'. As mother Ebla acknowledges, Sagal is afforded the luxury of
playing at politics because of her comparatively privileged status.

It is only when she is on the threshold of crossing over into the realm of
motherhood, inhabited by Medina, Ebla and now Amina, that Sagal begins
to appreciate how and why priorities must change. Ebla insists, 'you swim
as though you are wrapped in water, breathe as though you are the air. I
just want to remind you that some of us are mortal and realize we are. Have
you ever considered the position of the worrying mother who clutches her
daughter as though she were life?'(S: 34). As Foucault suggests in *Madness
and Civilization*, water provides 'an inexhaustible reservoir of operative
metaphors' (Foucault 2001: 160). This is certainly the case in the alternative
setting of *Sardines*, particularly in depictions of Sagal. Its fluid motifs seep and
ooze into much of Farah's subsequent work. Set against this, however, is the
more substantial fascination with and concern for the fleshy precariousness

of the body and relations between bodies. For Alden, this is captured in the variously ambivalent, often antagonistic relationships between mothers and daughters. There is also a correlation between these fraught pairings and the half-revealed mysteries of *Variations* as a whole: 'the text requires us to consider numerous interactions between mother and daughter … it does not do the work of synthesis for us' (Alden 2002: 372).

Sagal accuses Ebla of evading her dissident duties by falling back on tradition, stories and duck-and-dodge tactics to survive the current political climate. Yet, as is the case in both *Sweet and Sour Milk* and *Close Sesame*, Farah invites the reader to go beyond Sagal's blinkered critiques in order to appreciate both the nuances and necessity of such strategies. This once more corresponds with Gready's work:

> The kind of subject demanded by the state and those ranged in opposition to it were the same, an example of mimicry and reversal … But, for opponents of the state in particular, such formulations of identity were both embraced and rejected, continually reworked in their imposition and self-construction within an evolving political purpose and context on the underside of power. Alongside censorship and obfuscation, was the necessary secrecy, evasion, and disguise of oppositional self-preservation. (Gready 2003: 10)

It is the acute awareness of such 'oppositional self-preservation' that distinguishes figures such as Ebla and, as I argue in the next chapter, Deeriye in *Close Sesame*. Adolescent/adult tensions are rife throughout Farah's work, yet in *Sardines* it is the embodied urgency with which mothers conceive of their worldly relationships that is most striking. For Sagal, Ebla ultimately speaks with prudent clarity. It is disconcerting precisely because it cuts against the grain of her studied self-indulgence.

Hours after her ordeal, Amina is found by a young shepherdess who calls upon her fellow villagers for help. Before it can be offered, Amina is confronted with **that** question, the original answer to which sealed her abject fate in the eyes of her attackers: 'whose daughter are you?' (*S*: 119). Her response splits the reception of and reaction to her along clear gender lines. The men rely on the absolutist logic of the rapists. They seek recourse in clan, complicity and betrayal to authorise her abandonment in the name of the father: 'the men decided they would have nothing to do with the daughter of that great conspirator. 'Do you know how many innocent men of our clan your father has sent to prison, how many he has tortured?' … The men walked away. She had no energy to appeal to them, she lay where she had been raped' (*S*: 119).

Crucially, however, the reader is offered a vital counterpoint in the form of an elderly woman who comes to Amina's aid. She is the figurehead of a women's support group, prepared to disobey the men's orders by washing and feeding this abandoned sister. Amina's rape is transformed for and through them into a powerful emblem of wider struggles against insidious forms of patriarchal oppression. As such, it corresponds with the aim of texts such as *Somalia – The Untold Story: The War Through the Eyes of Somali Women* (2004), concerned as they are with gendered perceptions and experiences of conflict. Pre-empting Amina's own reflections on the event, Farah's nameless woman speaks with the kind of lucidity he often reserves for older spokespeople: 'the pain is ours, the fat and wealth and power is the men's. I am certain your father will not understand – but your mother will' (*S*: 119). Whilst the first part of her prophecy comes to pass, any murmurs of acknowledgement and/ or dissent raised by Amina's mother are quashed by the interests of clan and corruption embodied by her husband. The father tells his daughter that 'I haven't spoken to your mother. I've spoken to the General' (*S*: 120). As such, the depiction of the post-rape care provided by the women resonates with some of the most enduring concerns of Farah's fictional and non-fictional work, since *From a Crooked Rib*, through *Yesterday, Tomorrow* and on to *Knots*. In these and other texts, women are oftentimes conceived as skilled practitioners of evasive strategies, perfecting acts of micro resistance to accommodate the burdens of various oppressions.

The result is that Amina's traumatic recollection is associated with both these male rejections and the women's compassionate reception. For the latter group, they see all too clearly how the plight of 'Mother Somalia' is etched onto this broken young body. Once again, this micro/macro focus corresponds with Farah's assertions in 'How Can We Talk of Democracy?' 'I'm not one of those who fights a regime. If I did not make this clear [in *Variations*] I think I should have failed as a writer: that Siyad Barre was not a target for me. No dictator is born out of a vacuum. A dictatorship comes out of a society and therefore one must stand in that society and see it as part of an authoritarian program' (Farah 2002: 30). Such statements chime with those Foucauldian analytics of power alluded to above. References to 'standing in' and focusing on 'parts' of programs and thus power can be seen in terms of those links, chains and relays discussed in the opening chapter.

The Building Blocks of Resistance

Both Medina and Amina have the capacity to exist in contexts where previously stable orders, whether micrological or macrological, have started to crumble. Ostracised by the support networks of family and clan, Amina must seek alternative alliances. Similarly, Medina is presented as struggling to safeguard her own survival space amidst the disintegration of family, profession and political movements. To extend the mirroring motif that recurs at strategic points throughout Farah's oeuvre, Medina can be viewed as a prominent if problematic reconfiguration of Amina's elderly assistant. She too disobeys patriarchal dictates to head up another resistance group. The reader enters the narrative as Medina is relieved of her duties as editor of Somalia's only daily newspaper. Her fate is sealed when she alters a report on one of the General's speeches. She is confronted with the challenge of accepting and utilising this newly marginalised status. In many ways, it parallels Farah's own experience under a gagging order that, when broken, carried the threat of imprisonment if not death. In *Sardines*, as in the *Variations* cycle as a whole, pronounced tensions exist between oral and written forms of dissent. During the periods of personal and political, individual and collective re-evaluation following Soyaan's death, Medina refocuses her insurgent energies within the domestic sphere. Having been written and/or writing herself out of the nation's political narrative, she dedicates herself to raising precocious daughter Ubax whilst contemplating the production of an anti-General tract. For characters such as Amina, who she furnishes with radical reading ('Brownmiller's *Against Our Will*, Fanon, Richard Wright and Eldridge Cleaver', *S*: 120), Medina acts as a guide, seeming to embody their resistant aspirations. Amidst the Group of 10's ongoing fallout, she describes how 'the feeling returned, the feeling which had to do with ... being the one person who had survived a ruinous trauma, an arduous journey, a disastrous duel' (*S*: 49). Typically, the complications of Farah's critique of power arise as his educated elite demonstrate their own failings. Once more, therefore, Foucault's notion of a proximate power/resistance 'duel' is enabling.

Farah has expressed his inherent unease with the politics of grouping in the following terms: 'I could fight better not being a member of [the oppositional movements], because the moment I became a member of them, some of them would not want to openly associate themselves with me because of my well-known views' (Farah 2002: 32). Whilst writing from a different context, Said shared this ambivalence. In 'Wild Orchids and Trotsky', he states:

I have tended to resist the exigencies of politics – which have to do with
authority, with power, with confrontation, with rapid responses – simply
because I have always wanted to maintain privacy for my own reflections …
I have tried to remain outside of direct political office of one sort or another …
in order to be able to reflect in this literary way, which takes more time, requires
more solitude. (Said 2002: 173)

I suggest that both of these statements can be seen in relation to the following passage from *The History of Sexuality*. As I explore below, it is also
stimulating when thinking about the distinctive features of the Group of 10
throughout the *Variations* cycle:

Where there is power, there is resistance, and yet, or rather consequently, this
resistance is never in a position of exteriority in relation to power … These
points of resistance are present everywhere in the power network … there is a
plurality of resistances: … that are possible, necessary, improbable; others that
are spontaneous, savage, solitary, concerted, rampant, or violent; still others
that are quick to compromise, interested, or sacrificial; by definition, they can
only exist in the strategic field of power relations … the points, knots, or focuses
of resistance are spread over time and space at varying densities, at times
mobilizing groups or individuals in a definitive way, inflaming certain points of
the body, certain moments in life, certain types of behaviour … more often one
is dealing with mobile and transitory points of resistance, producing cleavages
in a society that shift about, fracturing unities and effecting regroupings,
furrowing across individuals themselves, cutting them up and remolding them,
marking off irreducible regions in them, in their bodies and minds. (Foucault
1990: 95–96)

Focusing on mobile, transitory points of resistance, alongside the embodied
rhetoric here is highly suggestive in the context of *Sardines*. Foucault's attention to disciplinary sites that intensify power is complemented by his analysis
of forms of opposition that are provisional. As such, it appears analogous
with Farah's loose, factionalism-prone priviligentsia. Whilst the intimate
power/resistance dialectic remains similarly attractive, Foucault's awareness
of revised oppositional tactics is particularly provocative in relation to this
central narrative.

In *Sardines*, Medina's unflinching stance ultimately contributes to the
Group's downfall. She wants to construct and ideologically invest in a caricature of her opponent. As such, she might be seen as a version of the naïve

dandy referred to by Foucault in 'The Eye of Power': 'it takes the rather naïve optimism of the nineteenth century "dandies" to imagine that the bourgeoisie is stupid. On the contrary, one has to reckon with its stroke of genius … which in turn re-inforced and modified the power apparatuses in a mobile and circular manner' (Foucault 1980a: 160). As Farah demonstrates, it is only once Medina begins to deconstruct her Manichean world view, acknowledging the Grand Patriarch as a Machiavellian manipulator and appreciating the mobile circulation of power, that she starts to decipher the code that might ultimately unlock his disciplinary labyrinth. Indeed, it is no coincidence that the General is described as Machiavellian throughout the novel. It is a loaded phrase employed by a host of commentators on Somalia. For Lewis, for instance, 'President Siyad, who had the skills of a practical Machiavelli and the mind of a political computer, was particularly adept at selecting token figures from obscure, minority segments of major clan groups who were flattered to serve him and present themselves as clan representatives' (Lewis 2002: 250). That Farah returns to the archetype in *Yesterday, Tomorrow* is similarly revealing: 'Siyad's studiedly Machiavellian tactics, combined with our mistrust of one another, made our pan-Somali position untenable' (*YT*: 111). Lastly, a considerable passage from Soyaan's copy of *The Prince* is rendered verbatim in *Sweet and Sour Milk*: '*There is nothing more difficult to take in hand, more perilous to conduct, or more uncertain in its success than to take the lead in a new order of things. Because the innovator has for enemies all those who have done well under the old conditions, and lukewarm defenders in those who may do well under the new*', (*S&SM*: 16).

Whilst the Medina of *Sardines* does not lose any of her determined indeterminacy, the reader is left with the impression that she has, however tentatively, undergone a certain development, most clearly in terms of bringing political discourse and resistance to it back within the domestic sphere. She identifies the embodied base upon which the General's despotic regime is, at one level, founded. This allows her to reassess it as a corporeal stage on which she might engage in small yet strategic acts of resistance. By the close of the novel, she is arguably the only Group member who manages to negotiate the metaphoric maze with anything like success. Whilst ultimately losing the bigger battle to usurp the General, she succeeds at the level of domestic, embodied politics by protecting the sovereignty of her young daughter from the pain of infibulation. Her critical act defines this central novel and the body-politics preoccupations of *Variations* as a whole.

Medina's life, at a distance from the male-dominated Group of 10, involves a constant struggle to get her own house in order. It is a metaphor to which

Farah will return in *Knots*. Medina surrounds herself with a kaleidoscopic assortment of female companions who, despite their largely petit-bourgeois status, continue to strain under the Grand Patriarch's authoritarianism. For Wright, however, 'Medina … is a rather weak symbol of the subjugated national self since she is too-Western-internationalist in her orientation, too privileged and protected a member of the elite, and too little oppressed as a woman' (Wright 1994: 73). A counter-argument to Wright can be taken from one of *Sardines*' key intertexts, Virginia Woolf's *A Room of One's Own*: 'this is an important book, the critic assumes, because it deals with war. This is an insignificant book because it deals with the feelings of women in a drawing-room' (Woolf 1967: 74). Farah's commitment to privileging 'the feelings of women' in turn allows him to offer a peculiarly embodied reappraisal of the (dis)order of things. As such, it produces one of the most explicit instances in which Medina's impassioned anti-General polemic blurs boundaries personal and political. At the beginning of *Sardines*, Medina leaves husband Samater. For Alden, 'Medina deplores his refusal to cut his ties to power … she sees him as someone who has learned too well in the bosom of the family to "bow his head" to authoritarian power' (Alden 2002: 368). The shift from subversive journalist to maternal martyr becomes all the more pressing as Medina questions her husband's ability to resist the tyrannical traditionalism she sees personified in his mother, Idil. In ways befitting the associative energy of her name, Medina turns her home into a defensive citadel in an attempt to ward off external threats. Idil's ominous promise to have Ubax circumcised prompts Medina to reassess her position, laying claim to and ultimately waging war over her daughter's body.

Arguably, therefore, Medina's unrepentant stance on corporeal sovereignty carries the greatest burdens of political significance. Like Farah, she refuses to waver on this issue: 'if they mutilate you at eight or nine, they open you up with a rusty knife the night they marry you off; then you are cut open and re-stitched. Life for a circumcised girl is a series of de-flowering pains, delivery pains and re-stitching pains. I want to spare my daughter these and many other pains. She will not be circumcised' (S: 59). As Amina becomes conscious of the intertwined relationship between her abjection and the disciplinary structures of the General's society, Medina concentrates her energies on neutralising the threat posed by Idil. It thus stands as a micrological act of defiance against more ominous forms of societal control. As such, the resistant energy devoted to safeguarding Ubax's body might be interpreted using Gready's formulation: 'the body represents a further area where constructions of truth and power are played out, the irrefutable and infinitely contestable evidence of a battle between state and opposition over truth and power, over life itself' (Gready 2003: 75). Whilst Medina may appear marginalised at the outset, it is the complex process by which she comes to terms with these macro/micro political negotiations that remains critical.

Foucault and FGM

Anthropological and political debates surrounding the practice of female circumcision, from Nawal El Saadawi to December Green, are as intense as they are complex.[1] If I can only touch on them here, it is striking that Foucault's work, from *Discipline and Punish* through *The Order of Things* and *The History of Sexuality*, plays such a prominent role. Alongside Said and Spivak, for example, he emerges as a key referent for many contributors to *Female Circumcision and the Politics of Knowledge: African Women in Imperialist Discourses*. Obioma Nnaemeka describes how the collection 'brings into the debate the suppressed voices of indigenous women, not by locating imperialism in far away periods in Africa, Asia, the Pacific or South America, but by focusing on a contemporary debate, circumcision, to show that imperialism is a will to dominate that haunts us even today' (Nnaemeka 2005: 7). Chapters from Vicki Kirby and Francois Lionnet, in particular, operate in the salvaging rather than savaging spirit discussed above.[2] For many, the aspects of Foucault's work most pregnant with possibility include notions of discourse, biopower and political technologies of the self. As such, it provides a more substantial framework within which to engage *Sardines* and Medina's defence of Ubax's corporeal sovereignty in particular.

Farah reconfigures the notion of family base refracting state superstructure for the pressing case of Somalia. Throughout, Medina views Idil's recourse to clannish traditionalism in relation to the General's increasingly hollow promises of progress. Taking an ideological stance that seemingly allows her to cross chasms personal and political, Medina attempts to solve various longstanding conundrums: 'did she not realize that a confrontation with Idil meant a direct challenge to tradition, to the General's generation?' (*S*: 99). Once more, such rhetorical questions capture the open-endedness of the *Variations* cycle. Aware that such a generational affront contravenes a sacred tenet of Somali culture, Medina sets about achieving a viable political result. Trying to implement change and launch resistance within her own space is one of the limited ways she can avoid the General's persecution. Her identification of Ubax's contested body as located at the nexus of power and resistance might, therefore, be seen in terms of Amina's reflections on rape.

Whilst Medina is a quintessential intellectual, she undergoes a similarly intense political education, coming to realise that the practice of female infibulation is always already linked to the General's hegemony. Just as Amina claims that every rape is political, Medina asserts that every act of infibulation is intimately associated with the dominant system of power. Farah's fictional exploration of these issues once more anticipates what has become a significant field of inquiry in its own right, as evidenced in works such as *Female "Circumcision" in Africa: Culture, Controversy and Change* (2000). To a significant degree, therefore, Medina's stance can be read in terms of El Saadawi's declaration in 'Imperialism and Sex in Africa': 'I oppose all attempts to deal with female circumcision or any other sexual problem in isolation, severing it from its links with historical, economic, and political factors, at national and international levels … the link is here. Imperialism as a patriarchal class system cannot survive without sexual and economic exploitation of women and the poor' (El Saadawi 2005: 22–23). For El Saadawi, it is imperative that these connections be exposed and explored. Read in this light, affinities between protagonist and author are once again striking.

As Farah states in 'How Can We Talk of Democracy?', 'what I am interested in is to be able to work within the family as a unit, and if there is no democracy in the house, there can certainly be no democracy in the capital' (Farah 2002: 31). Beyond the General's gaze, Medina begins to take measures pregnant with the kind of power that might ultimately topple regimes. The familiar, if bitter-sweet irony is that the implications of such acts might prove more effective than the grand schemes dreamt up by the Group of 10. As *Sardines'* epilogue announces, acts of evasion, concealment and coping never cease. Both the processes of resisting power and attempting to assay and recover the self are, by their very nature, incomplete. As Chowers notes, 'like the opposition between literature and discourse, the one between freedom and power offers no final victories, but rather demands ongoing, incessant struggle' (Chowers 2004: 165). Typically, form and content operate in an intriguing dialectic throughout *Sardines*. Towards the narrative's inconclusive close, Medina still faces the question; 'would she hold out any longer than the rest of them?' The only hope of arriving at an answer comes by considering the alternative: 'to get to them, to break them, the General's security took its time, choosing its victim … It was like this: the roulette-wheel turned and every time the ball dropped into a numbered chamber one of the ten was gone' (*S*: 241). For Maggi Phillips, Medina negotiates through the macro- to the microdynamics of politics. In so doing, she comes to the painful yet necessary realisation that 'there are no manuals nor formulae articulating the right way to demolish structures of injustice. Shadows and small acts exposing human vulnerability may be the answer' (Phillips 2002: 394). Once more, Foucauldian parallels are suggestive. As Colin Gordon maintains in his Afterword to *Power/Knowledge,* 'the schema of a strategy of resistance as a vanguard of politicisation needs to be subjected to re-examination, and account must be taken of resistances whose strategy is one of evasion or defence ... There are no good subjects of resistance' (Gordon 1980: 257).

Mourning Yet on Creation Day

In *Resistance in Postcolonial African Fiction,* Neil Lazarus offers an illuminating analysis of *The Beautyful Ones Are Not Yet Born* (Lazarus 1990: 46–79). He challenges the notion that Armah's allegorical exploration of the betrayal of Ghana's post-Independence dream is an exemplar of a 'literature of disillusionment'. Lazarus focuses on the micro-acts of resistance pursued by the anonymous protagonist, showing how they are suggestive in terms of setting the stage for future struggles. At the borders of a text seemingly consumed by postcolonial despair, he argues, hopes for revolutionary change still flicker. Lazarus refers to Farah in his concluding chapter, chiding his work for lacking the kind of radical urgency he sees in Armah's writing. Whilst his comments are fleeting, it is revealing that he focuses on *Sardines* (Lazarus 1990: 211–214). I suggest the approach Lazarus takes to defend Armah might be reappropriated to read against the grain of his own dismissal of Farah. The insistence on building blocks of resistance and initial engagement in 'not yet' struggles has a powerful resonance when considering *Sardines'* wider preoccupations.

Published in 1968, Armah's text emerged some eleven years after the advent of Ghanaian independence and a couple of years after the military coup that ousted Kwame Nkrumah, alluded to in the novel as '[n]ew people, new style, old dance' (Armah 1988: 157). *Sardines,* published approximately the same number of years after the Somali Revolution of 1969, still resounds with Armah-esque laments for a dream deferred, as it is referred to in Achebe's 'Africa and Her Writers' in *Morning Yet on Creation Day* (Achebe 1975: 38–45). Of greater significance in terms of the novel itself, however, are the repeated allusions to Medina's formative student experiences, with Soyaan, Samater *et al.,* in the revolutionary melting pot of Milan during 'the fabled year of

'68!' (*S*: 89). Immediately prior to the explosion of a supposedly new Somali order of things, Farah's diasporic intelligentsia are in European cities, their red flags fluttering in the breeze. If this appears wistfully ironic, Farah is more concerned with the complex conceptual process Medina undergoes over the course of a narrative brought back home in more ways than one. Accordingly, her conceptual realignment can be read in terms of the wider theoretical paradigms touched on by Michael Lambek and Andrew Strathern in *Bodies and Persons – Comparative Perspectives from Africa and Melanesia*: 'a focus on 'the body' perhaps also fits with a new materialism, disconnected from the more dogmatic side of Marxism but concerned with the domain of lived experience and the effects of the social realm on the human body' (Lambek & Strathern 1998: 5). Viewed from this perspective, the critical force of Farah's writing is arguably intensified. As such, if *The Beautyful Ones Are Not Yet Born* can be read in terms of its anonymous protagonist's attempts to build effective resistance from the bottom upwards, *Sardines* might be seen in a similar light.

Whilst Lazarus has bemoaned Foucault's excessive valorisation in postcolonial studies in *Nationalism and Cultural Practice in the Postcolonial World*, his methodological principles might, in Adorno's sense, be 'hated properly' and his approaches to power/resistance employed selectively to enhance the type of reading he proposes for Armah and I suggest for Farah (Lazarus 1999: 7–11). If there is a return to quotidian struggles in both, *Sardines* might be interpreted as having a sharper political edge as it focuses on contested corporeal realms. Bodily preoccupations are similarly pronounced in Armah's text. Yet, with its playful, at times pointedly grotesque representation of retching/wretched politicians, such motifs are largely employed to serve the fleshy functions discussed by Mbembe in *On the Postcolony* (Mbembe 2001: 105–116). Lazarus's critique might therefore be supplemented by considering Gready's South-Africa specific formulation:

> The ebb and flow of resistance and repression were locked together [during apartheid] in a relationship characterized by dependency, a paradoxical complicity and mimicry, and an unambiguous animosity. While acknowledging the imbalances of power characteristic of these interactions, this study seeks chiefly to explore a series of subversive potentials and processes: the mechanisms and techniques of resistance, specifically written and discursive strategies of resistance. The core argument put forward in relation to the interaction between oppression and resistance is that the architecture of one contained within it the building blocks of the other. (Gready 2003: 5)

Whilst Gready focuses on inscription as resistance, allusions to potentials, processes and oppositional building blocks remain enabling in terms of my approach to *Sardines*. If the reclamation of Ubax's contested body is accepted as a pivotal point in novel and trilogy, it is also striking that the architectural motifs, prominent in both, are employed in critical works concerning the symbiotic relationship between the female body and a wider body politic. At the outset of *The Hidden Face of Eve*, for instance, El Saadawi states that 'the "higher" politics of any country are a construction of many small bricks of details that weave themselves into a general pattern' (El Saadawi 1980: 1). Whilst construction and weaving motifs have a tendency to fall over themselves in Farah's fiction, this theoretical and rhetorical focus on building blocks of power and resistance meshes together at various instances with the wider concerns of his project. If such negotiations are essentially comparable with moving from the small to the big, they also have a peculiarly Foucauldian flavour.

In a further parallel with Amina's recollection, which galvanises her political consciousness, Medina is equally spurred by direct memory. She reclaims her daughter's body with an intimate urgency fuelled by her own experience of painful childbirth. She recalls Ubax's caesarean delivery in Rome at a formative stage in the narrative: 'the pain and the scissor-cut; and the complications which had arisen because she was circumcised. But the pleasure was huger … like a delicate touch on the dark rim of a wound' (*S*: 13). Crucially, therefore, these corporeal complications are different from those of *Sweet and Sour Milk* and *Close Sesame*. Borrowing from Gready once more, I find them powerful because double-edged: 'the somatic cartography of the state finds its contours in never-ending pain, unhealed wounds and scars, deformed posture, awkward movement, and immobility, in damaged senses, in physical and mental degenerations and illness, and more' (Gready 2003: 14). For Farah, it is imperative that the trauma of female genital mutilation be seen in similar terms. This is something explored from the perspective of a Somali woman by Saida Haigi-Dirie Herzi in 'Against the Pleasure Principle'.[3] Similarly, Medina's visceral recollection establishes the centrality of body-politics motifs within both personal and increasingly political spheres of being. It is equally revealing, however, that in a text devoted to displays of micrological resistance practised with comparative success, the body as a regenerative and regenerating entity is foregrounded.

If the pain/pleasure dialectic defines Medina's memory of Ubax's birth, it also captures the reaction of many of the novel's readers. Wright's exasperation and Philips' spirited defence are cases in point. Medina's 'priggish self-righteousness' is perhaps at its most exhaustive when she describes her sado-masochistic relationship with the General: '[the] General's power and I are like two lizards engaged in a varanian dance of death; we are two duellists dancing a tarantella in which they challenge their own destiny … He uses violent language and so do I. He calls me a "dilettante bourgeois", "a reactionary", I call him "fascist" and "dictator"' (S: 45). The reader can cut through Medina's overdetermined rhetoric by focusing on a particular term that is suggestive when it comes to thinking about Farah's suitably more Foucauldian conception and critique of power. The pivotal image figures Medina and the General as two dancing duellists. She makes a similar reference a few pages later (S: 49). It is no coincidence that the term is repeated within such a condensed narrative space. The manner in which she represents their relationship is strikingly corporeal and proximate. Rather than disclosing a chasm of difference between the two imagined antagonists, Farah obliges a comparative reconsideration, and thus probing, of binary oppositions (dominator and dominated) and moral absolutes. As such, the portrait is distinguished by the agonistic intensity noted in Foucault's own, strikingly physical definition: '[the] neologism ["agonism"] is based on the Greek … meaning "a combat". The term would hence imply a physical contest in which the opponents develop a strategy of reaction and mutual taunting, as in a wrestling match.'[4] Whilst Medina re-imagines this wrestling contest as a macabre tango, the conceptual attention to physical proximity serves similar ends. By figuring her in such close relation to the General at strategic points, Farah demonstrates how Medina's journey towards a more complex sense of self ultimately enables her to display the critical degrees of difference or, in Foucauldian terms, 'potential' between herself and the autocrat. Her battle to safeguard the sovereignty of Ubax's body might thus be read using the terms outlined by Chowers: 'Foucauldian resistance never contemplates an unblemished social predicament as its goal, never pictures a world devoid of power relations and mutual subjection. Resistance, in Foucault's view, takes the form of local confrontations that achieve limited ends and set the stage for subsequent struggles' (Chowers 2004: 187). Like *Sardines*' concerns once more, attempts to recover and assert the self are left deliberately incomplete.

One counterpart to Medina's exasperating verbal sparring comes as she recalls a confrontation with Atta, a crude caricature of African-American separatism. Over a meal where Medina and Samater play host to their foreign guest (a particularly prominent motif here as throughout Farah's later work), the conversation inevitably turns to politics. Atta infuriates Medina with her ethnic fetishism, insisting that suffering is a process of collective racial memory to which she has privileged access: 'one doesn't forget centuries of suffering. My race remembers this suffering, my race hasn't forgotten it. I remember this suffering, this pain. *Therefore I am*' (*S*: 185). More significant than her gestures towards her ample education is Medina's decision to confront Atta's warped notion of collective beyond individual suffering at an intimate level. Rather than attack her ignorance ('Atta praised Kenyatta, Haile Selassie, Senghor and Kaunda; in the same breath, she said the General was the greatest African leader she had ever had the pleasure to shake hands with' *S*: 184), Medina situates Ubax and her painful birth at the crux of their conversation:

> 'I suffer this humiliation, this inhumane subjugation of circumcision; you can never know how painful it is unless you've undergone the operation yourself. But must every woman in the world suffer this act of barbarism in order to know the suffering it entails? … A great majority of Africa's female population suffers complications arising from infibulation.' (*S*: 186–187)

This alternative use of 'complications' is again indicative of the conceptual and corporeal distance separating *Sweet and Sour Milk* and *Sardines*. At such disarming moments, they are employed to make more immediate, embodied claims. As the wince of pain spreads over Atta's face, it appears Medina has achieved her aim: 'it's not racial. Suffering is human' (*S*: 187). Medina's deconstruction of Atta's dangerously disembodied logic gives some indication of how she should be approached as a protagonist learning the importance of balancing micrological and macrological speculations.

If *Sardines* is centrally concerned with Medina's fraught struggle to protect her daughter's body, it is also charts her Woolfian attempts to build a room of her own beyond the reach of surveillance and the pressure of other insurgent aspirations. After she has provisionally triumphed in her war with Idil, Medina arrives at this existential space, with her restored family, in the novel's last scene. As with the body's sliding significance throughout Farah's work, construction themes are employed to represent what Wright calls 'the swift movement from microcosm to macrocosm' (Wright 1994: 74). At a macrological level, it recalls the archetypal design for disciplinary society as a penitentiary in which the judicial overlord/General occupies the panopticon position from which all subjects can be monitored and displays of dissidence neutralised. In more immediate textual terms, the construction motif serves as an earlier, pre-*Maps* meditation on inscription and silence. Farah exposes the architectural impulse that drives Medina's art of artifice from the opening pages: '[she] reconstructed the story from the beginning. She worked it into a set of pyramids which served as foundations for one another. Out of this, she erected a construction of great strength and solidity' (S: 2).

Medina uses her training, as both literature graduate and journalist, to establish some kind of narrative order from political turmoil and traumatised memory. For Phillips, 'the bricks and mortar of [her] imaginative castle are ideas bridging the ancient African world (pyramids) with the future through words constructed to puzzle and … foretell the narrative movement from one house to another until the central protagonist chooses a back door leading to an alternative space' (Phillips 2002: 386). By the narrative close, as Medina, Samater and Ubax walk away, it appears this alternative space is being explored. As above, there is a slippage between meditations on narrative constructions and disciplinary designs. From a Foucauldian perspective, the reader might build an alternative bridge connecting Medina's narrative speculations to his own on the artifice of power in *Discipline and Punish*: 'power in the hierarchized surveillance of the disciplines is not possessed as a thing, or transferred as a property; it functions like a piece of machinery. And, although it is true that its pyramidal organization gives it a "head", it is the apparatus as a whole that produces "power" and distributes individuals in this permanent and continuous field' (Foucault 1991: 177). Gready's notion of 'building blocks' becomes critical once more. It is only when reprising her storyteller role, in a way that foreshadows Duniya in *Gifts* and Cambara in *Knots*, that Medina illuminates the myriad connections between construction, in terms of both her own narrative and underlying national structures, and corporeality. In essence, therefore, *Sardines* announces its critical project through a trio of contested bodies.

The embodied significance of Amina's rape, the omnipresent threat of Ubax's circumcision and how these correspond with broader critiques have been considered. There is, however, a third corporeal instance where the abject female body is employed with various ends in mind. Medina recounts the story of her friends, a married couple visiting their native Somalia after twenty years. She tells her brother Nasser how 'they brought with them their daughter aged sixteen … American as ketchup and Coca-Cola' (S: 90). On arrival, however, they realise a more ominous fate awaits them. The monomaniacal paranoia of the General's regime becomes apparent as their immigration papers are seized amidst accusations that they are imperialist informants (S: 91). Upon their release from a sinister round of interrogation, the parents see the regime's power brutally inscribed on their daughter's body. In an apocalyptic inversion of the female solidarity experienced by

Amina, Medina reports how considerations of clan displace those of gender: 'the women hired by the newly-stipended chieftain plotted. One night, while the parents were asleep … they dragged the girl out of bed, tied her to the bed-post, gagged her mouth with a cloth and circumcised her' (S: 92).

Medina fulfils crucial roles in both performative and personal capacities, building narratives from the agony of others. If they are punctuated with silences and rhetorical flourishes, Farah is also susceptible to lyrical indulgence, describing how 'her silence crawled up [Nasser's] spine like an insect which has found its way onto one's bed when one's reaction is half-numbed by sleep and the darkness of the hour. Her silence gave a Hitchcockian touch to the story she was telling; the curtains blew in the wind; a door opened and slammed shut somewhere in his roomy brain; a silence deep as the night was opaque' (S: 90). Yet, whilst seeming to revel in this ambiguous space, Medina retains a trace and tragic affinity with the parents deprived of their daughter. In a fatal inversion of Amina's familial abandonment, Medina records how her two friends commit suicide, after learning that their daughter was circumcised to ready her for marrying a male member of the dominant clan. From this point onwards, the nightmarish tale assumes even greater significance within the context of Medina's own narrative, the critical project of *Sardines* and the trilogy as a whole.

The returnees' dark story is another instance where the interlocking complicity between clan and patriarchal state power is made visible. At the textual level, Medina employs the tragic tale to support her own, ongoing struggle with Idil over the sovereignty of Ubax's body. She is defiant when insisting to Nasser that Ubax will not fall victim to the circumcisor's knife, seeing in Idil an ominous counterpart to the tribal chieftain beholden to the General: 'I vowed I wouldn't let her go anywhere near Ubax … By then Ubax had begun to see Idil in her dreams, Idil carrying a knife in her hand every night'(S: 93–94). Nasser's stunned reaction, both to Medina's narrative reconstruction and its strategic use, mirrors the reader's. After all the labyrinthine rhetoric of her tale, this incisive declaration of intent is disarming: '[Nasser] appeared not to have accepted her explanations: too *simplistic*, he thought … She held back; and she didn't need him' (S: 94). Medina's penchant for architectural signifiers and her repeated desire to set aside her own sanitised space gives some indication that the only way she can achieve this is by building walls around herself and the narrative. As they serve to insulate and fortify her world view, they also exclude others. This dualism defines her relationships throughout the novel. However, whilst Nasser is understandably cautious when it comes to Medina's gestures towards transparency, he does come to the fundamental realisation that she is safeguarding her daughter. Perhaps now, with cracks emerging after the Group's disintegration, as she tries to solidify the super-structure of narrative and struggles with the expectations of motherhood, Medina considers such an embodied focus to be of more immediate concern.

'Writers don't give prescriptions, they give headaches!'

An analysis of *Sardines* lends credence to Ewen's assertion that 'the structure of all Farah's novels is that of a dialogue between the author and his charac-ters' (Ewen 1984: 206). Like Farah, Medina returns to and re-interrogates the microphysics of power in order to branch out into a more macrological critique. As such, it appears little coincidence that both Amina's rape and the ominous prospect of Ubax's circumcision fall either side of the U.S.-Somali girl's story. The previous citation concerning Medina's 'Hitchcockian touch' was left, like Foucault's visceral conception of agonism, deliberately incom-plete to illustrate the point. The full description reads:

> a door opened and slammed shut somewhere in [Nasser's] roomy brain; a
> silence deep as the night was opaque; another door opened (he remembered
> the anecdote she once wrote him about Amina who had been raped by two
> men and the political exploitation made of this and the hush-money paid by
> the government), the door creaked shut in strict obedience to the powers of
> nature. (*S*: 90)

Typically, Farah's depiction of these mental processes resonates with the read-er's; doors creak open, leading onto what appear to be connecting corridors, only to slam shut. The recollection is loaded with familiar ambiguities, rang-ing from the inappropriate use of 'anecdote', suggesting characters and their stories are mere props for Medina, to the slippery identification of two rather than three rapists. It is the juxtaposition of these three major body-politics moments, alongside its privileging of a more embodied critique, however, that suggests why the passage is so striking.

In various ways, therefore, Medina's narrative has a symbiotic relationship with Farah's wider project:

> Nasser was lost in the turbulence of the terror the story created in him. He
> felt small as an ant but had no hole in which to hide. Medina felt smaller and
> sadder: in her mind she blindly ran and ran and ran, until she came up against

a wall huge as the Himalayas. When she could go no further, she stopped
to reason. She decided to open up for her brother the portcullis which had
remained locked since the day she left Samater, a portcullis at whose entrance a
spider had woven a web. (S: 93)

The manner in which these images (Himalayas, portcullis and spider's web)
relate to each other is highly suggestive. Medina draws a self-consciously
definitive line after recounting the U.S.-Somali girl's story, announcing her
intention to disentangle the ornate web of motives and motifs that make up
her narrative. Whilst she never abandons the ultimate aim of usurping the
Grand Patriarch's rule, the decision to turn her existential attention towards
safeguarding Ubax's body does enable her to begin slicing through various
political conceits in the hope of arriving at a palpable objective. This peel-
ing-away process, the culmination of which comes in the final tableau as the
reconstituted family find room in which to walk (S: 250), refracts Farah's own.
For Alden, this notion of process is critical. It remains vital for those, such as
Wright and Turfan, who consider the trilogy's open-endedness a weakness.
It is just as important, however, for those who believe such ambivalence is
representative of a more substantial exploration of rather than detachment
from the turbulent dynamics of history. As such, Woolf's playfully provocative statement in *A Room of One's Own* is particularly apposite when it comes
to *Sardines*, if not the trilogy as a whole: 'women and fiction remain, so far as
I am concerned, unsolved problems' (Woolf 1967: 6).

Citing Achebe's statement that 'writers don't give prescriptions ... They
give headaches!', Alden juxtaposes the exasperating and enervating attributes of Farah's Medina with Woolf's Clarissa Dalloway. Commenting upon
the 'otherness' of indeterminacy within an African literary tradition, Alden
maintains,

with Medina the positive and negative perspectives are located within history:
the unresolved questions involve evaluating the efficacy of her actions in
history, and this cannot yet be established. Thus the indeterminacy of Farah's
novel keeps us engaged with historical process while Woolf tempts us to escape
it. It is important to see that the literary technique of modernism, critiqued
by Lukacs as a decadent form of bourgeois evasion, can in fact work to quite
different purposes in the African context. (Alden 2002: 379)

Such debates prefigure those that challenge the designation of *Maps* as
a thoroughly post-modern novel. Whilst they seem important within

literary-critical spheres, they might also be interpreted in the Saidian light of wider theoretical and political issues: 'there is a pleasure, there's a satisfaction of its own that comes with working through this particular type of irreconcilability … there's always the subsumption of contradictions and irreconcilabilities in the higher synthesis, and I don't believe in that synthesis at all' (Mitchell 2002: 48). This resoundingly chimes with Alden's comments on *Sardines*: 'the text requires us to consider numerous interactions between mother and daughter … it does not do the work of synthesis for us' (Alden 2002: 372). Medina's determined indeterminacy might thus be figured in relation to alternative processes, and in terms of Foucauldian conceptions of power and resistance.

Ideas of process and evasion are similarly vital when considering how this triad of images relates with more national structures. The intricate constructions of both the 'solid' portcullis and the 'delicate', yet equally durable, spider's web stand as figurative representations of Somali society as it is imagined by Farah under the General's rule. The process of disentangling the hegemonic interconnections between bodily abjection and the complicities of clan and state power is sparked by the revelation that the tribal chieftain is in the General's pay. Farah's use of the portcullis image is suggestive in terms comparable with those of disciplinary designs. As with the labyrinth, the protective opacity that both Medina and her protégé Sagal employ in discourse finds its ominous correlative in the General's reliance upon the competing claims of clan security/privilege to fortify his own tribal dominance. Whilst the grid blocks and seemingly forestalls the threat of invasion, its very design is predicated upon presence and absence (solid iron and gaps) and, by metaphorical extension, what can and cannot be said. Attempting to push beyond her own exasperating forms of evasion, be they political or prosaic, Medina begins to explore these holes in the societal structure more thoroughly. Typically, it is for Farah's reader to continue to probe such gaps in the grid. They reveal that the body, and its abject control, lies at the very heart of the disciplinary structure of society itself.

A return to the sovereign body, however, can also serve as the foundation from which to build an alternative order of things. The apparent solidity of the portcullis gives way to the spider's-web's fragility, where the removal of one silken strand threatens its collapse. This once more recalls Woolf's sense that 'fiction is like a spider's web, attached ever so lightly perhaps, but still attached to life at all four corners' (Woolf 1967: 43). Medina is a complex figurehead who is bound up in the ongoing process towards what Samater calls 'owning the truth' (S: 71). Once again, her tumultuous journey towards this more embodied sense of truth has profound connections with Farah's own:

> The 'truth' that matters, indeed! What if I argue that the truth must be 'spoken' whether in the privacy of one's chambers or in the presence of others? What if I argue that it must be given a body, a physical existence, that truth must be clothed in the bodied concepts of words, of motions – so that others may share it, challenge it or accept it? (Farah 2002: 11–12)

Another of Medina's symbolic abstractions, nestling amongst metaphors of fortification and evasion, corresponds with my sense of how body-politics imagery operates in *Sardines*. In her lofty manner, Medina teeters on the brink of appropriating the tragedy of others for symbolic ends. She tells Nasser how the parents 'cut tragic figures … The crack in the glassy superstructure that had been the heavenly dream they imagined their daughter would wake up in became bigger, a crack whose leakage they could stop with their collective suicide' (S: 93). Whilst the fissured image represents the Group's insurgent aspirations, it also captures the sense of schism that underpins Medina's rhetoric and her relations with others. The constant architectural motifs relied upon by Farah to articulate her reconstruction of narrative as well as to express her desire to occupy independent space suggest her attempts to rebuild from various sites of wreckage. She becomes obsessed with prolonged meditations and subsequently the active processes of construction, deconstruction and reconstruction within the intertwined spheres of her personal and political being. The result is that Medina is consistently viewed as both living with and exploiting the fault lines in the edifices built up around her.

The enduring emblem of fissure also represents the fine line Medina treads between deconstruction and destruction. It is here that Foucault's analytics of power again prove useful. This is perhaps best illustrated in Medina's final encounter with sister-in-law Xaddia. Having flown in from Rome, Xaddia launches a blistering attack on Medina as an anarchic architect pursuing her own designs regardless of others and at the risk of liquidating families. Inverting Medina's own image of the General who plays a fatalistic game of roulette, Xaddia maintains 'you are a gambler who having won once thinks that another win is in the offing' (S: 245). Warning Medina that she will not succumb to the same bookish distractions as Sagal and Amina, Xaddia crowns her tirade thus, 'you pawn and pawn and pawn until there is nothing or nobody left to put up to auction. Yesterday, it was Samater; today, Nasser and Dulman; tomorrow – who knows? – maybe it's my turn; the day after tomorrow, Sagal. When will you stop being obstinate and start seeing reason? Will you never concede defeat?' (*S*: 246). With the detachment of a returnee hearing of her brother's incarceration and her mother's ostracism, Xaddia does indeed smash through the portcullis of Medina's pretensions. She directs an uncompromising light on the complexities and contradictions that make Medina such an archetypal figure in Farah's work. Xaddia's critique of her sister-in-law's rigidity, in personal and political life, recalls a much earlier description. Wright's assertion that Medina is not so far removed from the Grand Patriarch himself is seemingly supported when she is portrayed as being 'unbending … as confident as a patriarch in the rightness of all her decisions' (*S*: 4).

Yet, it is the very qualities that exasperate Xaddia in the novel and Wright in criticism that define Medina in terms of Farah's more nuanced analytics of power. The accusation that she moves people around like pieces of furniture appears valid. Once again, however, this is precisely the point. It is the very proximity of these figures to the citadels and discourses of power that affords the reader greater insight into such mechanisms. As Farah renders Loyaan's desire for answers in terms of a torturer's sadistic temptation, so he presents Medina as a thoroughly frustrating, if all too accurate, power broker and manipulator in her own sphere. By rendering his protagonists thus, as he does up to and beyond Cambara in *Knots*, Farah simultaneously disarms the reader of any preconceived notion that power is a homogenous force exerted by a caricatured despot on an unsuspecting public. Once again, this effective disrobing of power conforms to something like Foucault's own sense in 'Power and Strategies': 'one should not assume a massive and primal condition of domination, a binary structure with "dominators" on one side and "dominated" on the other, but rather a multiform production of relations of domination which are partially susceptible of integration into overall strategies' (Foucault 1980b: 142). As with the epigraphs above, the rhetorical reliance on fluctuation, transience and fragmentation corresponds with Farah's critical project on a number of levels. For him, the key remains the degrees of difference that separate the autocratic General and his adversaries in the Group of 10. This again corresponds with the Foucauldian idea, as outlined in 'The Confession of the Flesh', that '[in] so far as power relations are an unequal and relatively stable relation of forces, it's clear that this implies an above and a below, a difference of potentials' (Foucault 1980c: 200–201). Seen in this light, Medina is a key figure in Farah's early trilogy. Defined as she is by pitfalls and paradoxes, she remains a protagonist in the process of becoming. Struggling with the awareness of her own entanglement in history-in-the-making, she comes to focus on the microphysics of power as a means of solidifying the building blocks of resistance.

For Alden, 'Farah's novels reflect the human condition: there are no positions outside history from which we can judge with certainty the acts of others. There are only interested perspectives, on resistance as on mothering' (Alden 2002: 374). For Medina, all gambles do not come off. Yet there remain some issues on which she, like Farah, will not waver. It is revealing, therefore, that Xaddia concentrates her ire on Medina's obstinacy. What at first seems a wholly negative trait might be reinterpreted in a more enabling light using the Foucauldian notion of 'essential obstinacy', as discussed in the Afterword to *Michel Foucault: Beyond Structuralism and Hermeneutics* (Dreyfus & Rabinow 1983: 225). Farah provides an insight into the personal/political tension that defines Medina's omnipresent struggle by giving shape to her thoughts during Xaddia's onslaught: *'if only Xaddia could understand that I'm fighting for the survival of woman in me, in her – while demolishing "families" like Idil's and regimes like the General's'* (S: 246). The enduring irony is that, for all the intellectual extrapolations that have gone before, she cannot articulate and therefore cannot solve this conundrum. For Ewen, however, this does not signal the end of critical debate: 'often the characters in these novels, recognizing the impossibility of reconciling opposite views, fall silent and say nothing to each other, or fall to scolding, a form of one-sided silence. Their author, however, continues to talk to them and the reader continues to overhear' (Ewen 1984: 206).

The unobtainable ideal Medina imagines for herself, as one-woman resistance to the personality cult of one-man oppression, does not, of course, demolish the General. However, in a far from utopian sense in this compact, thoroughly concentric work, the positioning of Medina's 'I' before that of 'her' (referring to Xaddia and then onto Somali womanhood more generally) signals a subtle shift in her thinking. It resonates with Farah's own centrifugal impulse, concerning the process by which the small must change before the big. Typically, the assertion sends the reader back to the opening of *Sardines*. Medina comes to realise that the mansions she desires to build, in terms of reconstructing both narrative and nation, can only be achieved once foundations are right and her own house is put in some kind of order. The last lines of the novel, therefore, are amongst its most poignant: 'the three walked away, refusing to play host to the guests who waited to be entertained with explanations, explications and examples. Medina, Samater and Ubax behaved as though they needed one another's company – and no more' (S: 250). Characteristically, Farah invites the reader to interrogate this playful notion of 'no more' in light of the sheer number of questions posed by *Sardines*. When Nasser delivers the following, for instance, he brings together those body, mirror and carceral motifs that have proved so central to this analysis:

> God is not in mosques made beautiful and covered from wall to wall with Saudi donations of silk … God lives in the crack of a mirror, the broken wing of a bird, He is in the lungs of a dog running away from the children who are stoning it to death … When a machine cuts off [a] worker's finger, it is in that finger, if restored, that you can find God: He is in the fold of the hurt joint of the finger, He is in the pained scar of memory. (*S:* 106)

The imagistic drift of this passage is particularly revealing. Nasser suggests that, rather than religious wholeness, subliminal beauty reveals itself in the corporeal capacity to overcome schism, to reconfigure and regenerate. Once more, Farah asks us to consider how and why the individual body might stand in for the national. The notion of collective homogeneity and exceptional identity is subject to the same degree of withering critique as that of the 'pure' political subject. The final image of the severed finger and its subsequent reconnection to the living organism is, therefore, the most profound. The 'pained scar of memory' at once resonates with Medina's recollection of the sensual experience during and after Ubax's painful birth, as well as Amina's ordeal, as some of their most embodied political memories.

The dialectical interplay between suffering and surviving bodies can once more be viewed as the resolute kernel of hope amidst Farah's exploration of political dystopia. Whilst the corporeal capacity to live with and move on from schism is personified in Medina's and Amina's resistance to subjection, fissure is also conceived as a productive catalyst at rhetorical, familial, generational and national levels. 'God lives in the crack of a mirror' as this allows individuals to differentiate themselves from oppressive hegemony, thus celebrating the 'difference of potentials' as well as the 'contradictions which breathe life into us' (*S:* 206). It is from here that the process by which alternative architectures of resistance are brought into being might begin. This again chimes with Foucault's argument in 'The Eye of Power' that 'if one wants to take seriously the assertion that struggle is the core of relations of power, one must take into account the fact that the good old "logic" of contradiction is no longer sufficient, far from it, for the unravelling of actual processes' (Foucault 1980a: 164).

To Guernica with Love

> My current obsession is one in which, as though in a reflected vision, I see
> the rest of the world in a broken mirror and discern the distorted truth of the
> things which I behold. Then I spot the fractured quality of souls reflected in the
> looking-glass; I see amputated limbs and am consequently overwhelmed with
> images suggesting Guernica.
>
> *(Nuruddin Farah – 'A Country in Exile', 1992: 5)*

Farah's Guernica obsession informs *Sardines*. The oftentimes fragmented
play of its narrative seems inspired by the dissonant quality of Picasso's art.
'God lives in the crack of a mirror', for Nasser and Farah, as hairline fractures spread to become key sites of productive contestation. As John Hawley
maintains, 'although [the Group's] plotting proves to be ineffective in over-
throwing the General, their resistance to his presentation of himself as the
center of meaning for Somalis offers readers something of a negative theol-
ogy: though they do not assert an alternative 'god', they at least can say what
their god is not' (Hawley 2002: 71). Set against the oppressive backdrop of 'a
country rife with internal intrigues, international conspiracies and local ma-
fiadom' (S: 208), 'God' reveals himself in the refractive process that compares
and ultimately distinguishes Medina from the General, as well as Samater
from Amina's father. Whilst the latter abandons his daughter to maintain
the regime's crypto-fascist status quo, Samater finally unites with his wife
to reject Idil's despotic claims of dominion over Ubax's body. Similarly, the
comparative cracks that separate mothers, daughters, sisters and sisters-in-
law are persistently seen as prerequisite, if painful, divides to be negotiated.
As such, Nasser's pregnant meditations capture the centrifugal thrust of
Farah's critique and the supplementary hope that resonates beyond his fictitious construction of the General's Somalia. Whilst *Maps* remains the most
popular and explicitly embodied of Farah's texts, his labyrinthine obsession
with body politics is just as central in this earlier work. As crystallised in the
sprawling song of *Sardines*, Farah asserts that only once the microdynamics
of power refract the oppressive dictates of the state will conditions exist for
real change. These concerns spill over into *Close Sesame*, the final instalment
of the *Variations* trilogy.

References

Achebe, C. 1975. *Morning Yet on Creation Day – Essays*. New York: Anchor Press.

Alden, P. 2002. 'New Women and Old Myths: Chinua Achebe's *Anthills of the Savannah* and Nuruddin Farah's *Sardines*'. In D. Wright (Ed.). *Emerging Perspectives on Nuruddin Farah*. New Jersey: Africa World Press.

Armah, AK. 1988. *The Beautyful Ones Are Not Yet Born*. Oxford: Heinemann.

Chowers, E. 2004. *The Modern Self in the Labyrinth – Politics and the Entrapment Imagination*. Cambridge, Mass.: Harvard University Press.

Dreyfus, H. & Rabinow, P. 1983. *Michel Foucault: Beyond Structuralism and Hermeneutics*. (2nd ed.) Chicago: The University of Chicago Press.

El Saadawi, N. 1980. *The Hidden Face of Eve – Women in the Arab World*. (S. Hetata, Trans. and Ed.). London: Zed Books.

El Saadawi, N. 2005. 'Imperialism and Sex in Africa'. In O. Nnaemeka (Ed.). *Female Circumcision and the Politics of Knowledge: African Women in Imperialist Discourses*. Westport: Praeger Publishers.

Ewen, D.R. 1984. 'Nuruddin Farah'. In G.D. Killam (Ed.). *The Writing of East and Central Africa*. London: Heinemann.

Farah, N. 1992. 'A Country in Exile'. *Transition*, Issue 57.

Farah, N. 2002. 'How Can We Talk of Democracy? An Interview with Nuruddin Farah by Patricia Alden and Louis Tremaine'. In D. Wright (Ed.). *Emerging Perspectives on Nuruddin Farah*. New Jersey: Africa World Press.

Foucault, M. 1980a. 'The Eye of Power'. In C. Gordon (Ed.). *Power/Knowledge – Selected Interviews and Other Writings*. Harlow: Pearson Education Ltd.

Foucault, M. 1980b. 'Power and Strategies'. In C. Gordon (Ed.). *Power/Knowledge – Selected Interviews and Other Writings*. Harlow: Pearson Education Ltd.

Foucault, M. 1980c. 'The Confession of the Flesh'. In C. Gordon (Ed.). *Power/Knowledge – Selected Interviews and Other Writings*. Harlow: Pearson Education Ltd.

Foucault, M. 1990. *The History of Sexuality, An Introduction*. (R. Hurley, Trans.). London: Penguin.

Foucault, M. 1991. *Discipline and Punish – The Birth of the Prison*. (A. Sheridan, Trans.). London: Penguin.

Foucault, M. 2001. *Madness and Civilization – A History of Insanity in the Age of Reason*. (R. Howard, Trans.). London: Routledge.

Gready, P. 2003. *Writing As Resistance – Life Stories of Imprisonment, Exile, and Homecoming from Apartheid South Africa*. New York: Lexington Books.

Hawley, J.C. 2002. 'Nuruddin Farah: Tribalism, Orality and Postcolonial Ultimate Reality and Meaning in Contemporary Somalia'. In D. Wright (Ed.). *Emerging Perspectives on Nuruddin Farah*. New Jersey: Africa World Press.

Juraga, D. 2002. 'Nuruddin Farah's *Variations on the Theme of an African Dictatorship*: Patriarchy, Gender and Political Oppression in Somalia'. In D. Wright (Ed.). *Emerging Perspectives on Nuruddin Farah*. New Jersey: Africa World Press.

Lambek, M. & Strathern, A. (Eds).1998. *Bodies and Persons – Comparative Perspectives from Africa and Melanesia*. Cambridge: Cambridge University Press.

Lazarus, N. 1990. *Resistance in Postcolonial African Fiction*. New Haven: Yale University Press.

Lazarus, N. 1999. *Nationalism and Cultural Practice in the Postcolonial World*. Cambridge: Cambridge University Press.

Lewis, I.M. 2002. *A Modern History of the Somali*. (4th ed.). Oxford: James Currey.

Mbembe, A. 2001. *On the Postcolony*. Berkeley: University of California Press.

Mitchell, W.J.T. 2000. 'The Panic of the Visual: A Conversation with Edward W. Said'. In P. Bové (Ed.). *Edward Said and the Work of the Critic: Speaking Truth to Power*. Durham and London: Duke University Press.

Ngũgĩ wa Thiong'o. 1998. *Penpoints, Gunpoints, and Dreams: Towards a Critical Theory of the Arts and the State in Africa*. Oxford: Clarendon Press.

Nnaemeka, O. (Ed.). 2005. *Female Circumcision and the Politics of Knowledge: African Women in Imperialist Discourses*. Westport: Praeger Publishers.

Okonkwo, C. 1999. *Decolonization Agonistics in Postcolonial Fiction*. London: MacMillan Press.

Phillips, M. 2002. 'To a Room of Their Own: Structure and Shadow in Nuruddin Farah's *Sardines*'. In D. Wright (Ed.). *Emerging Perspectives on Nuruddin Farah*. New Jersey: Africa World Press.

Rushdie, S. 2002. 'Notes on Writing and the Nation'. *Step Across this Line – Collected Non-Fiction: 1992–2002*. London: Jonathan Cape.

Said, E. 2002. 'Wild Orchids and Trotsky'. In G. Viswanathan (Ed.). *Power, Politics, and Culture – Interviews with Edward W. Said*. New York: Vintage Books.

Scarry, E. 1985. *The Body in Pain – The Making and Unmaking of the World*. New York and Oxford: Oxford University Press.

Woolf, V. 1967. *A Room of One's Own*. London: Penguin.

Wright, D. 1994. *The Novels of Nuruddin Farah*. Bayreuth: Bayreuth African Studies Series.

Endnotes

1 See Green, D. 1999. *Gender Violence in Africa: African Women's Responses*. New York: St Martin's Press and El Saadawi, N. 1980. *The Hidden Face of Eve – Women in the Arab World*. (S. Hetata, Trans. and Ed.). London: Zed Books, p. 36.

2 Kirby, V. 'Women's Rights, Bodies and Identities: The limits of Universalism and the Legal Debate Around Excision in France'. In Nnaemeka, O (Ed.). 2005. *Female Circumcision and the Politics of Knowledge: African Women in Imperialist Discourses*. Westport: Praeger Publishers, pp. 81–96 and Lionnet, F. '"Other" Bodies: Western Feminism, Race and Representation in Female Circumcision Discourse'. In Nnaemeka, O (Ed.). 2005. *Female Circumcision and the Politics of Knowledge: African Women in Imperialist Discourses*. Westport: Praeger Publishers, pp. 97–110.

3 Agosin, M. (Ed.). 1998. *A Map of Hope: Women's Writing on Human Rights – An International Literary Anthology*. New Jersey: Rutgers University Press, pp. 244–250.

4 'Translator's Note' to Foucault's 'Afterword', 'The Subject and Power', in Dreyfus, H & Rabinow, P. (Eds.). 1983. *Michel Foucault: Beyond Structuralism and Hermeneutics*. (2nd ed.). Chicago: The University of Chicago Press, p. 222.

4

Through the Maze Darkly: Incarceration and Insurrection in *Close Sesame*

[The aim of the public execution] is not so much to re-establish a balance as to bring into play, at its extreme point, dissymmetry between the subject who has dared to violate the law and the all-powerful sovereign who displays his strength … in this liturgy of punishment, there must be an emphatic affirmation of power and of its intrinsic superiority. And this superiority is not simply that of right, but that of the physical strength of the sovereign beating down upon the body of his adversary and mastering it: by breaking the law, the offender has touched the very person of the prince; and it is the prince – or at least those to whom he has delegated his force – who seizes upon the body of the condemned man and displays it marked, beaten and broken.

(Michel Foucault – Discipline and Punish, 1991: 48 – 49)

No one could account for Deeriye's movements for three solid days. And it took the best part of the fourth day to piece together stories stranded with gaps nobody could fill … Into what dark hole of mystery did he disappear between being seen with Khaliif and turning up, arrayed in army uniform, marching in rhythm with other soldiers – and standing at attention before the General who was awarding medals to heroes of the land, pulling out, by mistake, prayer-beads instead of a revolver to shoot the General dead? (Another version told how the prayer-beads, like a boa-constrictor, entwined themselves around the muzzle of the revolver and Deeriye could not disentangle it in time.) He was an easy target, now that he hadn't hit his.

And the General's bodyguards emptied into him cartridges of machine-gun fire until his body was cut nearly in half.

(Close Sesame: 236)

THE MADDENING BRILLIANCE OF THE LABYRINTH IS THAT ENDING AND beginning often seem to be one and the same. If *Sweet and Sour Milk's* prologue establishes its evasiveness with Soyaan's mysterious death, *Close Sesame's* epilogue captures its fascination with overt violence and strategic subterfuge. Foucault's sovereign is here reconfigured as Farah's punitive General, with Damiens' regicidal intentions re-imagined through Deeriye's abortive assassination attempt. As with Loyaan's enduring memory of the oppositional hope he and his brother invested in Ladan, Farah presents one of his major preoccupations in parentheses. An obsession with the processes and politics of narration defines the reports of Deeriye's death. If two fatalities buttress the trilogy, this suggests another vital connection; the competing claims and clashing voices that do battle over the 'truth'. This is played with in *Sweet and Sour Milk* where a dispute erupts as to whether Soyaan's final words were pro – or anti-regime. Loyaan: '[Soyaan] called my name three times … Those were his last words.' The Minister grinned. Then: 'We were given a different version. We prefer that' (*S&SM*: 42). Similarly, in *Close Sesame*, the reader confronts the same challenge as grieving family members: interrogating the slippages between various versions of the account of Deeriye's disappearance and ultimate demise. Such narrative tussles can be read both in terms of the fraught socio-political situation of Somalia itself and Farah's commitment to advocating greater tolerance and democracy through his writing.

'With the Portcullis Down', 'History through an Unfocused Lens' and 'A Door in the Darkness' are just some of the enigmatic chapter headings that feature in *Close Sesame*. They are part of an imagistic continuum that at once binds the trilogy, whilst also gesturing towards Farah's nuanced critique of power. As Wright maintains, images of doors in darkness hinge on the figurative dialectic of opening and closing, release and confinement, protection and prohibition (Wright 1994: 89–90). It is fitting, therefore, that Deeriye's description of his own period in Italian incarceration resonates with Ngũgĩ's metaphorical designation of the postcolonial state as penitentiary. Throughout, the aging protagonist reflects on the true liberation unwittingly afforded him by his colonial captors:

> Confinement in prison opened to Deeriye a vista of a wider, larger world: detention compelled him to think of the history and contradictions which the neo-colonial person lives in; detention forced him to see himself not as a spokesman of a clan, but made it obvious to him that he was a member of the world's oppressed; detention painted for him a different picture. (*CS*: 103)

This is repeated at strategic points throughout the novel: '[i]t was prison [under the Italians] which opened up a world which had been closed to him by virtue of his background' (*CS*: 89). When recalling his detention under the General, it is the refusal of reading material (especially the Koran) that impresses itself on Deeriye's memory. He is such a crucial protagonist in the *Variations* cycle as he straddles regimes both colonial and neo-colonial, thus bringing an extended historical perspective to proceedings. The 'dark room of [Deeriye's] isolation' (*CS*: 30) ensures that he has a room of his own in which to muse upon the mechanisms of power. Taking place against the backdrop of the Group's factional fallout, *Close Sesame* introduces the reader to a society where Soyaan's figuration of the Syracusan tyrant has been realised. Through the processes of rumour, reverberation and reiteration, a panopticon-style vision of the supreme surveillance society has been supplemented by a vast echo chamber with murmurs and malevolent gazes the order of the day. This once more recalls Perrot's description, in 'The Eye of Power', of the Panopticon in Foucault's work: 'essentially it's the gaze; but also speech, because he has those famous "tin tubes"' (Foucault 1980a: 154). Within the imaginative confines of the *Variations* cycle, Deeriye acknowledges the General's manipulation of Somali oral-based networks, provocatively describing them in terms of 'the acoustics which echo their fears' (*CS*: 98).

Both *Sweet and Sour Milk* and *Close Sesame* confront the reader with labyrinthine narratives designed to reflect the disciplinary designs of society itself. Unlike Medina, Loyaan and Deeriye have tangential relations with the Group of 10, having been dragged into its cellular struggles through the exploits of family members. Mursal, Deeriye's son, belongs to the Group and, by this stage in the fictional cycle, has committed himself, along with comrades Mukhtaar, Mahad and Jibril-Somali, to remove the General using any means possible. As Wright notes, 'Farah mischievously gives his four conspirators the names of the Koranic messengers' (Wright 1994: 101). Fittingly, therefore, Fanonian debates concerning the legitimacy of violent resistance punctuate *Close Sesame*. They also inform the rhetorical struggles between father and son. Like Loyaan, Deeriye offers a refreshing perspective on similarities in arrangements and activities between resistance and regime. However, whilst

Loyaan is relatively inexperienced, Deeriye draws from a personal history 'resplendent with contradictions' (CS: 180). As a result, his critique of poly-morphous power is one of Farah's most distinctive. His alternative depictions of incarceration speak of the shifting terrains of domination and resistance. Accordingly, questions concerning the most effective modes of opposition are left open ended. It is this very inconclusivity that recalls Foucault's stance in 'Useless to Revolt?': 'Is one right to revolt, or not? Let us leave the question open' (Foucault 2000: 452). In choosing to end *Close Sesame* with an unan-swered question, therefore, Farah signs off on the note of critical ambivalence that defines such large swathes of his writing.

As in the relationships between Ebla and Sagal in *Sardines* and Hilaal and Askar in *Maps*, Deeriye's wise council provides a tonic to some of the more overzealous pronouncements of youth. The bond he has with Mursal, how-ever, is seen in terms of two lucid, politically informed adults sharing the type of common ideology refuted by Keynaan in *Sweet and Sour Milk*. Before becoming a Professor at the National University of Somalia, Mursal's PhD concerned 'the political relevance of the Quran in an Islamic State' (CS: 8). Yet, as with all parent/child relationships in Farah's work, proximity between characters often results in complicated, if invariably compelling, tensions. In an exchange concerning the appropriate nature of resistance, Deeriye cau-tions his son. In so doing, he gestures towards the incremental critique of power Farah builds throughout his work:

> Mursal – 'The only difference, if there is a difference, is that in 1934 the enemy
> and the famine-creating power was colonial and foreign; and now it is neo-
> colonial and local. Have you not learnt your lesson? Which reminds me of
> something you used to say: that the history worth studying is one of resistance,
> not capitulation; and that all great men – Shaka Zulu, Ataturk, Nkrumah, Cabral,
> Garibaldi, Lenin, Cabdunnaasit, Gandhi, the Sayyid – have one thing in common:
> the shaping force of their lives has been resistance.'
>
> Deeriye – 'Between national and colonial governments there is this major
> difference: the enemy is obvious, the nation's priorities are clear on one hand;
> on the other hand, with national governments, things become unclear,
> priorities are confused. The enemy is within: a cankerous tumour. You die of it
> gradually; bloodless, pale and unmourned.' (CS: 166)

Whilst Mursal's Fanonian pronouncements appear justified, Farah invites the reader to challenge their totalising bent. Once again, it is the family dynamic that skews the kind of theoretical extrapolations that Mursal as well as Medina (*Sardines*) and Margaritta (*Sweet and Sour Milk*) are culpable of.

In *Close Sesame*, Deeriye effectively serves as Farah's critical mouthpiece, typically resorting to embodied rhetoric to make his point. He emphasises the shifting terrain upon which effective struggle must be waged, urging his son to look beyond the inchoate appearance of power rather than underestimate its workings. For Wright, Deeriye can therefore be placed in an oppositional continuum with Nkrumah and Gandhi as 'one of history's passive resisters; he is a moral rather than a military hero, who in a dilemma chooses the most difficult option because he believes it to be right' (Wright 1994: 98). When Mursal chides his father for sitting on the sidelines of real action, he shows his ignorance of different notions and strategies of opposition. As such, Deeriye might once again be read in relation to Colin Gordon's conception of a Foucauldian microphysics of resistance:

> The existence of those who seem not to rebel is a warren of minute, individual, autonomous tactics and strategies which counter and inflect the visible facts of overall domination, and whose … desires and choices resist any simple division into the political and the apolitical. The schema of a strategy of resistance as a vanguard of politicisation needs to be subjected to re-examination, and account must be taken of resistances whose strategy is one of evasion or defence … There are no good subjects of resistance. (Gordon 1980: 257)

Building from this notion allows the reader to ask more searching questions of the ethical as well as polyglot imperatives that underpin Farah's novels. This, in turn, enables us to appreciate how and why they play host to a series of substantive debates, both theoretical and pragmatic. In *Close Sesame*, the effective implementation of 'minute, individual, autonomous' resistance strategies on a narrower, domestic-political stage preoccupies both writer and protagonist. Deeriye's contingent position, as political prisoner under Italian and Somali regimes, leads him to insist on complicating links between powers rather than presenting them in reductive terms. It is revealing that Farah attends to this translational motif in the text. The Reich quote that provides the central epigraph in *Sweet and Sour Milk*, for instance, is distorted through Deeriye's errant memory, providing an acerbic aside on the current disorder of things: 'paraphrasing the ideas of a philosopher whose name eluded him … he said to himself: In the figure of the chieftain, the authoritarian state has its representative in every clan or tribe so the elders of the clan become its most important instrument of power' (*CS*: 104).

This playful misinterpretation has its more ominous counterpart in what Wright calls the General's 'monstrous perversion' of the Koran (Wright 1994: 101). It also gestures towards the problematic implications of the priviligentsia's desire to transpose the fruits of their colonial learning into a Somali setting. Whilst the rhetorical weapons of Lenin *et al.* are employed to bolster anti-colonial struggles, it is critical, for author and protagonist, that they are reconditioned in African hands. Typically, it is left to Deeriye to point out the bitter irony that the General's opponents now confront a power advertising itself in a hollow triptych of Grand Patriarch, Marx and Lenin. As the Foucault of *Discipline and Punish* reminds us: if hegemonic authority is circuitous, locking ruler and ruled in more complex, interdependent relations, it can never be sufficient to eliminate the head of that pyramidal power alone (Foucault 1991: 177). Seen from this perspective, it is necessary to initiate an analytics of power that traces flows of force from the bottom up as well as from the top down. Simply changing the cast is insufficient. As Foucault emphasises in 'The Eye of Power', it is the tower/power system itself that needs to be dismantled (Foucault 1980a: 164–165).

Considered from a perspective that takes account of the microphysics of resistance, alongside what Foucault, in 'The Confession of the Flesh', terms the 'capillarity' of power, the cautionary notes struck by Deeriye throughout *Close Sesame* are much more salient than submissive (Foucault 1980b: 201). He conducts his own life according to principles that, at an individual level, he holds dear. It is this preoccupation with the counter-hegemonic capacity of human nature at its most profound, politically personal level that animates Farah's work and makes Deeriye an exemplary protagonist. The knots and entanglements that define relations between power and resistance endow the individual with a responsibility to construct alternative designs so that they might 'cope', in as dignified a manner as possible, with the world. As such, it again chimes with Chowers' description of Foucauldian resistance. In what follows, I maintain that the utility of such a concept only intensifies as Farah's literary project evolves: 'Foucauldian resistance never contemplates an unblemished social predicament as its goal, never pictures a world devoid of power relations and mutual subjection. Resistance, in Foucault's view, takes the form of local confrontations that achieve limited ends and set the stage for subsequent struggles' (Chowers 2004: 187).

The Writer as Doctor: Revolting Bodies and the Optics of Surveillance

One of the most distinctive features of Farah's novels is the potted bibliographies that accompany them. Whilst intertextual references abound, from Walcott to Woolf, these border vignettes remain compelling in their own right. In *Close Sesame*, a preoccupation with all things bodily informs the author's note: 'on occasions, I did not hesitate to borrow the skeleton of a notion or phrases but have had to cover this body of information with flesh and skin of my own manufacture' (*CS*: 239). Once again, this foreshadows *Links*: 'I am grateful to all those I spoke to, and to the authors whose writings I read. Needless to say, I covered all borrowings with skin of my own manufacture' (*L*: 335). On one level, this fleshy rhetoric works in conjunction with Farah's diagnosis of Somalia's ailing body politic, as cited by Ewen: '[t]he writer in Africa … is the doctor and it is he who must diagnose and then prescribe the right drug for the nation's illness' (Ewen 1984: 192). When viewed in relation to the *Variations* cycle as a whole, it also corresponds with those intense corporeal concerns that lie at its heart. Farah's visceral vision only sharpens as the reader moves into the bloodier, more sexually explicit realm of his second trilogy. If the resistant pivot around which the *Variations* series turns is Medina's defence of Ubax's corporeal sovereignty, the key to unlocking Farah's critique of power throughout *Close Sesame* may be conceived in similarly embodied terms.

Deeriye is an asthmatic and the author acknowledges the useful information gained from *Asthma: The Facts*. As such, it is tempting to consider Farah's protagonist in relation to the carceral narratives of both Ngũgĩ and Soyinka. In *Detained*, Ngũgĩ reveals that 'what I dreaded most was a possible recurrence of my asthma. In Dakar, Senegal, in 1968, I had nearly lost my life after a very severe attack' (Ngũgĩ wa Thiong'o 1981: 103). Similarly, in *The Man Died*, Soyinka details how his time in prison compelled him to relearn his body: 'my body becomes of a new absorbing interest to me, a new occupation to while away the hours. I have not till now taken much notice of the physical fact of the body, only of its sensations. Now it has become a strange terrain where flakes come off every part merely by rubbing' (Soyinka 1972: 140). Seen within this discursive framework, *Close Sesame* seems haunted by these carceral accounts. They, in turn, explore the Foucauldian processes by which, through disciplining and punishing, the subject is perpetually forced to renegotiate their body. As such, Deeriye's asthma symbolically supplements an interpretation of the trilogy as one focused on confinement, entrapment and cellular space, in an anatomical sense as well as in architectural terms. Alden and Tremaine consider the claustrophobic politics of space in their study. Yet, with the notable exception of Wright, the significance of Farah's figurative conception of constriction has been somewhat underexplored (Wright 1994: 90–91). In essence, therefore, I suggest the possible outlets sought by all three protagonists in the *Variations* series cluster round the theme of release from claustrophobia and confusion. *Sweet and Sour Milk's* Loyaan strives to uncover answers to his numerous riddles and is ultimately posted abroad, the issue of whether this constitutes release or liquidation left unresolved. *Sardines'* Medina seeks a room of her own, moving family and furniture in the domain of her own architecture of power. The myriad moral, spiritual and political dilemmas of *Close Sesame's* Deeriye are conceived in terms of his struggle to breathe.

Whilst the metaphor might appear forced, I suggest it can be productively read in relation to Chowers' overview of Foucault's notion of entrapment:

> Foucault … [presents] human relations as war-like – with the embattled territory being one's body, conduct, or self-understanding … The inner conflict cannot be resolved because it is interwoven with the external one … Under entrapment, the most intimate dilemmas are also the most global and impersonal; *the internal and the external are hopelessly intermingled.* (Chowers 2004: 188)

A preoccupation with the hopeless intermingling of conflicts intrinsic and extrinsic lies at the heart of each and every Farah novel, with *Close Sesame* providing an intriguing early example. Whilst Farah explores similar political subject/subjectivity issues through the figurative body, he critically highlights a spiritual dimension as an alternative outlet from certain 'war-like' relations. For Chowers, Foucault's godless world permits no such release from the entrapment of modernity. For Farah, Deeriye's piety provides him with an opportunity to explore how a coherent and compassionate faith might provide the foundations for a highly politicised programme of resistance. As Anthony Appiah suggests, *Close Sesame's* counter-hegemonic portrait of an elderly Muslim has both subtlety and substance, qualities conspicuously lacking in certain other representations: '[Deeriye is] the most fully realized picture that I am aware of in English of the interior life of a devout Moslem – indeed, one of the richest representations of a prayerfully devout human being I have ever read' (Appiah 1998: 704). Deeriye's status as a widower, who continues to communicate with wife Nadiifa in dreams and visions, makes

Farah's portrait even more unique. When reflecting on his ailment, he recalls the spiritual balm provided by Nadiifa's words:

> 'All our lives … we misdescribe illnesses and misuse metaphors … Nadiifa … spoke of my lungs as my soul: she didn't speak of my lungs as though they were my face. Which perhaps means she believes that my soul is struggling, has been struggling to free itself and join its Creator … Why has this never occurred to me? In my lungs is my soul, struggling to be free from this body so it can join Nadiifa's and prepare for the eventual roll-call of names of the pious when these souls will be one with their Creator.' (CS: 235)

For Wright, in a passage reminiscent of Adonis' description of metaphor discussed in relation to *Sweet and Sour Milk*, the most suggestive qualities of these corporeal images are their instability. Deeriye's asthma, for instance, resists reductive interpretation, with the reader being cautioned against the sort of associative misuse identified by the protagonist. Once again, for a text littered with incomplete parentheses and unresolved questions, these open-ended qualities have multiple significance:

> [The] book's pervasive Islamic image-complex of breath, chants, ears and lungs – which also stresses Islam's link with oral tradition – keeps open the religious options of the asthma symbol … there is no attempt to read Deeriye's illness, in negative material terms, as an evasion of political defeat and a retreat into a private religious quietism, or to write off his problematic spirituality as the psychosomatic product of his bodily illness or his political despair. (Wright 1994: 90)

With Wright's caution in mind, Deeriye's respiratory problems may be interpreted as a symbolic precursor to the psychosomatic, if much bloodier explorations of *Maps*. Alongside the other aches and pains of old age, his asthma represents existential anguish as well as the moral asphyxiation caused by being a peripheral spectator as Mursal gambles with his life and, potentially, the lives of those around him. A representative moment comes immediately after trusted ally Rooble announces his suspicions about the young men's plans. Following this, Deeriye suffers an attack: '[his] head buzzed with whispering prayers for a while; it seemed he was becoming aware of his chest congesting … Something pulled at his inside, a pain, a terrible and dizzyingly real pain tugging at his lungs and emptying them of breath' (CS: 44–45). He tries to convince himself that the anxiety results not so much from ideological opposition to the proposed violence but rather because he feels the burdensome strain of 'heavy political secrets'. These have defined Deeriye's existence, leading to his earlier exclusion from the lives of his children. His physical condition therefore forces him to muse on alternative, more subtle modes of resistance. What might be called the psychosomatic politics of *Close Sesame* also chimes with Monica Greco's *Illness as a Work of Thought – A Foucauldian Perspective on Psychosomatics*. In acknowledging the contested discourses that frame the field of psychosomatics, Greco argues that re-engaging with Foucault's work 'enable[s] the space of problematization to be opened and unfolded, rather than settled and closed' (Greco 1998: 5). As I have argued above, it is precisely this sense of contesting what appears to be fixed, in the interests of providing space for alternative visions and voices, that characterises *Close Sesame*.

To pursue this 'problematization' argument further, it is one of the novel's pointed ironies that the aged, asthmatic Deeriye dies in an attempt to take the General's life. The Fanonian catalyst, of course, is the intrusion of murderous politics into his private, domestic life (Mursal has been killed in his own foiled assassination bid). In its wake, Deeriye enters into another dreamy discourse with Nadiifa whose voice, and/or Deeriye's imagining of her voice, bids him 'avenge your son. Let the powerful heart of anger persuade you, don't wait until it cools. Then come and join me ... *I am here, awaiting your arrival, I am the* houri *assigned to you – on earth as well as in paradise*' (CS: 227). For a text concerning existential doubt and obfuscation, it is fitting that the presentation of arguments for and against direct action is entangled in a way that foreshadows novels such as *Links* and *Knots*. Pangs of paternal guilt merge with Nadiifa's spectral indictment for 'having imagined a jungle of ideas in which our son Mursal has lost his way' (CS: 226). This serves as a metatextual comment on many of Farah's texts, resembling, as they do, sprawling mazes of ideas. Yet, in order to navigate a successful course through them, the reader must come to terms with how and why Farah anchors these debates in unremittingly fleshy terms.

The Optics of Malveillance

As the following chapters explore, the bloody pivot on which the body politics of both Farah's discourse and Somalia's national narrative turns is defeat in the Ogaden War. There are, however, intriguing links between concerns with carceral confinement in the first trilogy and bio-political (dis)orders in the second. If a discomfiting new reality is brought home to Misra when Askar refuses her maternal touch in *Maps*, the tipping point for Deeriye comes when neighbours start turning against one another. Harrassed and humiliated by the young, stone-throwing Yassin, Deeriye retreats indoors to muse upon the unravelling of Somalia's social fabric:

> These unneighbourly neighbours: a world stood on its head, he reflected, a world whose inhabitants live, like ants, in societies of total exclusiveness from one another, busy eating away at one another's foundation … It seemed that the Somali rationalism nowadays shared space with the materialistic cynicism based in fear of one another and suspicion … Neighbours spying on one another. God forbid! (*CS*: 150–151)

The image of the ant colony's 'total exclusivity' and cannibalistic fervour is precise and prophetic, paving the way for something similar in *Secrets*: '[t]ermites too have their way of hiding out in sandhills built with their own saliva, after they have destroyed one's timber construct' (*Sec*: 192).

As Wright argues, 'the General contravenes the Koranic code of trust and friendship by setting neighbour against neighbour' (Wright 1994: 101). Building from this, Foucault's notion of 'malveillance', as set out in 'The Eye of Power', is particularly instructive here: 'in the Panopticon each person, depending on his place, is watched by all or certain of the others. You have an apparatus of total and circulating mistrust … The perfect form of surveillance consists in a summation of *malveillance*' (Foucault 1980a: 158). Faced with this sombre normalisation of mistrust, Deeriye opts to stand apart. This once more foregrounds issues of autonomy, with Yassin's unruly behaviour threatening a newly constituted domestic order in which the elderly Muslim shares the same space as his Jewish-American daughter-in-law. The above portrait sees the disintegration of traditional codes of neighbourly affiliation as symbolic of societal atrophy more broadly. As such, it anticipates some of the central concerns of *Yesterday, Tomorrow*. In it, a Deeriye-type figure reflects how '[tradition] is a target, an honourable goal worth achieving … Ask yourself, "Whom do the warlords represent?" They represent a streak of anti-tradition, and they are the product of a plot to dishonour our centuries-old culture' (*YT*: 87). In *Close Sesame*, at various junctures both past and in the historical present, Deeriye chooses to 'define himself out of' (*CS*: 99) rather than in terms of such 'anti-tradition'. Conducting his relationships based on love and respect for family and friends, rather than in 'unthinking' deference to clan, he embodies the critical ambivalence that underpins Farah's oeuvre.

Deeriye originally falls out of favour with his kinsmen during the period of Italian occupation when he offers protection to a member of a rival clan. The deviant act is incomprehensible to tribal figures and colonisers alike. The price he pays is the period in detention that ultimately serves as an unexpected gift, opening his world and obliging him to interrogate interconnections between seemingly alternative technologies and operations of power. Yet, if this runs the risk of envisaging history as repetition, it is Deeriye's discriminatory awareness of colonial and neo-colonial power that prepares him for one final confrontation with clannish authority. To emphasise Deeriye's singularity and stoicism, Farah presents his adversaries in suitably anonymous terms: '[his] name could have been Ali, Ahmed, Abdulle, or anything; he didn't matter' (CS: 171). One faceless elder continues:

> 'I know that although [Deeriye's] rationale may be as incomprehensible to us as a madman's, he has stayed by and walked the same determined road these past forty-odd years. Never has he wavered; never have his actions demonstrated a moment's indecision or hesitation. People like myself have done so. We've been used time and again by whoever headed the government of the country.' (CS: 172)

In *Close Sesame*, fellow elders muse on their functions as complicit pawns in the General's game: 'someone said, "Isolate and rule, isolate each community, keep them divided, call the nationalist tribalist and the tribalist nationalist and use them. But rule them"' (CS: 172). The real tragedy, however, is that such moments of realisation remain fleeting.

Once again, Ali's testimony in *The Cost of Dictatorship* chillingly reinforces Farah's vision. In recounting a meeting with Barre upon leaving prison, Ali recalls that 'there were eight in our group, but Siyad ordered Dr. Mohamoud Hassan Tani to remain outside because he was of a different clan to the rest of us. This was typical of the man, who was always exploiting the clan divisions in Somali society to remain in power' (Ghalib 1995: 251). This chimes with *Close Sesame's* concern with the ways in which strategic, larger clan interests transcend any willingness to alter the rules of engagement set out by a General all-too-aware of the need to exploit such schisms. For Hashim, this is embedded at the level of collective consciousness. 'While, on the one hand, Somalis know that they are part of a Somali people, on the other, they perceive this to be secondary to the primary affiliation of group which is the essential part of that whole' (Hashim 1997: 68). These tensions run deep throughout Farah's fiction, leading him to explore how inculcating fear and fostering factionalism enables autocratic regimes to sustain themselves. This once more recalls the statement he made concerning the objectives of his *Variations* sequence: not a polemical attack against caricatured tyrants but a more sophisticated, necessarily sombre analytics of power as a system in which individuals and collectives are entangled in labyrinths of culpability, confinement and complicity. Clan, of course, is not the only target of Farah's critique.

Mnthali describes the solipsistic tendencies of Farah's priviligentsia in the following terms:

> [They] have been either politically marginalised by being isolated from the rest of society or co-opted into their countries' ruling and exploitative elites. In such a situation any meaningful attempt at influencing change is bound to lead to the sort of bizarre preoccupation with secret memoranda and 'kamikaze' attempts at assassinating the General which form the bulk of the 'detective' layers of both *Sweet and Sour Milk* and *Close Sesame*. (Mnthali 2002: 181)

Whilst there is extensive scholarship on oral power in Farah's work and Somali historiography, Mnthali's description of the Group's preoccupation with written material as 'bizarre' is revealing. A concern with writing might be misguided, as the inability to reach out to a wider audience consigns them to the exclusivist fate referred to by Deeriye. It is their communicative rather than specific failings that play into the General's hands, in turn passing over the heads of the oppressed citizenry. Deeriye's meditations on polymorphous power, therefore, resonate with those on the dissemination and denial of information itself. In *Close Sesame*, the key issue is not so much what is said but how it is said, by whom and through which channels.

> Information, Deeriye was thinking to himself, is the garden the common man in Somalia or anywhere else is not allowed to enter … information, or the access to that *power and knowledge*: power prepared to protect power; keep the populace underinformed so you can rule them; keep them apart by informing them separately; build bars of ignorance around them, imprison them with shackles of uninformedness and they are easy to govern … tell them the little that will misguide them, inform them wrongly, make them suspect one another so that they tell on one another. (CS: 74)

As the last line suggests, Deeriye's designation of an atrophying ant colony casts a substantial shadow over the novel. The priviligentsia, however, may offer some oppositional hope. As noted, Farah is concerned with the mechanics and processes of resistance, rather than a portrayal of revolutionary proportions. If ideological projects fail and the autocrat retains his panoptical powers, the resistant energy unleashed in the struggle itself is driven inward, internalised to bring the critique back home at the level of political subjectivity, embodiment and sovereignty. Once again, therefore, Chowers' Foucauldian interventions are enabling: 'the best we can do is to devise personal ways of *coping*' (Chowers 2004: 185). One approach to the entire *Variations* series, therefore, would consider it a prolonged, fictional investigation of how best to cope under autocratic rule, constantly speculating on relations between micrological and macrological body politics. *Close Sesame* offers an intriguing supplement to this imaginative exploration of coping via its Foucauldian meditations on madness.

Madness and (Un)Civilisation: Spectres of the 'Mad Mullah'

If Farah invites his reader to consider how his imagined metropolitan spaces replicate the cellular power manipulated by the General, he also suggests how the contested realities of Somali self-definition play themselves out on city streets. This once again corresponds with sociological commentaries on the country. Writing during the civil war that engulfed Somalia in the early nineties, Abdi Sheik-Abdi identifies a harbinger of disorder in the destruction of a key monument in his study *Divine Madness: Mohammed 'Abdulle Hassan (1856–1920)*: 'in the current chaos and factionalism in Somalia, the Mullah's statue overlooking Mogadishu was defaced and later toppled, to be sold for scrap – an unmitigated death-blow to Somali nationalism and even nationhood' (Abdi 1993: 212). Whilst debates rage over the Dervish leader's legacy, Abdulle Hassan occupies a critical place in both the national narrative and political consciousness of Somali people. Consider, for instance, Ahmed's counter-argument in *The Invention of Somalia*:

> … the construction of the monument unilaterally accentuates the Sayyid's stature as a national hero, irrespective of the fact that some of his poetical diatribes and his raids against other clans were motivated and shaped by his clannish world view. It is no wonder, therefore, that the monument was immediately destroyed by the masses after Barre's overthrow. The destruction of the monument does not only symbolize the overthrow of Barre, but it also

brings to an end the political supremacy of the Dervish followers. (Ahmed 1995: 138–139)

Fittingly, Hassan functions as a vital touchstone throughout *Close Sesame*. In his reflections on the present (dis)order of things, Deeriye continually refers to Hassan who, in a decidedly different context, served as a resistant figurehead for his generation. Going against the grain of Ahmed's argument, Deeriye reveres him as a leader who was able to manipulate the affiliations of clan, kith and kin in unifying appeals to resist 'infidel occupiers'. Then, the enemy was identifiably external, with the goals of any opposition to this occupying force common and transparent. This corroborates Hashim's sense that '[the] appeal to Somali national identity has generally been most effective when an overt external threat has existed' (Hashim 1997: 60). For many, therefore, Hassan is considered a master tactician who united disparate forces in the sort of coherent project that successive Somali leaders have only dreamt about. Farah's imagined General appeals to a distant clan lineage joining him to Hassan. He does so in a bid to strike an heroic chord in the national consciousness. As Wright crucially reminds us, however, the 'real' story is riven with revealing tensions: 'under Barre's regime the poems of the Sayyid were still banned because … they contained diatribes against families of the dictator's own Mareehaan clan who fifty years earlier had collaborated with the colonial authorities' (Wright 1994: 98). The dystopian situation presented by Farah throughout the *Variations* trilogy builds from this, showing how and why the General manipulates Somali social and clan structures to perpetuate the isolate-and-rule policies that secure his grip on power. In order to explore continuities between colonial and neo-colonial authorities further, he focuses on constructions of madness.

As with Farah's work, the title of Abdi's study has more than superficial significance. He shows how and why debates are framed between characterisations of divinity and madness, with the latter term carrying significant colonial baggage:

> Was the Mullah mad? He was mad to the extent that he was inspired, obsessed and single-minded in his enduring dual aims of 'reviving the religious spirit in his people' and driving the non-Muslim foreigners out of his country. He was far from mad when it came to the proper conduct of his own affairs … So why then was he called the 'Mad' Mullah? … The implication was that knowledge made the Mullah mad. According to the 19th-century English traveller, Richard Burton, too much learning tended to make the Somali mad: 'Like the half-crazy

Fakihs of the Sahara in Northern Africa, the *Widad* [i.e. *wadad*], or priest [in Somaliland], is generally unfitted for the affairs of this world, and the *Hafiz*, or Koran-reciter [memorizer] is almost idiotic.' In Somali society, the sobriquet 'mad' could also be given to men who are exceptionally brave or bright. (Abdi 1993: 51)

Besides being an almost literal transcription of *Close Sesame's* opening questions ('Was the Sayyid mad? Why did the British call him the Mad Mullah?' *CS*: 29), Abdi's work opens the way for another Foucauldian intertext. In *Madness and Civilization*, Foucault refers to 'qualitative simplifications of madness'. He goes on to argue that, seen through the prism of traditional discourses, '[the world] of mania was parched, dry, compounded of violence and fragility; a world which heat – unfelt but everywhere manifested – made arid, friable, and always ready to relax under moist coolness. The essence of mania is desertic, sandy' (Foucault 2001: 121–122). *Close Sesame* sees Farah playing with colonial tropes, particularly those linking intense weather conditions (invariably heat) and pathological disruption, in a way that recalls everything from *Jane Eyre* to *Heart of Darkness*. In contemporary discourse on Somalia, from news reports to sociological treatises, an implied relationship between 'parched' ecological and psychological landscapes still endures. When viewed within this Somali-specific context, Foucault's identification of a discursive association between aridity and 'friable' states of mind assumes fresh burdens of significance. Whilst, as Abdi maintains, the conflation of madness and exceptional intellect is familiar, it plays a particularly important role in *Close Sesame*. In the figure of Khaliif, the reader is provided with an ominous 'fool' who utilises his transgressive position at the margins of society to speak out against repressive power. He does so with a disruptive clarity that the Group of 10 can only envy. As Claudio Gorlier points out, 'the reader is induced to reflect ... on the question of folly, and of the mental asylum as a prison; on the basis of socio-psychoanalytic theories from Szasz to Foucault; on madness as an Orwellian classification of dissent' (Gorlier 2002: 424). Formerly a civil servant, Khaliif is an itinerant irritant. Deeriye's description of him once again speaks to the trilogy as a whole: '[he] was a mystery half-revealed' (*CS*: 16).

As Wright maintains, Farah is concerned, in much the same way as Foucault in *Madness and Civilization*, with social constructions of madness set against the backdrop of civil turbulence: '[in] *Close Sesame* madness is essentially a politically manufactured phenomenon and a measure of political despair' (Wright 1994: 91). Just as Medina indulges in a fatalistic display of bad faith by dismissing the General as unworthy, the larger body politic attempts to distance itself from the disquieting reminder of disorder made flesh by labelling it 'madness'. Likewise, just as the architectural lay of the land reflects the cellular structure and power wielded over it, the propagandistic and ideological links between colonial and neo-colonial authorities remain pronounced. The British 'infidels' needed to define the Mullah as mad to shore up the logic of occupation. As Colin Gordon emphasises, Foucault compels us to pay greater attention to the designation's discursive weight: '[*Madness and Civilization's*] working hypothesis could be taken … to be that 'madness' does not signify a real historical-anthropological entity at all but is rather the name for a fiction or a historical construct' (Gordon 1980: 235). In the context of colonial Africa, Megan Vaughan has focused scholarly attention on the 'African' in medical discourse in *Curing Their Ills*. Whilst I acknowledge key areas of divergence from Farah's fiction, I find the Foucauldian overlaps in both cases intriguing:

> … in British colonial Africa, medicine and its associated disciplines played an important part in constructing 'the African' as an object of knowledge, and elaborated classification systems and practices which have to be seen as intrinsic to the operation of colonial power. However, there are important differences between this colonial power/knowledge regime and the power/knowledge regime described by Foucault. (Vaughan 1991: 8)

By considering the figure of Khaliif more closely, and with due awareness of Deeriye's fascination with Hassan's legacy, the reader gains a clearer insight into how and why these power/knowledge contestations play such a significant role throughout *Close Sesame*. In the neo-colonial context of Farah's imagining, similar constructions of deviance are conceived, leading to them being either ignored or disciplined by a normalising power enacted by citizens on the ground. The spectres of subversive threat are dispelled by an audience to whom this speaking of the truth about power is designed to liberate from the 'shackles of uninformedness'.

As with *Xala's* vagrants or Foucault's lepers in his construction of a disciplinary utopia, Farah produces a compelling examination of Khaliif's transgressive reach. In a manner that recalls his interrogation of slippages between individual/collective, innocence/guilt, body/politics across the *Variations* sequence, Farah uses Khaliif to investigate the porous constructions of madness and sanity. For Deeriye, Khaliif's madness provides 'immunity' (*CS*: 60) from all-consuming fear: '[Khaliif] shunned human contact.

He showed intense dislike for any violence … [he] did not suggest a broken man on the fringes of society … he sold to everybody the very thing no one was prepared to buy, and bought from everybody the very thing no one was ready to sell' (*CS*: 16–17). In a Saidian sense, he speaks 'unsettling, antiutopian' thoughts to a crowd enclosed in the General's hegemonic cocoon. In an imagined context, where regulating the channels of communication and information ensures 'order', Khaliif murmurs discontentedly in the echo chamber of a society under surveillance. As such, he once more performs the oppositional function set out by Said in *Representations of the Intellectual*: 'intellectuals [are] precisely those figures whose public performance can neither be predicted nor compelled into some slogan, orthodox party line, or fixed dogma' (Said 1996: xii). Khaliif's performance is all the more unpalatable for the wider citizenry as he offers a damning indictment of their culpability and complicity. Whilst he spouts invective against the General as autocrat, he is aware, in a properly Foucauldian sense, that meaningful critique must target the mechanisms, systems and technologies of power:

> 'Now who is mad? Down with those that kill, who humiliate and torture! Down
> with those who make use of unjustified methods of rule.' And he burst into a
> guffaw of laughter which made everybody raise querying eyebrows. Scarcely
> had everyone relaxed than he startled them with 'Don't Arabs say, "Pinch
> wisdom, o people, out of the mouths of madmen."' Then a silence. (*CS*: 19)

This corresponds with Farah's own sense, informed by Arabic proverbs, that '[in] Islam madness occupies a mystical position … all people who receive wisdom from the mouths of the mad remain sane' (Wright 1994: 92). Once again, therefore, it is crucial that Farah not only draws his reader's attention to the unruly content of the message but also, and crucially, the willingness or otherwise of implicated parties to heed its warnings.

That Khaliif is a counter-hegemonic orator is critical both in the context of Somalia's national narrative and in terms of Farah being the son of a Somali poetess. Whilst Khaliif's outspokenness distinguishes him from the Group of 10's studious solipsism, it also places him in an ancient lineage that includes Hassan. For Abdi, the Sayyid's poetic prowess was proportionate to his skills as a master political tactician:

> A highly interesting facet of the Mullah, the importance of which cannot be
> overemphasized, is the poetic one … The ferocity of the language in this poem
> ['The Death of Richard Corfield'], which we can only translate in the roughest

and crudest approximation, is perhaps unparalleled in the annals of world literature. The only comparison that this present writer can think of are certain passages describing the desecration of Hector's corpse in Homer's *Iliad*. Even here Homer seems to betray a certain measure of compassion for the fallen Trojan hero. Not so the Mullah! (Abdi 1993: 65 & 77)

Deeriye returns to a recording of 'The Death of Richard Corfield' at various stages throughout the narrative. For Jacqueline Bardolph, Farah's decision to leave part of the poem in Somali is critical: 'all readers are reminded by the untranslated extract of the way [it] acts as a fundamental intertext for the whole of *Close Sesame* … each time giving meaning to present day events … the third book of the trilogy is thus entirely centred on this seminal national text, as if any relevant understanding had to be looked for essentially in Somali values' (Bardolph 2002: 409). Whilst, in the Abdi passage, Hassan is viewed in exceptionally visceral company, it is the notion of translation that resonates with *Close Sesame*, most particularly Farah's reflections on constructions, of both madness and space, confinement and the most effective modes of resistance. Seen in this light, the Homeric parallel is particularly instructive.

As with *The Iliad*, Hassan's poetry underwent a transformative process from oral to written long after its original composition. That there was no standard Somali orthography until 1972 makes matters even more intriguing. In the *Variations* cycle, the Group's written discourse is not engaged in such a translational project and the enemy is suitably more opaque. In *Close Sesame*, it takes a 'mad' prophet to deliver his critique outside the homes of those he views as culpable. For Wright, the times at which these outbursts occur are revealing: 'Khaliif … unleashes his vitriolic abuse at dawn and dusk, the transitional periods when the oral poet, in vituperative vein, casts his curse, the *cir-gaduud*, upon those who have wronged him, including his political enemies' (Wright 1994: 92–93). The transitional periods of dawn and dusk come to represent the ambiguous constructions of madness and sanity. This once again suggests how and why preoccupations with blurring are so prominent throughout Farah's work. Fittingly, it is Khaliif as public performer who voices a prophetic warning to a regime and society bent on processes of distortion rather than productive translation: 'he cursed those who kill, who never resign themselves to the will of the divine; he cursed those who never accept His word as the Sacred message but who force people to go to Orientation Centres instead of mosques and who asked to be worshipped in his place' (*CS*: 220). As such, he operates outside the codes that restrict the Group's discourse and actions. This once more chimes with

Ngũgĩ's *Penpoints, Gunpoints, and Dreams*. In it, he suggests that 'a mad person … can utter anything, ask any questions, and even link different situations. And just as sane people are disturbed by the presence of a crazed mind, the state with its certitude is irritated by the uncontrollable characters of dreams' (Ngũgĩ 1998: 19). At the narrative's close, one version of Deeriye's disappearance suggests he has united with Khaliif. In light of the above, the forging of a bond between a dreamer who continually questions his own sanity and a fellow 'deviant' is suggestive on a number of levels.

Staying true to the inconclusivity that pervades Farah's oeuvre, it is vital that what appears to be the certainty of the Group of 10's obituary is undermined. Crucially, Khaliif is left to report on their fate:

> 'May God bless the martyrs, may He grant them peace … And let me say this. They began as a community, a community of ten, and worked together as a community and suffered as a community of brotherhood. Can you think of anything better to say about a group of young people … they suffered on behalf of the suffering humanity' … He looked about him: no audience. But that did not worry him today. (CS: 220–221)

Whilst fallen intellectuals and visionary prophet operate in different spheres, they are joined through their enclosure within isolated cells sanctioned at the highest and sustained at the most quotidian levels of power. For Alden and Tremaine, Khaliif's intervention invites the reader to assess the effectiveness of the Group's incremental critique of repression, rather than any definitive insurrectionary act:

> Though the methods of those in the resistance often vary as the General's do, becoming increasingly subversive and violent, what strengthens and deepens in the course of the trilogy is these characters' inquiry into the interplay of multiple forms of power. It is by the strength of their analysis of political power, not the success of their attempt to overthrow that power, that the reader is invited to judge them. (Alden & Tremaine 1999: 86)

Accordingly, it is perhaps the complex issues of audience and agency that both haunt the Group and implicate the reader. The priviligentsia's flawed project might, therefore, be imagined in terms of their inability to communicate beyond the walls of their intellectual isolation. This is shown when, in the indeterminate period before learning of Mursal's death, Deeriye uncovers a group register: 'he had never imagined they were an organized group as such. (Neither did all the members know of one another. Each person knew the one other person who was in the same cell)' (CS: 203). In light of the argument pursued above, the reference to their 'cellular' nature is particularly revealing. Similarly, Mursal's epigraph speaks of the Group's factional structure, their battles with the social constructions of an authoritarian regime and, ironically, the subversive cover that the designation of 'madness' could have afforded them (CS: 127). Yet, whilst the means through which they debate and disseminate their resistant aspirations may be compromised, it is once again the 'essential obstinacy' of their guiding principles that endures. As Foucault maintains, 'if it is true that at the heart of power relations and as a permanent condition of their existence there is an insubordination and a certain essential obstinacy on the part of the principles of freedom, then there is no relationship of power without the means of escape or possible flight' (Dreyfus & Rabinow 1983: 225). That this statement problematises the archetypal image of Foucault as the 'scribe of domination' is significant, particularly when taking account of those 'power relations' at the heart of *Variations*. It also supports the argument that Farah's fiction pointedly refuses to offer any simple exit strategies, either for reader or protagonist. Rather, the suitably Foucauldian challenge is to determine how complex relationships of power might best be negotiated.

Whilst Farah's reliance on the Group of 10 has divided critics, I suggest it is charged with the productive tension between individual and collective responsibility that defines his oeuvre as well as its ethical underpinnings. Like Said, Farah does not pretend to have all the solutions. In conversation with Jacqueline Rose, Said maintains 'it's not that I have the answers which they claim that they have; it's that they are hiding the facts, which is a very different thing, and making promises that they can't keep, effacing bits of history that are embarrassing and complicated. I think it's important to say just that. In the interest of something larger than yourself to which you feel connected' (Rose 2000: 12). This complicated interest in 'something larger than yourself' becomes, for Farah and his protagonists, power as a system in which both autocrats and audience are embroiled, revealing the key battlegrounds, tensions and complications that might determine hopes for the future. As such, Farah operates in the spirit of what Foucault, in 'Truth and Power', calls the 'specific intellectual', probing issues of power and resistance at the microphysical level:

> Intellectuals have got used to working, not in the modality of the 'universal',
> the 'exemplary', the 'just-and-true-for-all', but within specific sectors, at the
> precise points where their own conditions of life or work situate them (housing,

the hospital, the asylum, the university, family and sexual relations). This has undoubtedly given them much more immediate and concrete awareness of struggles … This is what I would call the 'specific' intellectual as opposed to the 'universal' intellectual. (Foucault 1980c: 126)

The 'group' designation is inherently problematic, with the kind of scepticism Appiah demands the writer focus on 'tribe' and 'nation' in *In My Father's House* being turned on the insurgent faction itself: '[o]ur positions as intellectuals … make it impossible for us to live through the falsehoods of race and tribe and nation; [our] understanding of history makes us sceptical that nationalism and racial solidarity can do the good that they can do without the attendant evils of racism – and other particularisms; without the warring of nations' (Appiah 1992: 284). As the intensity of their internal schisms suggests, Farah's Group might be conceived as a quasi-tribe. As in the Medina/General relationship explored in *Sardines*, however, degrees of separation remain critical.

This relates to a key point made by Alden and Tremaine and taken up by Farah: 'it is individuals as individuals who oppose dictatorship and [Farah] recalls his strenuous disagreement with the practice of human rights' groups that give the clan name of victims of torture … "When someone is detained, tortured, dealt with rather savagely by dictatorial regimes, you do not belittle that person by giving the name of the clan from which they come"' (Alden & Tremaine 1999: 91). Whereas the anonymous clan elders are seen in a bleak continuum with those of the colonial era, Farah's trilogy suggests some progress and development within the Group. The hubris of collective association is stripped away, obliging a return to an individual and familial identity as the basis upon which effective, if still provisional, resistance might be built. Whilst Hashim contends that 'the [Somali] individual does not stand alone as he may appear to do in Western society', Farah is concerned with the problematic politics of autonomy and identification as an alternative to those of unthinking allegiance to groups (Hashim 1997: 31).

In a despotic state, the 'madman's' intense isolation retains a certain heroic quality for those charged with the similarly lonely business of writing as resistance to power. This is touched on by Said in *Representations of the Intellectual*: 'I had certainly become used to being peripheral, outside the circle of power, and perhaps because I had no talent for a position inside that charmed circle, I rationalized the virtues of outsiderhood' (Said 1996: 107). Once again, the parallels between Farah and Said are striking. In the *Variations* cycle, it is imperative that, in order to rage against the dying of the light on the General's badly lit stage, another set of theatrical directions be produced that take account of the cast of dramatic agents. The Thomas allusion is inspired by the epigraph to *Close Sesame's* final section. As in *Sweet and Sour Milk*, dramaturgical and luminary images are central to Farah's analytics of power. Similarly, when it comes to considering the axiomatic function of Khaliif, the Foucault of *Madness and Civilization* once again proves enabling: '[i]n farces and *soties*, the character of the Madman, the Fool, or the Simpleton assumes more and more importance. He is no longer simply a ridiculous and familiar silhouette in the wings: he stands centre stage as the guardian of truth' (Foucault 2001: 11). If this can be seen in relation to those theatrical allusions that pepper Farah's work, it is also revealing that Foucault draws on the kind of luminary motifs that recur throughout the Somali writer's work. They allow him to explore the idea of madness as 'reason dazzled':

> … with error, madness shares non-truth, and arbitrariness in affirmation or negation; from the dream, madness borrows flows of images and the colourful presence of hallucinations. But while error is merely non-truth, while the dream neither affirms nor judges, madness fills the void of error with images, and links hallucinations by affirmation of the false. In a sense, it is thus plenitude, joining to the figures of night the powers of day, to the forms of fantasy the activity of the waking mind; it links the dark content with the forms of light. But is not such plenitude actually the culmination of the void? (Foucault 2001: 100)

This in turn corresponds with Wright's description of *Close Sesame* as 'transitional', 'featuring phenomena that are simultaneously present and absent, dark in one order and light in another' (Wright 1994: 89). Towards the novel's close, Farah repeats his familiar conception of a dystopian drama with a culpable audience through Deeriye (*CS*: 214). Like the disruptive writer, Khaliif refuses to clap, opting instead to shuffle off stage with only the disquieting legacy of his performance left in his wake. From here, the onus falls on fellow audience members to find ways of resisting the abuses of power.

Fleshing Out the Truth about Power

> Among all the reasons for the prestige that was accorded in the second half of the eighteenth century, to circular architecture, one must no doubt include the fact that it expressed a certain political utopia.
>
> *(Michel Foucault – Discipline and Punish, 1991: 174)*

> When my period of internal segregation is over, I join in the same erratic, aimless
> circles and wanderings going everywhere and nowhere. The compound is too
> tiny to give anybody the feel of a purposeful walk or even the illusion of one. I
> am now one of the inmates of this once famed lunatic asylum.
>
> It is not a joke, really. The compound used to be for the mentally deranged
> convicts before it was put to better use as a cage for 'the politically deranged'. In
> a sense, we are truly mad. Imagine anyone questioning the morality of man-eat-
> man in a state of man-eaters? … Madness after all is relative. It depends on who
> is calling the other mad. In a state of madmen, anybody who is not mad is mad.
>
> *(Ngũgĩ wa Thiong'o – Detained, 1981: 120)*

Whilst I have speculated on potential parallels between Deeriye and Ngũgĩ,
the above passage details the ominous realities of penitentiary life as transposed by Farah into fiction. To flesh out his pronouncements concerning the
prison/postcolonial state, Ngũgĩ draws from haunting personal experience.
In doing so, he foregrounds a series of issues (construction, confinement, labyrinthine movement, spectres of individual and collective madness, the right
to interrogate doctrines of social cannibalism, to name but a few) central to
the *Variations* trilogy as a whole. In terms of *Close Sesame* more specifically,
the violence Deeriye unleashes to 'vindicate not my son but justice' (*CS*: 218)
does not adequately represent his ideological opposition to the regime. The
most subtle yet seismic changes take place within the home and are symbolised in intimate, embodied terms. Prior to the confirmation of Mursal's
death, Deeriye surveys the scene. Waiting with the women and children, he
sounds the Group's ominous obituary:

> Deeriye was thinking: was this a perverted image his own mind and eye had
> screened upon a reality so familiar by now: women with no men; and behind
> them … the elderly and children? With Soyaan dead and Loyaan exiled …
> with Mahad mysteriously held in one of those underground prisons, perhaps
> the same prison where Ibrahim Siciliano was being kept; with Mukhtaar killed;
> Mursal vanished and Jibril … (*CS*: 200)

When Mursal's death is confirmed, Deeriye consoles his foreign daughter-in-
law, who has been kept on the linguistic and political sidelines for much of
the narrative. In the very act of bending his knee before her, Farah metonymically captures the qualities that make Deeriye such an exceptional character.
Whilst the young men of the resistance have been either marginalised or
murdered, leaving domestic responsibilities in their wake, Deeriye attends to

matters on this other stage. Shifting props and protagonists in this alternative arena carries the resistant potential to precipitate much wider, more palpable change. This is because, as argued in my analysis of *Sweet and Sour Milk* and its portrayal of Keynaan in particular, one of the most crucial ways in which the General's regime shores itself up is by relying upon the perpetuation of abusive power within the home. The portrait of the pious, elderly Muslim gentleman prostrating himself before a white, Jewish, American woman carries a peculiar burden of significance. Farah's fundamental point, however, is that individuals must interrogate and, where necessary, adapt their own worldly designs before they can dismantle those of governance and/or collective identity.

With this micro/macro relationship in mind, Bardolph's critique is highly instructive. She considers how Deeriye is used to interrogate historical continuities and how this corresponds to the familiar ways in which Farah charges his reader as agent:

> *Close Sesame* is not … a 'historical novel' in the way there are 'ethnological novels' in Africa. History is questioned for the answers it may give for the present. Underlining all the book, as with the other works of the trilogy, is the certainty that there is a meaning in human lives which has to be deciphered … The novel underlines the idea that there is a latent pattern to history by pointing repeatedly at coincidences, parallels, echoes, facts that through decades seem to refer to one another … Farah also wants the reader to start looking for the pattern in the fiction which is both image and representation of the real historical world: there is meaning for those who try hard to make sense of fragmented experience, especially by interpreting cycles and situations which are repeated across the years. (Bardolph 2002: 412–413)

Bardolph's notion that Farah probes history 'for the answers it may give the present' is hauntingly similar to Colin Gordon's tribute to Foucault: '[i]f [he] poses a philosophical challenge to history, it is not to question the reality of "the past" but to interrogate the rationality of the "present"' (Gordon 1980: 242). As I explore throughout the remainder of this study, similarly interrogative impulses underpin Farah's work. Whilst creating fiction from the fabric of a national narrative that is now past, he does so with a view to placing the present on trial. This, in turn, is done so that more searching questions might be posed of the future. As above, therefore, there are patterns to be deciphered beneath the determined indeterminacy of *Variations*. In *Close Sesame*, it is Deeriye who, alert to the hegemonic ties between colonial and neo-colonial authorities alike, demonstrates the benefits of such an approach. Towards the end of the novel, he asks Zeinab, 'did I ever tell you why I conjure up interlocutors, why I have visions, why it is I invent histories, why I try to create symbolic links between unrelated historical events … did I ever bother to explain myself to you?' (*CS*: 229). Bardolph's notion of the patterning of both historical and fictional narratives is critical here. Deeriye's actions complicate matters, defying the authoritarian and flat worldview of Keynaan and, as Alden and Tremaine point out, 'becoming a model for how individuals can select from the materials of their social world those elements that they require for autonomous acts of self-definition' (Alden & Tremaine 1999: 89). Like the globe given to Ladan by the twins in *Sweet and Sour Milk*, Deeriye's action symbolises an alternative outlook. His act of prostration takes place before his grandson, Samawade. The suggestion is that it sets the stage for forthcoming struggles.

As such, Deeriye can be seen in terms of what Foucault calls the 'cerebro-spinal individual' in 'The Moral and Social Experience of the Poles Can No Longer Be Obliterated': 'I don't really know what they mean by "intellectuals," all the people who describe, denounce, or scold them. I do know, on the other hand, what I have committed myself to, as an intellectual, which is to say, after all, a cerebro-spinal individual: to having a brain as supple as possible and a spinal column that's as straight as necessary' (Foucault 2000: 473). When saluting his progressive vision, Elmi-Tiir recalls how his brother-in-law washed Nadiifa's feet (*CS*: 210). The comparative links that Deeriye refers to in conversation with Zeinab are made flesh in the transition between his sensual, sensitive handling of Nadiifa's body and the subversive symbolism of kneeling before Natasha. Once again, therefore, Deeriye can be read in terms of Said's *Representations of the Intellectual*:

> [The intellectual] is an individual endowed with a faculty for representing, embodying, articulating a message, a view, an attitude, philosophy or opinion to, as well as for, a public. And this role has an edge to it, and cannot be played without a sense of being someone whose place it is publicly to raise embarrassing questions, to confront orthodoxy and dogma (rather than to produce them), to be someone who cannot easily be co-opted … The intellectual does so on the basis of universal principles: that all human beings are entitled to expect decent standards of behavior concerning freedom and justice from worldly powers or nations, and that deliberate or inadvertent violations of these standards need to be testified and fought against courageously. (Said 1996: 11–12)

Rather than define Deeriye in Foucauldian terms of universal or specific, the reader is asked to position him between the two: a figure bringing universal principles to bear on the concrete struggles played out within the home. Farah obliges us to recall the double-edged critique levelled against Deeriye by the clan elders. The anonymous spokesman declares how '[Deeriye] has stayed by and walked the same determined road these past forty-odd years. Never has he wavered; never have his actions demonstrated a moment's indecision or hesitation' (*CS*: 172). This, however, is one further caricature. The reader experiences Deeriye's doubts, like Loyaan's and Medina's, as versions of their own. As with Khaliif and members of the Group, the road Deeriye walks is an uncertain and, at times, lonely one. It does, however, exist on a map plotted according to those coherent ideological coordinates that might allow for escape from the labyrinth. The *Variations* trilogy is buttressed by death and attempts to reclaim fallen bodies and identities. Yet it is this concentration on alternative micro- and macrodesigns for the world, ultimately conceived at an embodied level, that might represent the foundations for palpable change. These issues inform my analysis of *Maps*, a text described by Wright as 'the first African novel of the body' (Wright 1994: 118). In considering this claim more fully, I argue that the first instalment of the *Blood in the Sun* trilogy sees Farah move away from the carceral concerns of the *Variations* cycle to explore a series of issues that can be viewed through a bio-political lens. In the chapter that follows, I suggest how and why *Maps* benefits from a reading that traces similar shifts in Foucault's work.

References

Abdi, AS. 1993. *Divine Madness – Mohammed 'Abdulle Hassan (1856–1920)*. London: Zed Books.

Ahmed, A.J. 1995. '"Daybreak is Near, Won't You Become Sour?" Going Beyond the Current Rhetoric in Somali Studies'. In A.J. Ahmed (Ed.). *The Invention of Somalia*. New Jersey: The Red Sea Press Inc.

Alden, P. & Tremaine, L. 1999. *Nuruddin Farah*. New York: Twayne Publishers.

Appiah, K.A. 1992. *In My Father's House – Africa in the Philosophy of Culture*. London: Methuen.

Appiah, K.A. 1998. 'For Nuruddin Farah'. *World Literature Today*, Vol. 72, September.

Bardolph, J. 2002. 'Time and History in Nuruddin Farah's *Close Sesame*'. In D. Wright (Ed.). *Emerging Perspectives on Nuruddin Farah*. New Jersey: Africa World Press.

Chowers, E. 2004. *The Modern Self in the Labyrinth – Politics and the Entrapment Imagination*. Cambridge, Mass.: Harvard University Press.

Dreyfus, H. & Rabinow, P. 1983. *Michel Foucault: Beyond Structuralism and Hermeneutics*. (2nd ed.). Chicago: The University of Chicago Press.

Ewen, D.R. 1984. 'Nuruddin Farah'. In G.D. Killam (Ed.). *The Writing of East and Central Africa*. London: Heinemann.

Foucault, M. 1980a. 'The Eye of Power'. In C. Gordon (Ed.). *Power/Knowledge – Selected Interviews and Other Writings*. Harlow: Pearson Education Ltd.

Foucault, M. 1980b. 'The Confession of the Flesh'. In C. Gordon (Ed.). *Power/Knowledge – Selected Interviews and Other Writings*. Harlow: Pearson Education Ltd.

Foucault, M. 1980c. 'Truth and Power'. In C. Gordon (Ed.). *Power/Knowledge – Selected Interviews and Other Writings*. Harlow: Pearson Education Ltd.

Foucault, M. 1991. *Discipline and Punish – The Birth of the Prison*. (A. Sheridan, Trans.). London: Penguin.

Foucault, M. 2000. 'Useless to Revolt?' In J.B. Faubion (Ed.). (R. Hurley *et al.*, Trans.). *Power – Essential Works of Michel Foucault 1954–1984, Volume III*. New York: The New Press.

Foucault, M. 2001. *Madness and Civilization – A History of Insanity in the Age of Reason*, (R. Howard, Trans.). London: Routledge.

Ghalib, J.M. 1995. *The Cost of Dictatorship – The Somali Experience*. New York: Lilian Barber Press.

Gordon, C. (Ed.). 1980. *Michel Foucault, Power/Knowledge – Selected Interviews and Other Writings, 1972–1977*. (C. Gordon, L. Marshall, J. Mepham, K. Soper, Trans.). Harlow: Pearson Education Limited.

Gorlier, C. 2002. 'Mystery and Madness in *Close Sesame*'. In D. Wright (Ed.). *Emerging Perspectives on Nuruddin Farah*. New Jersey: Africa World Press.

Greco, M. 1998. *Illness as a Work of Thought – A Foucauldian Perspective on Psychosomatics*. London: Routledge.

Hashim, AB. 1997. *The Fallen State – Dissonance, Dictatorship and Death in Somalia*. Maryland: University Press of America.

Mnthali, F. 2002. 'Autocracy and the Limits of Identity: A Reading of the Novels of Nuruddin Farah'. In D. Wright (Ed.). *Emerging Perspectives on Nuruddin Farah*. New Jersey: Africa World Press.

Ngũgĩ wa Thiong'o. 1981. *Detained: A Writer's Prison Diary*. London: Heinemann.

Ngũgĩ wa Thiong'o. 1998. *Penpoints, Gunpoints and Dreams: The Performance of Literature and Power in Post-Colonial Africa*. Oxford: Oxford University Press.

Rose, J. 2000. 'Edward Said talks to Jacqueline Rose'. In P. Bové (Ed.). *Edward Said and the Work of the Critic: Speaking Truth to Power*. Durham and London: Duke University Press.

Said, E.W. 1996. *Representations of the Intellectual – The 1993 Reith Lectures*. New York: Vintage Books.

Soyinka, W. 1972. *The Man Died: Prison Notes of Wole Soyinka*. London: Rex Collings Ltd.

Vaughan, M. 1991. *Curing Their Ills – Colonial Power and African Illness*. Cambridge: Polity Press.

Wright, D. 1994. *The Novels of Nuruddin Farah*. Bayreuth: Bayreuth African Studies Series.

5

From the Carceral to the Bio-political: The Dialectical Turn Inwards in *Maps*

The dispute that leads to the war involves a process by which each side calls into question the legitimacy and thereby erodes the reality of the other country's issues, beliefs, ideas, self-conception. Dispute leads relentlessly to war not only because war is an extension and intensification of dispute but because it is a correction and reversal of it. That is, the injuring not only provides a means of choosing between disputants but also provides, by its massive opening of human bodies, a way of reconnecting the derealized and disembodied beliefs with the force and power of the material world.

(Elaine Scarry – The Body in Pain, 1985: 128)

Individual experience, because it is national and because it is a link in the chain of national existence, ceases to be individual, limited and shrunken and is enabled to open out into the truth of the nation and of the world.

(Frantz Fanon – The Wretched of the Earth, 2001: 161)

THE PROPHETIC FORCE OF FANON'S WRITING HAS ATTRACTED VARIOUS commentators concerned with the peculiarities of postcolonial state formation. In the case of Somalia during the latter stages of Barre's regime, the warnings he issued about the dangers of political nepotism would prove particularly apt. In 1986, the year *Maps* was published, Barre was returned to power with a purported 99.9% of the vote (Lewis 2002: 255). Fanon imagines precisely such a scenario in 'The Pitfalls of National Consciousness' (Fanon 2001: 146). Throughout what follows, I argue that his legacy casts a significant shadow over *Maps*. In Hilaal, Farah has created a pseudo-Fanonian character who researches 'the psychological disturbances the [Ogaden] war had caused in the lives of children and women' (*M*: 157). This recalls *The Wretched of the Earth*'s provocative final chapter, 'Colonial War and Mental Disorders' (Fanon 2001: 200–250). Hilaal's most significant case study is his young nephew, Askar, whose fractured narrative reflects the psychic and physiognomic pressures brought about by conflict. Askar's turbulent struggle to come to terms with the politics of identity and affiliation takes place against the backdrop of Somalia's anti-secessionist war with Ethiopia. As such, Farah is preoccupied with the uneven development of national consciousness as well as the complexities and complicities of subject formation in the process of what might be termed resistance. Alongside this, Fanon's notion of inextricable connections between individual, national and ultimately transnational experience is particularly enabling for the purposes of this chapter. With more than a hint of self-reflexive irony, Farah has Askar declare, 'no one has ever explained how to read maps, you see, and I have difficulty deciphering all the messages' (*M*: 116). When it comes to *Maps* the novel, this metatextual comment corresponds with the sheer number and range of analyses it has attracted. In the context of this study, I argue that its complex, increasingly visceral preoccupation with the body can be explored by expanding upon the Foucauldian framework I have employed throughout.

In *Curing Their Ills*, Meagan Vaughan casts a revisionist eye over Foucault's meditations on biopower, amending and extending them for her own biomedical purposes. In so doing, she invokes a *Black Skins, White Masks*-era Fanon for his exemplary insights into the psychological effects of racism and colonialism (Vaughan 1991: 204). Similarly, in *Race and The Education of Desire*, *Carnal Knowledge and Imperial Power* and *Tensions of Empire*, Stoler turns to Foucault's later work in *The History of Sexuality* and 'Society Must be Defended'. Following their lead, I find biopower a productive prism through which to trace certain paradigm shifts in Farah's oeuvre. This concerns a movement away from the carceral concerns of *Variations* to bio-political preoccupations in *Blood in the Sun*. In what follows, I suggest how and why this might be read in relation to significant events affecting Somalia's national narrative. This, in turn, demands a more panoramic view of Foucault's work in order to identify key discursive ruptures. With the renegotiation of the temporal and spatial coordinates of power comes a move away from an early preoccupation with the institutions, mechanisms and sovereignty of disciplinary control to the normalising procedures and politics of biopower. This leads Foucault to renew his fascination with a hermeneutics of the subject as well as to explore geographical questions more fully. Whilst not allowing him to engage with the dominant discourses of imperial knowledge and power with anything like the urgency demanded by figures such as Stoler, it marks an important departure in Foucault's work. As Clare O'Farrell suggests, this might be characterised by a critical shift away from individual sites of disciplinary power (prison, hospital, asylum) to larger questions of region, space and the wider body politic (O'Farrell 2005: 102–103). Accompanying this reorientation is the greater emphasis Foucault places on the ordering and management of the population itself, encompassing everything from the collection of birth and death statistics to the provision of adequate healthcare. Arguably, the key question upon which Foucault's exploration of biopower rests is that of 'making live and letting die', as discussed in *'Society Must be Defended'* (Foucault 2003: 247). In what follows, I consider how *Maps* is concerned with the life-and-death significance of these issues when set against the backdrop of conflict.

For Gilles Deleuze, Foucault 'should be seen not as a historian, but as a new kind of map-maker – maps made for use, not to mirror the terrain' (Dreyfus & Rabinow 1983: 128). Whilst scholars have stretched his speculations onto broader geo-political canvases, Foucault's influence has even found its way into critical analyses of *Maps*. In his contribution to *Emerging Perspectives*, for instance, Simon Gikandi alludes to the predominant concerns of contemporary African writers with networks of knowledge and power. He uses strikingly Foucauldian rhetoric, reconfiguring an analogy from *Madness and Civilization* to frame his Ngũgĩ-esque argument: 'to paraphrase Foucault's famous discussion of the relationship between madness and leprosy, colonialism had disappeared but its structures remained; thus the substitution of the theme of colonialism for that of neo-colonialism "does not mark a break, but rather a torsion with the same anxiety"' (Gikandi 2002: 452). For my purposes, the notion of 'torsion' is particularly suggestive when it comes to offering a reading of *Maps* that builds from some of the labyrinthine figurations discussed in relation to *Variations*. For Rossana Ruggiero, for instance, '*Maps* provides us with a further tile in a mosaic that is often explicit in Farah's fiction in the shape of a maze the exit of which is never possible to find, there being only innumerable and different entrances that merge into one another, thus creating a complex and intricate narrative whirl' (Ruggiero 2002: 560–561). Whilst enabling to a point, I argue that the imagined geography of power in *Blood in the Sun's* initial instalment is much changed. The reader moves from an autocratic world whose punitive control is unleashed upon quasi-regicide Deeriye to one where the despotic body is conspicuous by its absence. Thus, the Fanonian idea of a dialectical turn inwards remains critical. It is clarified by Francesca Kazan, who discusses how 'the intellectual concentrates on the "inside" space of the nation in order to move beyond, "outside" to the globe' (Kazan 2002: 471). For my purposes, 'Farah' is interchangeable with 'intellectual'. By this, I mean that the socio-political context of his most explicitly embodied work concerns a pivotal moment in the national narrative. As discussed by Louis Fitzgibbon in *The Betrayal of the Somalis*, defeat in the Ogaden War constituted the decisive blow to the irredentist dreams of pan-Somali nationalism, which, in turn, hastened the demise of Barre's regime (Fitzgibbon 1982: 52–61). For many, the seeds of impending civil war were sown in this political vacuum. In the absence of an external, identifiable adversary, the anachronisms of clan power, historically manipulated by various leaders, were turned divisively inwards to the tragic cost of the body politic. As the chapters that follow suggest, preoccupations with this kind of atrophy dominate the imagined landscape of *Secrets*, *Links* and *Knots*. It is, however, *Maps'* focus on the renegotiation of affinities, both cartographic and corporeal, that sets the stage for these novels.

With its at times graphic, taboo-shattering depictions of quasi-incestuous union, mutilation, rape, circumcision and menstruation, *Maps* certainly marks an amplification of the contested corporeality of *Variations*. The text explores the ways in which territorial disputes affect the personal and always already political relationships between protagonists. More specifically, in Scarry's sense, it examines how these fallouts are both inscribed on and negotiated by these bodies, with notional as well as national realities being consistently called into question. Parallels between the *Variations* series and *Maps*, therefore, might be made in relation to Farah's nuanced critique of power. Medina and Deeriye, for example, engage in strategic acts of resistance that allow them to arrive at a more complex sense of self whilst, perhaps, also laying the groundwork for future struggles. For the adolescent Askar of *Maps*, the road to self-awareness is decidedly rockier. If the representative symbol of *Variations* exists somewhere between maze and crossroad, it is the Borgesian image of 'the infinite garden of forking paths', referred to by Charles Sugnet, that is most fitting when it comes to *Maps* (Sugnet 2002: 525).

Whilst events in the bio-political sphere spiral out of control and seem to establish the rules of ethnic conflict, Askar is ultimately burdened with seeking out and pursuing his own choices. In keeping with the narrative's concentric structure, his inertia is represented by his perpetual inability to commit himself, on paper at least, to either the resistant forces of the Western Somali Liberation Front, charged with reclaiming the fallen Ogaden, or to what he hopes will be an enriching career at the National University of Somalia. Askar's typically overdetermined self-narration doubles back on itself, posing rhetorical questions that have few, if any, definitive answers: 'whether or not one should join the Liberation Front or choose a career in the world of academia? ... So would he take the gun? Or would he resort to, and invest his powers in, the pen?' (*M*: 55). Some time later: '[a]nd here I stand at the crossroads. Shall I leave Salaado and Uncle Hilaal for a freedom fighters' camp in the Ogaden? Shall I register as a student at the university?' (*M*: 181.) The third and final such reference comes towards the novel's close: '[h]e was back to the unplanned future ... back also to the unfilled, unsubmitted forms from the Western Somali Liberation Front and that of the National University of Somalia' (*M*: 255). As all three instances demonstrate, Askar is stranded between taking anti-colonial action and wallowing in ennui.

Whilst such uncertainty, which often borders on paralysis, is characteristic of many of Farah's protagonists, it is peculiarly intense in *Maps*. As such, it represents the author's refusal to portray a monolithic domination that holds its subjects in hegemonic thrall. As maps are revealed to be formulations embedded in particular networks of knowledge and power, both colonial and postcolonial, the identities individual characters attempt to pin their allegiances to over the course of *Maps* are susceptible to challenge and therefore change. As Jones and Porter once again point out, a similarly interrogative intensity sets Foucault's work apart: 'historians have particularly appreciated Foucault for his rejection of the common supposition that the objects of history are somehow "given" or "natural". Foucault's aim was to defamiliarize, to expose seemingly natural categories as constructs, articulated by words and discourse, and thus to underline the radical contingency of what superficially seems normal' (Jones & Porter 1994: 5). Whilst using fiction to defamiliarise, Farah is equally concerned with exposing the radical contingency of discursive constructs, from cartography to ethnic difference. As such, the exploration of intimate relations between constructions of 'truth' (corporeal, bio-political and mapped) binds the narrative together.

It is quite fitting that Farah's most specifically Somali novel should have received such international acclaim. In previous and later work, the diasporic element remains constant. Fictional figures are drawn from an upwardly mobile cadre, either flying back to Somalia after a period of higher learning in the former colonial centre (Koschin in *A Naked Needle*) or flying out to retake their place amongst the vast diaspora (Jeebleh in *Links*). In *Maps*, both protagonists and geo-political preoccupations are rooted, however precariously, on the very 'Somali' soil being contested by war. These spatial and temporal choices are indicative of what I consider to be the narrative's commitment to a dialectical turn inwards. At an immediate textual level, this can be seen by exploring *Maps'* treatment of pronouns. From Ebla in *From a Crooked Rib* through to Cambara in *Knots*, Farah's fictional terrain is populated by protagonists whose most pressing concerns are staged at the pronominal level. Theirs is a struggle to determine how the subjective 'I' defines or, more notably, fails to define itself in terms laid out by one or other dominant power. These pronominal tussles plumb new levels of depth and density in *Maps*. They are turned in on Askar's narrative, immediately framing the reader's engagement with the novel. In the Barthesian sense, it is the most 'writerly' of Farah's fictions, peppered as it is with a series of metafictional asides (Barthes 1990). In a manner reminiscent of Rushdie's *Midnight's Children*, both author and protagonist reflect on the reconstituted nature of the narrative: 'I cannot vouch for the accuracy of my memory here. Possibly I've invented one or two things, perhaps I have intentionally deviated from the true course of events. Although I tend to think that I am remembering in precise detail how things happened and what was said' (*M*: 84). The reader is thus obliged to consider and, where necessary, critique the fictionalising processes of those ideologies being reproduced at individual and collective levels.

Critical reception of *Maps* is distinguished by something akin to a geometric fascination with it. Rosemary Colmer, for instance, focuses on the three stages of separation (temporal, geographical and ideological) that constitute key ruptures in Askar's relationship with surrogate mother Misra (Colmer 2002: 499–500). Adopting his comparative literary pose, Sugnet conflates Farah's protagonist with his modernist and postcolonial counterparts to arrive at the 'Askar-Oskar-Saleem' formulation (Sugnet 2002: 528 & 538). At the most immediate level, Farah's deconstructive preoccupation with triads and tripartite structures is announced through the dominant jostling of pronouns signalled with a seemingly defiant 'you'. Told in what Wright calls 'the first, third and speculative second person', it is a purposively ambiguous mode of introduction (Wright 1994: 106). Numerous critics have attended to the ways it both gestures towards Askar's ongoing genealogical tussles, whilst also representing a narrowing of the distance separating reader and narrator. Yet, whilst Wright and Kazan remain variously illuminating, their speculations can be bolstered by the kind of Foucauldian supplement I offer in the rest of this chapter. This enables a consideration of the ways Farah's novel interrogates notions of liminal and deconstructive third spaces as well as body politics, both micrological and macrological.

The Bloody Pivot of the Ogaden War

The opening rupture in Askar and Misra's relationship comes before the former's journey from war-torn Kallafo to the quasi-bourgeois sanctuary of life with Hilaal and Salaado in Mogadiscio. Moving away from his intimately infant association with Misra as life-giving earth, Askar struggles to come to terms with the hegemonic and bio-political binary dictating where affiliations must lie during times of conflict. By conflating child's play and war games, Farah discloses the essentially triumphalist logic behind both: 'Askar became the child he was – he abandoned thinking philosophically, he gave up the thought whether or no Misra too needed a mother in the same way he did and ran and joined the boys and girls of his age. For them, it was fun to be on the winning side, it was fun to disarm the disheartened already defeated Ethiopian soldiery – for them, war was fun' (*M*: 103). In the aftermath of temporary military success, Askar reads the signs of war's fallout, both personal and political, on the faces of those Ethiopian refugees fleeing the embattled region. The young boy turns to his adoptive, Ethiopian-born mother for instruction at the precise moment he feels claims to an embodied politics of identification, and thus differentiation, beginning to be made. It is at this critical juncture that Askar starts to wrestle with the painful implications of rigid bio-political taxonomies established in opposition to what Wright calls 'the irretrievable hybridisation of cultural reality' (Wright 1994: 114). These clashes haunt him throughout, defining the indeterminate space between dream and reality that is so central to *Maps*. Such ambiguities also inform the agonistic terms in which Askar's relationship with Misra will now be conducted.

As eight-year old Askar muses on this exodus, Misra reprises her maternal role. With the securities of her personal and political worlds beginning to crumble, she directs her immediate focus not towards the biopolitics of blood and lineage, but on the boy's unclean body. It is Askar's subsequent refusal to be washed that strikes both Misra and reader as a defining moment in a relationship now embroiled in broader geo-political struggles. A key schism, it anticipates their forthcoming separation. The dirt gained from mock-guerrilla training with an equally young band of potential child soldiers is now valorised as a quasi-nationalist badge of pride. To have it removed at the hands of an avowed enemy, an 'Ethiopian', would be a patriotic dishonour. Misra consoles herself that 'the world is reduced to chaos; there's a war on; boys, because of this chaotic situation, have suddenly become men and refuse to be mothered' (*M*: 113). Preoccupations with chaos as well as precarious constructions of masculinity endure in both physical and metaphysical terms throughout *Maps*. On more than one occasion, Askar's formative dalliance with what Wright calls 'introverted ethnocentrism' fails to prepare him for the chaos that Misra and, by extension, the disputed Ogaden region comes to represent (Wright 1994: 125). At this stage in the reconstituted narratives of Askar and nation, the rules of engagement for both child's play and war are clear cut. Chilling confirmation of an alteration in the relative order of things is given when Askar associates the sovereignty of his dirty body with the right both to defend himself against and, if necessary, to kill his enemy. The incident allows Farah to focus the reader's attention on the intricate and highly significant triad of body, text and nation that will dominate his work from this point on.

Concealment and evasion characterise Askar's narrative, with the reader becoming complicit in the selective versions he tells Misra. Accordingly, we learn of the young gang's violent voyeurism as they watch men preparing to join the war effort: 'through the hole in the wall, the boys imbibed an ideology embodied in the dream they saw as their own, the dream they envisioned as their common future: warriors of a people fighting to liberate their country from colonial oppression' (*M*: 114). The Fanonian rhetoric is significant. Yet it is the notion that these sovereign national dreams have an embodied quality that is most critical in terms of those biopower concerns that characterise Farah's later novels. As with the rules for play and war, the Ogaden dispute concerns a series of conceptual binaries ultimately designed to distinguish victors from vanquished. In terms of the embattled logic outlined in Scarry's epigraph, the conflict results from one side calling into question the other's essential (and, for this, Farah invites us to read 'projected') 'truth'. Scarry's intervention is key, focusing as it does on the relationship between conceptual interrogations and their corporeal fallout. Farah's primary concern throughout the novel is how these notional and national projections of truth are themselves susceptible to the kind of interrogation and dispute considered throughout *The Body in Pain*. In the Ogaden context of *Maps*, as Lewis suggests, a sense of historical longevity and legitimacy is factored in by conceiving the territory as an amputated limb. It enters the social imaginary as something cut away from the wider Somali body politic with the divisive assistance of colonial cartographers. With revolutionary consciousness being forged in the furnaces of liberation struggle, so the socio-political duty presented to and subsequently accepted by these young men is that of re-constructive surgery. It is here, with the textual focus on such embattled and embodied claims, that a Foucauldian supplement proves enabling.

Misra, Biopower and Ethnocentrism

In *The History of Sexuality*, Foucault focuses on the shifting logic of war, trac-ing a movement away from the defence of individual sovereign power to the regulation and maintenance of normalising, 'massifying' biopower:

> The principle underlying tactics of battle – that one has to be capable of killing in order to go on living – has become the principle that defines the strategy of states. But the existence in question is no longer the juridical existence of sovereignty; at stake is the biological existence of a population. If genocide is indeed the dream of modern powers, this is not because of the recent return of the ancient right to kill; it is because power is situated and exercised at the level of life, the species, the race, and the large-scale phenomena of population. (Foucault 1990:137)

If Foucault's lack of specificity poses obstacles for some, it presents oppor-tunities for others. Here, the critical notion concerns a shift away from the protection of the sovereign leader as embodiment of the nation to a bio-po-litical position where the management and health of the wider body politic takes precedence. Of similar significance is the sense that these deployments are waged in the name of modern power, rather than ancient appeals to the right to kill. It is here that Gikandi's use of Foucauldian 'torsion' might be most productively linked to Farah's work. Whilst distinctions between the critical preoccupations of both trilogies remain blurry, *Maps* concerns the projection and ultimate disintegration of the dream of pan-Somali nation-alism largely divorced from the General's despotic dictates in *Variations*. Whilst Farah explicitly mentions Barre's regime for the first time since *A Naked Needle* in *Secrets* (*Sec*: 190–191), allusions in *Maps* are conspicuously few. For Alden and Tremaine, the General's omission corresponds with this wider, shifting order of things (Alden & Tremaine 1999: 103). It is reveal-ing, for example, that only Gikandi makes the connection between *Maps*' function as exemplary postcolonial critique and Farah's specific treatise on the failings of Barre's regime during this period (Gikandi 2002: 464). Whilst

Farah is writing fiction rather than political commentary, the paradigm shift in *Maps*, particularly in terms of who/what is subjected to the most withering analyses, might be superimposed onto developments traced by Foucault:

> Wars are no longer waged in the name of a sovereign who must be defended; they are waged on behalf of the existence of everyone; entire populations are mobilized for the purpose of wholescale slaughter in the name of life necessity: massacres have become vital. It is as managers of life and survival, of bodies and the race, that so many regimes have been able to wage so many wars. (Foucault 1990: 137)

Whilst commentators point to the predominance of embodied rhetoric used to justify the Ogaden offensive at the time, Farah's fictional intervention affords a more thoroughgoing analysis of power and resistance as channelled through and thus subject to alteration by politically conscientised agents. As such, the idea of a dialectical turn inwards appears useful once more.

As Sugnet maintains, the reading experience is only intensified by being locked in the pseudo-confessional chamber of Askar's unstable narrative (Sugnet 2002: 536). In a very immediate sense, it obliges the reader to consider how individual subjects might absorb and regurgitate dominant nationalist discourses. Considered in this light, such pronominal shifts may be read as one of the ways in which fiction can make oppositional interventions. For Francis Ngaboh-Smart, for instance, Farah is concerned with challenging the type of Fanonian 'idealism' that manifests itself through Askar's nationalist longings:

> While Fanon may have found the 'tribal' paradigm useful in analysing the collage that is Somalia, his vision sees such a paradigm, even for the individual, as likely to foster idealism. To avoid such idealism, Farah tries to show that the nature of the Somali national character, despite protests to the contrary, lies in its diversity or fluidity, paradoxical as that may sound. (Ngaboh-Smart 2001: 6)

At one level, Farah represents this fluidity through the pronominal jostling that makes Askar's narrative so formally distinctive.

Whilst silent on the role Foucauldian thought might play in her own work, Scarry maintains that there is a vital relationship between war waged on the basis of a disputed territory and the politics of the bodies involved:

At particular moments when there is within a society a crisis of belief – that is, when some central idea or ideology or cultural construct has ceased to elicit a population's belief either because it is manifestly fictitious or because for some reason it has been divested of ordinary forms of substantiation – the sheer material factualness of the human body will be borrowed to lend that cultural construct the aura of 'realness' and 'certainty'. (Scarry 1985: 14)

Whilst indulging in a moment of xenophobic triumphalism, Askar feels the schisms in his personal/political construction of identity being dragged into painful relief. If the adrenaline of nationalist euphoria temporarily safeguards him from the sort of psychosomatic capitulation he suffers elsewhere, this episode constitutes a decisive wrench. With a strategic eye on the future, his comrades point suspicious fingers at Misra or, more specifically, at an ethnic genealogy tracing her back to the Ethiopian highlands. Whilst they imagine themselves taking pre-emptive measures against a potentially damaging in-former, their underlying unease is rooted in a discriminatory (bio)politics of blood. The murky circumstances surrounding Misra's eventual murder serve as the opaque counterpart to this incident. In both, the reader remains deliberately uncertain as to the extent of Askar's complicity. In the final reck-oning, accounting for the bodies of victors and vanquished relies on clearly establishing identity and affiliation. Farah is concerned with the processes by which such absolute distinctions become blurred when necessarily unstable, individual and human elements encroach.

At a macrological level, the embodied dream is of pan-Somali unity and the restoration of the compomised body politic, as discussed by Scarry. One of the most effective ways of ensuring its normative health, therefore, is through a cleansing of 'foreign' contagion. Fittingly, Wright invokes Su-san Sontag's *Illness as Metaphor*, suggesting the cancerous growth Misra has removed in a mastectomy operation intersects with some of these broader concerns:

In Askar's narrative speculations, the tumour acquires the ancient punitive associations of the 'canker of guilt', something which she has both caused and deserved, and which her body, by its own inner logic, has brought upon itself. Moreover, cancer cells, in the mythology of the disease as described by Susan Sontag, becomes a besieged citadel infiltrated by enemy cells that represent the non-self. (Wright 1994: 109)

In Foucauldian terms, Farah is preoccupied with the dark underbelly of those bio-political procedures that reveal themselves through war. The result is that both body and nation are shown as besieged citadels and porous constructs. It is this realisation that Askar struggles to come to terms with. In a Saidian vein, it is only once the non-self can be identified and, where necessary, demonised that something like stability/ethnic essence can be claimed by and for the self. In Scarry's terms, it is the mechanics of these very processes that are being called into question, particularly in the arena of war. Seen from the Foucauldian perspective sketched out so hauntingly in *'Society Must Be Defended'*, Askar entertains the idea of destroying his adoptive, 'other' mother as a means of purifying and purging both himself and Somalia's wider body politic: '[it] is the relationship of war: "In order to live, you must destroy your enemies." But racism does make the relationship of war – "If you want to live, the other must die" – function in a way that is completely new and that is quite compatible with the exercise of biopower' (Foucault 2003: 255). Askar's asides on Misra as belonging to a different 'species' are particularly striking when viewed through this bio-political lens.

Constructions and Destructions of the (M)Other

As a Somali resident of Amharic descent, Misra resembles the Ogaden: an embodiment of the ambiguous zone differentiating Somali and Ethiopian ('my people and yours', M: 98). In the current disorder of things, she is constructed as a deviant to be normalised or neutralised in the process and subsequent aftermath of war. Askar recalls how, as he tracked the W.S.L.F.'s progress on maps of the disputed territory, Misra attempted to stabilise the slippages in her political and familial identities:

> 'I am an Ethiopian,' she said. But how was I to know what species an 'Ethiopian' is? I asked the appropriate questions and got the appropriate answers. The image which has remained with me, is that of a country made up of patchworks – like a poor man's mantle. She wasn't decided to go back to the Highlands or stay, she repeated. Although she no longer spoke the language of the area of Ethiopia in which she was born. (M: 98–99)

Strikingly, Farah places 'Ethiopian' rather than 'species' in inverted commas, suggesting that it is the torsion between the two that ranks amongst *Maps'* most pressing concerns. If the imagined patchwork corresponds with those narrative/stitching metaphors that litter Farah's oeuvre, it carries greater weight when considered in relation to Askar's political education. This derives from private tutor Cusmaan and Hilaal, and is dominated by issues including Somali linguistic and cultural homogeneity. In an ideological sense, Askar appears unable to stitch an alternative conception of heterogeneity and difference together with anything like the requisite skill. Misra finds herself caught on ethno-political cusps in spatial, corporeal and, critically, cultural-linguistic terms. Askar's inability to cope with the patchwork image might therefore be read alongside his psychological distancing from her as a multiply embodied remnant of his pre-literate, tactile childhood; a period crucially defined as being prior to the imposition of inverted commas.

As *Maps* interrogates lines of cartographic and ethno-political division, so those separating dream and reality remain fluid. It is thus revealing that Askar is haunted by visions of himself inhabiting different bodies. Arguably, they are liminal compensation for his inability to cope with the corporeal contests and sacrifices of war. In Misra's case, she once more becomes an orphan, stranded between two equally empty notions of home. She both embodies and clings to the patchwork for protection. Askar, by contrast, dismisses it as a dishonourable challenge to Somali exceptionalism. This critical difference remains between nominal mother and son. Typically, Farah employs Hilaal to gesture towards the complexities of such debates: 'Ethiopia is the generic name of an unclassified mass of different peoples, professing different religions, claiming to have descended from different ancestors. Therefore, "Ethiopia" becomes that generic notion, expansive, inclusive. Somali, if we come to it, is specific. That is, you are either a Somali or you aren't … What is at war are the generic and specific as concepts' (*M*: 155). Hilaal's notion that conflict is, to a significant degree, conceptual once again resonates with Scarry's epigraph.

In the process of exploring her functions within both private and public spheres, Misra disturbs Askar's self-serving, mythical depiction of her as not 'the type of woman who could lose herself in the eternity of a search for who she was – for she knew who she was' (*M*: 26). The undulating course of the Ogaden struggle precipitates remappings of allegiances both notional and national. It is again fitting that Misra, the interstitial irritant who challenges 'native/alien' definitions, concentrates her meditations on body rather than blood politics:

> There are a number of blind spots the body of a human has. We may not know them until we are self-conscious; we may not sense how helpless we are until

> we submit ourselves to other hands. A child's body's blind spots are far too
> many to count … They are difficult to live with, these blind spots, these blind
> curves in one's body, the curtained parts of one's body, the never-seen, never-
> visible-unless-with-the-assistance-of-a-mirror parts. (*M*: 114–115)

Whilst this conflation of individual and collective body politics might appear
a little clumsy, it does allow Misra to deliver an effective Fanonian critique of
the pitfalls of exclusive nationalism. As such, it anticipates a key intervention
from Nonno in *Secrets*: '[o]ur nation's predicament is our own predicament
too … Our challenge is to locate the metaphor for the collapse of the collective, following that of the individual' (*Sec*: 191). In *Maps*, Askar's struggle
centres around the difficulties of living with these various curves and complexities. Fittingly, as he attempts to come to terms with Misra's comments, a
bomb blast separates them. In its aftermath, the dirt of guerrilla child's play
is replaced with mortar dust. Emerging out of the confusion and dismissing
Misra's concerns for his wellbeing, Askar confronts her with the very riddle
he tries to solve throughout: 'who do you take me for?' (*M*: 115). Whilst this
is one of many abrupt, accusative questions, simultaneously directed at himself, others and the reader throughout, it is the precariousness of the potential
response that is both crucial for and serves to confound Askar. The difficult
blind spot he faces is that Misra takes him as a prospective son rather than
an ethnically 'other' Somali.

The counterpart to Misra's salutary lesson emerges during a key dream.
Confronted by a spectral refugee girl, standing in borrowed skin, without
country or name, Askar is scolded for being 'almost always satisfied with the
surface of things – a smooth surface being, to you, a mirror in which your
features, your looks, may be reflected, and so you see nothing in mirrors
save surfaces' (*M*: 136). As Askar reflects on his inability to cope with the
multiply embodied disorder of his new world, his unconscious is invaded by
the remnants of a critique he was both unwilling and unable to accept from
Misra. As Wright suggests, '[for Askar] Misra is a perfect image of the Ogaden insofar as both are mirrors in which the beholder sees his own desires
reflected, and maps, like mirrors, reflect the dispositions of their makers'
(Wright 1994: 119). In this most unstable of texts, Farah's enduring concern
is the process by which apparent certainties are revealed to be provisional
constructs. Such preoccupations, whether corporeal, cartographic, textual or
ideological, might be favourably interpreted in a Foucauldian light. As JM
Coetzee maintains in *Doubling the Point*, when it comes to writing-the-self,
'the only sure truth in autobiography is that one's self-interest will be located

at one's blind spot' (Coetzee 1992: 392). Caught up in the vociferous calls for a swift counter-attack, Askar runs with the crowd, leaving Misra and her careful critique of corporeal and conceptual blind spots in his wake.

Psychosomatics and War

The counterpart to Askar's refusal to be washed comes in the aftermath of the role reversal of victor and vanquished following the Tragic Weekend. Fanon's prophetic warning about the extent to which '[each] act of sedition in the Third World makes up part of a picture framed by the Cold War' is expressed through Askar's aside on the decisive hand played by the Russians and Cubans in securing Ethiopian victory (Fanon 2001: 59). With Mother Somalia defeated, Askar is consigned to his sick bed. More than an amplification of the existential anguish he wrestles with throughout, it is crucial that such a capitulation, be it psychosomatic or otherwise, comes in the aftermath of military failure. As a reconstituted Greater Somalia temporarily reigned supreme, Askar's body resisted fragmentary pressures, both internal and external. Now, with the psychological and militaristic order of things somewhat altered, peculiar tolls are being exacted from national and individual bodies. Faced with Askar's besieged condition, Hilaal explains that defeat will mean 'an influx of refugees' (*M*: 163). Once again, this is touched on by Lewis (Lewis 2002: 246–247). The association between military failure and waves of displaced peoples emerging over the horizon is striking. Whilst the designations 'winner' and 'loser' may have changed, structures and results remain the same. It is, therefore, similarly significant that, dishevelled as he is, Askar is unable to associate the influx with Somali defeat. Effectively the displaced peoples, like the exilic dream girl, have a liminal identity. As such, they exceed the limits of his understanding.

As I explore in a later chapter, Farah uses *Yesterday, Tomorrow* to examine transnational movements of people, considering how and why Foucauldian concerns with disciplinary mechanisms and bio-political taxonomies define the global order of things. If his diaspora study concerns the all-too material issues of identity papers, passports and surveillance, *Maps* is just as preoccupied with the normalising desire to inscribe or 'fix' identity on paper. In novels both before and after, elderly protagonists wrestle with the politics of self-definition and documentation from positions straddling the colonial/ postcolonial power divide. For Askar, the papers offered by Hilaal to shore up a faltering identity present him with more immediate, internal conflicts of interest. On presentation of the identity card, he muses on its literal and figurative power: 'here you are, [Hilaal] seemed to say, with another life all your own, one that you must take good care of, since it is of paper, produced by the hand of man, according to the laws of man' (*M*: 171). As he soon learns, however, the process of defining the self is as slippery as that of defining the nation. Appearing to offer ontological stability with one hand, it compels acts of exclusion with the other. For Askar, it enables psychological distancing from the 'refugee' or 'unperson' designations and attendant ambiguities that infiltrate his dreams. As all else crumbles, including those cartographic 'truths' also produced 'by the hand of man', he tentatively invests in the card's prescriptive power: 'after all, I was not a refugee! … looking at the photograph and, under it, like a caption, my name, I began to see myself in images carved out of the letters which my name comprised. It meant that I had a *foglio famiglia* and that I wasn't just a refugee from the Ogaden. It is unfair, I thought to myself, that Misra wasn't even given a mention on my identity card' (*M*: 172). This reliance on 'carved' echoes other, defining moments in *Maps*.

Whilst suggesting a process of honing or refining the self, 'carved' also connotes stripping away, as well as the potential pain this implies. Fittingly, these and other verbs have fleshy significance throughout *Maps*. For Wright, Farah is concerned with the ways cartographic products of the 'colonial carve-up' are either resisted or reinforced by postcolonial regimes (Wright 1994: 111). As with the identity card, the map is seen as a projection borne out of coercion and a deeper violence that is epistemic as well as geographical. This is implied when Hilaal asks Askar, 'do you carve out of your soul the invented truth of the maps you draw?' (*M*: 227). In relation to the European 'frenzy of conquest', Philip Gourevitch's *We Wish to Inform You That Tomorrow We Will be Killed With Our Families* argues that 'distinct [African] nations, with their own languages, religions, and complex political and social histories, were either carved up or, more often, lumped together beneath European flags' (Gourevitch 2000: 53). Whilst he discusses Rwanda, a notable referent in Farah's later work, Gourevitch also foregrounds the gruesomely divisive, bio-political role played by identity cards during colonial and postcolonial epochs (Gourevitch 2000: 56–57). In *Maps*, it is equally significant that 'carve' is used to capture the embodied intimacies of Askar and Misra's early relationship. Askar recalls how he functioned as 'part of the shadow [Misra] cast – in a sense I was her extended self … for years, I contemplated the world from the safe throne carved out of Misra's back' (*M*: 78). The ominous supplement to this description of conjoined bodies, with self effectively inhabiting other, comes after the mutilation and dismemberment of Misra's body. Having had her cancerous growth removed, the post-mortem confirms her heart was torn from her body. Farah therefore invites his reader to consider how Misra has been constructed and carved out of Askar's life in ethnic, embodied and epistemological terms. The loaded use of 'carved', therefore, suggests the peculiarities of Askar's journey towards a more complex, if unresolved, sense of self. In so doing, it also calls for a more substantial exploration of issues including identity politics and biopower.

This, in turn, corresponds with Colmer's assertion that 'Farah's continued insinuation [concerns] a legalistic construction of nationhood which fails to find a space in its definitions for socially and culturally nurturant relationships such as Misra's with Askar ... Farah consistently highlights the disjunction between the real world and the text that culture and national aspiration attempt to inscribe on it' (Colmer 2002: 502). In *Maps*, Misra is the hybrid irritant who cannot be accommodated by bureaucratic prescriptions. In response, Askar attempts to rationalise the personal/political exclusion they represent by introducing a temporal fracture, conceiving Misra as part of a 'non-literate past' (*M*: 172), prior to the 'authentication' of his identity on paper. Through his complicit narration, Askar presents a conceptual departure from the earlier belief that her exclusion was based on her ethnic status as Oromo, set against his as Somali. Yet, in the wake of ignominious defeat, this is precisely the kind of bio-political dividing line identity cards and associated documents are designed to police. The instability of Askar's response to Hilaal, therefore, is revealing: '"the truth of the matter is, Misra, being Oromo as you've explained to me once, belongs to a peripheral people ... as such, the Oromo have either to assume Somali or Amhara identity. Thank God, my ethnic origin matches the papers with which I shall be issued," I concluded' (*M*: 170). In ideological terms, this remains a suitably open-ended conclusion to Askar's conceptual 'development'. It allows Farah to invite his reader to set such either/or discourses against *Maps'* wider concern with potentially deconstructive third spaces and identities.

Whilst alluding to some of the body-politics issues considered above, I suggest that Colmer does not go far enough: '[i]t is under the patronage of Hilaal and Salaado that Askar acquires the carta d'identita ... which says in writing that he is a Somali national, but on which there is no room for Misra's name, because such documents deal with categories and classifications of the literate world, and take no account of the human relations of touch and nurturance' (Colmer 2002: 503). Such documents, particularly in light of Askar's conflictual context, not only preclude the transgressive politics of touch. They also define the terms in which ethnic identities and affiliations can be established or, in relation to Farah's wider project, constructed. In this pivotal section, Hilaal suggests it is a peculiar linguistic-cultural homogeneity that sets Somalis apart, rather than specifically ethnic issues. Yet for Askar, as Colmer intimates, the identity card appears to confer an essential, legal and fixed identity. It is thus multiply revealing that he entertains the idea that post-conflict solutions to his existential anguish and fraught association with Misra will come if she is granted Somali status. The whole issue of the identity card's legalistic and symbolic power gestures towards the central problematic in *Maps*. For Gikandi, it once again confronts the reader with critically contested issues around body politics:

> Does this mean that an Ethiopian who adopts the Somali culture and language can also be considered Somali? This is the problem posed by Misra in the novel: although she will not be accepted as a Somali, by all the indices used to determine a Somali, Misra is surely one. But since she will always be denied this identity because of her Ethiopian origins, Misra is the figure Farah uses to deconstruct the hegemonic doctrine of Somali national purity. (Gikandi 2002: 463)

Such identity card debates might also be read in light of Foucault's comments on the shifting role of the law when it comes to those normalising procedures of a bio-political state. As he states in *The History of Sexuality*:

> Another consequence of [the] development of bio-power was the growing importance assumed by the action of the norm, at the expense of the juridical system of the law. Law cannot help but be armed, and its arm, par excellence, is death; to those who transgress it, it replies, at least as a last resort, with that absolute menace. The law always refers to the sword. But a power whose task is to take charge of life needs continuous regulatory and corrective mechanisms. It is no longer a matter of bringing death into play in the field of sovereignty, but of distributing the living in the domain of value and utility. Such a power has to qualify, measure, appraise, and hierarchize, rather than display itself in its murderous splendor; it does not have to draw the line that separates the enemies of the sovereign from his obedient subjects; it effects distributions around the norm. (Foucault 1990: 144)

The notion of tabulating the living in regulatory discourse provides an intriguing prism through which to view *Maps*. Whilst identity cards and papers function as constant symbols of normative power, whether colonial or post-colonial, throughout Farah's fiction, it is the significance attached to them by individuals in turbulent times that remains striking. Whilst legally binding documents appear to represent the bio-political distinctions necessary for victory in the territorial dispute, it is the subjective process of struggling with concepts such as 'norm' and 'transgression' that impacts upon *Maps'* protagonist and reader most directly. Askar's true battle is to square the circles of his personal and political affiliations, to decipher where both he and Misra fit in. The tragic irony, of course, comes with the violent flourishing of 'absolute menace' and 'murderous splendour' towards the close of the text, as well as Askar's potential involvement in it.

In this light, Misra's alleged role as conspiratorial go-between can be viewed, more properly, as a thin veneer covering her position as an embodied go-between. She thus represents a contagion, like the cancerous tumour, to be removed and neutralised. Yet, a vital feature of Farah's portrayal of punitive biopower is his unwillingness to present it as monolithic. The reader is certainly invited to view the Somali soldiers who rape Misra, only to present their story in subhuman rhetoric, as agents of the State. Like Askar, however, they are also figured as individual combatants, caught within a power network that still affords them space to resist:

> 'The story these young men circulated (and everyone who believed that I was a traitor had no difficulty accepting it) was that I had been raped by baboons … The baboons, said the poet amongst them (and one of them was a poet), smelt the beast in her and went for it; the baboons smelt her traitor's identity underneath the human skin and went for it again and again. Thank God, we were there to save her body since, as a traitor, she had ransomed her soul.' (*M*: 195)

Typically, Farah frames some of his most provocative observations in parentheses. In a moment of narrative, if not emotional or embodied relief from Askar's retelling, Misra places herself centre stage. Her immediate audience comprises Askar, Hilaal and Salaado, yet it is the parenthetical reference to wider complicity that demands the reader's attention. As such, Misra's meditation is reminiscent of Khaliif's in *Close Sesame* or Amina's in *Sardines*. She attends to the sadistic affinities between her attackers, their construction of a narrative that in turn portrays her as a subhuman traitor and, critically, the all-too-willing acceptance of this version of events by the public. This, I maintain, is Farah's most suggestive point. Whilst the reader is given various versions of Misra's alleged crime (betraying a W.S.L.F. unit to rival Ethiopian soldiers), the 'truth' of the matter becomes a relative side issue. Her purported betrayal is effectively a ruse. For Hilaal, she is essentially constructed and destroyed, not only as a treacherous woman but also, in accordance with prevailing if perverted logic, as an ethnic other who, because of her Ethiopian roots, could do nothing but betray the Somali soldiers: 'women as whores, women as witches, women as traitors of their blood, women as lovers of men from the enemy camp – throughout history, men have blamed women for the ill luck they themselves have brought on their heads' (*M*: 186). Her interstitial identity, therefore, constitutes her true crime, with the result that, in gender and ethnic terms alike, her demotic depiction is the one preferred by various audiences. As such, this can be seen as a concentration rather than a dilution of the kind of nuanced, pyramidal critique of power discussed in relation to *Variations*. This development might also be interpreted in light of the Foucauldian shift Jeremy Moss identifies when outlining his ideas about the 'intransigence of freedom':

> A defining feature of power for the later Foucault is that subjects have the possibility of not just reacting to power, but of altering power relationships as well. Foucault moved away from the rhetoric of *Discipline and Punish* where power seemed to constitute individuals, without there being much opportunity to resist power, to a position where individuals have the scope to refuse the regulation of apparatuses of power … at the heart of the power relationship there lies what he calls the 'intransigence of freedom' … subjectivity in the later Foucault is a far more active constituent of power relations. (Moss 1998: 5)

Moss' attention to Foucault's privileging of active subjectivity is significant. Alongside this, it remains tempting to consider the discursive relationship between such 'hermeneutics of the self' concerns and those other, late preoccupations with State racism and punitive biopower. I suggest an enabling reading of *Maps* can emerge from the space between the two.

Like Moss, O'Farrell offers a synopsis of a key project that detained the later Foucault:

> In proposing a 'history of the subject', Foucault once again emphasises that, like 'truth', the subject is not prior to history … The subject is a form, not a thing and this form is not constant … the self that is created is a form that relies very much for its existence on its interaction with other people, history and culture. This is opposed to the notion of a true self that needs to be 'discovered' in introspective isolation … [Foucault] describes three forms of the

'exercise of thought' in Western history which relate to the acquisition of truth
and knowledge and to self-formation ... firstly, remembering or recognising
one's original truth (self-discovery); secondly, self transformation; and thirdly
discovering an external point of certainty and truth on which all else rests
(science). Foucault strongly favours the second process. (O' Farrell 2005: 113)

Characteristically Eurocentric, it appears little would be gained from trans-
lating these speculations. For me, however, Foucault's notion of an unstable
subject enmeshed in the processes of history, his conceptual disavowal of
a 'true self' and his provocative attention to three forms of the exercise of
thought are particularly enabling when it comes to reading *Maps*. As with
Misra's critique of bodily blind spots, O'Farrell is alive to the importance Foucault placed on the self engaging with and being engaged by others, rather
than remaining locked in a hermetic search for essence. These negotiations
are critical. As such, Askar's pronominal struggles, engaged at both narrative
and national levels, can be conceived as attempts, however forlorn, to construct a 'true self'. If fractures in these internal and external narratives are
painfully exposed when such bids falter, Foucault's three-point schema offers
a fascinating lens through which to view them.

As an orphan child of the Ogaden, Askar is obsessed with his origins.
Throughout *Maps*, he attempts to piece together a coherent version of these
beginnings from the fragments of his mother's journal. It falls to Hilaal to
deliver the quotidian truth in a letter: 'you didn't take shorter than a month
to be conceived and born … there was no eclipse of the sun or the moon.
I've read and reread your mother's journal for clues. I am afraid it appears
you completed your nine months' (*M*: 22). The projected remembrance of
his origins as mythic being is replaced by the recognition that he comes
from all-too-human stock. Whilst *Maps* concerns Askar's tumultuous bid
for self-discovery, this disavowal is formative and multiply significant. Foucault's third category concerns the desired revelation of 'an external point of
certainty and truth on which all else rests'. Whilst he focuses on science, the
principle holds true in relation to *Maps*' preoccupation with cartography.
As with the deflating discovery of his origins, Askar finds the geo-political
designs he falls back on to be 'truths' drawn up and disputed by man. As
Hilaal maintains, 'there is truth in maps. The Ogaden, as Somali, is truth. To
the Ethiopian map-maker, the Ogaden, as Somali, is untruth' (*M*: 229). As it
gradually dawns that little has fixed status in *Maps*' imagined landscape, it
becomes necessary to investigate the category between these empirical bids
for self-discovery and the perpetual groping after truth. For Foucault and

Farah, it is one that privileges self-transformation. Askar is challenged to come to terms with his earthy beginnings as well as the realisation that little is certain, before transforming himself and his actions accordingly. With the threat of incarceration hanging heavy over the novel's close, the reader is cast in the role of arbiter, judging whether Askar has successfully negotiated these transformative challenges by considering what he has both lost and gained in the process. Whilst others have advanced nuanced readings of Farah's sliding pronouns, I consider them in light of this Foucauldian subject in the process of self-discovery/transformation, embedded in the complexes of history itself.

Hallucinating Foucault/Transforming Farah

At the outset of his critique of *Orientalism*, Dennis Porter draws attention to a methodological tension between Said's use of Foucauldian 'discourse' and Gramsci's concept of 'hegemony'. To illustrate their incompatibility, he turns to TE Lawrence's *The Seven Pillars of Wisdom*. By focusing on the complexities and complicities of Lawrence's narrative mode, Porter suggests the text's generic instability is one of its most genuinely radical features. He uses the following definition of the literary to interrogate Said's rendering of Lawrence as a prototypical Orientalist:

> If I use the literary here … it is only to make a qualitative distinction between texts that are characterized by a self-interrogating density of verbal texture and those that offer no internal resistance to the ideologies they reproduce. I take the literary instance to signify all texts – traditionally literary, philosophical, historical etc. – which are of sufficient complexity to throw ideological processes into relief and raise questions about their own fictionalizing processes. (Porter 1983: 182)

Maps' pivotal status is in part due to the kind of textual density that, albeit in a different context, is being highlighted here, as Porter finds multitudes in Lawrence's 'I'. By buffeting his reader between pronouns from the outset, Farah demands an immediate focus on the constructed nature of Askar's narrative. It is only once wider debates concerning geo-political disputes and appeals to nationalist 'truths' as well as interrogations of the politics of cartography and corporeality are considered alongside them that the reader is charged with bringing a greater degree of critical scrutiny to bear. It is therefore revealing that Sugnet engages with another Said text to support his interpretation of *Maps'* pronominal play. Extending his comparative focus, he suggests *The Question of Palestine* 'contains more of the burden of history, emphasizing the political and geographical causes of pronoun instability, of a subject who apprehends himself literally *elsewhere*' (Sugnet 2002: 538). Read differently, Sugnet's analysis might also be viewed as an invitation to consider the potentially transformative role of fiction.

Central to Vaughan's critique of Foucault's Eurocentric concept of bio-power in *Curing Their Ills* is its incommensurability with the biomedical procedures implemented by colonial powers in Africa:

> In colonial medical discourse and practice colonial Africans were conceptualized … as members of groups (usually but not always defined in ethnic terms) and it was these groups, rather than individuals, who were said to possess distinctive psychologies and bodies. In contrast to the developments described by Foucault, in colonial Africa group classification was a far more important construction than individualization. Indeed, there was a powerful strand in the theories of colonial psychologists which denied the possibility that Africans might be self-aware individual subjects, so bound were they supposed to be to collective identities. (Vaughan 1991: 11)

For the Rushdie of *Imaginary Homelands*, one of the peculiarly postcolonial achievements of a novel such as *Maps* is the extent to which it goes against the hegemonic grain of African caricatures that still rely, in the age of global mass media, on the sort of generic, distorting discourses considered by Vaughan: 'here is a starving child, there is a mad dog; feed her, bomb him … information about Africa reaches us, most of the time, through a series of filters which, by reducing the vast continent to a cluster of emotive slogans, succeed in denying us any sense of complexity, context, truth' (Rushdie 1992: 201). At an immediate textual level, as with Porter's analysis of Lawrence, the instability and ambiguity of Askar's 'I' is the source of its richness. Farah's critique of power is facilitated rather than frustrated by the very creation of a speaking subject who, precisely because he is uncertain and fallible, obliges the reader to grapple with issues of 'complexity, context and truth'. In Rushdie's sense, novels such as *Maps* open up and explore interrogative spaces in the historical present by demanding greater attention be paid to the subject-in-process.

The claustrophobic confinement of Askar's narrative finds its correlative in what Kazan calls 'an unusually dense summoning of the mother-child dyad' (Kazan 2002: 477). Her interpretation is exemplary, moving as she does between dyads and third spaces, in both interpretative and ideological terms, to focus on the contested and potentially resistant body in *Maps*. As a child leaving the maternal womb, only to glimpse his mother before her untimely death, Askar clings to and is indulged by expansive 'cosmos' Misra in the earliest stages of his narrative. Whilst shunning bodily contact with paternal uncle Qorrax, he strives to annex himself to his guardian, tucking himself 'into the oozy warmth between her breasts (she was a very large woman, and I a tiny little thing), so much so I became a third breast … and I would find myself somewhere between her opened legs this time, as though I was a third leg' (*M*: 24). These 'crypto-incestuous' couplings are recalled after Misra disappears from hospital (*M*: 244). As with her consideration of Farah's fluid pronouns, however, Kazan invokes Fanon to reject the notion that images of corporeal excess are simply sensationalist:

> … while Askar's projection of himself as the 'third leg' or 'third breast' could possibly be read as a kind of grotesque representation, a distorted view of the filial, it can be read more productively as creating a site where 'third' does not signify 'less' in a vertical counting scheme, but rather counts for 'more' in a system of empowerment, a site where consciousness is nourished, to summon Fanon once more, both nationally and internationally; a site, then, which denotes a potentiality in the term 'Third World' and which enables Askar to be at home both in the body of the m/other, and in the body of politics. (Kazan 2002: 477–478)

As Kazan rightly points out, however, this notion of being at home in a liminal third space is problematised throughout Askar's narrative and, with Misra's violent obliteration, definitively shattered. She considers this critical rupture in terms of Askar's coerced substitution of the nurturing body's 'third world' for that of politics, social constructions of 'reality', hegemonic language and affiliation. There is, however, a more contested corporeal site that exists between these two spheres. Like Foucault, it is this interstitial, bio-political zone, when explored alongside constructions of race and ethnicity, which concerns Farah.

Foucault and/on Biopolitics and Race

One of the most significant features of *The History of Sexuality* is the attention paid to temporal and disciplinary differences between what Foucault terms an 'anatomo-politics of the human body' and a 'bio-politics of population'. He describes the increased attention paid to the general management of life in the form of regulatory or biopower controls (monitoring births, deaths and public health programs). In the concluding chapter, 'Right of Death and Power over Life', Foucault draws a distinction between the political primacy of what he terms the 'blood relation' and a society deemed to be 'with a sexuality':

> The blood relation long remained an important element in the mechanisms of power, its manifestations, and its rituals. For a society in which the systems of alliance, the political form of the sovereign, the differentiation into orders and castes, and the value of descent lines were predominant; for a society in which famine, epidemics, and violence made death imminent, blood constituted one of the fundamental values. It owed its high value at the same time to its instrumental role (the ability to shed blood), to the way it functioned in the order of signs (to have a certain blood, to be of the same blood, to be prepared to risk one's blood), and also to its precariousness (easily spilled, subject to drying up, too readily mixed, capable of being quickly corrupted). A society of blood – I was tempted to say, of 'sanguinity' – where power spoke *through* blood: the honor of war, the fear of famine, the triumph of death, the sovereign with his sword, executioners, and tortures; blood was *a reality with a symbolic function*. We, on the other hand, are in a society of 'sex', or rather a society 'with a sexuality': the mechanisms of power are addressed to the body, to life, to what causes it to proliferate, to what reinforces the species, its stamina, its ability to dominate, or its capacity for being used. Through the themes of health, progeny, race, the future of the species, the vitality of the social body, power spoke *of* sexuality and *to* sexuality; the latter was not a mark or a symbol, it was an object and a target. (Foucault 1990: 147)

There is much to admire in this dense passage. Yet there is also a question of how the self-assured 'we' is used and to whom it refers. There is certainly a temporal distinction created between an age predicated on the blood relation and one credited as being 'with a sexuality'. Viewed from a perspective that takes account of Foucault's own reference to a geo-political sphere 'outside the Western world [where] famine exists, on a greater scale than ever', an inquisitive eyebrow might be raised concerning the spatial and/or geographical distinctions being drawn (Foucault 1990: 143). The editors of the *Society* lectures are certainly keen to situate his work in a wider context, even if they too relegate African civil conflicts to a mere footnote (Foucault 2003: 285). The inclusion of familiar caveats and qualifications, however, breathes new life into Foucault's meditations.

Having constructed an apparent binary opposition, Foucault invokes the kind of torsion I have found useful throughout this analysis:

> While it is true that the analytics of sexuality and the symbolics of blood were grounded at first in two very distinct regimes of power, in actual fact the passage from one to the other did not come about … without overlappings, interactions and echoes … Beginning in the second half of the nineteenth century, the thematics of blood was sometimes called on to lend its entire historical weight toward revitalizing the type of political power that was exercised through the devices of sexuality. Racism took shape at this point (racism in its modern, 'biologizing', statist form): it was then that a whole politics of settlement … accompanied by a long series of permanent interventions at the level of the body, conduct, health, and everyday life, received their color and their justification from the mythical concern with protecting the purity of the blood and ensuring the triumph of the race … A eugenic ordering of society, with all that implied in the way of extension and intensification of micro-powers, in the guise of an unrestricted state control (*étatisation*), was accompanied by the oneiric exaltation of a superior blood; the latter implied both the systematic genocide of others and the risk of exposing oneself to total sacrifice. (Foucault 1990: 149–150)

Once again, there is much that appeals in relation to my consideration of Farah's work. Of most immediate interest is Foucault's willed problematisation of his own exclusive categories: 'analytics of sexuality' and 'symbolics of blood'. The Foucauldian focus on an interactive, transformative third space can be linked to the kinds of embodied, deconstructive sites attended to by various Farah critics. Seen from an alternative perspective that takes such blind spots into consideration, Foucault's unremittingly Eurocentric focus can be transposed anew to resist any conflation between the 'symbolics of blood' and a 'primordial' politics that might be ascribed to Africa.

As O'Farrell maintains, therefore, it is also critical to acknowledge the shifting significance of biopower in Foucault's thought:

> In volume 1 of *The History of Sexuality*, and also his lectures *'Society Must Be Defended'*, discipline becomes merely a subset of 'biopower'. The other side of the coin of this control over the life of populations was the control over their death and Foucault argues that never before in history had such bloody wars or such systematic practises of genocide occurred as under the regimes which adopted a strategy of 'biopolitics'. (O'Farrell 2005: 106)

In both the trajectories of Farah's fiction and the course of Somalia's national narrative, this sense of bio-political implosion endures. Whilst comments on the intertwined relationship between racism and 'colonizing genocide' have peculiar significance in relation to this part of the Horn of Africa, Foucault's attention to the dialectical turn inwards of this state racism can be put to work in terms of Farah's later fiction. For Wright, there is an enduring, almost Fanonian quality to this central novel, which draws attention to reciprocal processes as it resists any rigid identification of exclusively European or African guilt (Wright 1994: 127). For the Foucault of 'Society Must be Defended', the archetype of punitive associations between disciplinary and biopower comes in the murderous form of the Nazi 'final solution'. The critical if apocalyptic supplement, however, is that this ultimate bio-political dictatorship had power over both the life and death of the contagion-carrying 'other', as well as its own people: 'everyone in the Nazi state had the power of life and death over his or her neighbours, if only because of the practice of informing, which effectively meant doing away with the people next door, or having them done away with' (Foucault 2003: 259).

Whilst not advancing a biopower comparison between the racist, murderous and suicidal Nazi state and the Somali order of things constructed in Farah's fiction, I do find this notion of an atrophied turn inwards provocative. With defeat in the Ogaden, Barre's attempts to reconstruct the broken body politic were thwarted. The regime turned its punitive gaze inwards to identify and deal with domestic dissidents.[1] To a large extent, it was the hegemonic reanimation of competing clan hostilities that was manipulated to justify these policies. For commentators such as Lewis, Barre's scorched-earth raids against the Isaaq people of Northern Somalia constituted an incomplete genocide: 'the protracted history of neglect, capped by brutal ill-treatment ... culminated in the mass executions in Hargeisa carried out by Siyad's soldiers in the late 1980s' (Lewis 2002: 282). As Farah explicitly maintains in Secrets, it was from this region that Barre's ultimate overthrow would come: 'my mother did not wish our family to be caught by surprise, following the inhumane destruction caused to the people and property in the northern regions. The second largest city of the land was bombed by Siyad's regime, its residents massacred, almost all its buildings razed to the ground' (Sec: 22–23).

Foucault's increasingly sombre notion of bio-political *malveillance* finds a fictional correlative in the accusative fingers pointed towards Misra as an ethnic, cancer-carrying 'other' and potential threat to the normative health of the wider body politic. As such, Askar's reference to Misra's Ethiopian ethnicity, in terms of belonging to a different 'species' (*M*: 98–99), is once again extremely revealing when considered in the light of Foucault's intervention:

> What in fact is racism? It is primarily a way of introducing a break into the domain of life that is under power's control: the break between what must live and what must die. The appearance within the biological continuum of the human race of races, the distinction among races, the hierarchy of races, the fact that certain races are described as good and that others, in contrast, are described as inferior: all of this is a way of fragmenting the field of the biological that power controls. It is a way of separating out the groups that exist within a population. It is, in short, a way of establishing a biological type caesura within a population that appears to be a biological domain. This will allow power to treat that population as a mixture of races, or to be more accurate, to treat the species, to subdivide the species it controls, into the subspecies known, precisely, as races. That is the first function of racism: to fragment, to *create* caesuras within the biological continuum addressed by biopower. (Foucault 2003: 254–255)

Typically, the usefulness of this definition comes precisely from its lack of specificity. Foucault focuses on the fragmentations and schisms of racism as a strategic construct enmeshed in competing discourses of knowledge and power. His formulation emphasises the creation of racial fissures and how power seeks to present them as deriving from essentially biological domains. In *Maps*, the key relationship is between cartography and identity. In suitably Foucauldian terms, both are interrogated and dismantled as discursive constructs.

For Kazan, however, attempts to ascribe such a racial reading must be approached with caution: 'the first thing to note is that in *Maps* the *other* is not the racial *Other* … at least, not a racial *Other* in the sense that black and white are inevitably *other* to each … It is not a stable entity, but a more complex mutable force which rejects the oppositional, hierarchized *other* typical of Western thinking' (Kazan 2002: 475). The notion that Farah's text resists predominantly Western discourses remains attractive for those concerned with how it might write back on behalf of postcolonial critique. Yet, there is a sense in which this accommodating notion of liminality has veered a little too far from the novel's material, embodied preoccupations. The Foucauldian idea of created breaks is most strikingly exemplified through the fraught dynamics of Askar and Misra's relationship, as conducted against the backdrop of broader political struggles. Whilst this is primarily waged on the basis of disputed territory, it is, as Scarry suggests in an alternative context, always already anchored at a level that draws specific lines of corporeal division. For Gikandi, 'an important strategy of national formation in *Maps* is the use of the human body as a third site of national formation ... In examining the relationship between Askar and Misra, in "bodily" terms, the narrative questions the "wall" that is supposed to separate Ethiopians from Somalis' (Gikandi 2002: 463). As with the richly allusive 'carved', the use of this wall motif is striking. It variously captures the sense in which biological/ethnic differences are essentially hegemonic constructs. As such, the text suggests, they can both be built up and, crucially, knocked down. This again corresponds with Scarry, who alludes to the dialectical significance of these construction/deconstruction dynamics in her introduction: 'the title of the book ... designates as [its] subject the most contracted of spaces, the small circle of living matter; and the subtitle designates as its territory the most expansive territory, *The Making and Unmaking of the World*. But the two go together, for what is at stake in the body in pain is the making and unmaking of the world' (Scarry 1985: 22–23).

In *Maps*, Askar's narrative encloses him like a wall, locking him into the kind of isolated introspection that can be read in light of Foucault's own formulations about the individual trapped in a futile search for his 'true' self. Likewise, in a typically academic postscript following the handover of Askar's identity card, Hilaal speculates on the arguably unstable divisions separating Somalis and Ethiopians: '[for] all we know, there is no ethnic difference which sets apart the Somali from the Ethiopian – the latter in inverted commas' (*M*: 174). Taken on to *Maps'* concluding tableau, where biopower and disciplinary spheres arguably collide, Hilaal's musings appear even more significant. Brought in for questioning regarding his involvement in his adopted mother's murder, Askar finds himself enmeshed in the disciplinary mechanisms of a bio-political state in apparently all-too fine working order. The tragic irony is that Misra's neutralisation as ethnic, conspiratorial 'other' constitutes something akin to a suicide in the wider body politic, with the reader once again obliged to focus on depictions of the state as manager of the life and health of the population. Whilst I have repeatedly used Scarry's notion of being 'called into question' to approach *Maps*, it is this moment, when Askar himself is called in for questioning, that is multiply revealing. The resonant sense at the novel's close is that self and other, in their constructed forms, have definitively merged, so that the latter's extermination constitutes a decisive blow to the former. As such, Foucault's provocative notion of state racism's created biases might be called upon once more. The reader is left to consider the extent of Askar's failure to call into question the conceptual bases upon which various battles, notional and national, individual and collective, are fought. The implicit call, therefore, is for us to return to the opening sections of *Maps*, re-evaluating ambiguous depictions of Askar and Misra's 'crypto-incestuous' couplings as more than mere sensationalism on Farah's part. This once more allows us to appreciate the dialectical relationship between form and content in the novel, with the 'other' inhabiting and haunting the 'self' in both its uncertain beginnings and endings. The reader thus joins the narrator in cyclical acts of rereading and rewriting. In immediate and interpretive senses, such calls for narrative return and renegotiation are potentially transformative.

Bifurcated Bodies and Split Subjects

In an article written after the overthrow of Barre's regime, one of its most prominent architects bemoaned Somalia's failure to translate the despot's demise into a brighter new political dawn. For Ibrahim Samater, the nation is a 'bifurcated society, with a non-integrated personality' (Samater 1997: 40). Farah continually invokes this notion of psycho-political schizophrenia, in both novels and more autobiographical work. The creation of Askar signals his most intense fictional attempt to come to terms with these fissures at narrative, cartographic and corporeal levels. He is a protagonist who, in Mbembe's terms, is paralysed by 'a tragic duality and inner twoness' (Mbembe 2001: 12). Caught on the agonising cusps of not-yet man/not-quite boy, not-yet intellectual insurgent/not-quite resistance fighter, Askar is depicted as never quite able to live with the indeterminacies of his situation. The result is that his early 'awareness of the thin line separating the personal from the political' (*M*: 104) begins to desert him. As the war moves beyond the theatre of child's play and begins to take its toll on his life, body and concomitant relationships, the thin line turns to barbed wire. For Salaado, the result of living in this child/adult war zone is that '[Askar's] life has been a war of sorts' (*M*: 149).

This is most graphically brought to bear on Askar's body during circumcision. Misra initiates this symbolic and physiognomic rite of passage from boy to manhood, proclaiming, 'what we must do one of these days, so you can be a man, is to have you circumcised, have you purified' (*M*: 89). Demonstrating dutiful respect for the rituals of her host society, Misra casts her young charge into an arena where the body confronts discourses of power loaded with the propensity to (re)configure identities by (re)fashioning corporeal realities. To be a man, it seems, your rite of passage must be marked by, as it is cleansed through, violence. As the outbreak of war looms and the political stakes set by blood and national affiliation grow more significant, Farah signals Askar's entry into the 'horrid territory … of pain' (*M*: 92) by evoking the child's gaze distracted by a bird in flight: 'it became again the centre of my world and I was inside it, in flight … impervious to the realities surrounding me – and then, sudden as bushfire, ZAK!' (*M*: 92). Comparisons between this episode and the final incident I focus on here are striking, in more ways than one.

As in *Yesterday, Tomorrow*, Farah uses the interlude to bring several key concerns together. In *Maps*, the interlude traces Askar's journey out of Kallafo and away from Misra. Borne along by nationalist triumphalism and the 'joy of travel' (*M*: 125), Askar imagines himself substituting the geo-political disorder of things for a liminal zone between dream and reality, the metaphysical and the physical:

> [The singing], together with the speed of the lorry, transported your imagination to the high seas and you thought you were floating, one and all, in the pure silver water of total abandon. Nothing mattered any more … Beautiful voices that sing beautiful, nationalist songs beautifully are seldom found … it seemed you had bodily gained access to the buffer between reality and dream as you listened to the song. (*M*: 130)

As with so many features of Askar's narrative, however, this hiatus is cut short. The beautiful nationalist song, like the passing Somali triumph and finally his own journey, reaches its end with the inevitable result that the contested order of things, created and confounded by man, must be faced. In this instance, Farah draws the reader's attention to the critical torsion between Askar's desire for liminal transcendence and his ultimate inability to live with the indeterminacies of the reality surrounding him. As one of dreamy deferral, the third space is, in a Foucauldian sense, neither personally nor politically transformative.

If descriptions of both journey and circumcision represent palpably painful degrees of separation, they also capture the narrative's broader preoccupations. The post-circumcision pool of blood in which Askar finds himself alone becomes literally the least and figuratively the most significant of his concerns. As events unfold, his real difficulties are contrasted with the incision of this moment. If Askar learns that all divisions have the same traumatic potential, the conceptual struggle reminds him they are not all as clean cut. The ritualistic power to distinguish between boy and man, invested in circumcision and represented by the honed blade, is repeatedly interrogated throughout *Maps*. Typically, there is a literal and figurative double edge to the sharpened instrument used for a series of carving purposes through-out the text. The 'ZAK!' that effectively signals the '/' in the binary either/or formations of warring realities is cast into the sort of chaos represented by both Misra and the Ogaden. As the narrative progresses, the reader becomes increasingly aware of the rupturing significance of this event, in both physical and psychical terms. The 'territory of pain and manhood' it causes Askar to inhabit, therefore, is coterminous with the reconfiguration of borders as well as affiliations, personal and political. As a result, it is no coincidence that bouts of psychosomatic capitulation take place when geo-political lines on the map are drawn and redrawn with similar 'ZAK'-like, often bloody force. When Askar is finally implicated in Misra's mysterious death, it stands as the mutilated counterpart to his own, earlier disavowal. Critically, by suggesting her adoptive son become 'purified', Misra performs her role as cultural-political 'passer' a little too well. She thus becomes the interstitial crosser at a formative stage before Askar has reconciled himself with the politics of inverted commas and ethno-political affiliations. His true 'war of sorts' is an inability to call into question the various demands placed on him to define himself in unambiguous ways.

Whilst Askar's circumcision represents a clear severance from Misra, the specificities of his first person narration at this point bring together several of those issues considered above. The reader is once more drawn into his complicit confession, with the narrator admitting strategic acts of deception:

> When asked how I was, I lied. I said I was well and that the pain had more or less confined itself to the *de facto* boundaries of the wound. The truth I didn't tell anyone was that I had, in effect, become two different persons – one belonging to a vague past of which Misra was part … in which I felt so attached to Misra I couldn't imagine life without her. The other person, or if you prefer, the other half, was represented by the pain which inhabited the groin. I held the citizenship of the land of pain, I was issued with its passport and I couldn't envisage when it would expire or what would replace it or where the urge of travel away from it would eventually take me to, nor at what shores they would abandon me. In the territory of pain, there is a certain uncertainty, I thought, of a future outside of it. (*M*: 94)

The phrase 'certain uncertainty' relates to the textual body of *Maps* as well as its wider, deconstructive objectives. The reconstituted 'I' is all encompassing here, as Askar attempts to come to terms with his bifurcated self as well as the expression of all-too-intimate pain. As Scarry suggests, the coincidence of hurt and expression continues to haunt the artistic imagination: '[alarmed] by his or her own failure of language, the person in pain might find it reassuring that even the artist … ordinarily falls silent before pain. The isolated instances in which this is not so, however, provide a much more compelling (because usable) form of reassurance … that can be borrowed when the real-life crisis of silence comes' (Scarry 1985: 10). The quasi-onomatopoeic 'ZAK', therefore, is wince-worthily effective. The imagistic terms in which Askar seeks to render the experience are even more revealing. Alongside the familiar notion that this rupture alters the physical and metaphysical co-ordinates of his relationship with Misra, Askar's triple focus on numbers, travel and documentation is significant in relation to the above discussion. The embodied schism leads to a conceptual reconfiguration in both spatial and temporal terms. As with the rationale he relies on when presented with the identity card, Askar consigns Misra to an antecedent time characterised by corporeal plenitude, with the body effectively taking precedence over the pen. In typically narcissistic fashion, pain is envisaged as a spatial territory that, in this instance, only he can claim. Whilst Askar negotiates this territory, he emerges on the other side only to encounter the alternative pangs and problems of entry into manhood and Kazan's 'third world' of politics.

As in the identity card episode, this central and complex section is distinguished by the presentation of simultaneously instructive and intrusive gifts. Critically, it is Misra who recommends Uncle Qorrax buy Askar a globe and some maps to mark this transition. Once again, this allows Farah to address corporeal, cartographic and conceptual breaks in unison:

> During my brief sojourn in the land of pain, two things occurred: one, I lost myself in it (I wondered, was this why Misra suggested I was given a map of the globe and of the oceans?); two, I took hold of a different 'self', one that had no room and no space for Misra and no longer cared for her. I let go of Misra and, with self-abandon, roamed about in the newly discovered land, thinking not of her, but of pain. It rained a lot and the rain levelled the terrain which wiped out the readable maps, the recognizable landmarks and milestones. (*M*: 96)

There is a playful allusion to strategies of interpretation here. In the certain uncertainty of Askar's meditation, the reader roams in indeterminate zones between dream and reality, Somali and Ethiopian, self and other, unsure whether, in terms of Farah's overarching critique, the obliteration of maps should be read as apocalyptic or liberating. As such, it corresponds with Wright's sense that *Maps*' projected reality might ultimately be 'unmappable' (Wright 1994: 122). Key parallels with the identity-card passage can also be made in relation to the specifically spatial rhetoric employed by Askar. Once more, the narrowing of his conceptual scheme is accompanied by a corporeal counterpart. The result is that the reader penetrates a liminal third space between the personal and the political.

Gaping Open: Textual Cycles and National Bodies in *Maps*

> I make the same demands of people and fictional texts … that they should be open-ended, carrying within them the possibility of changing whoever it is they encounter.
>
> *(Patricia Duncker – Hallucinating Foucault, 1997: 111)*

Whilst Farah's text is preoccupied with mediations and meditations physical and metaphysical, the reader is cautioned against conflating them. With this caveat in mind, a concluding focus on cycles, at both corporeal and textual levels, privileges the kind of transformative space attended to in Foucault's tripartite history of thought. As Askar retrospectively notes, the periodic occurrence of Misra's menstrual cycles caused repeated breaks in their early intimacy (*M*: 50). Whilst Misra becomes almost homicidal during these times, it is a necessary, regulatory cycle through which she passes and re-emerges. In effect, the painful inevitability of menstruation is a consistent bodily process set against the volatility of war. Misra endures a debilitating corporeal cycle that purges her body and, once complete, enables her to perform her myriad roles. Excluded from this physical flow, Askar is caught in a metaphysical paralysis, the result not only of his inability and/or unwillingness to countenance the concentric circles made physically manifest through Misra, but also his failure to rid his body of bad blood: 'was life a poisonous potion which, if taken in the right doses, offers sustenance, but if not kills?' (*M*: 103). Whilst Askar fantasises about the possibility of menstruating to alleviate some of Misra's pain, it is crushed in a manner akin to that of his mythic origins. By indulging in such imagistic play, Farah might open himself up to the kind of accusations selectively levelled against his depiction of rape in *Sardines*. The reader, however, is asked to heed the dream girl's words and look beneath such surfaces.

As Margrit Shildrick maintains in *Leaky Bodies and Boundaries – Feminism, Postmodernism and (Bio)Ethics*:

> In monthly menstruation both the loss of vital blood and the confirmation
> of an internal build-up of noxious waste material further underlined the
> dissipation of women's bodily vigour and their reduced intellectual capacity.
> Moreover, the very sign of fertility, the menses, has been regarded as evidence
> of women's inherent lack of control of the body and, by extension, of the self ...
> women, unlike the self-contained and self-containing men, leaked; or, as Grosz
> claims: 'women's corporeality is inscribed as a mode of seepage.' The issue
> throughout Western cultural history has been one of female lack of closure,
> a negating coding all too evident in one of Sartre's many derogations of the
> gross materiality of the female body: 'the obscenity of the female sex is that
> of everything which "gapes open"'. The indeterminacy of body boundaries
> challenges that most fundamental dichotomy between self and other,
> unsettling ontological certainty and threatening to undermine the basis on
> which the knowing self establishes control. (Shildrick 1997: 34)

Foucault is referred to throughout Shildrick's book, yet she remains as alive to his manifest blind spots as Stoler: 'Like Foucault, I prefer the formulation that everything is dangerous; and particularly so when the microphysics of bio-power coalesce to support quasi-structural systems of domination such as patriarchy – the very thing that Foucault tends to ignore' (Shildrick 1997: 56). Whilst her own sphere of reference is resolutely Eurocentric, Shildrick's notion of leaky female bodies challenging dominant discourses of closure might be re-appropriated to read bodily and textual cycles in *Maps* in a more nuanced way. As Shildrick sees the oppositional potential in Sartre's pejorative notion of 'gaping open', so Farah typically obliges the reader to consider textual ambiguity and open-endedness as enabling rather than inhibiting. The physical process of oozing and seepage that Misra undergoes is amplified at a more conceptual level, throughout the narrative, in relation to identity and ethnicity. Misra-as-Ogaden comes to represent a chaos that confronts and ultimately confounds Askar's longing for conceptual control over the ways both self and other can be defined. In simultaneously physical, metaphysical and psycho-political terms, she embodies a critical lack of closure and a transgressive third space, disrupting the hegemonic binaries Askar invariably tries to impose on his life. Bodies and text, questions and conclusions 'gape open' in *Maps*. It might also be possible, however, to reconfigure

Shildrick's own finale to consider both Farah and Foucault as 'paradoxical postmodernists'.

Whilst borrowing heavily from Foucauldian and postmodern theories, Shildrick remains alive to the pitfalls of uncritically appropriating either:

> The fragmentation most usually associated with postmodernism and feared for its destructive potential is to be celebrated both for its shattering of masculinist certainties, and for the refusal to exclude the complication of fluid boundaries … The strand of postmodernist feminism that insists on the significance of embodiment turns away from the value-resistant and free-floating abstractions of an ultimately irresponsive postmodernism and asserts that it is not all immaterial. (Shildrick 1997: 216)

Such urgent qualifications are prerequisites for those engaged in feminist struggles, inevitably concerned with embattled and embodied politics. Similarly, for Said, in his 1995 Afterword to *Orientalism*, there is a concomitant need to distinguish between the cultural-political projects of postmodernism and postcolonialism:

> Whereas post-modernism in one of its most famous programmatic statements (by Jean-Francois Lyotard) stresses the disappearance of the grand narratives of emancipation and enlightenment, the emphasis behind much of the work done by the first generation of post-colonial artists and scholars is exactly the opposite: the grand narratives remain, even though their implementation and realization are at present in abeyance, deferred, or circumvented. This crucial difference between the urgent historical and political imperatives of post-colonialism and post-modernism's relative detachment makes for altogether different approaches and results, although there is some overlap between them (in the technique of 'magical realism', for example). (Said 2003: 351)

Like Farah, Said concludes with a key parenthetical observation. *Maps* has been variously heralded and hampered by the designation 'postcolonial/ postmodern novel', as well as being esteemed in the magical realist company of Rushdie and García Márquez. Yet its real power comes from the sort of interstitial, contested area identified by both Shildrick and Said.

At significant points throughout *Maps*, Askar tries to appropriate a corporeal process to avoid taking existential and ideological responsibility. As with his psychosomatic capitulation following the Tragic Weekend, Askar's body prevents him from undergoing the purifying cycle Misra experiences.

Locked in the cell of his own narrative by its open-ended conclusion, an alternative transformative cycle appears to present itself in the guise of constant acts of retelling. The bad blood of complicity and guilt resides within, and his attempts to piece together his fractured narrative can be interpreted as a tortuous bid to cleanse himself. As the narrative swirls back on itself, however, it becomes all too apparent that no amount of retelling will either exonerate him completely or wash the blemishes of conscience clean. In the Ngũgĩ sense, therefore, *Maps* certainly poses more questions than it provides answers. For Sugnet, however, this should be interpreted as one of the most enabling aspects of a work that 'calls all into question', at Scarry's geo-political and intimately textual levels. Perhaps more so than any other Farah novel, the choice of epigraphs, from Socrates to Conrad, with their privileging of doubt and scepticism, go beyond intertextual indulgence. Caught between the certain uncertainty of poles that might be labelled 'self-discovery' and 'science', in Foucault's formulation, Askar emerges as a protagonist in the agonistic process of trying to make sense of as well as transform himself through the act of narration. Tensions, fissures and instabilities riddle the version he eventually tells. Yet Farah places the onus on the reader to examine and then re-examine the text's broader concerns (national truth, maps, bodies, ethnic difference) with the same interrogative devotion they direct towards the patent artifice of Askar's account. In the circuitous spirit of *Maps*, therefore, I invite the reader to reassess the opening epigraphs from Scarry and Fanon.

Whilst extending some previous speculations on the respective projects of Farah and Foucault, I have also paid attention to some of the most nuanced readings of the former's seminal work. Sugnet offers a fitting conclusion. He refers to Wright's chapter in *The Novels of Nuruddin Farah*, questioning its desire to fix *Maps* into a prescribed literary category such as 'psychological realism or postmodern experimentalism'. Sugnet offers a critical alternative, employing the sort of third space rhetoric alluded to throughout this chapter:

> Perhaps the choice is not such a stark binary choice between two predetermined, off-the-shelf modes of writing … Farah is certainly formally daring and innovative, but his innovations seem ultimately responsible to the gravity of his situation. *Maps* is certainly a complex book, but what I find most striking about it is how emotionally moving it is to read – so much bodily closeness, so much pain, so much loss, is detailed and *felt* in its prose. (Sugnet 2002: 539)

If Farah's primary concern can be seen to lie with the biopolitics of identity and conflict, such tussles over literary classification are similarly revealing.

If *Maps* simultaneously confounds and captures the reader's imagination for 'gaping open', it remains critical that the subtle relationship between form and content be considered beyond the limits of any disembodied, playfully postmodern critique. For Sugnet, therefore, *Maps'* achievements are inseparable from 'the gravity of [Farah's] situation'.

Seen in this light, it is necessary to emphasise both Farah and Foucault's mutually fraught relationship with postmodern discourses. Wright has defined Farah as a 'paradoxical postmodernist', whilst David Couzens Hoy has described Foucault as 'a consistent postmodern in that he would never have called himself a postmodern' (Hoy 1988: 38). Throughout their respective projects, there remains a commitment to calling into question power, knowledge and discursive constructions. Whilst the answers to such interrogations often remain opaque, both demand their readers focus on the nuances of the political situation as compounded and contested on the ground. Vaughan alludes to Fanon in the conclusion of *Curing Their Ills*, suggesting that such (pre)postmodern debates have historically been and continue to be of more than merely academic interest in relation to Africa:

> There is a sense … in which colonial peoples and marginal groups in metropolitan societies discovered the postmodernist subject long before a postmodernist theory of subjectivity was elaborated in academic and literary circles. The experience of being a fragmented and fluid self was, if Fanon is correct, a common experience of colonial people … For many people in Africa the fluidity of identity and the necessity of constructing new individual and collective identities for political purposes are real and immediate experiences. Nationalism, after all, was and is about just such processes. (Vaughan 1991: 204)

Maps is centrally concerned with such intense, ongoing debates.

From shifting pronouns to contested body politics and the privileging of liminal or, more specifically, deconstructive corporeal spaces, the emphasis incessantly shifts from binaries to tripartite structures in *Maps*. This idea of more than either/or divisions has a peculiar resonance with Farah's own narrative. For Charles Sugnet, there are intriguing parallels with what he terms Samuel Beckett's 'triple deterritorialization' (Sugnet 2002: 530–531). There is even a sense that their shared affinity for trilogies might have certain roots in their own experiences. Similarly, Francesca Kazan points to the cultural, linguistic and spatial dynamics that distinguish both Farah and his work: 'to be a Somali outside Somalia, writing prose rather than poetry, and in English rather than Somali, is to be triply outside. (Perhaps, even, three worlds removed). Small wonder, then, that borders are the issue' (Kazan 2002: 472–473). Yet it is the way these critiques complement rather than consume *Maps* that distinguishes them. Neither Kazan nor Sugnet is concerned with advancing a reductive biographical interpretation of the text, yet both demonstrate how the personal plays an always already political role in Farah's work. These and other enabling readings have provided a basis from which to extend my own Foucauldian interpretation. It is the conceptual torsion between meditations on biopower, state racism and the hermeneutics of the subject that has, with due qualification and caveats, provided an intriguing third space. I pursue this bio-political approach throughout my reading of *Gifts*.

References

Alden, P. & Tremaine, L. 1999. *Nuruddin Farah*. New York: Twayne Publishers.

Barthes, R. 1990. *S/Z*. (R. Miller, Trans.). Oxford: Blackwell.

Coetzee, J.M. 1992. 'Interview'. In D. Attwell (Ed.). *Doubling the Point: Essays and Interviews*. Cambridge, Mass.: Harvard University Press.

Colmer, R. 2002. '"This is a pen": Writing in *Maps*'. In D. Wright (Ed.). *Emerging Perspectives on Nuruddin Farah*. New Jersey: Africa World Press.

Dreyfus, H. & Rabinow, P. 1983. *Michel Foucault: Beyond Structuralism and Hermeneutics*. (2nd ed.). Chicago: The University of Chicago Press.

Duncker, P. 1997. *Hallucinating Foucault*. London: Picador.

Fanon, F. 2001. *The Wretched of the Earth*. (C. Farrington, Trans.). London: Penguin Classics.

Fitzgibbon, L. 1982. *The Betrayal of the Somalis*. London: Rex Collings.

Foucault, M. 1990. *The History of Sexuality, An Introduction*. (R. Hurley, Trans.). London: Penguin.

Foucault, M. 2003. *'Society Must Be Defended' – Lectures at the Collège de France 1975–1976*. In Bertani, M. & Fontana, A. (eds). (D. Macey, Trans.). New York: Picador.

Gikandi, S. 2002. 'The Politics and Poetics of National Formation: Recent African Writing and *Maps*'. In D. Wright (Ed.). *Emerging Perspectives on Nuruddin Farah*. New Jersey: Africa World Press.

Gourevitch, P. 2000. *We Wish to Inform You that Tomorrow We will be Killed with Our Families – Stories from Rwanda*. London: Picador.

Hoy, D.C. 1988. 'Foucault: Modern or Postmodern?' In J. Arac (Ed.). *After Foucault – Humanistic Knowledge, Postmodern Challenges*. New Brunswick: Rutgers University Press.

Jones, C. & Porter, R. 1994. 'Introduction'. In C. Jones & R. Porter (Eds). *Reassessing Foucault – Power, Medicine and the Body*. London: Routledge.

Kazan, F. 2002. 'Recalling the Other Third World: Nuruddin Farah's *Maps*'. In D. Wright (Ed.). *Emerging Perspectives on Nuruddin Farah*. New Jersey: Africa World Press.

Lewis, I.M. 2002. *A Modern History of the Somali*. (4th ed.). Oxford: James Currey.

Loxley (Eds). *The Politics of Theory, Proceedings of the Essex Sociology of Literature Conference*. Colchester: University of Essex.

Mbembe, A. 2001. *On the Postcolony*. Berkeley: University of California Press.

Moss, J. 1998. 'Introduction'. In J. Moss (Ed.). *The Later Foucault – Politics and Philosophy*. London: Sage Publications.

Ngaboh-Smart, F. 2001. 'Nationalism and the Aporia of National Identity in Farah's *Maps*'. *Research in African Literatures*, Vol. 32, No. 3.

O'Farrell, C. 2005. *Michel Foucault*. London: Sage Publications.

Porter, D. 1983. '*Orientalism* and its problems'. In F. Barker, P. Hulme, M. Iversen & D. Loxley.

Ruggiero, R. 2002. '*Maps*: The Faint Borderland of a Warrior of Words'. In D. Wright (Ed.). *Emerging Perspectives on Nuruddin Farah*. New Jersey: Africa World Press.

Said, E.W. 2003. *Orientalism*. London: Penguin.

Samater, I.M. 1997. 'Light At the End of the Tunnel: Some Reflections on the Struggle of the Somali National Movement'. In H.M. Adam & R. Ford (Eds). *Mending Rips in the Sky: Options for Somali Communities in the 21st Century*. New Jersey: The Red Sea Press Inc.

Scarry, E. 1985. *The Body in Pain – The Making and Unmaking of the World*. New York and Oxford: Oxford University Press.

Shildrick, M. 1997. *Leaky Bodies and Boundaries – Feminism, Postmodernism and (Bio) Ethics*. London: Routledge.

Sugnet, C. 2002. 'Farah's *Maps*: Deterritorialization and the Postmodern'. In D. Wright (Ed.). *Emerging Perspectives on Nuruddin Farah*. New Jersey: Africa World Press.

Vaughan, M. 1991. *Curing Their Ills – Colonial Power and African Illness*. Cambridge: Polity Press.

Wright, D. 1994. *The Novels of Nuruddin Farah*. Bayreuth: Bayreuth African Studies Series.

Endnotes

1   See *Somalia: A Government at War With Its Own People: Testimonies About the Killings and the Conflict in the North*. 1990. New York: Africa Watch Committee, pp. 27–29.

6

'A Call to Alms'[1]: *Gifts* and the Possibilities of a Foucauldian Reading

[The global doctor] is too busy feeding rice to hungry mouths to listen to what these mouths are saying. Words do not concern him. He turns his attention to murdered populations, not to eloquent voices, to the transparent language of complaint, not the opaque tongues of individual nations. The bodies he cares for are disembodied.

(Michael Barnett and Thomas Weiss – Humanitarianism in Question: Politics, Power and Ethnics, 2008: 45–46)

[Somalia] was one of the most generously aided in the world but the donors were having a negligible impact on either the policies of the regime or the capacities of the country. Supply-driven aid carried donors' trademarks and the landscape was littered with some of the starkest relics of aid failure: broken tractors, silted pumps, fuel-less turbines, vacant schools, darkened hospitals, and crumbling new roads to nowhere. Typical of 'capacity-building' was a large bilateral programme at the National University of Somalia, worth more than the total national education budget. The main beneficiaries were the expatriate professors from the donor country who enjoyed lucrative six monthly tours of duty in the capital.

Somalia began to implode in the late 80s ...

(Stephen Browne – 'Aid to Fragile States: Do Donors Help or Hinder?', 2010: 165)

WHEN VIEWED IN RELATION TO FARAH'S FICTION AS A WHOLE, *GIFTS* IS something of an anomaly. Set against the backdrop of the kind of post-Ogaden-War misery depicted by Stephen Browne, it interweaves reflections on everything from the apocalyptic realities of famine in the Horn of Africa to the complicity of international aid agencies and global donors. If this provides the foundation for later novels, where new worlds of disorder are explored in all their macabre complexity, it is the love story element, unconventional as it is, that sets *Gifts* apart. More than a simple leavening of the text, I argue that Farah's decision to foreground Duniya and Bosaaso's burgeoning relationship, seen in conjunction with their all-too-brief adoption of an unnamed foundling child, has more interrogative significance. In this chapter, I explore how and why a dialectical relationship exists between narrative reflections on both the complicities and complexities of global aid, with Somalia as a compelling case study, and the equally complex unfolding of *Gifts'* central romance. The opening epigraph, therefore, serves as a provocative catalyst.

Finkielkraut's concern with the ways in which the individual voices and stories of 'victims' are often drowned out by the reductive rhetoric of both media outlets and aid agencies resonates with one of Farah's most crucial and defamiliarising motivations here and throughout his later fiction. Why, *Gifts* challenges us, does it take such an imaginative leap of faith to envisage love stories taking place against, and thus serving as profound counterpoints to, those of conflict and famine? Building on this, I argue that, to a significant extent, the novel returns the reader again and again to those corporeal preoccupations that have informed Farah's vision since *From a Crooked Rib*. What are the political implications, *Gifts* seems to ask, of reducing the human body to one that is denied agency, one that is always inscribed with pain rather than pregnant with desire? In what follows, I once again make the case for a dialectical appreciation of the relationship between body politics, on a micrological level that accounts for both the emaciated and the erotic, and the body politic, in terms of Farah's enduring fascination with diagnosing certain Somali ailments. Of supplementary interest is the way he frames this diagnosis in relation to a global anatomy of power. By turning his attention to the always compelling issues of international aid, development and the complexities of gift-giving, both individual and collective, Farah's longstanding preoccupations with the channels and networks through which power flows, is used and often abused, are galvanised anew throughout *Gifts*.

As this talk of power suggests, Foucault continues to cast a lengthy shadow over this analysis. For my purposes, there are three key areas of interest.

The first considers how and why Foucauldian thought has been put to use by scholars concerned with the trajectories of development studies, particularly in relation to those issues of humanitarian intervention and aid around which *Gifts* is built. If Elaine Scarry's *The Body in Pain* was a key intertext for the reading of *Maps*, Arturo Escobar's *Encountering Development* is similarly central here. Just as the full title of Scarry's text is *The Body in Pain: The Making and Unmaking of the World*, so Escobar's is *Encountering Development: The Making and Unmaking of the Third World*. As this suggests, both are concerned with intertwined processes of construction, deconstruction and reconstruction. In their own ways, and with their own aims in mind, Scarry and Escobar both maintain that if the world can be made through discourse and design, it can also be unmade and remade anew. As the reader navigates through *Gifts*, the significance of this idea only intensifies, on both micrological and macrological levels. Alongside this, however, is the importance that Escobar, amongst others, places on Foucauldian interventions. As I demonstrate, it is once again Foucault's insistence on a more nuanced analytics as well as a relational conception of power that has most appeal. This is yet another example of the ways in which his thought and legacy have been put to use by those interested in the possibilities that arise once his work has been translated and transposed. For the purposes of this study, therefore, Escobar's Foucault-inflected approach offers an enabling framework within which to explore *Gifts*. I maintain that Farah's foregrounding of certain Somali voices shows his enduring commitment to exploring the ambivalences, interstices and negotiations of power in terms of the home, the nation and the global body politic.

The second Foucauldian preoccupation that informs my reading is discourse. *Gifts* can be seen as a natural successor to *Maps* as it is concerned with the processes of, and potential barriers to, storytelling. It also ends in a circuitous manner, bidding the reader, like protagonist Duniya, to return to the narrative's beginning. Whilst this can be seen in terms of Foucault's more identifiably literary concerns, including those of authorship and authority, I am more interested in the entangled relationship between this, at the textual level, and those broader discursive strategies used to frame 'the third world', 'humanitarian intervention' and 'famine in Africa'. As Escobar reminds us,

> ... terms – such as overpopulation, the permanent threat of famine, poverty, illiteracy, and the like – operate as the most common signifiers, already stereotyped and burdened with development signifiers. Media images of the Third World are the clearest example of developmentalist representations. These

> images just do not seem to go away. This is why it is necessary to examine development in relation to the modern experiences of knowing, seeing, counting, economizing, and the like. (Escobar 1995: 12)

Building on this, I explore the extent to which *Gifts'* concern with dominant discourses, particularly those of the media, invites its readers to reconsider the very processes of (in)visibility and normalisation, as well as their relationship with power, foregrounded by Escobar. It is significant, for instance, that *Gifts* does not feature the intertextual borrowings of other Farah novels. Rather, most usually at the end of chapters, there are simulations of Reuters-style reports, international dispatches and/or policy frameworks. They entice the reader into a contrapuntal reading. We are asked to place them alongside the on-the-ground, in-the-flesh immediacy of *Gifts'* other narrative preoccupations, most prominently that of Duniya, and her various familial and extra-familial relationships. I argue that Farah is principally concerned with the kind of discursive tropes that pepper international development agendas and news reports alike. For many commentators, Foucault's speculations have allowed them to uncover the compelling, invariably complex connections between the reliance on certain rhetorical mainstays (setting out what can and cannot be said about famine-afflicted Somalia, for instance) and modalities of power.

The third and final Foucauldian concern is bio-politics. If *Gifts* addresses the same question ('who has the right to live and who must be made to die') as *Maps*, I explore how and why the bio-political coordinates have shifted between the two texts. Whilst conflict still rages in Farah's fictive landscape, it is the aftermath of various violent disorders, most notably famine, that dominates *Gifts*. As Peter Redfield, drawing from *'Society Must be Defended'*, maintains in his contribution to *Humanitarianism in Question*, 'the exercise of productive forms of power fostering life implies the inverse possibility of withholding care, of "indirect killing" through expulsion or rejection. The absence of a government clinic or international neglect can therefore represent a violation of political responsibility. In this sense, the humanitarian worldview is thoroughly biopolitical, even in its oppositional form' (Redfield 2008: 201). By drawing on such interventions, I consider the ways in which Foucault's speculations on biopower and sovereignty have been transposed to probe newly globalised (dis)orders. As *Gifts* suggests, decisions about the right to live and the necessity of dying are often made far from the spaces where their consequences, for good or ill, are realised. Whilst published some twenty years ago, Farah's novel still makes for haunting reading today. The

Horn of Africa, and Somalia in particular, continues to experience the ravaging effects of drought-induced famine. It is with a renewed sense of urgency, therefore, that we revisit many of the novel's reflections and precarious hopes for the future.

The (In)Visibility of Giving

To give a sense of *Gifts'* circuitous form and content, I begin at its close. By this stage, readers have been exposed to a thoroughly ambivalent portrait of gifts and gift-giving, whether it is the exchange of presents among family members, oftentimes for self-serving ends, or in relation to those transnational, sometimes equally nepotistic networks relied upon by donors and non-governmental organisations. For a novel that probes the ethical or otherwise motivation for gift-giving, large and small, its concluding lines are appropriately ambiguous. On the narrative surface, *Gifts* ends with a union (between Bosaaso and Duniya), symbolising comparative hope for the future. This provides a striking counterpoint to many other Farah novels, which invariably sign off on notes of dissolution, despair or departure. When considered in relation to the *Blood in the Sun* cycle, *Gifts* closes with a suitably metatextual flourish, aimed at foregrounding the complexities of beginning, concluding and piecing narratives together. Once again, therefore, it is somewhat disingenuous to talk of Farah drawing any of his novels to a close. For a work so centrally concerned with cycles of dependency as well as relationships characterised by complex, often unseen interconnections and interests, it is entirely appropriate that *Gifts* ends by inviting the reader to return to its opening. Similarly, in light of the novel's enduring preoccupations with female agency and autonomy, the contested sovereignty of women's bodies and the peculiarly gendered inscription of pain, it is vital that Duniya's role as narrative producer is privileged throughout its final pages:

> Duniya, the chronicler, is no longer certain how to go on, and nothing short of a much longer pause will enable her to look back on the events as they took place in order for her to describe them accurately.
>
> At one point Nasiiba said to someone, 'Don't all stories end in marriage or the dissolution of such a union?'
>
> Abshir was chain-smoking while speaking; among other things, he was saying that all stories are one story, whose principle theme is love. And if the stories feel different, it is only because the journeys the characters are to

> undertake take different routes to get to their final destination ... 'All stories,' concluded Abshir, 'celebrate, in elegiac terms, the untapped sources of energy, of the humanness of women and men.' Then Duniya smelt Bosaaso's odour, because he had come round to where she was sitting, and they were kissing while the others toasted them again and again. The world was an audience, ready to be given Duniya's story from the beginning. (*G*: 246)

For all its clunkiness, Nasiiba and Abshir's dialogue features several of the novel's distinctive elements. Whilst Farah's presentation of narrative time is nothing like as playful and/or disorientating as it is in *Maps*, his decision to mix present and past tenses here is revealing. Lines separating then and now are definitively blurred to jolt the reader from their interpretative comfort zone. That this is bound up with questions of the often arduous, invariably unstable business of building and telling stories only intensifies with intertwined references to distance and perspective. Duniya's narratological uncertainty results from the tumultuous events that surround and, to a certain extent, define her. As she attempts to make sense of a period marked by the joy of her brother's arrival and the prospect of future happiness with Bosaaso, alongside the trauma of the foundling's recent death set against the imploding nation beyond, the disorder of the present leaves her craving some breathing space. Only once this has been granted will she be able to impose a certain order on, and thus gain a greater understanding of, these various narrative entanglements.

It is also significant that Duniya does not speak. Her communication, such as it is, comes through the intimacy she shares with Bosaaso. For a novel that has been preoccupied, at strategic points, with the corporeal impress of often agonising pain, the decision to end with a gesture of love and a potentially regenerative union for both parties is key. Of arguably greater significance, however, is the notion that Duniya's narrative is a gift to be given by her, and her alone, to a now receptive audience. The final sentence, therefore, turns on this notion of 'readiness'. For Duniya's tentative telling to have any impact, her desire to tell must be matched by the willingness of others to listen. As such, it serves as a variation on those donor/recipient negotiations so central to *Gifts*. This becomes clearer when taking the novel's broader political concerns into consideration. It is precisely the sense that most recipients of gifts are not fully aware of the terms on which they are accepting these 'donations' and the motivations or agendas behind them that underpins *Gifts*. This is applicable to both Duniya and Bosaaso in their role as surrogate parents as well as famine victims whose plight is eased by humanitarian intervention and aid. This can be seen by considering the role played by certain motifs throughout the novel. As above, a critical example is the circle/cycle. If the narrative itself operates in a circular fashion, it also has symbolic resonance with concerns expressed by individual characters about the situations they find themselves in as well as their thoughts on the (dis)order of things within Somalia more generally. In essence, they are variations on the theme of cycles of dependency.

Farah's decision to place a single-mother protagonist at the centre of a text probing issues of power and indebtedness is significant on a number of levels. He once more zooms in on the individual, micronarrative in order to probe those sociological and economic discourses that inform *Gifts* as a whole. That he does so in the guise of Duniya, suspicious as she is of the whole business of 'no-strings-attached' giving, only intensifies subsequent, much broader meditations on donors and donations. If the text's concluding image suggests a loving union, ultimately symbolised by the ring, its opening one is a chain that threatens to compromise autonomy: '[w]as this some sort of male trap that would be impossible to undo at a later date, like links of an invisible chain?' (*G*: 7). Whilst the reference is to a seemingly innocuous car ride and cinema invitation from Bosaaso, it immediately suggests a female protagonist who has been wounded by previous encounters with overbearing, invariably patriarchal power. As the narrative unfolds, the nature and extent of this damage becomes clear. Justification for an interpretative approach that transposes these early images of traps and chains from the Duniya/Bosaaso context to that of international aid comes by heeding the structural peculiarities of several of *Gifts*' chapters. The first, for instance, ends with an imagined news report warning of 'impending disaster and famine in Somalia unless immediate action is taken to terminate the breeding cycle of the desert locust' (*G*: 9). Having quoted figures relating to the required aid budget, Farah challenges his reader to speculate on potentially provocative linkages between 'love' and 'aid' stories in *Gifts*. As such, the most suggestive term associated with the chain image is 'invisible'. One of the reader's many tasks is to bring a series of implied links into a field of greater visibility, considering how and why Duniya's anxiety about entering into another relationship, defined, as it threatens to be, by various cycles of dependence, overlaps with the text's pressing concerns with international aid and debt relief. In the spirit of what Jonathan Glennie has called 'aid realism', numerous commentators working on and/or in these fields have analysed how and why it is often in the strategic interests of donors, particularly those reliant upon big business, to conceal the true motivations behind their 'altruistic' acts (Glennie 2008: 7). Farah's reliance upon a series of loaded motifs, therefore, works alongside this fascination with the politics of (in)visibility.

One way of mapping both the thematic similarities and arguably even more significant differences between the *Variations* and *Blood in the Sun* cycles is to consider the alternative deployments of labyrinthine metaphors. It is no coincidence that a certain symbolic unity defines *Gifts'* opening chapters. By confronting the reader with multiple images of interlocking circles (as in the chain), alongside other spatial tropes used to represent frustrated journeys and the refusal of easy exits, Farah reconfigures some of the strategies he employed throughout *Variations*. The following details another fractious exchange between Bosaaso and Duniya early on. Again, the bone of contention is the offering of a lift. In this instance, however, it falls to the central protagonist to make connections, between the seemingly innocuous and the much more important, all too visible:

> 'Why do you accept lifts from me?' [Bosaaso] asked.
>
> 'That's a foolish question, since your giving precedes my acceptance or rejection. My accepting your gift of a lift is itself a reciprocal gift. So may I now ask why you accept my gift?'
>
> 'Why are you hesitant about receiving gifts from others?'
>
> 'Because unasked-for generosity has a way of making one feel obliged, trapped in a labyrinth of dependence. You're more knowledgeable about these matters, but haven't we in the Third World lost our self-reliance and pride because of the so-called aid we unquestioningly receive from the so-called First World?' (G: 22)

If the presentation and prose are a little leaden, the exchange once more invites the reader to speculate on those links gestured towards above. For example, whilst familiar preoccupations with entrapment are foregrounded, it is done with a twist. Here, entrapment has shifted from the private to the public, from the intimately personal to the intensely political. It is only when the central question of (in)visibility is addressed, however, that these and other such reflections can be seen in terms of debates within development, post-development and humanitarian studies.

As previously discussed, the maddening beauty of the labyrinth is that there is a way out. At its centre, of course, that visibility is obscured. Were you able, like a prison warder looking down at his charges, to take an aerial view of the maze before entering it, you could imagine an exit strategy. This, however, would defeat its whole playful purpose. In essence, similarities and shifts between Farah's first and second trilogies come into clearer focus by considering the relationship between portraits of a sovereign, carceral society in *Variations* and *Blood in the Sun*. In the later series, we are given a suggestive picture of a much more transnational order of things. It is still, however, one that, to a significant extent, is administered according to certain carceral principles and systems. In *Gifts*, Farah sketches a narrative backdrop against which multinational firms, Western donors and UN-sanctioned programs wield substantial, if still largely invisible power. The suggestion is that the panopticon has spilled beyond the boundaries of nation-states. Surveillance, whether in the form of statistical data collection, the rules governing debt repayment or the formulation of various league tables monitoring global performance, is internationalised. This line of inquiry is central to the work of Morgan Brigg, amongst many others. In an article entitled 'Post-Development, Foucault and the Colonisation Metaphor', Brigg shows how some key Foucauldian ideas inform one of the most pressing concerns of our globalised present:

> The [World] Bank renders Third World nation-states visible through processes of surveillance, evaluation and judgement carried out by personnel and consultants during Bank missions and consultancies ... These are exercises in examination which mobilise the relations of power and knowledge of developmentalist social science to observe hierarchically and judge against the developmentalist norm embodied by the Bank. (Brigg 2002: 432)

I find Brigg's foregrounding of the relationship between power (in this case the 'surveillance' of the IMF and other bodies), visibility, discourse and normalisation most enabling when it comes to *Gifts*. Remove the capacity to measure, assess and rank, and the bases upon which development principles, policies and practices are founded begin to crumble. As such, Farah's reliance on the labyrinth motif invites his reader to confront some of those questions that have haunted Brigg and Escobar, amongst many others. They include the following: Who has designed the maze of international aid? For what purposes? Who needs an exit strategy? Where is it to be found and how long will it take to achieve? Before suggesting how answers to these questions can lead to a more substantial engagement with the Foucauldian work represented by *Encountering Development* and its associated critiques, I consider Farah's suggestive deployment of another motif.

The end of Chapter 3 features a spoof Reuters report:

> Millions of people in the developing world have starved to death as a result of the policies of Western creditor nations, a United Nations Development Programme spokesman said. In a gloomy annual assessment, the spokesman argued that the finely woven economic tapestry could be unravelled at any time, causing calamitous suffering in the Third World. It was unfair, he added, that poor countries have been made to depend totally on what happens not in their own economies but in those of richer, more economically developed countries, whose debts they are unable to service, let alone repay. (G: 33)

If such sections appear a little heavy handed, reducing international aid to yet another branch of abusive, globalising power, it is arguably Farah's use of the 'finely woven economic tapestry' image that is most suggestive for my Foucauldian purposes. As such, overlaps with the 'invisible chain' metaphor discussed above are key. Lose one link and the chain is broken. Pull at a loose thread in the tapestry and the whole thing threatens to come apart at the seams. In terms of framing discussions of international aid and humanitarian intervention alongside discourses of power, the underlying questions concern the identity of those weaving the tapestry and their motivations for doing so. If many of Farah's novels are preoccupied with the complex, often violent unravelling of Somalia's national narrative, he places much greater emphasis on its transnational fallout from *Blood in the Sun* onwards. The darker, post-9/11 reality of what Christine Sylvester calls 'a globalised, mutually implicating and interrogating postcolonial time' means that ruptures in one geo-political sphere, be it economic turbulence or regime change, will inevitably ripple across borders (Sylvester 1999: 711). If too tightly wound an attachment to the strings of dependency threatens to strangle developing countries, so the argument goes, it may not be long before the global oxygen supply is at risk.

Foucault and the Tapestry of Aid

With a little imagination, the tapestry motif provides another opportunity to consider how and why Foucault's legacy has influenced debates within and beyond development and post-development studies, particularly in terms of reciprocal relations between discourse and power. In doing so, it calls upon us to think more carefully about the manner in which certain archetypal images of the Third World have been woven into the fabric of everyday perception. Whilst, as Susan Moeller points out in *Compassion Fatigue: How the Media Sell Disease, Famine, War, and Death*, this is nothing new, it is the processes by which these tropes become normalised, in turn impacting policy and related decisions, that are most intriguing. This enables a return to *Encountering Development* to consider how it provides an interpretative frame for *Gifts*. In his introduction, Escobar states that, 'this book can be read as the history of the loss of an illusion, in which many believed. Above all, however, it is about how the "Third World" has been produced by discourses and practices of development since their inception in the early post-World War II period' (Escobar 1995: 4). This resonates with *Gifts'* prominent concern with the constructedness of various narratives, in terms of which stories are allowed to be told, by whom and how. It also relates to Farah's fascination with the ways international aid and other organisations rely on certain discursive formations, drawing from a repository of Third World tropes, with a view to projecting them onto, rather than taking account of, invariably more complex realities. In acknowledging his debt to Foucault, Escobar refers to a number of the writers and thinkers discussed above:

> Foucault's work on the dynamics of discourse and power in the representation of social reality, in particular, has been instrumental in unveiling the mechanisms by which a certain order of discourse produces permissible modes of being and thinking while disqualifying and even making others impossible. Extensions of Foucault's insights to colonial and postcolonial situations by authors such as Edward Said, V.Y. Mudimbe, Chandra Mohanty, and Homi Bhabha, among others, have opened up new ways of thinking about representations of the third world. Anthropology's self-critique and renewal during the 1980s have also been important in this regard. (Escobar 1995: 5)

Alongside its concerns with labyrinths of dependence, in which nations like Somalia often find themselves disorientated by development packages and emergency aid relief following drought and famine, *Gifts* also turns on one of the central axes of Farah's oeuvre. This concerns the ways in which, from a colonial era, through a postcolonial one and into its necolonial variant, certain representations of Somali social reality have been deemed permissible, whilst others have been disqualified. As I have argued throughout this study, the counter-hegemonic current that bubbles beneath the surface of all Farah novels compels him to at once foreground and thus explore some of the systems of power upon which these representations rely. In turn, he offers alternative narratives in order to challenge their more reductive bases and biases. This once more works in relation to the tapestry motif. If certain fabrications can be brought into being, they can also be unstitched and restitched anew. Typically, *Gifts* stages a series of dialogues, between characters as well as in the form of newspaper opinion pieces, to foreground these pressing issues. Whilst they are by turns provocative and instructive, they also enable Farah to locate discussions about the peculiarity of Somalia's experience of famine in relation to an expanded genealogy. This allows him to gesture towards some of the key issues, regarding the post-World War Two institutionalisation of the concept of poverty as well as that of international development, so central to Escobar:

> ... poverty became an organizing concept and the object of a new problematization. As in the case of any problematization ... that of poverty brought into existence new discourses and practices that shaped the reality to which they referred. That the essential trait of the Third World was its poverty and that the solution was economic growth and development became self-evident, necessary, and universal truths ... [this] accounts for the 'developmentalization' of the Third World, its progressive insertion into a regime of thought and practice in which certain interventions for the eradication of poverty became central to the world order. (Escobar 1995: 24)

For my purposes, such interventions are appealing as they draw attention to and thus expose a series of more compelling, often cyclical relationships, both conceptual and practical. The essential point is that it is not sufficient to talk about the identification of a problem (in this case, poverty), the creation of an associated discourse and the formulation of a series of policies to reduce, if not eradicate it. As Escobar illustrates, a Foucauldian approach compels us to conceive of a much more dynamic, mutually constitutive relationship between discourse, conceptualisation and practice. What is said, represented and thought about 'poverty' cannot be divorced from our understanding of it. When viewed through this lens, the motivations behind Farah's decision to use significant sections of *Gifts* to pass comment on and/or pose questions regarding the mediatisation of Somalia in relation to broader Third World discourses are as clear as they are urgent. Whilst references to the eviscerating effects of famine punctuate the reading experience, it is the economical way they are used that ensures their impact. Take the following, for example: '[o]ne saw skinny cows whose bones stuck out so visibly that crows, mistaking these for dry eucalyptus twigs, alighted on them' (*G*: 57). Dystopian as this freeze frame is, the more pressing concern in *Gifts* runs parallel to that of Escobar's study: the production, consumption and persistence of these tropes and the degree to which they prop up rather than problematise certain ways of 'imagining' the world. I refer back to this critical intervention in the section that follows, which foregrounds dialectical relationships between individual body politics and the wider body politic throughout the novel. Prior to this, I consider a substantial section from *Gifts*, using it to explore the links between hegemonic representations of social reality and the use and abuse of international networks of power.

As has been the case at strategic points throughout the novel, Farah privileges Taariq's robust critique. In an article entitled 'Giving and Receiving: The Notion of Donations', he stages a provocative juxtaposition between the media exposure given to an international athletics event, presumably the Olympics, and that of escalating famine in the Horn of Africa. Whilst such a contrast might seem a little overdetermined at first, the reader is invited to probe the figurative significance of those competitive, survival-of-the-fittest principles that pertain in both contexts:

> Last week, while the non-starving people of the world ran, taking part in the self-perpetuating media exercises of TV performances, Africa waited in the wings, out of the camera's reach, with an empty bowl in hand, seeking alms, hoping that generous donations would come from the governments and peoples of the runners. Empty brass bowls make excellent photographs. Video cameras take shots of them, from every imaginable angle. To starve is to be of media interest these days. Forgive my cynicism, but I believe this to be the truth. (G: 195)

If this section resonates with much of the most provocative work that has been done in relation to the mediatisation and/or selling of death, disaster and disorder, it also plays with those discursive tropes of stasis and movement that have embedded themselves from the colonial era to the present. The argument seems to go that, then as now, individually and collectively, nothing moves, nothing progresses, nothing changes for those included in the nebulous construction 'Africa'. The seemingly unending stream of images that accompany reports of drought and famine reiterate the hegemonic message: these are bodies to which things are done, to which donations are given rather than bodies that do and give. Through Taariq's piece, however, I argue that Farah makes a suitably ambivalent intervention into these complex debates. They chime with some of the subtler, arguably Foucauldian undertones found in much post-development scholarship.

As explored above, it is precisely Foucault's challenge to the idea that power is monolithic, flowing in a unilateral way, that has appealed to succeeding generations of writers and thinkers. This is something usefully foregounded by Brigg. Taking issue with what he considers to be some of Escobar's more reductive conclusions, he argues that:

> Foucault's productive and relational understanding of the operation of power, framed through the notions of *dispositif* and normalisation, strengthens the analytical and critical purchase we can bring to bear on development ... The reliance on the colonial metaphor and a sovereign conceptualisation of power leads some post-development writers to overly aggregate the operation of power, to ascribe intentionality to a singular historical force such as 'the Americans', and to take an untenable oppositional stance. The engagement with Foucault shows that the generation of overall effects through development need not be reduced to such simplistic terms. (Brigg 2002: 433)

These and associated issues inform my approach to Taariq's lengthy reflections in *Gifts*. Whilst he appears to state his case with Escobar-esque conviction (declaring international aid to be an extension of U.S. neo-imperialism), Farah does not allow him to re-entrench the archetype of the Third World as passive victim:

> We give in order to feel superior to those whose receiving hands are placed below ours. We give to corrupt. We give to dominate. There are a million reasons why we give, but here I am concerned with only one: European and North American and Japanese governments' donations of food aid to the starving in Africa, and why these are received. (G: 194)

If the critique is unequivocal, a supplementary reading takes into account the role played by the collective pronoun as well as the connecting 'and'. The strategic, deliberately burdened use of 'we' immediately problematises the binary opposition between 'them' (power-hungry Americans, masking their true motivations) and 'us' (innocent Africans in need of outside intervention owing to an historically determined inability to fend for themselves). When considered alongside the bridging 'and', Farah's implication is even more suggestive. It is not sufficient to analyse the processes by which giving takes place and/or the motivations behind them. It is just as important, if not more so, that the reasons behind the acceptance or otherwise of certain gifts, complex as they often are, also be examined. It is significant, therefore, that Taariq's meditation comes towards the close of the novel, premised as it is on the notion that gift-giving is contingent and circumstantial. That the reader is invited to reflect on this in terms of the dialectical relationship between the micro and the macro in *Gifts* is purposive and effective. The gifts of love, life and instruction, for example, are given with little or no expectation of recompense. The act of imparting knowledge about how to drive or swim, crucial aspects of the text to which I return below, is not without a certain reciprocal benefit, however. Particularly when taking gender and power inequities into account, such gifts confer rather than compromise autonomy. As such, their value only increases. Alongside this, however, the narrative is equally concerned with the potential of gifts, invariably material, to corrupt and dominate. As illustrated throughout, the benefits of gift-giving, reciprocal or otherwise, are often compromised when certain conditions are attached.

Key elements of Taariq's frequently fervent critique reflect his awareness of the dialectical need, as discussed in the previous chapter, to turn the critical eye inwards. In essence, he demonstrates a quasi-Foucauldian sensitivity to providing a more nuanced analytics of power based on mutually implicating relationships and a reality that is often defined through complicity. Brigg is once more useful in this regard, foregrounding a relational notion of power in the context of development discourse. As I have argued throughout, greater sensitivity to this model can provide an enabling prism through which to view Farah's work, from *Sweet and Sour Milk*, through *Yesterday, Tomorrow* and beyond:

> the oppositional and negative conceptualisation of power fails us. Viewing power solely as imposition leaves us, as Foucault states, with 'the insubstantiality of the notion of the master, an empty form haunted only by the various phantoms of the master and his slave, the master and his disciple' (Foucault, 1980: 139). (Brigg 2002: 425)

Writing in an imagined Somali newspaper, for a predominantly Somali audience, Taariq's article anchors a critique of the forces of globalising hegemony by privileging the 'we' and all it implies. Accordingly, it can be read as a variation on those politics of collective pronouns that haunt Farah's fictional scapes. By grounding his reflections at this local level, Taariq simultaneously makes links between certain domestic and international agents more visible. This also enables him to probe the complex, at times disconnected, at others mutually implicating relationship between a bureaucratic elite and the masses:

> In Somalia, there are people who bear the names of the years of the drought. People adjusted the holes in their belts, but they did not beg ... Those who had the people's mandate to rule were united in their belief that he begs who has no self-pride, and he works responsibly who intends to be respected. But we know that a great many of the men at the helm of the continent's power do not have the people's mandate to be there in the first place, and have no self-pride or foresight ... Are we therefore up against the proverbial wisdom that people get the government they deserve, and we deserve beggars to be our leaders? (G: 195–196)

The soul-searching power of this critique once again derives from the use of the collective pronouns 'we' and 'our'. A sense of personal dignity and/or stoicism in the face of the most desperate circumstances is contrasted with a political class that has effectively reneged on the social contract binding rulers and ruled. As such, it is reminiscent of Fanon's critique in *The Wretched of the Earth*. In it, he attacks those intermediaries who, through obfuscation, bewilder the people:

> The economic channels of the young state sink back inevitably into neo-colonialist lines ... The budget is balanced through loans and gifts ... The former colonial power increases its demands, accumulates concessions and guarantees and takes fewer and fewer pains to mask the hold it has over the national government. The people stagnate deplorably in unbearable poverty; slowly they awaken to the unutterable treason of their leaders ... The new caste is an affront all the more disgusting in that the immense majority, nine-tenths of the population, continue to die of starvation ... [The leader] acts as a braking-power on the awakening consciousness of the people. He comes to the aid of the bourgeois caste and hides his manoeuvres from the people, thus becoming the most eager worker in the task of mystifying and bewildering the masses. (Fanon 2001: 134–135)

If this captures the mutually implicating nature of international development and aid relief, the prominence given by Farah to the Fanonian idea of a buffer zone adds piquancy to a critique designed to probe the links between certain aid packages and a more pervasive, neo-colonial order of things. Once more, Taariq's piece is used to defamiliarise and provoke: '[f]amines awake a people from an economic, social or political lethargy. We've seen how the Ethiopian people rid themselves of their Emperor for forty years. Foreign food donations create a buffer zone between corrupt leaderships and starving masses' (*G*: 196). Here, the collective trauma of famine is imagined as a catalyst to dislodge corrupt and corrupting power. This section, therefore, is distinguished by the dual energies, Foucauldian and Fanonian, running through it. Taariq's assertion that external intervention, in this case food donations, can retard systemic change is fairly conventional, particularly given those disclosures that have revealed discomfiting connections between Western donors/governments and tyrannical regimes, whether in the form of arms trading, foreign assets or international terrorism. If this covers the Fanonian side of things, it is in the following, incendiary reflection that Taariq traces the most damning continuities between the nepotistic incompetence of national regimes, the terms dictating the reservicing of international debt payments and the strategic interests of global hegemony. Given the pressing context out of which he writes, Taariq again concentrates his critique through the prism of famine:

> [It] follows that when the bread-winner's earnings do not meet everyone's needs; when the land isn't yielding, because insufficient work is being put in to cultivate it; when hard-currency earning cash crops are grown and the returns are paid to service debt; and just when the whole country is preparing to rise in revolt against the neo-colonial corrupt leadership: a ship loaded with charity rice, unasked for, perhaps, docks in the harbour – good quality rice, grown by someone else's muscles and sweat. You know the result. Famine (my apologies to Bertolt Brecht) is a trick up the powerful man's sleeve; it has nothing to do with seasonal cycles or shortages of rain. (*G*: 198)

If, for successive generations of Western readers, their social consciences piqued by Live Aid and Live8, this has a defamiliarising, if not plain disturbing intensity, I would again argue that this is precisely Farah's aim. Taariq's intratextual interventions throw the notion of self-contained, apocalyptically African disasters into chaos. Rather than reiterate a, by-now, familiar narrative, affirming the necessity of co-ordinated, international responses to crises such as famine, Farah compels his reader to confront the question of global entanglement, complicity and thus culpability at the inception stage. In essence, his decision to shift focus away from effects to causes is motivated by oppositional urgency. Once more, therefore, it is the image of the interlocking, interlinking chain that captures Farah's conception of a world that, by its very nature, is mutually dependant in ways often obscured by dominant discourses and media representations. If aid relief functions as a way of salving the guilty conscience of the West, an exposure of both root causes and the favourable terms on which assistance packages are sometimes based provides critical food for thought, in more ways than one.

Towards a Foucauldian Genealogy of Humanitarianism

In what follows, I offer a closer reading of those sections of *Gifts* that focus on disorders, in their various corporeal, ontological and political guises, framing them in relation to some of those contemporary debates within development and post-development studies, as well as international humanitarianism, gestured towards above. I argue that the relationship between individual, invariably contested body politics and those wider tensions that inscribe themselves on both the national and global body politic are as suggestive here as they have been at any other stage in Farah's fiction. To do this, I first provide a brief genealogy of humanitarianism, arguing that *Gifts* intersects with and comments on many of these Foucault-inflected concerns. The novel's presentation of characters whose lives are defined by disorder, turbulence and their ability, or otherwise, to cope is inextricably linked to the wider discursive and geo-political contexts I have gestured towards throughout.

In their compelling introductory chapter, 'Humanitarianism: A Brief History of the Present', Michael Barnett and Thomas G. Weiss offer robust critiques of the business and discourse of humanitarianism. Crucially, however, they balance them by recognising and paying tribute to those who would give their lives in the service of others. For Barnett and Weiss, the ethical clarity captured by such potential sacrifice is even more striking when viewed against a backdrop of global disorder and cynicism: 'many aid workers are drawn to humanitarianism precisely because it makes a clear political statement in a world that needlessly sacrifices so many. In this way, they live Michel Foucault's admonition that "the misfortunes of men must never be the silent leftover of politics." Their refusal to be silent is itself political' (Barnett & Weiss 2008: 37). It is significant that this is their only direct reference to Foucault. In order to circumvent the negative hermeneutics with which he is associated, Barnett and Weiss invoke a statement as haunting as it is prescient. If it is a riposte to the cynical self-satisfaction of many an armchair commentator, it is also revealing that the spectre of Foucault hangs heavy over those sections of their introduction that, as is the case throughout *Gifts*, subject both humanitarian principles and practices to greater scrutiny. The following is critical in this regard:

> Any consideration of politics requires a discussion of power. Humanitarian organizations have been in painful self-denial about their relationship to power, preferring to see themselves as weak and vulnerable as those whom they are helping. But their growing resources, their broader ambitions, and their relationship to global structures puts front and center the issue of power. Humanitarianism is largely understood as the ultimate of ethical acts, but a range of ethical positions leads to a range of different evaluations of humanitarian action, suggesting that one person's noble act might be another's sin. (Barnett & Weiss 2008: 9)

This early, cautionary note is striking on a number of levels. Repeated references to power are designed to drag what might have been those invisible chains, binding humanitarian organisations and global structures into a field of starker visibility. As such, it resonates with the kind of ethically interrogative probing enacted by Taariq and others in *Gifts*. As discomfiting as certain revelations might be for practitioners and patrons alike, it is only through the continual re-evaluation and, where necessary, exposure of what are deemed to be uncritically ethical acts and broader systems of power that humanitarianism's real gifts can be assessed and, from there, delivered. Once more, therefore, this model resembles a kind of Foucauldian analytics of power. By attending to connections, flows and networks, it makes the case that it is simply inadequate to place humanitarian organisations on one side of the ethical balance sheet and global structures on the other. It is only by exploring the overlaps between them that the real work of informed critique can begin. Rather than rely upon the tried and tested formulation of power as pyramidal, it becomes imperative to account for its diffuse potentialities. The final part of this description corresponds with a key concern foregrounded at strategic points throughout *Gifts*: the slippage between signifier and signified. Just as, given the contingencies of context, one person's idea of a gift might morph into that of a burden, so one notion of a noble act might, in alternative circumstances, be seen as ignoble at best. Crucially, however, Barnett and Weiss' intervention does not disavow humanitarianism, its principles or its ultimate aims. It is rather more an ontological call-to-arms, probing this penchant for self-denial so that the practices it was designed to inspire might be carried out more effectively. As such, their contribution is imbued with the kind of critical ambivalence that characterises *Gifts*.

In an important chapter entitled 'The Imperative to Reduce Suffering: Charity, Progress, and Emergencies in the Field of Humanitarian Action', Craig Calhoun offers a chronological mapping of humanitarianism's development and associated discourses, suggesting that 'the roots of this argument are older than is usually thought, and more deeply embedded in modern social imaginaries' (Calhoun 2008: 75). He maintains that it is only through revisiting these histories that we gain a greater understanding of the implications of what many perceive to be the defining question confronting humanitarianism today: 'how best to restore "order" to the disorderly scenes of humanitarian emergencies' (Calhoun 2008: 74). Building on this, the remainder of this chapter aims to show how and why similar kinds of order/disorder negotiations lie at the heart of Farah's fictive concerns, both in *Gifts* and beyond. If Calhoun's intervention enables us to frame humanitarianism in terms of a much more expansive, more intertwined historical narrative, it demands we do the same with geography. He shows us, for instance, how humanitarian organisations emerged out of a Europe buffeted by the storms of reformist zeal:

> Humanitarian reform movements transformed prisons, poor relief, mental hospitals, schools, and the relationship of European powers to 'primitive' peoples. Humanitarian ideals merged with the idea of philanthropy to encourage efforts to assimilate immigrants and mitigate the impact of new forms of inequality. In every case the implementation of these ideals was based on a sense among the well-off that they owed some obligation to improve the lot of the less well-off. In nearly every case the understanding of this obligation and the selection of courses of action were self-righteous and in part self-serving – but never simply reducible to self-interest. (Calhoun 2008: 76)

Whilst the chronotopes of Foucault's disciplinary society dominate here, it is once more the 'and' of the opening sentence that carries most significance. In order to gain a fuller appreciation of the evolution and impact of these domestic humanitarian reforms, it is necessary to situate them within an imperial framework. The context evoked by Calhoun is one in which travel, in terms of both leisure, economic necessity and, oftentimes, coercion, plays a pivotal role. Fast forward to the final sentence, and the qualifying note it strikes can be seen to resonate with *Gifts*, as it does with many of the most provocative interventions in development, post-development and humanitarian studies. If self-aggrandisement compelled certain philanthropic acts in the interests of opening up and exploiting new markets, Calhoun calls upon us to consider them in relation to much more diffuse, arguably productive networks and negotiations of power. If the histories and geographies of humanitarianism as a set of ideals and practices were intertwined, their motivations were similarly varied. Just as the inclusion of Taariq's journalistic reflections allows Farah to offer a more suggestively entangled portrait of both the roots of and responses to humanitarian crises, Calhoun's genealogy disavows the temporal and spatial myopia that plagues certain myths about humanitarianism. He shows that, as it is today, so it has always been: intrinsically concerned with the dialectical, mutually dependant relationship between the internal/domestic and the external/international.

Calhoun invokes the spirits of Weber and Foucault, arguing that humanitarian reforms can only be fully appreciated in this relational way. By focusing on the impact of rationalising and normalising discourses, he demonstrates how it was the production, rather than simply the maintenance, of order that remained most crucial:

> It is not so much that the ills were ended as that action in response to them was made orderly and goal directed. We should not be cynical about this, for there were genuine improvements. Michel Foucault notwithstanding, modern prisons are not obviously worse than public hangings or the drawing and quartering of earlier times. But as Foucault has suggested, humanitarian reform brought with it new forms of managerial orientation and governmentality in which a variety of agencies took on the challenge of producing order. (Calhoun 2008: 77)

As countless commentators have suggested, it is the exportation of this model of governmentality, building on foundations laid by Foucault in *The Order of Things*, that proved so central to the colonial project and its labyrinthine bureaucracy. Of more pressing concern here, however, is the extent to which certain lines of continuity can be traced from a colonial period valorised, however mythically, for its propriety and order, and a post/neo-colonial epoch conversely typified as an age of global disorder.

The Poetics and Politics of (Un)Conditional Giving

To suggest how these meditations might inform a reading of *Gifts*, I explore the ways in which Duniya's own contests with and within herself perform allegorical functions, both in relation to individual body politics and the broader body politic, in its national and global guises. In addition, I also speculate on how this intersects with contemporaneous debates concerning the roles and responsibilities of international humanitarianism, aid and development agendas, as well as the increasing attention being demanded by, and given to, those working in post-development studies. This serves to bolster my central argument: that *Gifts* is imbued with the same sense of ontological insecurity (individually and collectively, publically and privately, within family units and beyond, intrinsic to national spaces and extrinsic), that has gripped and continues to grip practitioners in and commentators on the above fields. It thus seems fitting to preface a re-engagement with the novel by foregrounding the notion of what Barnett and Weiss call 'contested humanitarianism'. As they ask, if all that once seemed certain has been thrown into doubt, where do we go from here? 'What are the forces that have so thoroughly shaken the humanitarian sector that they have unleashed this ontological insecurity? Why is there such anxiety amid all these accomplishments? What, precisely, has changed?' (Calhoun 2008: 8). To gain a greater sense of the enduring fascination Farah has with the dialectics of order and disorder in *Gifts*, and how these correspond with its geo-political backdrop, it is again useful to analyse later parts of the novel. As above, I work backwards from them.

Farah's decision to foreground a female protagonist in *Gifts* corresponds with those wider political and ethical imperatives that underpin the novel as a whole. As Escobar, drawing on Mohanty, reminds us, 'women in the Third World are represented in most feminist literature on development as having "needs" and "problems" but few choices and no freedom to act. What emerges from such modes of analysis is the image of an average Third World woman, constructed through the use of statistics and certain categories' (Escobar 1995: 8). A single mother and property owner, to a large degree financially autonomous, Duniya immediately destabilises this archetype. Whilst she cannot be accommodated under Spivak's subaltern sign, there is a sense, as there has been since *From a Crooked Rib* through *Sardines* and right on to *Knots*, that Farah is all too aware of the prominence afforded such tropes, within inter-related fields such as colonial discourse, postcolonial theory and development studies. For him, the novel is a vehicle through which to interrogate and, where appropriate, dismantle these notions. As Christine Sylvester provocatively asserts, 'the subaltern not only cannot speak in much development studies but she is rarely asked to do so in a way that might contradict what a development agency has already framed or decreed' (Sylvester 1999: 717). In light of this, it is vital to assess the role played by Nasiiba, Duniya's daughter, in the text. Whilst her overzealousness is, like her young predecessors in *Variations*, cloying at times, she is afforded some of the most substantial and searching lines in *Gifts*.

A key example comes towards the close of the novel. Nasiiba relays an anecdote about dogs, a subject whose symbolic stock rises as Farah's fiction develops. The dog's tale serves as an analogy through which reflections on the negotiations of and connections between colonial, postcolonial and neo-colonial eras can be framed. It is, therefore, worth quoting in full. Whilst it comes at the end of *Gifts*, it provides the basis for a more substantial discussion of those order/disorder dialectics referred to above:

> You see [dogs] everywhere, foraging in the very garbage bins the urchins have emptied of everything except the bones they cannot chew; these dogs attack pedestrians minding their own business, especially after dark. Have you any idea where these terrifying beasts come from? ... According to Taariq ... most of these dogs at one time or another belonged to Europeans or Americans with plenty of food to spare and human affection to indulge on these beasts that actually live in the same spacious and well-to-do houses as their children. Now the truth is, these dogs received more food and attentive love than most Somalis, and then, between one weekend and the next, the masters went home, leaving behind these spoiled creatures. This has been a pattern, too much love, then with frightening suddenness, homelessness and a hostile Islamic community ready to stone them on the slightest pretext. In short, the dogs are turned into schizoids ... This is that level of reality in which you might discern a certain similarity between dogs and some Third World dictators who receive the pampered approval of their European and American masters until their usefulness has ceased, dictators who are abandoned to the dogs of bad fortune. On a personal level, the Europeans and Americans living in Africa behave in a manner akin to that of their governments on a national level. (*G*: 238)

If the apocalyptic undertones of this section are only matched by the clunkiness of its prose, it is the impact of the all-too sudden shift in the order of the dogs' universe that is most notable. The dislocation is such that it wreaks internal havoc, rendering the animals 'schizoid'. As discussed above, tropes of schizophrenia and bifurcation pepper much of the discourse relating to Somalia's turbulent national narrative, particularly following defeat in the Ogaden War. As such, it again corresponds with those Fanonian speculations concerning the internal havoc wreaked upon 'colonised' subjects by their rulers and through the experience of conflict. Substitute 'colonised' for 'postcolonised', and the correspondence with Nasiiba's story is highly suggestive.

As many commentators concerned with development and post-development studies have maintained, once more attesting to Fanon's powers of prophecy, aid packages and other forms of support were deployed with unusual frequency throughout the Cold War. Bolstering certain, often autocratic regimes (such as Barre's in Somalia) ensured that strategic objectives were met. Fifty years after the publication of *The Wretched of the Earth*, *Gifts* reminds us, and we confront strikingly similar questions. In this instance, however, Farah uses Nasiiba's story to foreground concerns that will only become more prominent and pressing in terms of both fictional and national narratives: How to cope, on individual and collective levels, with the chaos of aftermath? What happens when the colonial powers, the neo-colonial stooges, the despotic dictator, the aid agencies and the media crews withdraw? In the final part of this chapter, I work my way back through *Gifts*, attempting to show how and why its order/disorder motifs slip and slide. As I do so, I reflect on their links to some of the most pressing debates within post-development and humanitarian studies.

As argued above, *Gifts* is a palimpsest of a narrative, made up of many different layers. If the concern with international aid should be seen in relation to a wider discourse, centred on attempts to reimpose order on a world of global disorder, a similar imperative underpins Duniya's own story. Her entire existence seems poised between the forces of certainty and chaos, in terms of family and relationships, as well as her private, public and professional identities. The entry of the foundling into her life, effectively an unsolicited 'gift' that threatens to become an onerous burden, merely adds to her complications. Of greater interest, however, is the way Farah plots her journey towards a sense of ontological security in the wake of the baby's death. This is captured in a multiply revealing reflection: '[Bosaaso] looked miserable. It would do no good to tell him to cheer up. He was as highly strung as her, but she had the self-control to contain her tension. She was a woman who knew how to accommodate all life's contradictions without going insane' (G: 214). Typically, we have an inversion of traditionally gendered power relations and archetypes here. Duniya is portrayed in sovereign charge of her body and desire. It is only through the process of reconnecting with this sense of self that a certain harmony, crucially denied Bosaaso at this juncture, can be restored. For my purposes, however, the most telling aspect of this description recalls an idea introduced much earlier in Farah's work: the notion that true knowledge of the self can only come about through the acceptance, rather than the erasure, of those contradictions that define life in all its often maddening glory. Approached from the Foucauldian standpoint outlined above, it is not simply an oppositional case of order versus disorder, but rather an understanding of the relational bonds between them.

For Duniya to arrive at this realisation, however, she has had to endure many disruptions. In the opening of *Gifts*, she is presented in her professional role, with the hospital in which she works providing the setting. A normalising, disciplinary chronotope *par excellence*, it serves as an early spatial representation of the desire to impose order on that, be it in terms of individual or collective bodies, which has become overwhelmed by certain disorders. In terms of discourses pertaining to aid and international development, it recalls the 'global doctor' epigraph with which this chapter began. With regard to Duniya's portrayal, however, Farah offers an early, revealing glimpse of how and why she is used by others, in both personal and professional capacities, to shore up their own, invariably faltering senses of self. Consider the following, for instance:

> Dr Mire was a man of strictly observed habits; he was fond of developing a more intimate relationship with rituals than with people. He was easily upset when small things went wrong, which in a place like Somalia occurred with annoying frequency. If irritated in a big way, he was depressed. To ensure the world didn't fall to pieces about him, Dr Mire depended on Duniya, who was never clumsy in her faithful observance of the details of these rites. He couldn't imagine working in Mogadiscio without her by his side, she who helped him understand his personal short-comings, who taught him to be tolerant, forgiving and forgivable. (*G*: 14)

For Mire, Duniya provides anchorage in a world where the only certainty is uncertainty. His observance of ritual is such that he has lost touch with the very fleshy, material reality of life itself. As we discover, this is in large part due to the tragic deaths of his wife and child. It is precisely Mire's inability to deal with a life defined by 'things going wrong' that results in his comparative ossification. This, in turn, means that he runs the risk of evading certain existential responsibilities. Duniya thus emerges as the figurative axis around which his professional and, it appears, personal worlds turn. It is, however, not long before his ideal of her is profoundly shaken. In the following exchange, Farah characteristically relies on the body-as-text motif, presenting Mire as an uncanny reader of that which, to Duniya, remains inscrutable:

> 'Be my mirror for a change,' [Duniya] said, 'and tell me what I can't have seen.'
> [Dr Mire] said, 'You hurt easily today.'

> 'How do you *see* that?'
> 'I sense you are open sores all over,' he said.
> 'On the contrary,' she smiled, 'today I don't hurt at all.'
> 'I'll be specific,' he said.
> Her eyes wouldn't focus. 'Are you psychoanalysing me?'
> 'Why haven't you changed into your uniform, for instance?' No longer defiant,
> Duniya was angry with her colleagues. 'But why didn't anyone tell me?' (*G*: 17)

Whilst many familiar Farah tropes are on display here (mirror/reflective imagery, the figurative reliance on the wounded body only revealing itself to gifted readers), it is perhaps the final reference to Duniya's failure to don her uniform that is most significant in terms of the discursive framework employed throughout. Her annoyance, I suggest, is piqued by more than a simple oversight in professional etiquette. The uniform is, of course, a normalising symbol like no other. Accordingly, Duniya's nonobservance of what, on every other day, is a ritual taken for granted, at once serves to show the cracks in Mire's image of her whilst, in turn, becoming a catalyst for attempts to fathom the complexities that define her. It is the simple yet essential realisation that one size does not fit all that galvanises a gradual appreciation of the more nuanced sense of self referred to above. Whilst it may seem a leap too far, I want to explore how this early privileging of Duniya's ontological insecurity, in terms of her struggles to accommodate her defining disorderliness within those normative frameworks symbolised by the uniform, corresponds with Farah's critical ambivalence towards the processes and practices of normalisation that inform international aid agendas.

In a provocative article entitled 'Bare Life as a Development/Postcolonial Problematic', Christine Sylvester makes a convincing case for the interrogatory role fiction can and, at times, must play in relation to some homogenising tendencies within development and associated discourses. It suggests that novels such as *Gifts* occupy an enabling position at the interstices of these discursive practices:

> Professionals engaging development problems often work from a laudable
> sense of urgency and impatience, but many with the greatest resources are
> tangled in an economic paradigm of development ... Postcolonial fiction writers
> have fewer illusions. Their vantage points on the postcolonial development
> situation are close range rather than remote and abstract. The politics they
> record is messy, often nasty. Even those who do not live in the societies they
> depict – and there are many of these – often produce work that emphasizes the

complex humanity of local people, often poor people, as against development reports that provide cases, numbers, needs, and theorizations of always deferred human capabilities. (Sylvester 2006: 70)

Much of this description resonates with the peculiarities of Farah's own situation as well as the particular concerns of *Gifts*. First, there is the sense that, whilst 'postcolonial fiction writers' might not live in the place they are writing about, it is, to a certain extent, this very distance that enables them to create. Added to this is Sylvester's sense that, for all the altruistic intentions of development specialists and associated bodies, the reality they confront is one defined by entanglements of invariably economic and political power. In the spirit of critical ambivalence, however, she does not simply denounce development paradigms or practices. Rather, Sylvester invokes the writer to suggest that their privileging of and sensitivity to much 'messier' realities can provide a salutary counter to certain normalising tendencies. When it comes to speculating on potential connections between Sylvester's reflections and *Gifts*, attending to loaded and oft-repeated terms proves instructive once again.

If Duniya's own arrival at a more comprehensive sense of self comes from her realisation of and acquiesence to certain defining contradictions, there is an analogous call throughout much of the scholarship associated with post-development and humanitarianism that greater attention be paid to those defining complexities of situations that are often airbrushed from, as they cannot be accommodated by, normalising grids. As Glennie maintains, 'while most people in rich countries consider aid to be a simple act of generosity, Africans understand its far more complex nature' (Glennie 2008: 5). Whilst not doing justice to the richness of Farah's novel, there is a sense in which this single sentence captures one of the driving motivations behind *Gifts* as well as debates concerning its consumption by predominantly Western readers. It once more prompts us to reconsider the rhetoric of visibility. If one of Farah's critical objectives in *Gifts* is to defamiliarise the notion of international aid/gift-giving, through an exposure of alternative narratives and voices, it can usefully be framed in the context of ongoing debates within post-development and humanitarian studies regarding the necessity, however discomfiting, of unveiling certain rather more complex entanglements with power. These tensions are once more foregrounded by Barnett and Weiss:

> Being apolitical is a convenient fiction that can only be sustained through
> rhetorical flourishes and discursive practices that allow for a particular category
> of politics ... Humanitarian workers traditionally saw themselves as apolitical
> insofar as they defied the dominant systems of power and were in solidarity
> with the victims of a 'sacrifical order'. As they become increasingly implicated
> in governance structures, they find themselves in growing collaboration with
> those whose influence they once resisted. Such a development means that
> humanitarianism's 'politics' are now more visible, and the relationship between
> humanitarianism and power is now more complex. (Barnett and Weiss 2008: 38)

Immediately prior to the foundling's unexpected entry into her life, Duniya
begins to review her recent, unsettling behaviour within a much longer time-
frame. It is one in which the battle between the forces of order and disorder
waged intense, oftentimes internal war:

> What was making her so blundering and unsteady? She stumbled at the
> memory of knocking things over in Dr Mire's cubicle yesterday. She also
> remembered tumbling headlong over Taariq's brick barrier on the night they
> decided to marry. And there was no avoiding recalling the image of Zubair,
> her first husband, wobbling his way about, toppling things with a blind man's
> walking-stick. Duniya solemnly vowed to herself to keep her balance and not
> fall. (G: 63)

As above, the anxiety caused by Duniya's faltering sense of self only deepens as she reflects on how her identity, personal and professional, is and has
been defined in relation to, as well as often by, others. Dr. Mire, Taariq and
Zubair have all profoundly shaped Duniya's experiences and consciousness.
They have also led her to become obsessed with potentially dangerous cycles
of dependency. As we come to discover, of course, Farah introduces another
male presence into her life, in the form of the foundling baby. The dependence
he has on Duniya, however, is of a different kind. As the narrative unfolds, the
relationship comes to be seen in reciprocal terms, with both, in ways at once
literal and symbolic, giving the other a new lease of life. Before this discovery
can take place, however, there are a series of profound jolts to Duniya's understanding of herself and her various functions. The picture of her life morphs
into one she cannot read according to those prescriptive structures, systems
and normalising grids that have governed it as well as her sense of self up until
now. As discussed above, certain forms of unlearning and/or unmaking need
to occur before vital reconstruction efforts can begin. Inevitably, this involves

Duniya undergoing the painful realisation that she is not always in absolute control. Invariably, discomfiting changes have to take place before a new order of things, with often greater potential, can establish itself:

> Meanwhile Duniya was thinking about something that worried her: her knocking things over, spilling drinks, kicking her toes sore. The fact that this was becoming routine with her, almost boringly predictable, rankled in her mental picture of herself. Had she lost control of a certain brain nerve, causing imbalance both in mind and body? She did not like being associated with leaving falls, crashes and wreckages in her wake. Why, shapes were becoming vague in her vision. Walls at times retreated. Her hands would bend athletically at the wrist, strong like a javelin thrower's. She reminded herself that in Somali mythology the cosmos balances on the horns of a bull, a beast that is forever staring at a cow tied to a pole right in front of him. It is said that the bull's body loses equilibrium whenever his love, the cow, turns its eyes elsewhere, and this physical shift is responsible for the earthquakes around the world. Was she, Duniya, subduing the universe by breaking things into bits? (G: 94)

If this mythological aside is a little overdetermined, it does allow Farah to make a point pivotal to both Duniya's evolving sense of self and, I would argue, many of the discourses and debates surveyed above. The seismic force of earthquakes and the intensity of love are imagined to balance out, suggesting that, before new ways of being and seeing can be instituted, old modes must fall away.

For my purposes, it is the manner in which Farah traces Duniya's increasingly complex awareness of her own corporeal and ontological being that is most intriguing in terms of potential connections with *Gifts'* other narrative preoccupations, namely the complexities and complicities of international aid and development. Crucially, this relies upon certain associations between corporeality and textuality. In many respects, therefore, the following could just as easily come from Misra in *Maps* as from Duniya in *Gifts*: '[t]he human body has its inherent mysteries and one cannot always account for its behaviour, neither are all its self-expressions and manifestations an open book to medical practitioners' (G: 184). The point is a simple yet essential one. Set against the universal claims of medical science, the human body reveals itself in all its disorderly glory, doggedly refusing to relinquish the enigmatic mysteries that define it. Seen from one perspective, the idea that we do not have all the answers is to be celebrated rather than feared. Openness and order cannot exist without that which is closed and, at times, disorderly. Whilst it may be something of a stretch, I suggest that the 'medical practitioner' as necessarily-limited-reader image might be analogous both with Finkelkraut's 'global doctor' and thus some of those development and humanitarian policy makers and practitioners referred to throughout.

To continue the analogy: if the specificities of the human body, in pain or otherwise, can be framed within and fathomed using a particular set of medical discourses and practices, there will be times at which these fall short in the face of its unruly secrets. To transpose this within the context of development, post-development and humanitarian discourses, there is a parallel sense that, whilst seemingly universal frameworks and mandates go so far, their universality is, at the very least, questionable. Failure to take this into account, alongside insensitivity to the peculiarities of situations on the ground, can have much more long-lasting, often detrimental effects. Once again, therefore, Duniya's reliance on images figuring the body as text and its 'readability' or otherwise can, with some imagination, be seen to resonate with those core, Foucauldian concerns with practices and discourses of normalisation that have preoccupied many commentators and actors within the development and humanitarian sectors. As Escobar provocatively reminds us: if a certain picture appears chaotic, dark, disorderly and/or unfathomable, it invariably has something to do with the lenses through which it is being viewed (Escobar 1995: 56). If no room is provided for a more self-reflexive critique, which analyses such prisms in the interests of questioning their supposed universality, the efficacy of both their governing principles and practices is severely compromised.

'O my body, make of me always a man who questions!'[2]

To conclude this chapter, I once more follow Farah's example by grounding broader speculations, concerning macrological debates ranging from debt repayment to humanitarian relief, at the level of the micropolitical. After battling with the sense that her own clumsiness is, in some way, a reflection of the wider disorder that defines her life, Duniya comes to a crucial realisation. That this occurs with Nasiiba watching and pivots around a reorientation of the self by re-anchoring to the sentient body is multiply significant:

> Somehow Duniya came to realise there was no turning back and what had to be done had to be done, reminding herself that the twin's father, being blind, had never set eyes on her body, and that it was ironic now that his

daughter was undressing her. She also drew strength from the memory that she, as a midwife, had seen many a woman naked, women whose bodies she had handled, whose most private parts she touched with panache. Her gaze worried, her body trembling, she flung aside the robe with which she had been covered, saying, 'There you are,' speaking the words with flamboyance. (G: 139)

Sections such as these showcase the imagistic continuities that underpin Farah's fiction. The female body is once more presented as a textual palimpsest which, when handled with deference, exposes some, if not all, of its secrets. The tenderness with which Nasiiba performs the ritualistic act of undressing/unveiling, therefore, is vital. Such passages also, of course, intersect with key questions of visibility and power. Duniya situates herself within personal and professional narratives that are defined by certain vulnerabilities and, most crucially, the presentation of relationships that rely on reciprocal respect to prevent abuse. By this, I mean both allusions to the blind Zubair and Duniya's role as a midwife. In the case of the former, we are told that, despite his impairment, stoicism combined with ingenuity so that his dependence on his young wife was not all-consuming. In turn, their partnership was defined in complex terms of power and visibility. If Zubair could not 'read' Duniya's body, he could interpret it at the level of touch. Likewise, the memory of her experiences as a midwife recalls moments at which Duniya took charge of other, female bodies, exposed to her in their most vulnerable states. As is the case throughout Farah's work, the human being's corporeal reality is imagined as a complex, compelling text precisely because it is inscribed with both pain and the possibility of joy:

Bosaaso approached Duniya's body as if it were a door whose combination locks required the performance of a certain number of feats, before being allowed in ... Only when he proved himself to be a charmer, did she let him in.

And then the doors of her body opened wider, and she lay on top of him, the mistress conducting the speed and flow of the river of their common love. Earlier, he had wanted to know if she had taken the necessary precautions. She had said, 'Of course, I have,' making it plain that she wanted no more children, thank you.

He followed the rhythmic dictates of her orchestrated movements, concentrating on the dents on her body, which were like those on stone steps leading to a frequently used door. Her body felt a lot younger than his own, and was undeniably more athletic. (G: 210)

If this shows Duniya as an active, autonomous woman taking charge of the sexual encounter, it is similarly important that Farah juxtaposes it with a section where the male body bears the impress of pain: '[s]he felt the marks [Bosaaso's] trouser belt had left round his waist, body marks that were as prominent as a woman's stretch marks following the delivery of a number of children. He had far too many burns and scars, even for a Somali. Had his mother cauterized every inexplicable complaint, thinking only that curative surgery made any sense?' (G: 211)

As with Bosaaso, so it is for the expectant mothers in this section. The joy of birth, easy as it might be for a man to say, is only intensified by the struggle of labour. Once again, the essential point is that these relationships are inherently and necessarily dialectical. You cannot have one without the other. This is captured in the closing lines of the above section, where Farah literally and figuratively leaves his protagonist exposed. Gone are the uniforms of her profession and her role as mother. In their place is a naked body, trembling and vulnerable. In turn, however, this only amplifies Duniya's triumphant declaration ('There you are'). As such, it emerges at a point in the novel where Duniya claims her body and all that comes with it. The oftentimes painful traces of the past it bears are not in any way erased. Duniya's evolving sense of self comes both from a realisation and an acceptance that certain uniforms, be they of outward appearance or perceived roles, do not fit comfortably and that, in order for human relationships to function, those often invisible bonds of mutual dependence must be revealed so that they can be celebrated.

To my mind, two of the most suggestive practices and processes invoked by Farah throughout *Gifts* are those of driving and swimming. In closing, I suggest how they might offer a figurative bridge between what I consider to be the dominant concerns of the novel as a whole: Duniya's ultimate acceptance of a new idea of herself as well as questions of international aid and relations of dependency. If, at the start of *Gifts*, we are presented with a central protagonist who is uneasy about accepting lifts as well as gifts from others, we can track her development in terms of her dedication to learning how to drive. If its figurative power might be dulled by overuse (autonomy, determining your own direction, going forward or moving backwards *et al.*), it becomes more intriguing when situated in relation to *Gifts'* overarching preoccupations. Once again, we are presented with a hierarchical relationship premised on power and its potential abuse. Bosaaso is the teacher and Duniya the student; without him, she cannot move. I suggest what Farah is once more urging us to consider, however, is the dialectical nature of this relationship. Without Duniya, Bosaaso's role as teacher becomes null and void. The gift we are really asked to focus on, therefore, is the transmission of knowledge. If Bosaaso equips Duniya with the necessary skills, framed in relation to a series of normalising rules and practices without which the whole idea of driving implodes, it is with the aim that she will be able to plot her own journey without having to rely on others. The potential analogies between this and some of the most pressing debates within international aid and other circles are suggestive. Again, therefore, Foucault's attention to conceptual power relations is vital. It is quite simply too reductive, whether thinking about learning to drive or the dissemination of international aid, to conceive of power in terms of a rigid, unilateral, trickle-down model. As Morgan Brigg reminds us, negotiations take place within much more complex and compelling networks.

The process of learning how to swim, laden as it is with symbolic potential, is equally suggestive. As in the case of driving, the relationship is based on the imparting of instruction. Crucially, however, this is supplemented by the kind of provisional, burgeoning corporeal awareness that defines significant portions of Duniya's journey throughout *Gifts*:

> Under Marilyn's supervision she swam back and forth, becoming more and more confident, and urged on by the success story her body was telling her. Then Marilyn sensed a tremor of worry in Duniya's body. It was like a traveller coming upon a sudden bend in a road, a turning not signposted. Marilyn placed her outspread palm further up, closer to Duniya's chest. A little later, Duniya's body regained its lost balance. (G: 188)

Whilst I am not interested in anything as reductive as reading the swimming motif in relation to those development discourses and debates touched on above, there are certain elements here that, again with some imagination, might be productively read back into them. The first concerns the reiterated image of the body as text. This time, however, it is not being read by anyone else. Instead, Duniya's body is narrating a success story to her as it comes alive through the process of learning about its own potential. As her figure moves through water, so it grows in confidence. Whilst this takes place under Marilyn's watchful eye, it is an action that Duniya can only perform herself.

Typically, however, the appearance of stability is quickly undermined by Farah. As the tremor of worry threatens to discompose Duniya, a familiar spatial motif is relied upon to capture the relationship between her internal distress and an outward disorder that threatens drowning and therefore death. Whilst Marilyn's hand intervenes at the vital point, of even greater interest is the fact that, in her role as supervisor, she does not actually guide her pupil. Rather than point her in a particular direction, Marilyn adjusts her own position to deal with Duniya's specific requirements. The result is that she is able to regain the confidence that has been jolted, achieving a bodily balance that allows her to chart her own course. Again, Farah's reliance on particular motifs can be seen as a distillation of many of his most pressing concerns throughout *Gifts*. Here, Duniya's sense of self is jeopardised by a disorder with potentially disastrous consequences. Marilyn's response, however, is not one that disempowers by wresting more agency and responsibility away. Were this to happen, the text seems to suggest, she would be evading her own duties as a supervisor as well as compromising the quality of a gift that is premised on reciprocity rather than dictating the terms on which it is to be given and received. As I hope to have suggested throughout this chapter, *Gifts* provides an intriguing fictional prism through which to consider a host of issues as pertinent to the oftentimes dark reality of our globalised present as any other. As such, I have tried to suggest ways in which it might be productively framed within those Foucauldian-inflected discourses that have proved stimulating to a host of commentators and practitioners within the international aid and development fields. This provides a platform from which to consider *Secrets*.

References

Barnett, M. & Weiss, T. 2008. 'Humanitarianism: A Brief History of the Present'. In M. Barnett & T.G. Weiss (Eds). *Humanitarianism in Question: Politics, Power and Ethics*. Ithaca and London: Cornell University Press.

Brigg, M. 2002. 'Post-Development, Foucault and the Colonisation Metaphor' in *Third World Quarterly*, Vol. 23, No. 2.

Browne, S. 'Aid to Fragile States: Do Donors Help or Hinder?' In Mavrotas, G. (Ed.). 2010. *Foreign Aid for Development: Issues, Challenges and the New Agenda*. Oxford: Oxford University Press.

Calhoun, C. 2008. 'The Imperative to Reduce Suffering: Charity, Progress, and Emergencies in the Field of Humanitarian Action'. In M. Barnett & T.G. Weiss (Eds). *Humanitarianism in Question: Politics, Power and*

Ethics. Ithaca and London: Cornell University Press.

Escobar, A. 1995. *Encountering Development: The Making and Unmaking of the Third World*. New Jersey: Princeton University Press.

Fanon, F. 2001. *The Wretched of the Earth*. (C. Farrington, Trans.). London: Penguin Classics.

Foucault, M. 1980. *Michel Foucault, Power/ Knowledge – Selected Interviews and Other Writings, 1972–1977*. Gordon, C. (Ed.). (C. Gordon, L. Marshall, J. Mepham, K. Soper, Trans.). Harlow: Pearson Education Limited.

Glennie, J. 2008. *The Trouble with Aid: Why Less Could Mean More for Africa*. London, Zed Books.

Redfield, P. 2008. 'Sacrifice, Triage and Global Humanitarianism'. In M. Barnett & T.G.

Weiss (Eds). *Humanitarianism in Question: Politics, Power and Ethics.* Ithaca and London: Cornell University Press.

Sylvester, C. 1999. 'Development Studies and Postcolonial Studies: Disparate Tales of the 'Third World'' *Third World Quarterly*, Vol. 20, No. 4.

Sylvester, C. 2006. 'Bare life as Development/ Postcolonial Problematic.' *The Geographical Journal*, Vol. 172, No. 1.

Endnotes

1 With thanks to Slim, H. 2004. *A Call to Alms: Humanitarian Action and the Art of War.* Geneva: Centre for Humanitarian Dialogue, February 2004.

2 Fanon, F. 1967. *Black Skin, White Masks.* (Markmann, C., Trans.). New York: Grove Press, p. 232.

7

Trajectories of Implosion and Explosion: The Politics of Blood and Betrayal in *Secrets*

Just before the Ogaden debacle, he changed masters, without adjusting himself to his new circumstances, a defeated man at the helm of a people desperate for a statesman. Siyad Barre might have prevented a worsening of the crisis if he had resigned then. He was a tragic figure, a victim of his own small-mindedness.

(Secrets: 191)

Somalia has … produced a number of global security problems. The country has been an incubator for two serious diseases which have spread beyond its borders, one a threat to humans (drug-resistant tuberculosis), the other a threat to both humans and livestock (Rift Valley Fever) … [the] outflow of Somali refugees and illegal immigrants from Somalia to Europe, North America, Australia and the Gulf has constituted one of the most vexing political problems emanating from Somalia's collapse.

(Ken Menkhaus – Somalia: State Collapse and the Threat of Terrorism, 2004: 52–54)

IN THIS AND THE CHAPTER THAT FOLLOWS, I REFLECT ON HOW AND WHY Foucault's meditations on politics, war and surveillance have been used to explore issues relating to what has been called 'postmodern conflict'. Like-wise, I consider how some Foucauldian interventions on AIDS, as well as the microphysics of power and struggle, provide an intriguing prism through which to view *Secrets*. If Foucault's meditations on disciplinary procedures can inform a reading of the *Variations* sequence, this final instalment of the *Blood in the Sun* cycle begins to probe similar questions in relation to the body as hosting viruses that spill over various geo-political borders. Whilst I do not seek to draw any easy lines of equivalence, it seems sufficient to note that the trajectories of both Farah's and Foucault's later discourse are, for varying reasons, increasingly preoccupied with the 'global equalizer' of AIDS.[1] As I suggest throughout my analyses of what comes after *Blood in the Sun*, Farah will explore some of the avenues of inquiry tentatively set up here in both fiction and non-fiction. As Menkhaus' epigraph suggests, issues ranging from global security to international migration and the threat of pandemics have dominated contemporary discourse on Somalia. As such, they inform much of Farah's most recent work.

Of equal significance is the fact that, as illustrated in the opening epigraph, *Secrets* is the first novel since *A Naked Needle* to refer to Barre directly, taking the implosion of his autocratic rule as its narrative backdrop. As such, it marks an intensification of the bloody body politics and interrogations of individual and collective identities that characterise *Maps*. Early on in the text, for instance, explicit reference is made to the scorched-earth policy pursued by Barre in Northern Somalia to quell insurgent forces: 'my mother did not wish our family to be caught by surprise, following the inhumane destructions caused to the people and property in the northern regions. The second largest city in the land was bombed by Siyad's regime, its residents massacred, almost all its buildings razed to the ground' (*Sec*: 22–23). The reference to implosion and explosion in the title of this chapter, therefore, chimes with Mbembe's notion in *On the Postcolony* as well as Farah's own conception of the novel (Mbembe 2001:44). In 'How Can We Talk of Democracy?' he maintains that:

> *Secrets* … terminates the process with which *Maps* begins. *Secrets* ends the internal civil war. The external combustion of the civil war was external because Somalia, Somalis, invaded Ethiopia. With the defeat, with their return, there is an implosion. There was an explosion, because it went outward, out of Somalia into Ethiopia, and then there is the implosion. (Farah 2002: 46)

As argued above, the explosion of the General's disciplinary labyrinth in *Variations* precipitates the increasingly visceral, bio-political preoccupation with the contested bodies of protagonists and polities that haunts the *Blood in the*

Sun cycle. In their various ways, *Maps*, *Gifts* and *Secrets* explore how and why the parameters of their protagonists' bodies are shaken and reconfigured with something approaching the intensity of geo-political borders.

If *Blood in the Sun* is awash with internecine conflict, to an extent only hinted at throughout the *Variations* cycle, Farah's preoccupation with comparative elites remains undimmed. Kalaman is a young professional, managing his computer business amidst civil strife. As in *Gifts*, therefore, there is a defamiliarising commitment to showing how life can and must go on, even against the most apocalyptic of backdrops. In *Secrets*, Farah once more considers the role played by female members of this new entrepreneurial vanguard. We are told, for instance, that Talaado, Kalaman's on-off girlfriend, 'sold "space," placing ads in newspapers or mural ads on people's walls. With socialism out of fashion and with capitalism still in an embryonic state, billboards became the possibilities of custom' (*Sec*: 90). The days when the General's face would beam from bullet-pocked walls alongside Marx and Lenin are very much those of a bygone era. Similarly, Kalaman's mother, Damac, is a successful artisan whose status as primary earner gives her the means to buy her own car. Like Judith Gardner and Judy El Bushra in *Somalia – The Untold Story*, Farah is interested in how '[one] impact of the [civil] war is that women are increasingly replacing men as the breadwinners of the family' (Gardner & El Bushra 2004: 10). Ousseina Alidou, amongst others, has placed Damac in the unconventional line-up of female figures that dominate Farah's fiction (Alidou 2002: 675). As well as destabilising certain gender roles and expectations, as he does with Duniya in *Gifts* and Cambara in *Knots*, Farah demonstrates how Damac's position safeguards her from being dragged into the disorder of things being played out on the streets of Mogadiscio. 'She could date the day when she became certain that there would be civil strife in Somalia … "The man's accent told me he was not familiar with cars and how they worked and would be frightened of speed"' (*Sec*: 22).

A fine line seems to exist between the protection afforded by such class-specific privileges and a kind of paralysing detachment from the troubling political dramas unfolding beyond. As I explore in forthcoming chapters, this renewed concern with a politics of detachment, dislocation and displacement corresponds with the undulations of Farah's own narrative. It is telling, therefore, that *Secrets* was published the same year he returned to his homeland after 20 years in exile. The result is that an obsesssion with the politics of disconnection and reconnection haunts every text from *Blood in the Sun*'s final instalment on. In *Secrets*, the venture-capitalist ethos that serves Kalaman so well on the outside also comes to define his dealings with extended family members. It thus impacts on the concomitant business of attempting to define himself out of the kind of identity politics being increasingly oriented around clan:

> I occupied a first-floor two-bedroom apartment in one of Mogadiscio's most sought-after residential zones, and seldom entertained anyone claiming to be from either side of my parents' extended families, clansmen and clanswomen whose demands would range from being put up and fed for months to having their medical and their children's school bills footed. I would remind them that I was no member of a clan, that I was a professional. (*Sec*: 27)

As argued in a previous chapter, Farah's imagined Group of 10 can be seen as a quasi-clan, prone to the sort of factional fallouts suffered by families as well as governments. The special role he reserves for older figures suggests that the progressiveness of the post-Independence generation might benefit from degrees of historical perspective they invariably dismiss as regressive because traditional. In *Blood in the Sun*, the pseudo-intellectual clan has been supplemented, if not supplanted, by an emergent petit-bourgeoisie.

It is therefore significant that the preoccupations and trajectories of *Close Sesame* and *Secrets* (both final instalments of their respective trilogies) resemble each other at various points. In *Secrets*, the Deeriye figure is reimagined through Nonno, whose experiences under colonial and neo-colonial regimes make him a suitable guide for his 'grandson'. Kalaman's desire to define himself in opposition to an increasingly clannish order of things is driven by his entrepreneurial convictions. Yet, particularly in a world where pre and post modern values collide, rejecting the insights offered by historical perspective and experience is fraught with danger. In a fictional foreshadowing of *Links*, it is not long before Kalaman's doggedly guarded 'I' is set against the demands and expectations of the 'we'. As Alamin Mazrui states in '*Secrets*: The Somali Dispersal and Reinvented Identities', it is this self-consciously postmodern struggle (in both its playful and political variants) that frames the novel as a whole: '[t]he civil war and the consequent collapse of the state of Somalia generated two seemingly contradictory processes within the Somali(an) body politic: clannization, on the one hand, and globalization, on the other hand' (Mazrui 2002: 617). The apparently progressive pairing of Damac and Talaado morphs into a more complex triptych with the arrival of another figure who, with due controversy, enables Farah to explore these processes further.

The Poetics and Politics of Revulsion

The sense of a never fully resolved tension between implosion and explosion is embodied by the anthropomorphic Sholoongo. She is a significant and distant other, bursting back onto the scene to reprise the at once fixating and frustrating role she played in a youth shared with Kalaman. Her re-entry shakes the seemingly impenetrable fortresses of dwelling, liminal and lived, that he has constructed around himself. As Farah adapts the quasi-detective model of *Sweet and Sour Milk*, the reader gradually discovers that she holds the keys to the real secrets behind Kalaman's identity. As he does throughout his other novels, Farah once again conceives the tension between implosion and explosion in corporeal terms, staging it as a battle between living flesh and all-too brittle bones:

> In a manner of speaking, the questions are comparable to bones with no flesh
> on them. Questions age, they lose their relevance, but do bones? Do skeletons
> hidden in closets age, on account of the dust with which they are covered?
> The marrow in these bones may have dried, but they are not lifeless. And when
> bones have remained buried for years, it may be unwise to dig them up, for they
> may have changed shape, so will the questions about them. (*Sec:* 74–75)

The notion of narrative as body is once again critical. Recently arrived from America with her brother Timir to bury their late father, Sholoongo encroaches into Kalaman's bachelor pad only to berate him for his bourgeois seclusion. The allusion to things changing shape is similarly loaded. Trained as a shamanic shape-shifter in the States, Sholoongo is a spectral figure who, to some extent, performs a role akin to that of the indeterminate Beloved in Toni Morrison's eponymous novel. Like Beloved, she forces various characters to confront their shadow selves by remembering unsettling parts of their past.

While Sholoongo insists that her return is, in part, motivated by a desire to fulfil a childhood pledge to have Kalaman father her child (*Sec:* 36), she attacks him as a changeling who has forgotten how to think big. Her impact is even more disturbing when she probes Kalaman's past: 'why on earth was this woman making me revisit in memory some of the things I had clean forgotten?' (*Sec:* 33). As commentators have noted, Sholoongo embodies the novel's slippery terrain, occupying those fraught spaces between pre and post modernity with which Farah, in both symbolic and geo-political spheres, is so fascinated. At various points, she is framed within the mythological discourse of the Somali queen Carraweelo 'to whose reign may be traced the period when the male order of society … replaced the country's matriarchal tradition' (*Sec*: 15).[2] Similarly, her transnational voyage from the States to Somalia can be seen as anticipating the returnee quests that characterise the *Past Imperfect* trilogy. It is arguably her entrepreneurial re-appropriation of exotic animism within the global village, however, that captures the relationship between *Secrets'* politics and its playfulness most strikingly.[3]

For Michael Eldridge, Sholoongo allows Farah to present a parodic critique of the very processes of globalisation:

> [At the conclusion of the text] Sholoongo, presumably, withdraws to America, from whose impressionable unconscious she seemingly sprang, to resume her role as flim-flam woman peddling spiritual mumbo-jumbo to gullible 'yoga-practicing latter-day hippies' (p. 53). If individual Somalis and their African neighbours snag a proportionately larger share of the blame for the country's annihilation, then here is an indication that America will not be let off the hook entirely. To begin with, Sholoongo's mere presence tweaks our nose for deciding to peer into the closet of Somali letters only after the body politic has become a skeleton. But beyond that, her return reminds us that in the wake of all imperial adventures comes a stream of refugees; in that sense, and not just in our narcissistic imaginations, the Somali story really *is* part of America now … Quite literally, then, Somalia now resides deep in the American heartland. (Eldridge 2002: 655)

As I explore more substantially in the chapters to come, this corresponds with the increasingly diasporic and entangled concerns of Farah's latest work. Whilst Eldridge employs the kind of fleshy rhetoric used throughout *Secrets* and earlier novels, it is his focus on Sholoongo as a disruptive presence, transgressing geo-political and liminal space, which is most illuminating. This interest, in what Paul Virilio has termed '[the] fateful geographic confusion of the local and the global', informs the *Past Imperfect* trilogy (Virilio 2002: 128). In relation to the intensification of visceral imagery here, however, it is revealing that Kalaman associates Sholoongo's invasion of his psychic and domestic space with bodily rupture: '[n]ow she is here, in my kitchen, a real blood-and-bones irritation' (*Sec*: 32). This recalls the title of Lewis's study, *Blood and Bone – The Call of Kinship in Somali Society*. Sholoongo's transatlantic arrival acts as a corporeal catalyst, setting our protagonist on an Askar-esque search, at once existential and intimately physical, to uncover the tangled roots of his own beginnings and identity. When thinking about the relationship between the text's form and content, therefore, Eldridge's description of it as 'sinuously circuitous' is once more effective (Eldridge 2002: 638).

Knots, Links and the Processes of Globalisation

I previously compared Askar's besieged body in *Maps* with the subtler, psychosomatic exploration of confinement, in anatomical as well as architectural terms, found in Farah's portrait of asthma-afflicted Deeriye in *Close Sesame*. Similarly, *Secrets'* shifting body politics must be set against the dissolution of what Timothy Brennan, citing Foucault, calls the nation's 'discursive formation' (Brennan 1989: 4). Farah's recent, if controversial, compulsion to explore taboos and transgression using such a visceral repertory, therefore, comes from a more-than-merely sensationalist desire to shock. Thus, whilst Nonno's sexual prowess stands in explicit contrast with Deeriye's Muslim piety, seemingly representing the gulf between both trilogies, an abiding concern with designs personal and political remains. This is shown in Farah's treatment of corporeal and, in particular, blood images throughout *Secrets*. A revision of the tangled strands of affiliation symbolised by the spider's web, lattice or maze in earlier work, it is the motif of knotting, with its simultaneous suggestion of the gallows and the tying of protective bonds, that carries greatest significance throughout *Secrets*. It also anticipates the concerns of *Links*, *Knots* and *Crossbones*. Following Sholoongo's early inquisitions, Kalaman attempts to chart a course through 'a world of sperm-and-blood uncertainties' (*Sec*: 204–205). What becomes clear to the reader early on, however, is that the journey will further jolt his provisional sense of self:

> Blood oaths there were, the veins of fingers cut, flints used, vows taken, till-death-pull-us-asunder promises made. Put it down to a sense of guilt weighing on my conscience, but the truth was I felt trapped in a universe of knots, which the more I tried to undo, the more the clove hitches loosened up and the more the reef knots and the bowlines got more and more entangled. (*Sec*: 32)

Whilst Kalaman's imagistic focus appears somewhat indulgent, the choice of knotting motifs operates at various levels. As I have argued throughout, concerns with the pronominal politics of affiliation, in relation to Somalia's lineage system, cast their shadow across Farah's work. In *Secrets*, such tensions are staged between the stayee figure of Kalaman and returnees

Sholoongo and Timir. 'At this stage of the strife, almost every act appeared to be informed by the politics of the parties waging a struggle. I let it go as I often have let foreigners' throwaway remarks spoken in ignorance, foreigners who hold the view that "Somali politics is clan politics." It would take me years to convince them otherwise' (*Sec*: 43). Interventions such as these challenge those who would define Farah as an unswerving critic of Somali genealogy. With a nod to scholars who have bemoaned the binary structures of Western epistemologies, *Secrets* is primarily concerned with the material fallout resulting from the perversion of clan logic rather than its structuring principles. Once again, therefore, the defamiliarising impulse that drives novels such as *Gifts* and *Knots* is robust here.

As Eldridge argues, Farah's concern with the politics and processes of globalisation cannot be dismissed as mere rhetorical play. With characteristic insight, he draws attention to Farah's oblique reference to an Iman-esque Somali supermodel, Waliya (*Sec*: 211), who generates income by cashing in on 'famine morphed, mollified, into famine-*chic*' (Eldridge 2002: 638).[4] Such concerns with the reified and fetishised body, commodified in order to meet the demands of various global consumers, are intriguing supplements to Farah's longer-standing body politics project. They also resonate with studies such as Dan Plesch's *The Beauty Queen's Guide to World Peace: Money, Power and Mayhem in the Twenty-First Century* (2004). The comparative reader is tasked with considering the discursive, arguably hegemonic connections between depictions of emaciated bodies in *Gifts* and a multinational industry turning profits by parading 'famine-*chic*' on a catwalk. Beyond such loaded allusions, *Secrets* gestures towards more-than-merely cosmetic repercussions for all inhabitants of a taxonomically ordered global village. As Eldridge maintains,

'Clan,' Farah has repeatedly asserted, in this novel and elsewhere, is merely a fig leaf, a thin shred of kinship allegiance covering over naked opportunism and egomaniacal thuggery, a manmade perversion masquerading as a natural phenomenon. The lesson of *Secrets* is not, as several reviewers would have it, that had those primitive Somalis only cast off their bafflingly backward notion of clan (as the author, evidently an improved specimen, did), they might have had a healthy nation founded in more heterogeneous kinds of community (like ours!) and saved their country from ruin. No: Somalia did not crumble because of some ancient, fundamental notion of 'clan' or 'tribe'. On the contrary: as in Rwanda, the Balkans, Nazi Germany and elsewhere, the late Somali incarnation of the idea is thoroughly, regrettably, modern. Moreover, 'clan' ... is itself a

> category no more intrinsic to Somalia than to the rest of the world. Like some
> sort of flesh-eating staph bacterium, it's endemic to all human societies, living
> right there on their skin. (Eldridge 2002: 652)

The Foucauldian thrust of this intervention is crucial. By situating Somalia in relation to those geo-political spaces that have borne witness to some of the twentieth century's gravest crimes, Eldridge disturbs archetypes of Somali exceptionalism. When seen through the bio-political prism, he suggests, the notion of 'clan' is one that confuses borders as it crosses them.

Whilst it remains imperative to foreground the manifest differences and contextual contingencies separating Nazi Germany and Rwanda, Eldridge does suggest how this kind of qualified comparativism might be enabling. If the terminology shifts, from 'clan' to 'tribe' to 'race', the bio-political paradigm remains largely intact. Once more, it governs orders of life and taxonomies of death. As such, Eldridge's strikingly embodied meditations invite speculations as to how and why the knot motif works in *Secrets* at global, local and individual levels. Essentially, as in *Gifts*, Farah's critique concerns the apocalyptic agency of those responsible for tying. With the blurring of global and local, personal and political, the reality of such tangled webs is beyond question; it is the revelation or concealment of such connections that becomes key. In light of Eldridge's qualified juxtaposition of Nazi Germany and Rwanda, we might consider the poignant, knotted rhetoric employed by Claudine Kayitesi, a survivor of the 1994 genocide:

> I also think that no one will ever write all the ordered facts about this mysterious
> tragedy; neither professors from Kigali or Europe, nor intellectuals or politicians.
> Any explanation as to what happened will fall down one side or the other like
> a rickety table. A genocide is not a bad patch of scrub rising from two or three
> roots, but it is a cluster of roots which have gone rotten underground without
> anyone noticing. (Hatzfeld 2005a: 150)

Kayitesi testifies to the haunting need to illuminate such connections rather than bury them under labels such as ancient (read barbaric) ethnic rivalries. Whilst operating in a fictional mode, Farah is similarly committed to challenging those dominant discourses that reduce the specificities of the larger African polity and the Somali body politic in particular. This preoccupation with entanglement only intensifies in his study of the Somali diaspora and throughout the *Past Imperfect* cycle.

In *Yesterday, Tomorrow*, Farah refers to the cul-de-sac of Italian colonial rule. Yet it is in *Secrets'* fictional setting that this at-once spatial and disciplinary metaphor is first invoked. Kalaman's struggle to pin down his identity and define himself in relation to what he believes to be his family is prompted by the existential anguish caused by his cul-de-sac of a name. It is Nonno, his supposedly paternal grandfather, who gives him this title. Kalaman's primary anxiety is that he cannot define himself in terms of the dominant order of things, where son can be traced to father and so on. Once again, as with Farah's preoccupation with distorted clan politics, it is the corruption of such genealogical inventories that causes most distress:

> I thought about my cul-de-sac of a name. Years earlier, I had come around
> to the idea that there were atavistic stresses in the string of names a Somali
> child recites as his or her own, emphases of a linear listing of ancestors in the
> male line … But what makes one kill another because this mythical ancestor
> is different from one's own: this has little to do with blood, more with a history
> of the perversion of justice. What makes one refuse to intermarry with a given
> community has to do with the politics of inclusion and exclusion. Forming a
> political allegiance with people just because their begats are identical to one's
> own – judging from the way in which clan-based militia groupings were arming
> themselves – is as foolish as trusting one's blood brother. Only the unwise trust
> those close to them, a brother, a sister, or an in-law. Ask anyone in power, ask a
> king, and he will advise you to mistrust your kin. (*Sec*: 76)

Sholoongo's arrival precipitates the probing of opacities, silences and unasked questions. The result is that Kalaman's ontological doubts gnaw away at him more intensely. Other commentators have surveyed this terrain effectively, exploring how the frame narrative encompasses this central struggle to reveal the roots of his patrilineal descent. Yet, as with Loyaan's quest to uncover those responsible for his brother's demise, it is the turbulent process of this exploration, rather than any definitive discovery, that Farah obliges both protagonist and reader to focus on. A juxtaposition of fleshy images from both trilogies proves illuminating in this regard. Whilst Soyaan, in *Sweet and Sour Milk*, depicts the besieged if still intact body politic suffering from a hernia of inefficiency, Kalaman's preoccupations are much more internal and personal. When he invokes corporeal metaphors, it is to give shape and substance to his own fraught sense of self. As the narrative unfolds, however, the reader situates Kalaman's quest in its always already political context. This is one in which relationships, micrological and macrological, familial and bio-political, are being constantly redefined. Farah's use of alternative narrative perspectives in *Secrets*, therefore, is highly significant.

Rather than imprison the reader in Kalaman's first-person narrative, Farah invites us to piece a more complex picture together from the insights of Damac, Sholoongo and Nonno. In the following, the task falls to the aged 'grandfather': 'I remembered Kalaman comparing secrets to growths on the body, boils maturing to the pus-forming stage, at which they might burst. Then one day, one moment, something happens' (*Sec*: 143). As Eldridge maintains, whilst it may cause the reader to wince, such eruptive imagery is essential to Farah's overarching objectives in *Secrets*:

> The whole thing seems to boil down … to 'sperm and blood' – and if pornographic traces of such intimate fluids are what Kalaman thinks he's sniffing for, then they are precisely what Farah will rub his nose (and ours) in at staggered intervals, in a prurient pageant of obscene ostentation … Yet Farah's purpose is on the whole quite serious: like the young Kalaman, like Sholoongo, he means – casually, wantonly – to shock, to provoke, to break taboos (a subject on which the book conducts a running, complicated debate). (Eldridge 2002: 646)

This once more recalls Said's pronouncement that 'the whole point [of the intellectual] is to be embarrassing, contrary, even unpleasant' (Said 1996: 11). Whilst the fiercest critics have questioned the political dimensions of *Secrets*' 'unpleasantness', it is imperative that Farah persevere with the rupturing body metaphor. Once more, the comparative reader is invited to think about the provocative connections between individual and collective body politics. In *Secrets*, however, it is crucial that the revelation of what we are tempted to believe is the narrative's defining secret does not fundamentally alter the order of things.

The Disorder of Things: Normalisation and Taboo

The reader learns that Kalaman was conceived during the vicious gang rape suffered by Damac. As in *Sardines*, whilst the brutality of rape is made explicit, the text foregrounds the various coping strategies employed by characters during and after the ordeal. Once this disconcerting truth is grappled with, the reader is invited to cast a more critical, revisionary eye over *Secrets*' characters. As in *Maps*, Farah disturbs our expectations regarding the cumulative revelation of a defining truth through Kalaman's contested narrative. Whilst the novel effectively builds to this point of dramatic disclosure, it is, as Alden and Tremaine suggest, of somewhat secondary significance at this late stage:

> The point of Kalaman's learning the 'truth' of his identity – that he is illegitimate and begotten in violence – is instead that it turns out not to be the truth at all, or not a significant truth. Rather, he rejects the principle by which social identity is constructed through bloodlines – whether genuine or forged – and insists that he is indeed the child of Damac and Yaqut by virtue of the commitments they choose to make to one another. Nonno responds to the revelation in the same manner, proclaiming Kalaman his rightful heir before his death at the end of the book. (Alden & Tremaine 1999: 77)

This fleeting treatment of the documentary circumstances surrounding Kalaman's discovery corresponds with my own sense that it is supplementary to, even as it serves to structure, a more engaged reading of *Secrets*. In this respect, it foreshadows the frame narrative of *Links*. In both novels, the reader's imagination is captured by the swirling body politics and identity interrogations that take place, involving the exposure of Kalaman's genealogy in *Secrets* and a somewhat spurious kidnap plot in *Links*. Crucially, when the former cracks the seemingly life-altering, because secretive, code of his identity, it is thoroughly anti-climactic. As referred to previously, Farah has been quick to point to the affinities between the opening and closing instalments of *Blood in the Sun*. Indeed, for both Askar and Kalaman, it is the gradual removal of these layers of indeterminate identity that disrupt their notions of exceptional birth. These fictional preoccupations are thus contiguous with Farah's long-standing commitment to challenging notions of Somali exceptionalism. Consider the implied relationship between individual and collective in the following, for instance: '[s]omething of a debilitated quality takes over the life of a Kalaman, who piques himself on his uniqueness, when he discovers that there is nothing special about his beginnings' (*Sec*: 189–190).

The reader accompanies Kalaman as he deconstructs himself, revealing his own complicity with those perversions of personal/political definition he conveniently opts to critique when it comes to clan politics. The explosion of myths surrounding his identity precipitates a more sobering, internal re-visioning. He thus renews his appreciation of the progressive environment in which the truly traumatised agents of the piece (the nominal parents he attacks for their strategic silences) nurture him. Prior to learning the painful truth behind his bloody beginnings, he defines himself as a child locked out by their whisperings. 'Starving a child of knowing the loving side of its parents is more cruel … You feed the child on self-mistrust. Paranoia eats into the heart of the unliked. In the end, such a child will imagine all kinds of untruths' (*Sec*: 153). It is only once he has come to terms with his unsettling news and attempts to imagine the situation from the perspectives of those involved that he revises his too-hasty judgements.

> I thought it is a wise father who knows when to tell what to his son. It is a wise parent who digs up the skeletons of a secret at the proper time, or knows when to allude to a scorpion by its name … [surrounded] by the uncertainties of life, my parents were wise to encircle themselves with a thread visible only to themselves, and which bound them together, a man and a woman who made a secret pact, their vows forever sealed in silence. (*Sec*: 263)

In the process of appreciating the insights of this wise father, Kalaman comes to read his mother's 'overwhelming neurosis' anew (*Sec*: 260). In so doing, he reinterprets her looks of revulsion and indifference towards him. As becomes clear, the scorpion reference serves as a cryptic clue for the narrative as a whole. Kalaman's review of events presents the decision of his adoptive parents to forge a mutually supportive union as being genuinely exceptional. Once again, it is the historical consciousness represented by Nonno that places these individual choices within contextual and collective frames, in turn imbuing them with oppositional importance. 'The nineteen sixties saw many such secret matrimonies, as the ideas of family authority over the individual were being renegotiated, following society's transformation from a preponderantly nomadic and rural one to an urban one' (*Sec*: 234). Interventions such as these give some sense of how and why preoccupations with renegotiation and redefinition, at once bio-political and social, mark the terrain of *Secrets* as a whole.

Suitably Foucauldian connections with *Maps*, therefore, can be extended in relation to Farah's complex portraits of seemingly central protagonists. Askar's rhetorical bluster is betrayed when he confronts the mutilated corpse of his adoptive mother Misra. Likewise, for all his existential navel-gazing, Kalaman must confront the reality that, whilst he was the product of the most intimate violence, it was not his body that was being targeted. Whilst he wallows in a metaphorical malaise, imagining his fractured identity in terms of dismemberment ('I sat down, not knowing what to do with my fragmented self. Highly uncoordinated images invaded my mind', *Sec*: 146), Farah once more privileges the incisiveness of a female intervention. It is the more circumspect and powerful meditation of Kalaman's adoptive mother that has the greatest impact on the reader. Prior to the not-so-grand revelation, Damac confides in Nonno, 'I am telling you that there are types of secrets which we choose not to disclose, secrets we prefer not to part with, secrets about dimly lit areas of one's lives, the lay of our bodies, the territories of our pain' (*Sec*: 174). Damac imagines a fence around her violated being, effectively reclaiming it in symbolic defiance. Like her fictional forbears in *Sardines* and *Maps*, and anticipating key figures in *Knots*, the act undermines the poisonous logic of the rapists. In so doing, Damac establishes comparably solid foundations for her union with Yaqut.

Fittingly, it is Nonno who supports the idea that there are intimate connections between harbouring secrets and alienating the self from the body (*Sec*: 173). Just as Askar's spiralling narrative prompts him to reassess his part in Misra's death, so Kalaman comes to revise his central belief that the revelation of patrilineal descent will restore order to that which is chaotic. Like Hilaal and Salaado in *Maps*, the pairing of Yaqut and Damac offers an alternative vision of human relations. The subversion of traditional gender roles is extended even further in this latter couple, with Damac's wage-earning capacity outstripping her husband who, in turn, performs largely domestic duties (*Sec*: 78–79). As previously argued, this destabilisation resonates at levels personal and political throughout the novel. It has also provoked heated debates about its Somaliness. I maintain, however, that this critical furore both mirrors *Secrets*' slippery nature and throws the whole, problematic notion of authenticity into crisis. In a world increasingly defined by the processes of glocalisation, Farah seems to ask what it means to invoke authentic discourses. Accordingly, the implosion of totemic phrases such as '*fathers matter not, mothers matter a lot*,' leads to the acknowledgement that there are 'no easy matters' (*Sec*: 111), in either existential or experiential terms, both within and beyond *Secrets*.

In a familiar manoeuvre, Farah conceives the turbulent evolution of Kalaman's more complex sense of self through a series of architectural motifs. Evicted from his world of petit-bourgeois comfort, his descent into the whirlpool of bloody uncertainties gives him a discomfiting insight into the violence being enacted on the body politic. Set against this collective atrophy, Yaqut and Damac's relationship is seen to be even more exemplary:

> He had no right to blame his parents or Nonno or others for his own failures. Nor had he the right to blame Sholoongo, a classical other. You could apply the same yardstick against which you could assess the contributions others

had made to the construction of the collapse, brick by destructive brick. Give people a chance to speak their pieces, and many will display their personal and collective hurts: Kalaman, his parents, Nonno … they all see themselves as ill used by the dictatorship. Press them further into a corner, ask them for their contribution to the struggle against one-man tyranny, and they fall silent, many unable to deny being accomplices in the ruin. Quick in self-defense, they blame the former colonialists, and they blame both the Soviet Union and the United States for bankrolling the cold warriors, gamers in weapons of mass destruction. Our challenge is to locate the metaphor for the collapse of the collective, following that of the individual. (*Sec*: 191)

References to weapons of mass destruction aside, it is the allusion to the construction of collapse that gestures towards trajectories of implosion and explosion, as well as the twin existential burdens of building personal and political identities. Whilst this is reiterated a little too explicitly in the final line, the above extract once again works in accordance with the guiding principle of Farah's oeuvre: 'it's just starting with the small and moving towards the big' (Farah 2002: 31). Repeated references to 'them' and 'they' prefigure the contentious debates surrounding the cult of blamocracy to be explored in *Yesterday, Tomorrow*. Yet, the swirling moral vortex at the centre of *Secrets* concerns the contested body itself and its attendant privileging of a politics of responsibility. Set against the collapse of a repressive yet centralised citadel of power, Farah presents a ground-zero scenario in which, like the *Variations* series, relationships must be renegotiated within the domestic sphere before being transposed onto the national stage. As he prepares for his own curtain call, it is the aged figure of Nonno who is left to speak one of the narrative's key truths to power. 'We were being made to rethink our relationships, what Somalia meant to each of us, the smaller unit succeeding where the larger unit, that of nationhood, had failed' (*Sec*: 227). The indeterminate allusion to 'we' blurs the dividing lines between savage actors and detached directors and, more widely, debates surrounding exilic writer and national subjects. It is the manner in which Farah attends to such contentious issues that continues to define the reception of one of his most provocative and problematic works. Seen from a Foucauldian perspective, however, it is arguably the idea that failure at the level of macrological narratives (in this case 'nationhood') has precipitated a change in focus onto the microphysics of power, struggle and resistance that is most essential. That said, it is too simple to conflate this shift towards micropolitical negotiation with quietism and/or fatalism. I suggest that, in their distinctive ways, the micropolitical strain that runs throughout Farah and Foucault's respective projects corresponds with their preoccupations with effecting immediate, local change. It is only once these negotiations take place, within the self, the family and/or a particular disciplinary space, that their real impact might be felt on a broader level.

Reconfiguring a Symbolics of Blood: Taboo and Transgression in *Secrets*

As he allows the dramatic tension to simmer before Sholoongo's entrance, Farah foregrounds the socio-material privileges that set the scene for her first encounter with Kalaman. It is Lambar, Kalaman's domestic worker, who reports her disconcerting presence: '[your] visitor has the quiet, confident look of someone who has chosen to be, if you follow my meaning. It was as though she chose to be a woman today, but that she could as well have been a man in another life, or a ghost or a goat' (*Sec*: 28). Whilst the spectral allusions support associations with Morrison's liminal character in *Beloved*, welded to Somali-specific, pre-Islamic myths, it is the relationship between this fluid description and Kalaman's gestures towards other designs that is significant. '[She] had too short a neck for a human, more like a bird's and just as agitated, forever moving back and forth, up and down, perhaps tracing mystical sevens, or else tying the knots of eights, or drawing the top loop of a nine' (*Sec*: 30). The association between a polymorphous being and a figure who has 'designs' on the lives of various characters, intent on tying them in knots from which they might never escape, is one Sholoongo will occupy throughout the text. The fraught nature of her relationship with Damac, for instance, is critical. As with Qumman and Beydan in *Sweet and Sour Milk*, Farah once more explores those tensions that compromise dreams of gender and generational solidarity.

When, for instance, Damac declares her intention to banish the 'half-human-half-animal deviant' (*Sec*: 74) she believes is disrupting her dreams, it is the older, wiser Nonno who points out the pitfalls of scapegoating. He urges Damac to look beyond the *duugan* (malevolent Somali spirit) label, in the interests of acknowledging Sholoongo as a fellow wronged woman:

> There are far too many strong minds working the same territory. Sholoongo is the territory we are tilling, a most fertile soil, dark as the good earth is yielding. She is the territory, she is the cause, she is the source of much ill will. Each member of our immediate family is involved … Add to this the fact that in

America, she has trained as a shape-shifter, able to tap into the energy of her shamanic powers. Shamans heal, they do not harm. (*Sec*: 141)[5]

If the imagery of woman as dark, sensuous, unmapped territory is troubling, Farah plays with it in order to gesture towards the sexual arena in which Sholoongo will prove herself dominant rather than dominated. In addition, loaded references to 'territory' invite the reader to forge connections between the two, links that Damac, initially at least, is unwilling to entertain. Their longstanding animosity is shown to date back to their battles for Kalaman's affections as well as Sholoongo's purported role in guarding a vital identity document. Like Deeriye once again, it is Nonno who sees the turbulent fate of the nation writ large in the alternative mistreatments suffered by these two women. '[The] crisis that is coming to a head in the shape of civil strife would not be breaking on us if we'd offered women-as-mothers their due worth, respect and affection' (*Sec*: 243). If Sholoongo can now cross international borders in a globalised village that rewards her professional, if parodic, status as an exotic animist shape-shifter, Farah, like Nonno, adds dimensions to her character by viewing it within a specifically Somali context. On her return, she finds herself framed by familiarly malevolent associations. Alongside battles to free herself from the historical chains of the past, this sets the stage for more visceral struggles.

Towards the close of *Secrets*, Sholoongo and Nonno share the bed denied her by Kalaman. 'Share', however, does not tell the whole story as it is the setting for *hor-gur* (female rape of the male). Mazrui maintains that this troubling scene works in accordance with the complex play of global/local, postmodern/pre-Islamic, post-national/quasi-mythic that distinguishes Farah's novel: '[i]t is [Nonno's] historical consciousness ... that Sholoongo, the collective representation of the Somali(an) woman turned-American, rapes in order to reproduce Somalia in its new globalized womb' (Mazrui 2002: 625). He argues that Farah's turn towards this specifically Somali cultural practice indicates his desire to challenge the rigidly patriarchal order he sees as largely responsible for the current, clannish disorder: '*hor-gur* is itself a symbolic challenge to the patriarchal dispensation within which Somali(an) identity is framed. It is also an attempt to reappraise and perhaps celebrate the matriarchal face of Somaliland that has been eradicated by Islamic and European intrusions' (Mazrui 2002: 624). Whatever the reader's take on this interpretation, it seems oddly fitting that, for a book concerned with the collisions of cultures, the impassioned debates it has sparked have been largely disseminated via Internet chat rooms and social-networking sites. For many

Somalis, living in a truly post-national context, such communicative forums are invaluable.[6]

Of arguably greatest significance, however, is the manner in which Farah's negotiation of those geo-political and cultural discourses surrounding globalisation always return us to contested corporeal terrain. Once Sholoongo has got what she wants (supposedly the right amount of sperm to become a mother), she imagines wandering lost in 'the labyrinths of my capital joy, my motherhood' (Sec: 274). Considering the various connotations of the labyrinth motif gestured towards throughout, the use of it in Secrets, in relation to sexual activity, is an intriguing variation on a key metatextual theme. Sholoongo may initially appear in charge of hor-gur. Crucially, however, Farah undermines this by once more invoking the body inscribed with pain. In so doing, he compels the comparative reader to place Sholoongo within a corporeal lineage that stretches back to Ebla in From a Crooked Rib through to Cambara in Knots. For all her transnational border crossing and anthropomorphic play, Sholoongo cannot get beyond her painfully fleshy reality. Beneath the appearance of sexual agency, therefore, is the sense that her body is a marked labyrinth from which she can never fully escape: '[Nonno] fondled the tip of an area which might have been my clitoris if I hadn't been infibulated, wherein I might have been easily aroused' (Sec: 272).

An exploration of further parallels with the indeterminate figure of Beloved in Morrison's novel, therefore, proves instructive. Whilst the reader is not permitted to pin down her identity or specific function with any degree of certainty, her liminal being is always already rendered in terms of the bloody infanticide of which she was the victim. Like Sholoongo, she too is first conceived and then dispatched to absorb and then absolve the associated traumas of other characters caught in the narrative's web. As Farah points out in Secrets, Sholoongo's name 'alludes to an ancient precapitalist form of banking among women; these contribute each to a collection, to share out once a week' (Sec: 171). In effect, therefore, she serves as a receptacle into which the community invests its collective hurt, guilt and shame, only to take and take until she has nothing left to give. To extend the image further, the comparative havoc stirred by Sholoongo's return can be interpreted as the settling of some older, darker debts from which, as Nonno suggests, nobody is exempt. 'Why blame her? Why not blame yourself?' (Sec: 142). Once again, this foreshadows the provocative idea of blamocracy so central to Yesterday, Tomorrow.

As in Beloved, a similar oscillation between spheres liminal and lived, polymorphous and political, subversive and scapegoated is gestured towards through the figure of Sholoongo. Critically, for Farah's predominantly Western readership, the uncertainty of her meaning not only results from the density of Somali-specific cultural and mythological allusions. It also corresponds to the turbulent socio-political context in which she is imagined. As such, Nancy Diaz's comments about the truly 'fantastic' qualities of figures in various Latin American texts might be productively transposed:

> [A] mutable narrative world will be one in which phenomena are often strangely altered in form and therefore in meaning, in which the line between what is supposed to be real and what is not becomes blurred, and in which the reader may be asked to question his or her own sense of stability and stasis in the objective world. (For unlike the fantastic narratives described by Tzvetan Todorov, the Latin American narratives [considered here] … assume a vital political and historical relationship between the configurations of the narrative world and those of the external world.) (Diaz 1988: 4–5)

In terms of the infibulated female body gestured towards above, I argue that the critical preoccupations of the *Variations* and *Blood in the Sun* cycles productively blur at key points. At every juncture, underwriting dense allusions to transnational flows of culture and capital, and what Samater defines as distorted reference to the intricacies of Somali belief systems, there remains a resolute concern with the kind of fleshy materiality central to El Saadawi's *The Hidden Face of Eve*, amongst other studies. 'A college student told me that her brother had been wont to caress her sexual organs and that she used to experience acute enjoyment. However after undergoing circumcision she no longer had the same sensation of pleasure' (El Saadawi 1980: 36).

It is therefore vital that Sholoongo's role is not just that of a quasi-liminal being, forcing characters to face their own dark secrets. Of equal importance is the way she is used to confront the reader with a series of decidedly uncomfortable issues. At one significant level, Farah employs her to shine an interrogative light on the darker side of those politics underpinning notions of taboo, deviance and abnormality. As Sholoongo's desire for sexual fulfilment/motherhood is checked by the reality of her infibulated body, she also worries that Nonno might be just another man in her life, following her husband and father, ravaged by AIDS.[7] Nonno alludes to 'containing waste'. The reader therefore shares Sholoongo's uncertainty as to whether these are the words of a man who knows he is on the verge of death or as the result of a retroviral disease or both. With reference to her quasi-mythic upbringing as an orphan cast out by society to live amongst animals, Sholoongo concludes 'it's been my ill luck to keep courting men on the verge of extinction, myself a returnee from the precipice of death, surviving it thanks to the kindness of a wolf, the maternal instinct of a lioness, the protective motherliness of an ostrich' (*Sec*: 271). Whilst these allusions to animalistic/animist origins might gesture towards Farah's attempts to synthesise 'pre' and 'post' modern concerns, they also support Nonno's claims about the bestial treatment meted out to her as an orphan by a culpable society (*Sec*: 143).

In terms of the approach I have adopted throughout, of greater interest is the way Farah tackles discourses surrounding the truly globalised phenomena of AIDS. This is, of course, an area in which much of the most stimulating scholarship has been inspired by Foucault.[8] In the South African context, for instance, Didier Fassin's interventions, such as 'The Politics of Death: Race War, Bio-Power and AIDS in the Post-Apartheid', have been key (Fassin 2008: 151–165). If I can only gesture towards this vast field, I maintain it provides yet another, inherently bio-political lens through which to view *Blood in the Sun's* concerns with conflict, famine and the globalisation of disease. Farah orients the AIDS narrative around the figures of Sholoongo and her brother. With reference to Yoweri Museveni and Robert Mugabe, Mazrui suggests that Farah's introduction of Timir, an openly gay figure, intersects with discussions concerning homosexuality and its place within African society more widely:

> [Tensions] and accommodations between the dispersed and the 'stayees' are also played out in the arena of the global equalizer, AIDS. Timir and Sholoongo came home to attend the funeral of their father who, in his last hour, had wasted away like an AIDS victim. On the other hand, it is those who have been in contact with the West, returnees like Timir and Sholoongo, who are suspected of being the likely carriers of the AIDS virus. The West sees AIDS as a disease that originated in Africa. Africans see it as a Western-borne disease. Each perception inscribes a particular identitarian quality in the 'other'. (Mazrui 2002: 633)

Mazrui is also quick to point to the fact that it is Sholoongo, as transgressor of liminal and lived borders, who is invested with the most progressive powers. Similarly, he considers how and why Farah endows her with the diasporic propensity to make such connections rather than accept the rigid binary model: '[it] is only Sholoongo who recognizes AIDS as a trans-national, global phenomenon. As she entertains the possibility that Nonno (with whom she is engaged in sexual union) may be HIV positive, she reminds herself that her own Maghreb husband in the USA is also HIV positive' (Wright 2002: 633). This, in turn, works in conjunction with, as it also anticipates, much contemporary scholarship on the globalisation of various pandemics, such as *Urban Health: Global Perspectives* (2010. Eds. D. Vlahov *et al.*). Indeed, the notion that Sholoongo serves as a representative gateway, opening onto the politics of a more-than-merely sensationalist series of taboos, is critical in relation to the trajectory of Farah's most recent work.

Responding to the reactions of some readers following the publication of *Secrets*, Farah maintains:

> [it's] interesting … that there is a certain openness about lots of taboo material in *Secrets*, much more than in much African fiction, where there is a certain prudishness about it. And my view is if the members of a society can do unto each other such savageries, then who are they to remain prudish? Who are they to say there are no longer virgins, there is no honesty, there is no truth, there is no trust, nothing, and therefore it's a world in which every acceptable truth can be challenged? (Farah 2002: 44)

With these sentiments in mind, it is unsurprising that the spectres of national meltdown hang heavy over the *Past Imperfect* trilogy. Whilst Farah's work, particularly from *Secrets* onwards, is marked by the pronounced tensions between exilic writer and stayee subjects, there is a sense that his gestures towards interrogating taboos in a globalised context derive from the same central source. He constructs an ornate network of taboos, in which the contentious issues arising from this foundational 'perversion' spill over into the similarly transgressive and, crucially, embodied arena of homosexuality and AIDS, amongst others.

As Eldridge asserts and Samater quibbles, *Secrets* is an all-or-nothing text. Imagistic showers of blood and sperm create understandable unease in certain readers. For Farah, such disturbing preoccupations exist in a genuinely aberrant hierarchy where bio-political paradigms such as ethnicity are manipulated, leading to the bloody entanglement of political allegiances. Towards the narrative's close, for instance, Kalaman attempts to define the role Sholoongo has played or, rather, that others have coerced her into playing throughout. When read in terms of Farah's societal critique, the link Kalaman imagines is not as distorted as he at first supposes: 'I think of her as a shaman who has come not to heal but to dispossess us of our secret ill wills. I compare her, wrongheadedly, to one's idea of the clan: a notion difficult to locate, slippery, contradictory, temperamental, testing one's capacity to remain patient during one's trying times' (*Sec*: 294). Set against the promotion of absolute blood lineages by new oligarchs seeking to consolidate their power bases, Sholoongo's intermittently transgressive and fluid qualities are her most radical weapons. Having obliged a host of characters to review, however tentatively, certain occluded parts of themselves, Sholoongo embodies the very dynamics that Kalaman draws from as he comes to define himself anew and in opposition to the distortion of clan affiliation.

As such, the bio-political rhetoric relied upon by Innocent Rwililiza, a survivor from another bloody fallout, resonates here. As she recalls in *Into the Quick of Life*: '[in] certain ways, ethnicity is like AIDS, the less you dare talk of it, the more ravages it causes' (Hatzfeld 2005b: 77). Whilst contextual caution must be exercised, embodied contests concerning the entangled roots of power and identity feature prominently in the cases of both Rwanda and Somalia. As in the Eldridge analysis above, the notion that such maladies are indigenous is reductive at best. As Gourevitch points out, it was the Belgian colonial practice of insisting on identity cards, defining each Rwandan in accordance to a prescribed ethnic taxonomy, that exacted the bloodiest toll in the historical present:

> [In] 1933–34, the Belgians conducted a census in order to issue 'ethnic' identity cards, which labelled every Rwandan as either Hutu (eighty five percent) or Tutsi (fourteen percent) or Twa (one percent). The identity cards made it virtually impossible for Hutus to become Tutsis, and permitted the Belgians to perfect the administration of an apartheid system rooted in the myth of Tutsi superiority … Whatever Hutu and Tutsi identity may have stood for in the precolonial state no longer mattered; the Belgians had made 'ethnicity' the defining feature of Rwandan existence. (Gourevitch 2000: 56–57)

Referring to progressive steps taken by the post-genocide administration, Gourevitch points out that '[one] of the first acts of the new government was to abolish the system of ethnic identity cards, which had served as death tickets for Tutsis during the genocide' (Gourevitch 2000: 223). In the context of *Secrets*, it is similarly significant that, amidst the bloody swirls of identity conflict, personal and political, two pivotal incidents concern the processes by which identities are translated into documents. In light of the Foucauldian approach I have pursued throughout, it is their written quality that seemingly holds out most hope of restoring order to that defined by disorderliness.

Reconfiguring his earlier preoccupation with cryptic codes and conundrums, Farah fleshes out the details surrounding the circumstances of

Damac's rape, paying particular attention to the role played by paperwork in constructing official identities. Arbaco, mother of supermodel Waliya and Damac's former friend, fills in the narrative blanks for Kalaman by explaining how a forged marriage certificate led to this formative attack. A previously spurned suitor arrives at the home Damac shares with her aunt, carrying a document that appears to prove their union. The innocent girl's protestations fall on deaf ears and she is cast out. Meanwhile, the hapless suitor loses the forged document, which he bought on the understanding it would guarantee him a wife in a card game with an underworld group skilled in processing false papers. They arrive at Damac's doorstep, suitor in tow, to collect their loot. When she refuses to give herself over, she is gang-raped. At this narrative juncture, the reader acknowledges the significance of references likening secrets to scorpions lurking under stones (Gacme-Xume, the lead rapist, is described as having scorpion hands, *Sec*: 174). Once again, therefore, rather than providing the central revelation in Kalaman's genealogical quest, it is a discovery that gives the reader another perspective on the animosity between Damac and Sholoongo: the former mistakenly believing it was the latter who had stolen the document, thereby holding the ultimate power to take her 'son' away. All falls into place when the initials of the originally rejected suitor are revealed as Y.M.I. When Arbaco hears of the crime, she tracks down who she believes to be the culprit. Mazrui is typically alert to the playfully coded question that Farah poses in the midst of this concentric narrative, with Y.M.I operating as an acronym of Kalaman's primary question: 'Why am I?' (Mazrui 2002: 622). In a case of mistaken identity, Damac is introduced to Yaqut and a mutually supportive relationship results. Whilst this summary does not do justice to its careful disclosure in the text, it gives some sense of the narrative preoccupation with unstable meanings and identities (*Sec*: 230–231).

Following this seismic revelation, Nonno, like Medina before him, attempts to put his house in order. In an inversion of Damac's realisation of the radical contingency of documents, he turns to the supposed certainty of his old identity papers. In much the same way as his adopted grandson as well as Askar in *Maps*, he seeks respite from the fluid pronominal politics that define the wider political sphere and encroach upon his home by revisiting an earlier version of himself:

> I am searching for the first identity card the Italian authorities issued to me
> in my true names, mine and my father's and my grandfather's, in that order
> ... tragedies have a humour to them too. In fact, such was the Italian clerk's
> ignorance that I am described in that first Identity Card as *Inglese*, apparently

because I hailed from what was then the British Somaliland Protectorate. His superior officer, when signing the ID card, crosses out the word *Inglese* and in its place writes in his clumsy hand the word *Britannico*. Other Somalis of my acquaintance had their clan names where I had *Britannico*. Fancy that! (*Sec*: 241)

If, as I have argued throughout, preoccupations with the politics of passports, identity papers and cards are pronounced features of Farah's work, it is the peculiarly embodied juxtaposition between ethnicity and AIDS, as alluded to by Innocent Rwililiza, which shapes how Kalaman sees his search for identity. With typical introspection, he reflects on his status as a changed man, struggling to come to terms with those family allegiances shifting beneath his feet: 'Nonno not my grandfather. Yaqut not my father. I thought ahead to the moment when my mother would give me her version of what occurred. How would people react to the news that I was the issue of a gang rape? I didn't want sympathy or pity from anyone, I wanted to see palpable anger' (*Sec*: 236). In terms of staging a wider textual debate between Somali-specific pronominal politics and their globalised counterparts in *Secrets*, it is revealing that Kalaman-the-capitalist frames his crisis using a host of first-person singulars. Like Askar, he pays comparatively little attention to the vast territory of pain in which his supposed mother roams. Whilst this self-absorption affects his existential interrogations, it is Kalaman's conceptual and class-specific attempt to fathom a nearest equivalent that is most revealing:

Naturally, it would confound a lot of simpleminded clan-obsessed persons who might feel cheated of their right to know the name of the rapist, my biological father, if only to assign me to one of the clans. If they had pitied me, it would be because I was the poor sod who hadn't a blood family to be loyal to, to kill and die for, in this epoch of clan-kill-clan! I wondered how someone like Qalin, my deputy at the firm and once my lover, might react to this. How would my employees receive the news? I could only compare it in my experience to learning that X, a friend, had AIDS. We didn't know what to do, at least I didn't. So what do you say to someone afflicted with an identity crisis like mine, akin to AIDS in that it points to a kind of death? (*Sec*: 236–237)

Whilst, on one level, such instances appear to invite the reader to trace the development of Kalaman's increasingly complex sense of self, they also allow us to differentiate between the perspectives of author and protagonist. The above extract captures Kalaman as contradiction, showing how and why he projects his own confusion onto others. He effectively denounces them in the name of his own shortcomings. In as much as the drawing of equivalence between AIDS victim and existentially anguished protagonist concerns the embodied intricacies with which Farah's work has long been concerned, the comparison is effective. It is crucial, however, that the reader be called upon to attend to the difference between terminal patient and living, breathing, political agent. The great, deflating irony that Kalaman's dismissal of an ordering of society through clan, blood and bio-political lineages comes up against is the example of his 'parents'. It is therefore significant that Nonno frames his 'grandson's' search for identity in terms of a crossroad rather than a labyrinth. Before his death, he invests resistant hope in an upcoming generation to exercise the kind of agency abused by their counterparts:

> 'As a citizen of the crossroads where several worlds meet … you will find the weight of contradictory signs beginning to appear. You will come upon footpaths forking in all sorts of directions, signposts giving you confusing directions to where there is no return.' … Ill at ease in my company, or so I thought, his eyes evasive, [Nonno] looked withdrawn. He had known me as his grandson. Now I wasn't his grandchild anymore? There was I: the offspring of a gang rape. I had nothing of certainty linking me, as his own blood, to him. (*Sec*: 236)

Kalaman's most profound challenge, to be problematically amplified throughout the *Past Imperfect* cycle, is to expose the schisms and cope with the contradictions. To escape from the labyrinth, as in the *Variations* series, or to make the counter-hegemonic choice confronting him at the crossroad, he must bear the burdens of responsibility: 'There I was, dumbfounded, tyrannized – the summation, the symbol of many a Somali in a worse condition than I was. I wasn't what I had always believed myself to be, a man able to locate his truth in half truth, and able to live with the contradictions' (*Sec*: 250). As always, complexities, contradictions and confusion abound in Farah's fiction. Yet, however cryptic their signposting, alternative outlets remain.

'There Must Be Some Way Out of Here'

Interventions by scholars such as Sara Ahmed have provided some of the most provocative work at the intersection of feminist and postcolonial studies. They include *Differences that Matter: Feminist Theory and Postmodernism* (1998) and *Thinking through the Skin* (2001). In *Strange Encounters:*

Embodied Others in Postcoloniality (2000), Ahmed lends fleshy substance to her observations on stranger danger:

> In my analysis of strangers and knowledge … I discussed Plato's understanding of philosophy as a sneeze: the guard dogs and philosophers 'smell' the strangers (again, they have to be close enough) and by sneezing (a practice so habitual that it has become an automatic reflex), expel the strangers from the philosophical body, or the body of the good philosopher. Other forms of bodily expulsion might be shitting and vomiting, both of which imply a process of partial incorporation as well as expulsion: the other/stranger must be taken in, and digested, before what is desirable is both transformed and expelled. (Ahmed 2000: 136)

The implosion/explosion dynamics so central to *Secrets'* various concerns can also be seen as reworking these inhalation/exhalation, consumption/rejection tropes. If Farah's besieged body imagery is overdetermined at times, the 'histamine inelegance' (*Sec*: 28) Kalaman suffers appears analogous with the stranger danger sensations Ahmed, borrowing from Audre Lourde, traces on the surface of the skin: '[the] reforming of bodily and social space involves a process of *making the skin crawl*; the threat posed by strange bodies to bodily and social integrity is registered on the skin' (Ahmed 2000: 46). This can be seen in relation to one of Kalaman's earliest reflections in the narrative: 'I stood right in the center of an open parenthesis, in a time without past or present or future. Then I felt something scratchily pulling at the hairs inside my nostrils, and sneezed so loud the world shook on its stilts. My nose was runny with mucus, my lips were wet with saliva and the palms of my hands moist with a motley of discharges' (*Sec*: 28). Alongside allusions to jinn-like disruption, Farah once more relies on the open bracket image he has used for identity searches stretching from *Sweet and Sour Milk* to *Links* (*L*: 322). As Sholoongo confirms herself as a more than passing presence, Kalaman's sneezing fits intensify. 'I sensed I itched all over as if I had come into contact with a poisonous ivy. Maybe the thought of having [her] as my guest had brought about an allergic tendency in me. I sneezed' (*Sec*: 52).

Typically, Mazrui urges the reader to look beneath the surface of such metaphors. He suggests they be viewed in conjunction with Farah's more pressing engagement with what I argue to be a biopolitics of globalisation, shuttling between pre- and postmodern spheres. Following their final, troubling copulation, Sholoongo bemoans the insatiable irritation she has contracted from Nonno:

> Now I was full of self-loathing. I picked up objects with sharp edges, pencils, pens, any items with the shape of a phallus. I scratched and scratched … I tore madly at my insides, dragging my claws at the walls of my person, my sex ... Had Nonno filled me with self-loathing? Was my body refusing to hold it? The thought that my body was resisting against Nonno's poison provided me with a short-lived sense of comfort, an instant of respite. (*Sec*: 282)

If such sections might cause eyebrows to be raised, the comparative reader will reflect that Farah has always placed the politics of contested female bodies at the heart of his work. As in *Maps*, therefore, it is critical to note that images of oozing and seepage are accompanied by gestures towards the material pain of infibulation. 'I oozed. I held my legs closer together and tighter in the uncomfortable posture of a young girl sore from a recent infibulation' (*Sec*: 281). Indeed, if Kalaman's 'histamine inelegance' (*Sec*: 28) can be likened to Ahmed's notion of stranger danger, further discursive connections might be forged in relation to this notion of oozing. As argued above, feminist scholars such as Margrit Shildrick have made much of the counter-hegemonic propensity of the female body that oozes, flows and refuses containment. As Ruth Holliday and John Hassard maintain in *Contested Bodies*:

> instead of spending time refuting the claim that women's bodies leak, ooze, intermingle and are far from self-contained, we must accept this proposition and theorise from it …The postmodern subject with its fuzzy boundaries and interdependent subjectivities has more in common with the conventional associations of womanhood than it does with the masculinist rational individual. Postmodernist subjectivities might be thought of as leaky subjectivities. (Holliday & Hassard 2001: 7)

If *Secrets* is a coda to *Maps*, productive links might be made between the similarly transgressive figures of Sholoongo and Misra. Yet, whilst such associations are enabling up to a point, the nature of Farah's corporeal project demands we avoid apolitical fantasies of bodies that are all fluid, no substance. This is achieved, at one level, by reading Sholoongo against those Somali-specific mythologies and cultural traditions reworked by Farah. Therefore, whilst Mazrui maintains that the fleshy fissures in the faux-relationship between Nonno and Sholoongo represent 'the love affair between Somalia and its Diaspora [as coming] to a painful, itching, oozing end, like a body that has rejected its transplanted part', it needs to be set against a more substantial socio-political backdrop (Mazrui 2002: 626).

The disruptions in Kalaman's personal narrative can, to a certain extent, be seen as dovetailing with that of the broader blood-and-bones irritation being played out at the national level. As with every other novel before and since, therefore, the success of *Secrets* is to be judged according to the effectiveness with which it probes dialectical relations between the personal and the political. In showing how and why one is prevented from being subsumed by the other, it also explores how old certainties begin to buckle:

> There is a Somali proverb that says that mothers are a certainty. To paraphrase: if there is a parent of whom we tend to be certain, it is the mother. But we are in an epoch in which mother-as-certainty no longer holds true: babies are abandoned in garbage bins. I read in a local paper the other day about a casualty of uncertainty, a mother committing suicide because her Somali-born daughter, now an American citizen, had borne a test-tube child. Why did the mother take her own life? Is it because she couldn't bear living any longer in a world where the mother-as-certainty was questioned, undermined as it was by the secret-derived science of today? (*Sec*: 196)

Self-reflexive nods to *Gifts* aside ('babies are abandoned in garbage bins'), specific attention is paid to those fraught dynamics of the North American/ Somali diaspora focused on by Mazrui and that will become more prominent in the *Past Imperfect* cycle. The above also functions as a reworking of the American-Somali girl narrative recounted by Medina in *Sardines*. Yet it is the sense that there is a constantly changing face and place of a politics or symbolics of blood that is most striking in relation to the Foucauldian approach of this book. As Eldridge maintains, if we subscribe to the epistemological notion of postmodern networks of communication and flow, conceptions of pure national sovereignty and/or primitive blood feuds become similarly fluid. Viewed from a post-9/11 perspective, Farah's allusions to the destabilisation of the United States' sense of self are eerily prophetic. This said, however, they appear more invested in the radical possibilities that might be unleashed by a truly interrogative critique. 'Are we speaking of a community's certainty shaken to its rock foundation, the essence of its collective survival? What of ascertaining paternity, of DNA, blood-to-blood? Science-derived secrets have delved into this uncertainty, helping to push the frontiers of certainty' (*Sec*: 196). The rhetorical opacity is crucial here. It once more challenges the reader to reflect on who this 'we' refers to and whether the notion of a 'community's certainty' relates to Somalia, America or both as occupants of a bio-political global village. If *Secrets* marks a point of departure, in terms of Farah's preoccupation with body politics, I hope to have suggested how and why those enduring, fleshy imperatives that underpin his work still hold firm.

Mixed-up Confusion

I know the case of a Hutu boy who fled into the marshes with the Tutsis. After two or three weeks they pointed out to him that he was a Hutu and so could be saved. He left the marshes and was not attacked. He had spent so much of his time with Tutsis in his early childhood that he was a bit mixed up. His mind no longer knew how to draw the proper line between the ethnic groups. Afterwards he did not get involved in the killings. That is the sole exception. The only able-bodied person not forced to raise the machete, even coming along behind. It was clear his mind was overwhelmed and he was not penalized.

(Jean Hatzfeld – A Time for Machetes, 2005: 114)

The blood relation long remained an important element in the mechanisms of power, its manifestations, and its rituals. For a society in which the systems of alliance, the political form of the sovereign, the differentiation into orders and castes, and the value of descent lines were predominant; for a society in which famine, epidemics, and violence made death imminent, blood constituted one of the fundamental values. It owed its high value at the same time to its instrumental role (the ability to shed blood), to the way it functioned in the order of signs (to have a certain blood, to be of the same blood, to be prepared to risk one's blood), and also to its precariousness (easily spilled, subject to drying up, too readily mixed, capable of being quickly corrupted). A society of blood – I was tempted to say, of 'sanguinity' – where power spoke through blood: the honor of war, the fear of famine, the triumph of death, the sovereign with his sword, executioners, and tortures; blood was a reality with a symbolic function.

(Michel Foucault – The History of Sexuality, 1990: 147)

In conclusion, I suggest that *Secrets* can be situated in the discursive territory between these two citations. Jean Baptiste's reference to the boy who 'was a bit mixed up' is as poignant as it is provocative. His inability to operate according to the dominant, bio-political order of things led to the label 'exceptional'. This inadvertently placed him beyond the arena where blood was spilled in the name of ethnic hatred. On the alternative, yet not wholly other terrain of *Secrets*, Kalaman faces the challenge of consciously defining himself out of what he sees as the bloody 'perversion of justice' (*Sec*: 74) and affiliation. It is multiply revealing that Jean-Baptiste conceives of the boy's psychological confusion in geometric terms. His disturbed state resulted in a pronounced failure to draw the necessarily rigid dividing lines, metonymically represented by the machete blade. When asked for her thoughts on the genocide itself, it should be recalled that Claudine Kayitesi offered a markedly more entangled vision than that suggested by a world imagined along angular lines. Her clustered roots image invites a more critical recognition of those who tie the knots, who draw the lines and who benefit from these processes, their revelation and/or concealment. Whilst I do not seek to dilute these geo-politically specific concerns by lifting them out of context, I have used this and preceding chapters to suggest that a host of similar, bio-political issues haunt Farah throughout his *Blood in the Sun* novels. Time and again, I have relied upon tropes of blurring, mixing and knotting. Viewed from this perspective, Farah's reflection on *Maps* is as applicable to *Secrets* as it is to the trilogy as a whole: 'nothing is straight. No line is drawn straight, because every line goes through mined territory of information, of truth, of philosophy' (Farah 2002: 45).

If Sholoongo and Nonno's union is the culmination of a series of apparent transgressions, it is significant that Farah presents it in terms of order and disorder:

> She slipped into my bed … and I let her. I thought to myself that in a world turned upside down, in which brothers are gathering deadly weapons to kill brothers, a world with no sense of morality, a society with no sense of taboos, no knowing where we are ending up and what has become of us – I asked myself, is it worth my while to remain true to my moral sense, when no one is? (*Sec*: 294)

Just as the open-parenthesis motif runs throughout Farah's work, so the reference to a world turned on its head will be familiar to seasoned readers. If Deeriye functioned as the noble, stoic exemplar in *Variations*, the more brooding figure of Nonno conveys some of the author's own deeper, darker convictions regarding the ultimate taboo-breaker: the perversion of clan logic and the lineage system itself. For Nonno, the separation between human and animal is once more conceived in spatial and geometric terms:

> We reason, we construct a mechanism of self-restraints, of guides, we construct further constraints into our logic of being ... Compare these to the lattice in a wall, crossed laths overlooking an open space, the political merges with the personal, the good cancels out the bad. Since other animals haven't developed their sense of taboo insofar as we understand the notion, it follows that a bull may mate with his mother, a carrion bird feed on the flesh of its own offspring, and so on and so forth. It is only in exceptional cases that humans feed on other humans, to survive. Taboos cover a wide area ... When crowds, advancing the interests of a clan or fighting in the name of one, turn into a mob and, animal-like, kill and kill indiscriminately, then we are entering the area of taboo, of things not done under normal circumstances. (*Sec*: 202)

For Alden and Tremaine, the distance separating Deeriye and Nonno seems to represent the apocalyptic turn in both Farah's fictional discourse and the national narrative more widely:

> The novel and the trilogy end with the death of Nonno, who dies lamenting, '[My] hopes of Somalia surviving the disasters are nil. Like me – and I am on my deathbed – she is as good as gone.' This is in notable contrast to the end of the first trilogy, in which Deeriye, another grandfather and unconventional patriarch, dies in an effort to defend both family and nation from dictatorship. (Alden & Tremaine 1999: 78)

As is the case with Farah's own work, however, they include a crucial caveat:

> In *Secrets*, however, the family as a sphere of identity is at last set free of constraint by the claims of the nation (and of its avatar the clan). The 'orphan' Kalaman … produces 'a we of hybrid necessities, half real, half invented', but one that does not demand his own sacrifice, one in which, on the contrary, his own life at last 'takes shape' and commitment: a decision to marry Talaado, a wish to produce a child, and a determination to participate in the construction of his family as a legitimate ground of identity. (Alden & Tremaine 1999: 78)

If Farah's treatment of various broken taboos aims to do more than simply shock the reader, the bleak portrait presented at the close of *Secrets* is also charged with political expediency and urgency. Nonno passes away, his vision of Somalia imploding before him. Yet, just as he urged his grandson to seize the resistant choices offered at the crossroads of his adopted identity, a sense of agency, perhaps even hope, is conveyed from one protagonist and, by extension, one generation to another. In the chapters that follow, I pursue the trajectory of that hope, precarious as it often is, through *Yesterday, Tomorrow* and the *Past Imperfect* cycle. I argue that, in significant ways, they bring together some of those disciplinary and bio-political concerns that inform Farah's *Variations* and *Blood in the Sun* trilogies.

References

Ahmed, S. 1998. *Differences that Matter: Feminist Theory and Postmodernism.* Cambridge: Cambridge University Press.

Ahmed, S. 2000. *Strange Encounters: Embodied Others in Postcoloniality.* London: Routledge.

Ahmed, S. & Stacey, J. 2001. (Eds). *Thinking through the Skin.* London: Routledge.

Alden, P. & Tremaine, L. 1999. *Nuruddin Farah.* New York: Twayne Publishers.

Alidou, O. 2002. 'Boundaries of Fatherhood in Nuruddin Farah's *Secrets*'. In D. Wright (Ed.). *Emerging Perspectives on Nuruddin Farah.* New Jersey: Africa World Press.

Brennan, T. 1989. *Salman Rushdie and the Third World – Myths of the Nation.* London: MacMillan Press.

Diaz, N. 1988. *The Radical Self: Metamorphosis To Animal Form In Modern Latin American Narrative.* Columbia: University Of Missouri Press.

El Saadawi, N. 1980. *The Hidden Face of Eve – Women in the Arab World.* (S. Hetata, Trans. and Ed.). London: Zed Books.

Eldridge, M. 'Out of the Closet: Farah's *Secrets*'. In D. Wright (Ed.). *Emerging Perspectives on Nuruddin Farah.* New Jersey: Africa World Press.

Farah, N. 2002. 'How Can we Talk of Democracy? An Interview with Nuruddin Farah by Patricia Alden and Louis Tremaine'. In D. Wright (Ed.). *Emerging Perspectives on Nuruddin Farah.* New Jersey: Africa World Press.

Fassin, D. 2008. 'The Politics of Death: Race War, Bio-Power and AIDS in the Post-Apartheid'. In A. Dillon & M. Neal (Eds). *Foucault on Politics, Security and War.* Basingstoke: Palgrave Macmillan.

Foucault, M. 1990. *The History of Sexuality, An Introduction.* (R. Hurley, Trans.). London: Penguin.

Gardner, J. & El Bushra, J. 2004. 'Introduction'. In J. Gardner and J. El Bushra (Eds). *Somalia – The Untold Story: The War Through the Eyes of Somali Women.* London: Pluto Press.

Gourevitch, P. 2000. *We Wish to Inform You that Tomorrow We will be Killed with Our Families – Stories from Rwanda.* London: Picador.

Hatzfeld, J. 2005a. *A Time for Machetes – The Rwandan Genocide: The Killers Speak.* (L. Coverdale, Trans.). London: Serpent's Tail.

Hatzfeld, J. 2005b. *Into The Quick of Life – The Rwandan Genocide: The Survivors Speak.* (G. Feehily, Trans.). London: Serpent's Tail.

Holliday, R. & Hassard, J. 2001. 'Contested Bodies: An Introduction'. In R. Holliday and J. Hassard (Eds). *Contested Bodies.* London: Routledge.

Mazrui, A. 2002. '*Secrets*: The Somali Dispersal and Reinvented Identities'. In D. Wright (Ed.). *Emerging Perspectives on Nuruddin Farah.* New Jersey: Africa World Press.

Mbembe, A. 2001. *On the Postcolony.* Berkeley: University of California Press.

Menkhaus, K. 2004. *Somalia: State Collapse and the Threat of Terrorism.* Oxford: Oxford University Press for the International Institute for Strategic Studies.

Plesch, D. 2004. *The Beauty Queen's Guide to World Peace: Money, Power and Mayhem in the Twenty-First Century.* London: Politico's.

Said, E.W. 1996. *Representations of the Intellectual – The 1993 Reith Lectures.* New York: Vintage Books.

Virilio, P. 2002. *Desert Screen: War at the Speed of Light*. (M. Degener, Trans.). London: Continuum.

Wright, D. (Ed.). 2002. *Emerging Perspectives on Nuruddin Farah*. New Jersey: Africa World Press.

Endnotes

1   See Gilman, S. 1988. *Disease and Representation: Images of Illness from Madness to AIDS*. Ithaca: Cornell University Press and Sontag, S. 1991. *Illness as Metaphor, and, AIDS and Its Metaphors*. London: Penguin.

2   Consider Said S. Samater's uncompromising assault on the text. 'Are there Secrets in *Secrets*?' 2000. *Research in African Literatures*, 31.1, pp. 137–143. He points out that Farah, perhaps an exile for too long, has misrepresented or failed to translate the 'Carraweelo' myth in *Secrets*.

3   Consider Harvey, G. 2006. *Animism: Respecting the Living World*. New York: Columbia University Press, specifically the literary examples he invokes: Soyinka, Achebe and Morrison, p. 25.

4   For a real-life account of a Somali girl emerging from compound to catwalk see, for example, Dirie, W. 2003. *Desert Dawn*. London: Virago. Also consider the murderous calls, on various diaspora blogs, for Iman, Waris and Farah to be killed for their supposedly un-Somali celebrity conduct. See www.somalinet.com (in particular, blogs from October 2000).

5   Consider the chapter entitled 'Shamans' in Harvey, G. 2006. *Animism: Respecting the Living World*. New York: Columbia University Press, pp. 139–152.

6   Many bloggers speak of Farah as a traitor to his country for broaching subjects such as homosexuality and bestiality (www.somalinet.com). Indeed, one contributor thought it necessary to reprint the entire text of Samater's critique, presumably to lend some academic credibility to the debate.

7   See Holliday, R. & Hassard, J. (Eds.) 2001. In particular, John O'Neill's chapter 'Horror Autotoxicus: The Dual Economy of AIDS,' in *Contested Bodies*. London: Routledge.

8   Patterson, A. (Ed.). 2005. *The African State and the AIDS Crisis*. Burlington: Ashgate. Barnett, T. and Whiteside, A. 2002. *AIDS in the Twenty-First Century: Disease and Globalization*. Basingstoke: Palgrave Macmillan. Baldwin, P. 2005. *Disease and Democracy: The Industrialized World Faces AIDS*. Berkeley: University of California Press. Kalipani, E. (Ed.). 2004. *HIV and AIDS: Beyond Epidemiology*. Malden: Blackwell. Erni, J. 1994. *Unstable Frontiers: Technomedicine and the Cultural Politics of "Curing" AIDS*. Minneapolis: University of Minnesota Press.

Bringing It All Back Home: Theorising Diaspora and War in *Yesterday*, *Tomorrow* and *Links*

The growing dissociation of birth (bare life) and the nation-state is the new fact of politics in our day, and what we call *camp* is this disjunction ... [it] is the hidden matrix of the politics in which we are still living, and it is this structure of the camp that we must learn to recognize in all its metamorphoses into the *zones d'attentes* of our airports and certain outskirts of our cities. The camp is the fourth, inseparable element that has now added itself to – and so broken – the old trinity composed of the state, the nation (birth), and land.

(Giorgio Agamben – Homo Sacer, 1998: 175)

Let me turn ... to the contemporary acts of state before returning to Foucault, not to 'apply' him ... but to rethink the relation between sovereignty and the law that he introduces ... With the publication of the new regulations, the US government holds that a number of detainees at Guantanamo will not be given trials at all, but will rather be detained indefinitely. It is crucial to ask under what conditions some human lives cease to become eligible for basic, if not universal, human rights. How does the US government construe these conditions? And to what extent is there a racial and ethnic frame through which these imprisoned lives are viewed and judged such that they are deemed less than human, or as having departed from the recognizable human community?

(Judith Butler – Precarious Life, 2006: 56–57)

THE FINAL SECTION OF THIS BOOK CONCLUDES AS IT BEGAN: CONSIDER-
ing how and why Foucault's work continues to be deployed across a
range of discursive fields. Whilst Giorgio Agamben and Judith Butler's investigations are separated by the socio-political schism of 9/11, both use
Foucault to explore issues of biopower, sovereignty and taxonomies of the
flesh through the shifting 'camp' paradigm. Agamben traces provocative
connections between the classification and treatment of 'bare life' in Nazi
concentration camps and refugee settlements from the Balkans to Rwanda,
flagging up blind spots in the writings of Arendt and Foucault as he goes. This
is discussed by Warren Montag in his contribution to *Michel Foucault and
Power Today* (Montag 2006: 13–22). For Butler, the erasure of certain obitu-
aries is central to the operation of what Sontag calls 'the new, international
carceral empire run by the United States' (Sontag 2007: 137). This chapter
examines Farah's journalistic study, published in the period between *Homo
Sacer* and *Precarious Life*. A mix of candid autobiography, travel narrative
and excoriating critique of the failures of both Somali guests and Western
hosts, the research for *Yesterday, Tomorrow: Voices from the Somali Diaspora*
directly feeds into the concerns of the *Past Imperfect* trilogy. As a turning
point in Farah's oeuvre, however, it warrants fuller exploration in its own
right. I draw on the biopower and camp debates gestured towards in these
epigraphs to consider how and why lines of Foucauldian continuity exist between Farah's novels and reportage.

From the outset, Farah draws on the same body-politics repository that
has dominated his writing:

> I thought that in the throes of dying, the body-politic that *was* Somalia
> displaced a leviathan. The leviathan in turn begat a monster with unsavoury
> character traits … The contagion spread, corrupting civil society, which in turn
> caused the death of the body-politic. A virus begotten out of violence infected
> the land with a madness. (*YT*: 9)

In essence, *Yesterday, Tomorrow* can be viewed as a prolonged attempt to
come to terms with a series of events from which Farah has been distanced.
If corporeal motifs provide points of contact with his fiction, they also correspond with commentators, including Hashim, who rely on tropes such as
'viruses' to describe the Somali situation (Hashim 1997: 127). In addition,
Farah recounts the testimony of Hussein Mohamed, whose passage to Britain
was facilitated by familial finance and prestige. His reply to the 'how would
you define a refugee?' question recalls many of Farah's novels:

'I recall one of my daughters asking her mother, my wife, what her first delivery was like … She replied that it being a stillbirth, it was the worst pain she had ever experienced in her life, a pain so acute, she explained, that it pierced her body, entered the perimeters of her mind, numbing it. And when the pain was gone, what did it feel like, our daughter wanted to know. The pain dissolved like burning gas vanishing in the air around it … she felt the loss of the stillborn, buried without her getting to know him. A pain for nothing, the pain we suffered.' (*YT*: 120)

This is one of several incidents where Farah finds a kindred spirit amidst the Somali diaspora's professional classes, with a significant proportion of his interviewees coming from the kind of petit-bourgeois group privileged throughout his novels. As he defends this fictional choice by admitting they represent the social milieu he knows best, the similar sense is that Farah feels more at home amongst this wandering, educated elite. With the distinction of a well-schooled modernist, Farah expresses his unease when around large groups. He recounts one particularly revealing incident when, following suggestions that the Islamic clergy bore heavy responsibility for the country's implosion, he was heckled by a crowd of Somalis in Lucerne, Switzerland (*YT*: 129). This again dovetails with the irate postings of bloggers following the controversial publication of *Secrets*. It is not only at the level of body-politics imagery, however, that the preoccupations of Farah's fictional and documentary worlds intersect. Adding flesh to the patriarchal critique voiced by several female protagonists in prior novels as well as foreshadowing *Knots*, Farah considers the role played by Somali women battling to safeguard their families. In *Yesterday, Tomorrow*, the enforced dispersal of peoples in the wake of Somalia's civil war provides certain opportunities for stoical women. Whilst they are presented as rising to various challenges in times of extreme adversity, husbands and fathers are invariably shown in neglect of their responsibilities. As Farah maintains early on, 'the generous-spiritedness of our womenfolk never failed to allay our worse fears, the women mending the broken, healing the wounded, taking care of the elderly and sick, martyrly women' (*YT*: 5).

Whilst this reliance on the collective pronoun raises thorny questions, reminiscent of his novels, the reader cannot disentangle these meditations from the intriguing personal reflections interwoven by Farah. He recalls meeting his father for the first time in seventeen years in a Mombasan camp for displaced people, bemoaning their ongoing failure to agree on anything. Oedipal readings apart, Farah's patriarchal critique is supplemented by the

testimony of Caaliya Muxummad, a former principal of a Mogadiscian secondary school. As robust as any Farah protagonist, Caaliya rails against the
post-conflict deficiencies of Somali men. She conjures images of breakages
and bodies, citing men's abject behaviour in an attempt to destabilise archetypes of masculine supremacy:

> 'Whether men like to hear it or not, exile abroad, the difficulties inside, these
> have both shown the weak stuff of which our men are made. No longer the
> chosen heirs to temporal power, and no longer endowed with the benediction
> of being closer to God than the womenfolk, the men fall apart like toys a child
> has glued together … like beggars showing their amputated arms, the men
> pointed to the harsh conditions consequent on the civil war.' (YT: 72)

Aside from the conscious or otherwise allusion to Achebe, the reader is
struck by the rhetorical force of such interventions. If questions of fidelity
and/or editorial intervention linger, connections between scribe and subject appear profound. More precise parallels, at the level of recording and
transcribing various testimonies, come into focus when attention turns to a
particular informant.

Farah interviews a man taking the adopted name Ciroole. His recollection
of the circumstances in which he and his family fled Mogadiscio at the height
of the civil war offers an alternative to Caaliya's critique. It is his focus on the
body, however, that provides the most intense counterpoint. In the process
of unsettling Farah, it reveals the extent of his physical and psycho-political
detachment from events:

> Another version had it that he had adopted a new identity once he got to
> Mombasa so he would distance his old self from the memories associated with
> it, and from what had happened to his female folk, all raped, including his four-
> year old granddaughter. Shocked, I had asked why anyone would rape a small
> child, and was told that it was the done thing, the rapists feeling safer that they
> would not contract AIDS from the rape victim. (YT: 11)

Whilst attention is paid to competing versions of the narrative, in a manner
that recalls Farah's fiction, it is the viscerality of the account that leaves writer
and reader shaken. Familiar debates over the legitimacy of subaltern representation continue, with the voices of the victims themselves conspicuous
by their absence. Revealingly, however, the painful recollection Ciroole tries
but fails to forget informs his subsequent comments. He goes on to consider

'how a part of [him] saw the nation raped' (*YT*: 12), bidding the reader to reflect on the more-than-sensational ends served by this imagistic choice. Farah subsequently interviews a member of Aideed's youth militia. Whilst doubting the veracity of the young man's testimony, Farah includes his comments on the punitive practices of groups roaming Mogadiscio's streets: 'a soldier would be reprimanded if he were caught asking moral questions. There was the day, for instance, when he didn't feel like raping an old woman in her seventies. Penalized by the head of his cell, he was offered a young girl of five' (*YT*: 23). Such fragments support the accounts of older exiles including Ciroole. They also offer disconcerting insights into the post-Barre power void, described in suitably Foucauldian terms as 'violence [assuming] a ruthlessness … something akin to violence-as-a-spectacle, violence to one's faculties' (*YT*: 17).

Taxonomies of the Human: Globalisation and Displacement

Further informant/interviewer parallels emerge as the text develops. Ciroole is a former Science lecturer from the National University of Somalia who, like the displaced Kalaman, now runs a computer business. He also speaks of his desire to lay claim to an identity that protects him from the pejorative associations of 'refugee', as used in the host society. With Askar-esque intensity, Ciroole insists the pen will aid and abet his distancing strategies: 'so as not to "become" a refugee, I have chosen the vocation of a researcher, and I am busy writing about the refugees' (*YT*: 13). The same, politically charged inverted commas that pepper Farah's fiction are present here, making the reader once more sensitive to questions of authorial intervention. That they surround verb rather than noun is key, linked, as it is, to Farah's own musings on the refugee condition: 'I've always considered countries to be no more than working hypotheses, portals opening on assumptions of loyalty to an idea, allegiance to the notion of a nation … During the long travel out of one hypothesis to another, one journeys further away from one's self. And somewhere between fleeing and arriving at the new destination, a refugee is born' (*YT*: 48). For both interviewer and informant, the focus is on *becoming* a refugee. Farah inquires, 'you are writing things down so as to understand things?' Ciroole's reply is provocative, obliging the comparative reader to reconsider the oral/written debates that frame Farah's fiction: 'writing things down imposes a sense of self-moderation. Composing poetry in the oral form, on the other hand, poses no restrictive aesthetics on its practitioner with regard to its truth content, only form' (*YT*: 13–14). Reflections on the process of becoming a refugee, alongside writing's restorative function as a personal yet always already political way of controlling disorder, chime with statements Farah has made throughout his career. Yet, as his preface suggests, it takes on added urgency here: 'if I haven't let go [of this project], it is because I wish somehow to impose a certain order on Somalia's anarchy … Here is a nation of narratives held to ransom. Here is an ocean of stories narrated by Somalis in a halfway house' (*YT*: viii). If a little overwrought, such statements offer an insight into the motivations behind the study. As in *Variations*, the presentation of competing and clashing voices reflects those calls for tolerance and democracy that have endured throughout Farah's oeuvre.

There are also revealing structural connections between Farah's fictional and journalistic work. In *Maps*, the interlude serves a didactic function by surveying the complexities of Somali-Ogaden history, whilst also setting the stage for Farah's most excoriating critique of the use and abuse of biopower. The central section of *Yesterday, Tomorrow* performs a similar role, even to the extent that, like the novels, it is introduced by a literary epigraph: 'I will not serve what I no longer believe in … silence, exile and cunning' (James Joyce). The silence is definitively shattered as Farah engages in the kind of pronominal sparring that distinguishes his fiction. If the epilogue provides a quasi-Foucauldian analytics of power, in the guise of what he calls 'blamocracy', the interlude enables him to analyse the culpability of European hosts in relation to more longstanding socio-political relations with their Somali guests. The result is that the rhetoric of reception, confinement and architecture is as marked as in a novel such as *Sardines*. In this context, it is reconfigured to interrogate one of the most pressing questions of our globalised present:

> Two world wars and a century later the inhabitants of that world are standing at the crossroads yet again. Where now are the architects of empire? Or do we confront a world divided, a world of desiccated empires and small minds, islands of insularity? Or are we witnessing a sorrier spectacle, one in which the West abandons ship at the 'end of history', at the moment it claims to be its undisputed captain? … For how does one explain this 'return' to 1930s politics; how does one explain the rise of the neo-Nazi right? How, indeed, can one explain the recourse to blood, the cultivation of ethnic absolutisms? … But if refugees are a challenge as well as a reproach to our humanity, if refugees are a lament raised, a cry spoken, if refugees are the bastards of empire, then how can

one blame this highly disenfranchised, displaced humanity for all Europe's ills?
(*YT*: 54–55)

If such incessant questions exasperate readers of his fiction, they serve alternative ends here. As well as offering a salutary reminder that the 'end of history' is an idea (su)stained by neo-colonial hegemony, Farah effectively flaunts and then harnesses his role as transnational citizen. In doing so, he is able to challenge the closeted convictions of both guests and hosts. Like people, ideologies and their distortions navigate various crossroads, breaching geo-political lines to establish themselves elsewhere. Read in terms of the Foucauldian approach I have pursued throughout, the bio-political drift of Farah's meditations is revealing, once again linking his preoccupation with individual body politics to those of broader national and transnational body politics. The interlude thus enables him to conjoin meditations personal and political. As in his finest fiction, it is the productive tension between the two that sets his writing apart.

Reflections on Blamocracy

In coining the term 'blamocracy', Farah offers another version of the Foucauldian, because relational, conception and critique of power that recurs throughout fictional work before and after *Yesterday, Tomorrow*. If the interlude offers a balance-sheet of interventions into the Horn of Africa, both imperial and neo-imperial, alongside a consideration of the transnational traffic of peoples, the epilogue is an equally provocative supplement:

> When an individual blames the community, and the community blames a leader, and the leader in turn blames his followers; when a well-meaning American blames the Somalis and not the Americans for what occurred in Mogadiscio: then it is clear that everyone is shying away from being responsible for his or her actions … This is a testament to our collective failure … Being blamocrats par excellence, Somalis do not place themselves, as individuals, in the geography of the collective collapse, but outside of it. It is as if they did not inhabit the territory in which the disaster occurred, many ascribing the collapse to Siyad's dictatorship, or more recently to the warlords and their politics … In short, the self is not to blame … The foreigners who have had dealings with Somalis as refugees indulge in blamocracy too. In Switzerland, Sweden, Britain,

Kenya, the men and women who look after the Somalis key in to a catch-phrase, 'the clan is malady!' (*YT*: 188)

Preoccupations with the existential and political weight of individual and collective identity, failure and responsibility have haunted Farah's work. In later novels, the idea that clan affiliation provides insulation from blame becomes more explicit as tensions between competing notions of the nation become more pronounced. If 'blamocracy' appears a hopeless designation from which none are exempt, it is arguably underpinned by an investment in the regenerative hope that might emerge once shared culpability has been acknowledged. As such, its function is comparable with Arnold Davidson's sense of a Foucauldian analytics of power. Davidson maintains that 'Foucault was never interested in providing a metaphysics of Power; his aim was an analysis of the techniques and technologies of power, where power is understood as relational, multiple, heterogeneous and, of course, productive' (Foucault 2006: xvi). Transposed onto the Somali narrative, this corresponds with Farah's sense that, following the removal of Barre as despotic figurehead, a necessarily sombre, introspective reassessment of the order of things has to take place as a precursor to more systemic change.

One burning issue, however, concerns the relationship between Farah's 'I' and these blamocratic tendencies. Once more, a return to fleshy materiality proves instructive. It is revealing that Farah draws attention to his own body. Metonymically, it captures the difference, and distance, between himself and his fellow Somalis: 'the food they eat [in London] is the food the poor eat anywhere, foods eaten not to please the tongue but to fill the stomach. I ate it, and it did damage to my constitution, not robust at the best of times. From then on, I called at non-eating hours of the day, and still they prepared ghee- and butter-rich meals for me, which got my stomach a-running' (*YT*: 103). In many ways, this seemingly innocuous observation gestures towards one of the text's critical, Foucault-inflected features. Despite the pseudo-Orwellian note of disdain, Farah does display a refreshing degree of class honesty.[1] This in turn leads to a critical re-grounding, oftentimes absent in other meditations on the metaphysics of exile. His engagement with other voices, experiences and, here, cuisines serves as a necessary counterpoint. Whilst expressing how Somalia is lost to him with characteristic lyricism, Farah acknowledges the importance of rigorously differentiating his own exilic passage from those of his fellow Somalis.

Bare Life and Transnational Travels/Travails Through a Bio-political Lens

> He was handsome … yet he was humble and fearful and made himself as small as his gigantic frame allowed. Seeing him with his back bent double, folded in on himself, with the air of someone apologizing for existing, it was obvious he'd already slipped into the skin of a refugee. Perhaps we should have done the same and got into training for the future … learn to keep in the background, to be nobody … or even a cockroach. That's it, yes, learn to be a cockroach.
>
> *(Mahi Binebine – Welcome to Paradise, 2003: 66)*

Whether 'cockroach' is used by the British National Party to describe asylum seekers or by Hutu Power extremists seeking to legitimise the extermination of their Tutsi neighbours, it is revealing, if disconcerting, that such tropes are relied upon by disparate groups. In *Welcome to Paradise*, it is similarly significant that Binebine focuses on the refugee's physical being. The body becomes a simultaneous shield against and sanctuary from the world, blending into its new surroundings with chameleon-like ease. Burdened by the negative connotations of 'cockroach', however, this other body is represented as carrying a contagion threatening the health of the wider body politic. In a chapter entitled 'Illness, Suffering and the Body', from *The Suffering of the Immigrant*, Abdelmalek Sayad offers a fascinating analysis of the differential body politics of immigrants (Sayad 2004: 177–215). Whilst Farah alludes to the disturbing resurgence of European neo-fascist parties and their appeals to pure blood, the following section intensifies this biopower focus whilst also considering how he, at times unwittingly, explores the material differences between intellectual and interviewee, writer and refugee. As such, some of the most intriguing moments in *Yesterday, Tomorrow* come when Farah is refused experiential access by his informants. They in turn lead him to reflect on his own position.

A representative incident occurs early on. Having arrived in Mombasa, Farah visits a refugee camp housing members of his own family, amongst many others. An exchange between an official in the Kenyan Civil Authority and the author is recounted: 'he ventured, "But you don't look like a refugee yourself." I asked, "How do refugees look?" Smiling wisely, he said, "They don't look like you" ' (*YT*: 8). Set against a broader backdrop of human suffering, Farah's is a conspicuous presence. When challenged to define a refugee, the official falls back upon the 'people in a halfway house' explanation that recurs throughout. Anticipating what will come to be the arguments of his bureaucratic counterparts in Europe, the official refers to specific tensions between Kenyan hosts and their Somali guests. Prior to being dismissed for suggesting that the geo-political tables might be overturned in future, Farah alludes to the twist of fortune that spared him such a fate, as discussed above. From this moment, the reader follows his various attempts to situate himself in relation to the diasporic community as a comparative outsider. Instances of metaphysical reflection, therefore, are balanced by refreshingly candid observations: 'there were areas of their lives that I had no access to, because I was not there when the horror came to visit their homes. They were part of a 'we', sharing the communal nightmare. That I was not included in the 'we' was made clear to me. But then I was not assumed to be part of the 'they' either' (*YT*: 5). Central as pronominal tussles are to Farah's novels, their significance is particularly acute in this documentary foray. Accordingly, they correspond with some of the most pressing, Foucault-inspired debates within postcolonial studies.

Confronted by metaphors of migrancy, images of itinerancy and the exoticisation of exile, scholars have renewed calls to attend to the material specificities of travellers and their travels.[2] Rey Chow, for instance, challenges intellectuals to 'unmask [themselves] through a scrupulous declaration of self-interest' (Chow 1993: 117). Revealingly, Foucault provides additional support for Chow's purposes: '[w]e need to remember as intellectuals that the battles we fight are battles of words ... (When Foucault said intellectuals need to struggle against becoming the object and instrument of power, he spoke precisely to this kind of situation)' (Chow 1993: 17). Other pioneers continue to recuperate Foucauldian meditations for their own ends. For the editors of *Uprootings/Regroundings*, for example, 'embodiment is crucial to any investigation of the effects of migrations, exiles and displacements on identity and community ... [we might come to] rethink the relationship between bodies, places and mobility by regrounding these concepts in specific histories, locations and forms of displacement and emplacement' (Ahmed *et al.* 2003: 11). For more than one contributor, returning to and, where necessary, resisting Foucault's speculations on biopolitics remains an all-too-urgent task. Farah's analysis of the Somali diaspora can be seen as an intriguing supplement to such debates. *Yesterday, Tomorrow* is the product of its author's particular propensity to travel. As he consistently points out, this transnational movement, and the prospect of freely willed escape, is at an otherwordly remove from the experiences of the diasporic majority he visits and talks to. There are certain instances, however, in which even the passage of an internationally renowned author is impeded. Throughout the account, Farah expresses his exasperation with being continually detained at security on presentation of his Somali passport. The following occurs at Zurich Airport:

> When I finally boarded the aircraft, I was aware that everyone was avoiding my eye, as the British have a habit of doing. Except an elderly man with a heavy German accent, maybe a Jew. He indulged me with his interest, telling me that he was only too familiar with the expression 'Step aside', being the only family member who had survived the Nazi Holocaust. I doubted if he thought the comparison ended there. (*YT*: 160)

Whilst an eyebrow may be raised over Farah's final speculation, the seasoned reader will find it noteworthy that he does end the Holocaust comparison here. This is the last paragraph of one section. Its stark presentation becomes an invitation for the reader to muse on points of bio-political convergence and, crucially, divergence between the treatment of Jews in Nazi Germany and refugees/migrants in contemporary Europe. As such, Farah's authorial restraint is vital.

Whilst attention is given to the all-too-pertinent politics of passports, identity papers and embodied notions of transnational movement (an area in which Foucault has been deployed by scholars such as John Torpey in *The Invention of the Passport – Surveillance, Citizenship and the State*), the above incident represents a critical tension between author and his subject/subjects (Torpey 2000: 122–157). Despite being inconvenienced, the book-promoting Farah does move through passport control and departure lounge rather than Her Majesty's Customs and detention centre. For many of his fellow Somalis, it is undoubtedly the latter experience rather than the air-conditioned nightmare of the former that defines their brush with this other form of travel and reception. As Kaplan argues in her contribution to *Uprootings/Regroundings*, 'if theory can be defined as a kind of travelling, travel can be defined as a manifestation of pain or work. Etymologically, *travel* is linked to *travail* or "labour, toil, suffering, trouble" … in addition to the more commonplace meaning of taking a journey, *travel* evokes hard labour (including childbirth) and difficulty' (Kaplan 2003: 208). The imagistic link to Hussein Mohamed's refugee definition is striking (*YT*: 120). As with 'travel', 'reception' has provocative multiple meanings.

Reception, Rejection and the Brotherhood of Man

Switzerland once again provides the setting for a revealing encounter with bureaucratic power. As he recalls the obstacles he also faced when travelling, Farah considers the strategic silences that litter the refugees' narratives. As in the airport anecdote, however, his description pivots around a deliberately loaded term:

> I doubt that the residents at the Horow centre opened their hearts fully to their Swiss minders, trust being one of the first things refugees part company with … If I use the word 'minders' to describe the Swiss administrators of the camp, it is because the Somalis made it clear that they were in a gulag whose key was deposited not with those who ran the centre on a day-to-day basis, but with a more powerful Swiss oligarchy, whom the refugees have no chance of ever reaching. (*YT*: 141)

It is significant that 'minders' rather than 'gulag' is placed in inverted commas. Whilst Farah interpreted the Jewish man's Holocaust reflections for his own ends, he here presents himself as messenger for a subaltern group of Somali refugees detained in an Agamben-esque camp. In the absence of supporting references, however, the carceral image appears to be his own. The reader is again invited to reflect on the provisional nature of Farah's 'I' separated here, as at other key points, from the disenfranchised majority. His intermediary role is confirmed as he is received by the Swiss oligarchy. Portraying himself as an intrepid spokesman, Farah seizes his opportunity to point out the differential treatment meted out to displaced peoples:

> In Berne, I had lunch with two Swiss immigration officials, Mr Tomasi Konrad, of the Federal Office for Refugee Affairs, Africa, and Mr Groppo, responsible for everything to do with Somali refugees … By the time our hors-d'oeuvre were served, I put forward the idea that the Swiss political menu to refugees was smeared with the partisan blood of choice. Bosnians, being of European stock, were shown preference over Somalis, who are African and black. (*YT*: 145)

The culinary reference provides a metaphorical bridge. In this setting, it is not the nauseatingly butter-rich dishes of the poor that are served, but somewhat tastier, bureaucratic morsels. Yet, in a manner reminiscent of Basil Davidson's comparative critique, it is the more unpalatable reference to a discriminatory politics of blood that defines the encounter (1992: 266–289).

With hors-d'oeuvres presumably sticking in their throats, his hosts defer to the Geneva Convention on first-country asylum before referring to the Somalis' unsettling and unassimilated presence on Swiss soil. As Farah suggests, anticipating Sontag's revealing reflection in *Regarding the Pain of Others*, such logic is a thin veneer over more longstanding notions of European geo-political fraternity (Sontag 2004: 100–101). Whilst 'gulag' runs the same associative risks as 'holocaust', it has profound Foucauldian resonance. The notion of the panopticon's imaginary intensity remains useful, as Farah evokes ominous images of a disciplinary mechanism founded on obfuscation and detachment. The dark room has been transposed onto a transnational stage where, as Didier Bigo suggests, 'a more globalized surveillance' defines the new (dis)order of things (Bigo 2006: 55–59). Once again, as Agamben, Bigo and Butler, amongst others, push Foucault in intriguing new directions, their concentration on bare life, taxonomies of the flesh and new configurations of biopower provide an enabling prism through which to view Farah's study. From Switzerland to Sweden, therefore, these issues strike at the heart of some of Europe's most progressive nations. In the process, they are invoked to interrogate some of their most purportedly progressive notions. The testimony of one exile reveals key connections between disciplinary mechanisms and spaces:

> As the slow cogs of Swedish asylum-related bureaucracy turned and as he waited, [Dr. Hashi] reflected that though he had evaded detention in Africa, he found himself in a different kind of confinement, a Swedish one this time. This feeling of moving from one 'prison' to another, with only the frontiers of his incarceration changing, was to persist beyond his many months in the camp. The feeling would pervade his life as a political refugee in the wider Swedish society. (*YT*: 177)

If some of Foucault's speculations on discipline, power and resistance provide an interpretive framework for Farah's early fiction, this shows how some of the bio-political concerns that underpin the *Blood in the Sun* series assume peculiar urgency in the geo-political present. At an immediate textual level, however, the Horow camp incident refocuses attention on the writer's role, as well as his propensity to move between various spheres of influence. From refugee camp to reception hall, detention centre to departure lounge, Farah's is a particular form of travel.

In 'Traveling Cultures', James Clifford reconfigures the Bakhtinian chronotope, defining it as 'a setting or scene organizing time and space in representable whole form'. He suggests the hotel or, more specifically, the hotel lobby might operate as an effective chronotope for contemporary culture: 'the chronotope … comes to resemble as much a site of travel encounter as of residence; it is less like a tent in a village or a controlled laboratory or a site of initiation and inhabitation, and more like a hotel lobby, urban café, ship, or bus' (Clifford 1997: 25). Clifford draws from a Foucauldian toolkit, admitting he is proposing research questions rather than conclusions:

> Another problem with the hotel image: its nostalgic inclination. For in those *parts* of contemporary society that we can legitimately call postmodern (I do not think, pace Jameson, that postmodernism is yet a cultural dominant, even in the 'First World'), the motel would surely offer a better chronotope. The motel has no real lobby, and it's tied into a highway network … Other ways in which the hotel chronotope – and with it the whole travel metaphor – becomes problematic have to do with class, race, and sociocultural 'location'. What about all the travel that largely avoids the hotel, or motel, circuits? The travel encounters of someone moving from rural Guatemala or Mexico across the United States border are of quite a different order; and a West African can get to a Paris *banlieu* without ever staying in a hotel. What are the settings that could realistically reconfigure the cultural relations of these 'travellers'? (Clifford 1997: 32–33)

It is significant that Clifford takes on Frederic Jameson here. Clifford not only identifies tensions in Jameson's designation of third world allegories, but also interrogates the idea that cultural postmodernism prevails in the West. Crucially, he introduces a taxonomical trinity of race, class and gender in order to challenge this notion. Even more striking is his differentiation of space, place and, specifically, borders. Clifford refers to those Mexican/U.S. border relations that Gloria Anzaldúa has draped with such figurative flesh ('where the Third World grates against the first and bleeds'), as well as the West African migrant who never makes it through the hotel door (Anzaldúa 1999: 25). The territory we are presented with, therefore, is one in which discourse itself is considered problematic, laden with ideological baggage. Clifford's theoretical explorations are important: first setting up and then exploring such discursive tensions, most notably in relation to 'travel' itself:

> I hang on to 'travel' as a term of cultural comparison precisely because of its historical taintedness, its associations with gendered, racial bodies, class privilege, specific means of conveyance … I prefer it to more apparently neutral,

and 'theoretical', terms, such as 'displacement', which can make the drawing of
equivalences across different historical experiences too easy. (The postcolonial/
postmodern equation, for example.) And I prefer it to terms such as 'nomadism',
often generalized without apparent resistance from non-Western experiences.
(Nomadology: a form of postmodern primitivism?). (Clifford 1997: 39)

Presenting the reader with the kind of semantic battles that rage beneath the
surface of *Yesterday, Tomorrow*, Clifford acknowledges that travel is tainted.
It is, however, precisely this awareness that allows for cautious and therefore productive use. His Saidian reference to the fraught borderzone that
marks work in postcolonial/postmodern fields is equally pertinent. For Clifford, 'displacement' elides crucial, material differences. From calls to resist
a 'neo-orthodoxy' that fetishises fragmentation, whilst dismissing appeals to
fixity or essence, to explorations of etymology, much of the finest scholarship within this interdisciplinary field is underpinned by such interrogative
commitments.[3]

   If, in *Questions of Travel*, Caren Kaplan applauds the impulse behind
Clifford's investigations, she is less forgiving of Baudrillard's concept of a
postmodern desert in which we are all nomads (Kaplan 1996: 66). Given the
Somali-specific context of *Yesterday, Tomorrow*, such indiscriminate appeals
are highly problematic. Nomadism takes on a distinctly other meaning when
used within the agro-pastoralist context of the Horn, just as real desert conditions impact your life differently when you can't feed your children. As such,
it seems particularly appropriate that, on the very page Kaplan foregrounds
this argument, she chooses the statement from Farah's 'A Country in Exile'
discussed in my introduction: '[a]lthough one often links a person in exile
to a faraway locality, the fact is I felt more joined to my writing than to any
country with a specific territoriality' (Kaplan 1996: 105). Having cited Farah,
Kaplan goes on to argue that:

   Contemporary theories of exile must delineate the material conditions of
   displacement that generate subject positions … the alienation of writers or
   intellectuals from the abuses and injustices of their 'home' location can generate
   an 'unhousedness' or displacement that brings them in solidarity, if you will,
   to meet the involuntary exile on the terrain of textual and political affiliation.
   Such a solidarity or affiliation is political, however, and cannot simply be
   assumed through the articulation of aesthetic principles of literary exile or the
   deployment of generalized metaphors … one task of cultural criticism [is] to

> participate in the formation of practices that will make these political links more visible and meaningful. (Kaplan 1996: 105)

When read in light of such critical debates, a final incident from *Yesterday, Tomorrow* assumes particular significance.

After visiting the Mombasa camp, Farah details the reception he receives at one of Kenya's premier hotels. For the purposes of my Foucauldian approach, his reference to a new kind of disciplinary labyrinth brings together those preoccupations with punitive and bio-political power that have underpinned Farah's entire oeuvre:

> From the bus depot in Mombasa, I took a taxi to Manor Hotel, where I put up. The hotel had the formal air of the colonial era, the manager extending to me much warmer hospitality on discovering that I was a friend of Professor Ali Mazrui, Mombasa's most famous native son. After a decidedly hot, long shower, a taxi arrived to take me to the Utange refugee camp in Mombasa, where my father, my son, my nephew and my sister had their allotted space in a rooming set-up, a maze of ill-designed facilities organized along the lines of gender, family affiliation and age-group. (*YT*: 40)

As with the Horow camp incident, Farah alludes to his propensity to travel between the two spheres: hotel and camp, concluding, as he began, with a revealing personal aside. Faced with the prospect of the Somali Embassy's closure in Rome and the related threat that his soon-to-expire passport will not be renewed, he muses on the difficulties this might pose 'if I am to pursue my career as a professional novelist able to travel' (*YT*: 192). In this globalised age, Farah's authorial function cannot be divorced from his capacity to move across international boundaries and through other spaces. I maintain that, by concluding with reflections on his provisional 'I', he broadens rather than limits the interrogative appeal of a study that lends itself to an interdisciplinary and interdiscursive treatment. *Yesterday, Tomorrow* can be read alongside Kaplan and Clifford's work as it asks the reader, however subtly, to focus on definitions that distinguish travellers and travel. Farah's subsequent reference to his non-refugee status, therefore, is as obvious as it is necessary. As he seeks to come to terms with Somalia's turbulent national narrative, Farah displays a grounded awareness of the need to resist conflating his own experiences of exile with those of significantly less-privileged countrymen. Typically, *Yesterday, Tomorrow* poses more questions than it provides answers. Yet, as in his strongest fiction, this is done in the interests of promoting and refining critical thought. Demands are placed on the reader to travail in order to travel through the labyrinth of those invariably bio-political, always pertinent issues that confront them in *Yesterday, Tomorrow*. In the spirit of Kaplan's links, the section that follows explores how these preoccupations are dealt with in Farah's eponymous novel.

Malawi and/as Disney: Reflections on *Links*

> There are none so ignorant of geography as those with their military bases in every quarter of the planet. It is possible to have satellites which survey every square inch of the globe while producing schoolchildren who think Malawi is a Disney character.
>
> *(Terry Eagleton – Holy Terror, 2005: 85)*

> The final challenge – drawing on theorists as diverse as Foucault (1977), Agamben (1998), Deleuze and Guatarri (1987), Gregory (2004) and Said (1978) – is to expose in detail the ways in which urbanized RMA (Revolution in Military Affairs) weapons programmes – and the discourses which fuel them – embed stark biopolitical judgements about the varying worth of human subjects, according to their location, beneath the intensifying transnational gaze of militarized surveillance. Such a theme must be at the very core of any re-theorizations of the links between corporeal, urban and transnational power in what Derek Gregory has called our 'colonial present' (2004)
>
> *(Stephen Graham – 'Surveillance, Urbanization, and the US "Revolution in Military Affairs"', 2006: 265–266)*

The following analysis of *Links*, the first instalment of the *Past Imperfect* trilogy, emerges from the discursive space between these two epigraphs. Whilst I explore the novel in relation to the imagined post-Operation Restore Hope setting it takes as its backdrop, I also consider its significance as Farah's first post-9/11 text. As such, I make generous reference to some of the discourse that has been produced around the 'War on Terror', particularly that which, as in the Graham citation above, draws on Foucault's legacy. My principle argument is that, by offering a fictional retrospective on America's military misadventure in Somalia in the early 90s, Farah poses some rather more searching questions about the entangled genealogies that define the contemporary (dis)order of things. For Graham, the methods called upon to police

such realities combine those carceral and surveillance techniques I have discussed in relation to Farah's earliest work with the bio-political paradigms
that inform his more recent writing. To a significant extent, therefore, *Links*
is a novel that exists in the discursive shadow of *Yesterday, Tomorrow*.

If *Links* is primarily concerned with conflict and its aftermath, of equal
significance is its preoccupation with the role played by the media, both in
laying the foundations for the initial, humanitarian intervention into Somalia and in streaming real-time images of a nightmare that would haunt the
popular and political consciousness of the United States well into a post-9/11
world. In many ways, therefore, *Links* stands in contrapuntal relation to *Gifts*.
Both texts deal with those mediating discourses and images that accompany
news about Somalia, be it famine, internecine conflict or as antagonist to
American hegemony. As John Hattendorf puts it,

> At the end of the decades-long Cold War, the United States displayed its military
> capability in a positive manner by responding to a severe humanitarian crisis in
> Somalia ... Regrettably, the best of intentions could not prevent a continuing
> drift towards disorder, and the American relief effort devolved into conflict and
> bloodshed. (Ohls 2009: v)

As a counterpoint to the kind of reductive, partisan rhetoric Farah seeks to
challenge throughout *Links*, Slavoj Zizek is typically compelling. In *Welcome
to the Desert of the Real*, he considers how events surrounding 9/11 were
disseminated to global mass media consumers. For Zizek, notable features
included airbrushing the visceral reality of the attacks. Alongside this, his
introduction of a much broader, transnational bio-political framework is
particularly stimulating for the purposes of this analysis:

> The same 'derealization' of the horror went on after the WTC collapse: while
> the number of victims – 3 000 – is repeated all the time, it is surprising how
> little of the actual carnage we see – no dismembered bodies, no blood, no
> desperate faces of dying people ... in clear contrast to reporting on Third World
> catastrophes, where the whole point is to produce a scoop of some gruesome
> detail: Somalis dying of hunger, raped Bosnian women ... These shots are
> always accompanied by an advance warning that 'some of the images you
> will see are extremely graphic and may upset children' – a warning which we
> never heard in the reports on the WTC collapse. Is this not yet further proof of
> how, even in this tragic moment, the distance which separates Us from Them,

from their reality, is maintained: the real horror happens *there*, not *here*? (Zizek 2002: 13)

With their respective attention to geography, surveillance, the mediatisation of trauma and bio-political taxonomies of value, the interventions of Eagleton, Graham and Zizek provide a more substantial framework within which to discuss *Links*. As Foucauldian thought has been variously reconfigured, so too *Links* suggests how and why Farah's concerns with the fraught processes of cultural and political globalisation both build on and depart from earlier work (Gregory 2004: 1–5). In essence, I argue that this novel sets the tone for what will follow throughout the *Past Imperfect* series: balancing the disciplinary preoccupations of *Variations* with the bio-political contests that lie at the heart of the *Blood in the Sun* cycle.

Links is variously concerned with transnational travel, postmodern conflict, rupturing bodies, both individual and collective, and the hegemonic reach of global media providers. In comparison with earlier novels, the journey motif also assumes greater significance, operating in relation to those geo-politically broader concerns with displacement, detachment, distance and (dis)location so central to *Yesterday, Tomorrow*. Emerging from the same U.S.-based Somali diaspora as Sholoongo in *Secrets*, Jeebleh is a key returnee protagonist in Farah's work. Flying in for his first visit to Somalia in 'more than two decades', Jeebleh's visit to his mother's desecrated grave prompts him to both settle her outstanding accounts and attempt to order his own life. This is set against a backdrop of broader, national disorder, leading him to imagine that only carrion birds are adequately fed. After disembarking, Jeebleh attempts to justify his return to himself and those around him. Farah again plays with pronouns, exploring the interrogations endured by his protagonist at the hands of host patrons:

> 'I had returned to reemphasize my Somaliness – give a needed boost to my identity … I was fed up being asked by Americans whether I belonged to this or that clan … many assuming that I was a just-arrived refugee …It's irritating to be asked by people at the supermarket which clan I belong to … You see, we Somalis who live in America, we keep asking one another where we stand on the matter of our acquired new American identity. I've come because I want to know answers.' (*L*: 36)

As the narrative unfolds, answers to these complex questions remain typically open-ended. If this serves as a revision of the kind of existential labyrinths that have dominated Farah's fictional landscape from *Sweet and Sour Milk* to *Maps*, the comparative reader will benefit by staging a more nuanced textual conversation across *Secrets*, *Yesterday, Tomorrow* and *Links* respectively. In the former, stayee Kalaman expresses his weariness with returnee misrepresentations of the intricacies of the Somali lineage system. In the latter, it is the diasporic figure who expresses his concerns with the disorder of things in light of the transnational tensions that define him. These and associated issues are addressed by Tim Allen in *The Media of Conflict – War Reporting and Representations of Ethnic Violence* (Allen 1999: 31). In a foreshadowing of similar negotiations in *Knots*, Jeebleh seeks to patch the schism in his hyphenated identity by bearing firsthand witness, discomfiting as it invariably is, to conditions on the ground. Accordingly, Jeebleh echoes many of the most exasperated moments in Farah's diaspora study. Pronominal strains between 'I', 'we' and 'our' characterise passages such as the one above. If *Secrets* is played out between pre-Islamic myth and postmodern global village, the diasporic dynamics of *Links* only amplify these competing claims and loyalties.

In an early survey, Ewen anticipated that Somalia would gradually lose its status as the backdrop against which Farah's fiction was set (Ewen 1984: 209). That this prediction has been grounded by Somali-centric preoccupations corresponds both with Farah's intention to keep his country alive by writing about it as well as with the fictional mileage he has got from its turbulent national narrative. Ewen's thematic wager might, however, be renegotiated in light of the publication of *Links*. Farah's fictive maps have been redrawn in accordance with the opening up and subsequent dissolution of the nation in post-dictatorship and then post-interventionist contexts. As such, the newly globalised labyrinth of *Links*, preoccupied as it is with travel, media networks, communication and the surveillance that accompanies them all, mirrors the explosion of Somalia and its diaspora onto international canvases. With Zizek in mind, the substantial references to a politics of media, travel and conflict in *Links* exist in an intertwined triptych purposely designed to focus attention on issues of distance and disparity, transnational traffic, time and space. Considering *Links* in the post-Restore Hope and 9/11 contexts in which it was conceived, the reader is struck with this new focus. With the realignment of global power following the lifting of what Daniel Moynihan calls 'the fog of cold war', the Soviet insignia of *Variations* have been replaced with more globalised fetishes (Moynihan 1993: 9). On his return to Mogadiscio's once familiar, now disorientating streets, Jeebleh's own pronominal struggle is presented in temporal and spatial terms. Wandering, and wondering, on what he imagines to be the blood-soaked soil of his homeland, he recalls watching Somalia's dramas unfolding on CNN:

> 'But despite everything, and despite the prevailing obfuscation, I've come to assess the extent of my culpability as a Somali.' And he imagined seeing corpses buried in haste by his kinsmen, the palms of the victims waving as though in supplication. Similar images had come to him, several times, in the comfort of his own home, in New York, and on one occasion, in Central Park, he had been so disturbed that he had mistaken the stump of a tree for a man buried alive … This was soon after he had watched on television the corpse of an American Ranger being dragged through the dusty streets of Mogadiscio. These images had given him cold fevers for months. Now he felt the strange sensation of a many-pronged invasion, as if his nightmares were calling on him afresh. His throat smarted, as with an attack of flu coming on. (*L*: 32)

If besieged body metaphors are a little overwrought in *Maps* and *Secrets*, Farah extends his psychosomatic interests in *Links*. It is multiply revealing that Jeebleh's own anxieties back up and betray his body as a result of the virtual reality projected onto his television screen. The sanitised representation of distant events he both craves and fears (the Zizekian '"derealization" of horror') causes him to reflect on the schisms that define his political being. Jeebleh feels his flesh crawl, in a manner reminiscent of Ahmed's stranger danger, as he attempts to come to terms with his own detachment from events as well as the indeterminacies of his Somali-American identity. It is highly significant that the media replay leaves him stranded in a desert of the virtual real, leading him to confuse a tree trunk with a human corpse. Such emotional and bio-political blurrings emerge as symbolic counterparts to the very uncertain terrain which, at various levels, he now roams.

Farah unveils this spiralling chronology in revealing detail. Jeebleh stumbles in the newly disorientating wasteland of Central Park following his encounter with what Andrew Hoskins has called the 'media "flashframe"' that seared itself into the American collective consciousness during the Somali debacle (Hoskins 2004: 6). The critical, Zizekian point is that this haunting image of a mutilated U.S. Ranger captures the corporeal fracture between distant, seemingly postmodern militaristic engagement in a far-flung out there and an all-too-material corporeality brought painfully back home. As Michael Ignatieff maintains, '[if] the consensus in favor of humanitarian interventions can be shaken – as it was in Somalia – by the sight of a single American serviceman's body being dragged through the streets of

Mogadishu, then keeping those images off the screen becomes a central objective of the military art' (Ignatieff 2000: 191–192). The graphic representation of such flashframes captures the defining paradox of the situation of transnational audiences who are connected to one another through their very disconnection from events. As he bids the reader accompany Jeebleh on his problematic return journey, Farah invites us to consider those broader political questions, such as clinical precision killing, that have come to dominate contemporary discourse. By foregrounding Jeebleh's reactions to Operation Restore Hope, as viewed through his television and then his visceral reaction upon returning to Somalia, Farah getures towards trenchant debates concerning re-embodiment, rematerialisation and reterritorialisation. In critical interventions concerning what has become known as postmodern conflict, scholars and diplomats alike have pointed to strategic links between operational failures in Vietnam and Somalia. For U.S. envoy Richard Holbrooke, for instance, 'the scars from [the Somali disaster] would deeply affect our Bosnia policy. Combined with Vietnam, they had what might be called a "Vietmalia syndrome" in Washington' (Peterson 2001: 163). Building from this, I suggest *Links* can be provocatively read alongside an early J.M. Coetzee text, showing how and why it supplements those concerns with body politics that underpin Farah's oeuvre.

'The Vietmalia Syndrome': The Poetics of Postmodern Warfare

Eugene Dawn, a military scientist commissioned to research the fallout of the Vietnam War by the American administration, is the first-person narrator of Coetzee's 'The Vietnam Project'. After harming his son, he is consigned to a mental institution where he takes solace in assisting his therapists with their diagnosis:

> When it comes to my turn I point out that I hate war as deeply as the next man. I gave myself to the war on Vietnam only because I wanted to see it end ... I believe in life ... Nor do I want to see the children of America poisoned by guilt. Guilt is a black poison. I used to sit in the library in the old days feeling the black guilt chuckling through my veins. I was being taken over. I was not my own man. It was insupportable. Guilt was entering our homes through TV cables. We ate our meals in the glare of that beast's glass eye from the darkest corner. Good food was being dropped down our throats into puddles of corrosion. It was unnatural to bear such suffering. (Coetzee 1982: 48)

The most intriguing connection with *Links* is the manner in which the relationship between the militaristic aspects of postmodern warfare and its representation via the global media is foregrounded. Consider, for instance, Coetzee's passage in relation to the words of then White House Press secretary, Marlin Fitzwater. Commenting on the U.S. deployment to Somalia, Fitzwater recalled how 'we heard it from every corner, that something had to be done … the pressure was too great … TV tipped us over the top … I could not stand to eat my dinner watching TV at night. It made me sick' (Robinson 2002: 50). If Vietnam represented the decisive chapter in the U.S.'s post-war interventions, for both Dawn and Fitzwater, mediated representations are most disturbing of all, leading to physiognomic disruption, be it literal or figurative. Parallels between Dawn and Jeebleh are intriguing. Both experience what Sontag calls 'a tele-intimacy with death and destruction' (Sontag 2004: 18). Fast forward to present-day Iraq and Afghanistan, and debates concerning the intricacies of postmodern warfare and its mediatisation remain similarly charged.

In *Postmodern War*, Chris Gray interrogates notions of cynically/clinically detached conflict, citing Vietnam as a cataclysm. He links his experience with what Jameson calls the 'first terrible postmodernist war' to the original Gulf conflict, an event coterminous with American interventions in the Horn of Africa (Jameson 2001: 1 971):[4]

> A few years ago I visited an embalmed Titan missile silo in Green Valley, Arizona.
> It floats on giant springs for riding out a near-miss. I sat in one of the easy
> chairs. I reached for the key. I pushed the red button. A year later I watched TV
> in horrified fascination as my country technologically dismembered Iraq, killing
> hundreds of thousands. Since then there have been many wars … It haunts me.
> The sheer weight of war's materiality and the violence of the inscription on the
> body politic, as well as my own body, force me to seek an explanation for the
> strange danse macabre of our age, war. (Gray 1997: 7)

Gray's gestures towards a relationship between conflict, representation and a resistant attention to corporeal materiality work well alongside Zizek: '[w]e should note the structural homology between this new warfare-at-a-distance, where the "soldier" (a computer specialist) pushes buttons hundreds of miles away, and the decisions of managerial bodies which affect millions … in both cases, abstraction is inscribed into a very "real" situation' (Zizek 2002: 35–36). Viewed through this lens, *Links* can be seen as emerging from the conceptual interstices of conflict as abstraction and a very real, corporeally inscribed situation. Scott Peterson's *Me Against My Brother* can be used to extend these Zizekian parallels further. In it, a Somali fighter makes explicit reference to an insurgent Vietnamese precursor: 'looking up while a US reconnaissance plane passed overhead, he defined the American predicament: "We can fight like the Viet Cong," he said. "How can that airplane stay in the air without fuel and without money? But I can stay here forever"' (Peterson 2001: 111). Whilst referring to Mark Bowden's partisan account *Black Hawk Down* in his author's note, Farah has one of his fictional combatants deliver a critique of the 'infidel' invaders in strikingly similar terms to Peterson's informant: 'as fighters, there was a major flaw in their character … They thought less of us, and that was ultimately the cause of their downfall' (*L*: 268). When considered in light of the above, this idea of 'downfall' carries great significance. At one level, *Links* is concerned with how a seemingly postmodern conflict is brought down to an all-too-material level. The spectre of the mutilated U.S. soldier haunts Jeebleh and the global viewing public, providing abject evidence of the all-too-contested, corporeal terrain on which war is waged. Like Coetzee's Dawn, Farah's Jeebleh experiences a physiological shock following his encounter with the freeze-frame image. Through the figure of a diasporic protagonist attempting to negotiate these comparative divides, Farah obliges the reader to consider broader debates about engaging in as well as representing military conflict. As such, the body-politics motifs of earlier novels are galvanised anew, shifting in accordance with the turbulent geo-political narratives of our time.

Revisioning Black Hawk Down

> Whatever has a body can be smashed to smithereens … Like finance capitalism, political terrorism is also diffuse, ubiquitous, and largely invisible … Yet if it deploys avant-garde technologies, it is in order to strew the flesh of men and women on the streets ... In this combination of technology and body, the impalpable and the grossly carnal, global terrorism is quintessentially postmodern.
>
> (*Terry Eagleton – Holy Terror, 2005: 82–83*)

Like *Maps*, *Links* is postmodern, in something like Eagleton's sense, concerned as it is with the confusion of rigid boundaries determining personal/political behaviour and affiliations. When Ali reminisces to Jeebleh about 'times … when you knew who was bad and who was good. Such distinctions are now blurred. We are at best good badmen, or bad badmen' (*L*: 41–42), he is referring to the disorder of things in a post-dictatorship power vacuum. Farah uses Jeebleh to show how and why these disruptive pressures are driven inwards, creating a pronominal war zone between 'me' and 'we' generations:

> He thought of how it was characteristic of civil wars to produce a multiplicity of pronominal affiliations, of first-person singulars tucked away in the plural, of third-person plurals meant to separate one group from another. The confusion pointed to the weakness of the exclusive claims made by first-person plurals, as understood implicitly in the singled-out singular. (*L*: 42)

That this is one of Farah's most sustained considerations of pronominal politics cannot be divorced from either this national sense of dissolution or the personal impact of his documentary excursion. Such struggles are manifest as, in this globalised environment of compressed time and space, the politics of antagonistic affiliation assume trans-, if not post-, national urgency. This diasporic dimension is alluded to in the final segment of this long meditation.

Jeebleh regrounds his complex, divided feelings at the personal and familial levels that seem to hold out most promise, precarious though it often is, in Farah's fiction: 'he was sure that he did not love Somalia the way he used to love it many years before … Maybe love did not enter into one's relationship with one's country? … Can one continue to love a land one does not recognize anymore? He had never asked himself whether he loved America. He loved his wife and daughters, and through them, was engaged with America' (*L*: 42). Such rhetorical equivocations are once more appropriate for an author preoccupied with the notion that countries are working hypotheses. The text's central tension is alluded to in the above passage, with the loaded reference to a psychic-political engagement with the U.S. For all the attendant indeterminacies, tensions and flaws of *Links*, the challenge confronting its reader is comparable to that faced by protagonists throughout Farah's novels: to live with complications by seeking to cope with them in the best way possible. This corresponds with Alex de Waal's sense that had the architects of Operation Restore Hope considered the distinctive order of things in Somalia with greater sensitivity, American forces might have experienced a different outcome:

> the political situation was more complex than the label 'anarchy' implied, and the factional leaders, as well as being 'warlords', also possessed political constituencies. The advocacy narrative diverged from the realities in Somalia

> in important respects … the trajectory of Operation Restore Hope cannot be understood outside the context of how the crisis was originally represented, such that a universal principle of international (American) salvation triumphed over other ethical concerns and sociopolitical narratives … As with other complex civil wars intertwined with organized criminality, the Somali conflict should be analyzed as a system in which those who control the means of violence can pursue their interests, often in collusion with their supposed enemies. (De Waal 2010: 301)

De Waal's analysis offers an intriguing frame within which to read *Links*. With his Foucauldian call to explore power as a more complex system, he also suggests how and why discourse surrounding Operation Restore Hope should be defamiliarised. Farah's novel is a significant attempt to factor in some of these more complex and compelling narratives.

The standing of *Links* within Farah's oeuvre as a whole, therefore, might once more be judged in terms of how he negotiates personal and viscerally political spheres. NGO worker Seamus, for instance, is used to deliver the broadest critique of post-Cold War imperialism:[5]

> 'Everything that could've gone wrong for the Yanks had gone wrong because they saw everything in black and white, had no understanding of and no respect for other cultures … They were also let down by their intelligence services, arriving everywhere unprepared, untutored in the ways of the world; he brought up the collapse of the Soviet Union and the former Yugoslavia, Iraq's invasion of Kuwait, and the disintegration of several ramshackle states in different parts of the globe.' (*L*: 260–261)

Concerned with remapping coordinates of power from Russian betrayal during the Ogaden War to ever bloodier Western intervention, Farah also draws the reader's attention to some longer lines of continuity:

> It was from the ocean that all the major invasions of the Somali peninsula had come. The Arabs, and after them the Persians, and after the Persians the Portuguese, and after the Portuguese the French, the British, and the Italians, and later the Russians, and most recently the Americans … In any case, all these foreigners, well-meaning or not, came from the ocean. The invaders might be pilgrims bearing gifts, or boys dispatched to do 'God's work.' (*L*: 124)

Whilst the function of historical-consciousness bearer has passed from figures such as Deeriye and Nonno to the next generation, counter-hegemonic appeals to Abdulle Hassan's resistant legacy endure. In the historical present, neo-imperialistic invaders still seek to inscribe their dominance in the pages of books. Post-9/11, references to 'God's work' appear even more loaded (*L:* 123–124). As such, it becomes crucial to read Bush senior's statement in the context of events clustered around the first Gulf conflict. Seamus continues:

> 'The Americans came to show the world that they could make peace-on-demand in Somalia, in the same dramatic fashion as they had made war-on-demand in the Gulf. They came to showcase peace here as a counterpoint to their war effort elsewhere. Iraq and Somalia had one thing in common: both were made-for-TV shows ... the prime-time performance was their focus all along.' (*L:* 261)

A strikingly similar portrait of these events appears in Linda Polman's *We Did Nothing – The Untold Story of the Modern Battle for Peace* (Polman 2003: 28). In *Links*, Seamus comes from Northern Ireland, and so brings a convenient amount of conflict and resolution baggage to his non-governmental work in war-ravaged Somalia. Whilst questions may arise, his introduction does allow those interested in representations of struggles, defined in neo-colonial/neo-ethnic terms, to make some provocative links. Moynihan, for example, cites Horowitz as he reflects on those tangled webs of ethnic tension spun from Burundi to Belfast: '"connections among Biafra, Bangladesh, and Burundi, Beirut, Brussels, and Belfast were at first hesitantly made – isn't one 'tribal', one 'linguistic', another 'religious'? – but that is true no longer. Ethnicity has fought and bled and burned its way into public and scholarly consciousness"' (Moynihan 1993: 11). In an alternative study, cited by Gready amongst others, Allen Feldman adopts a Foucauldian approach to stress that contests over the body itself remain at the heart of these struggles: 'I have turned to the sociohistorical site occupied by the body in Northern Ireland in order to approach power from its point of effect and generation – agency' (Feldman 1991: 3). As such, this supplements a critical, bio-political point made in the preceding analysis of *Secrets*. The notion of clan and its attendant conflicts are not exclusive to the Horn of Africa. Whilst assigned different labels according to geo-political context, the paradigm is saturated in the hierarchical discourses and practices of biopower.

Such broader references also refocus attention on the diasporic dimensions of *Links*, elevating it beyond any simple exercise in America-bashing.

This is particularly significant given the post-9/11 context in which it was conceived. As the Persian Gulf excerpt demonstrates, Jeebleh's intellectual perspective offers the kind of spatially and temporally entangled version of events demanded by Alex de Waal. Once more, therefore, the use and abuse of power on the transnational stage itself comes to be seen in Foucauldian and relational terms. As I argue in the concluding chapter, it is no coincidence that Farah has opted to call the central novel of his latest trilogy *Knots*. Whilst the means of global hegemony may appear new, the dominant ends exist in an ominously intertwined web, from which neither European, American, Arab nor African power players can free themselves. This informs the paratextual features of *Links*. Whilst the author's note, invariably featuring corporeal metaphors, plays an increasingly important role in Farah's later fiction, the bibliographical survey in *Links* also illustrates his renewed attention to globalisation and its discontents. Whilst referring to the Bowden account that provided the template for Ridley Scott's Hollywood revisioning of the Black Hawk Down incident, it is equally significant that Farah pins his allegiance to Dante. In contrast to the intertextual eclecticism of previous works, all epigraphs in *Links* are taken from *The Inferno*. This detail suggests a more nuanced engagement with the journey motif as a form of entanglement itself. Having left America for dystopian and disorientating Mogadiscio, Jeebleh, who has a doctorate on Dante, finds himself reliant upon a Virgil-esque guide in the shadowy form of Af-Laawe. In this ninth novel, Farah appears to be playing with a Dante-esque conception of hell. As Peterson suggests, this has a peculiarly Somali resonance: 'defined by centuries of hard parched existence, in which the human presence was ever but the smallest point of life struggling in the midst of an inhospitable threatening desert, the Somali world order is delineated by a series of concentric rings, designed to ensure survival' (Peterson 2001: 118).[6]

Peterson refers to the ways in which certain tangled webs of political affiliation re-emerged following the implosion of authoritarian rule, relying on thoroughly Dantean imagery to make his point. In relation to Farah's novel, links between micro- and macrospheres are once again suggestive. In this instance, the association is between both the courses taken by and the fates of protagonist and polity. When Jeebleh suggests that a 'poet might have described Somalia as a ship caught in a great storm without the guiding hand of a wise captain' (*L*: 18), the reader is invited to apply the description to the wanderer himself. The nautical imagery echoes that in *Yesterday, Tomorrow* (*YT*: 54–55). In *Links*, it is Af-Laawe's (mis)guiding voice that disturbs

Jeebleh. He focuses on the opaque world of political and personal affiliations, into which his charge has stepped and in which he now finds himself lost:

> 'Some of us are of a "we" generation, others a "me" generation. You mix the two modes of being, and things become awkward, unmanageable. I belong to the me generation, whereas my clan elders belong to the we generation … while our European counterparts belong wholeheartedly to the me idea, you and I belong at one and the same time to the me and the we … You and I … are made up of competing ways of doing things.' (*L*: 139)

Reading Jeebleh's final departure from Somalia in this light, it is his very inability to deal with ontological contradictions, complexities and mixtures that results in unbearable pronominal confusion. Typically, Farah's attention to, rather than evasion of specific class privilege adds to the political dimensions of a text preoccupied with the blurrings and entanglements of globalisation. A more-than-parodic sense of the hegemonic reach of global culture charges an early scene, for instance, in which young militia members are depicted 'standing with their backs to each other, in imitation of what they must have seen in American movies' (*L*: 23). This corresponds with scholarship such as Douglas Kellner's *Media Cultures – Cultural Studies, Identity and Politics between the Modern and the Postmodern* (1995).[7] Elsewhere in *Links*, Jeebleh dwells on pan-African comparisons with civil wars in Rwanda and Liberia, before indulging in a speculative juxtaposition between American ghetto and Somali shantytown. He concludes that even the chaos of poverty has a certain order: windows in the former context would at least be boarded up (*L*: 70). A macabre Mogadiscio is envisaged where those Somali corpses strewn across streets exist in sombre simultaneity with action movies being beamed into crumbling buildings. The presentation and subsequent blurring of a series of apparent juxtapositions (representation/reality, machine/body, commodity/conflict, displacement/engagement, returnee/stayee, linear journey/entangled reality) frames the textual action. At the same time, it captures a number of *Links*' broader preoccupations.

As Derek Walcott, another of Farah's intertextual favourites, maintains '[the] antecedent of cinema is Dante' (Fumagalli 2001: 277). This gives a sense of what I consider to be the discursive backdrop of *Links*, preoccupied as it is with the conjuncture and/or collision of Dante and CNN. This informs both the novel's central obsession with the politics of pronouns and its all-too-pressing concerns with postmodern warfare. Invariably, these and associated tensions are represented by those who stayed and those who left:

'he thinks our reliance on blood kinship is backward and primitive. He is saying that he has money, that his family is safe and in America, that he belongs to the twenty-first century, while we belong to the thirteenth' (*L*: 30). As in *Secrets*, this once again obliges the reader to think about the political implications of postmodern blurring. Not only does this character go on to allude to the resistant role he played in the struggle against the Americans, from which Jeebleh was absent; he also couches his reflections in temporal as well as spatial terms. Reading *Links* post-9/11, this twenty-first and thirteenth century standoff is presented in strikingly similar terms to what has passed for informed comment on the War on Terror. It is crucial, therefore, that Farah highlights an obvious if pointed irony for the reader. With acknowledgement of operational and symbolic parallels between Vietnamese and Somali debacles, *Links* alludes to the fact that it was the very strategies of this 'thirteenth century' force that defeated the military might of the twenty-first century's only remaining superpower. In *Links*, the whole binary logic underpinning civilised and barbaric is thrown into confusion. As such, it is a novel very much of the contemporary moment as characterised by John Berger: 'I'm tempted to say that the world has never been more confused. Yet this would be untrue. The world has never had to face such global confusion' (Roy 2002: xxii). This is picked up by I.M. Lewis and James Mayall. In their contribution to *United Nations Interventionism: 1991–2004*, they offer the following assessment of Operation Restore Hope:

> The huge gap between traditional Somali methods of dealing with foreigners and US high-tech put most of the UN staff at a great disadvantage in their local dealings. This is perhaps most graphically illustrated by US helicoptors dropping leaflets on a population with a primarily oral tradition whose sensitivity to radio broadcasting is famous in Africa. (Lewis & Mayall 2007: 134)

If this corresponds with areas I have touched on throughout this study (productive tensions between the oral and the written, the collisions of the local and the global, the relationship between pre- and postmodernity amongst them), it is once again worth considering how and why it has a certain Foucauldian resonance. Just as Foucault provided archaeologies of prisons, asylums, clinics *et al.*, deciphering their traces in the historical present with a view to investigating contemporary discourses and disciplinary practices, so Farah uses fiction to compel us to consider a much more intertwined cluster of historical narratives. In light of the above, I consider *Links* as a text set in opposition to the epistemological quietism of much that passes for postmodern thought, pervasive as it is in the fields of cultural studies, global security and/or military science.

Contagion, Chaos and Confusion in *Links*

'American movies, English books – remember how they all end? ... The American or the Englishman gets on a plane and leaves. That's it. The camera leaves with him. He looks out of the window at Mombasa or Vietnam or Jakarta ... He's going home. So the war, to all purposes, is over. That's enough reality for the West. It's probably the history of the last two hundred years of Western political writing. Go home. Write a book. Hit the circuit.'

(Michael Ondaatje – Anil's Ghost, 2000: 285–286)

Whilst Jeebleh fleetingly reconnects with his homeland, Somalia's blood-and-bones irritations ultimately prove unbearable and he departs. There are, however, other reasons for his exit. He finds himself being dragged into what he sees as the bloody whirlpool of the national narrative. Typically, Seamus cautions him to resist: '[my] only advice is that if you won't quit it, you watch out and make sure you don't get sucked into the vortex' (*L*: 215). This spiral-ling imagery is significant. Whilst Peterson draws attention to the concentric structures, if not strictures, of Somali society and the apparent security that comes from being closest to its centre, here that nodal point is situated at the heart of a whirlpool. With appropriate allusions to Dante, Jeebleh con-ceives himself teetering on the edge of an abyss. Once more, the suggestion is that individual and collective body politics have become intertwined. At one significant point, Jeebleh risks becoming a version of the gangster who haunts his family's Americanised archetypes of this supposedly savage land. In a reworking of Loyaan's brush with brutality in *Sweet and Sour Milk*, it is the sadistic sensation of gun cradled in hand that, at one level, triggers his desire to return to what he now considers to be home. In Ondaatje's sense, it is 'enough reality': 'perhaps he wasn't as exempt from the contagion that was of a piece with civil wars as he had believed ... He knew he was capable of pulling the trigger if it came to that. His hand went to his shirt pocket, where he had his cash and his U.S. passport' (*L*: 69).

As argued throughout this section, *Links'* triptych of concerns covers travel, conflict and media. Yet it is the replacement of these broader issues with a more concrete, class-specific and corporeally imagined ensemble that shows how Farah, at his evocative best, negotiates between the personal and the political, the micrological and the macrological. The new trinity comprises wallet, passport and gun. Typically, Farah has his protagonist and, by extension, his readers think again about the precariousness of their moral fortresses, besieged as they are from without. As such, it is crucial that Farah relies upon 'contagion' here, a term he will use again in *Knots*. It carries a peculiar burden of significance, corresponding, as it does, with those preoccupations with borders, cartographic, corporeal and/or ethical that haunt this novel, as they do Farah's entire oeuvre. Put simply, the boundaries separating good and evil, American and Somali, returnee and stayee, moral citizen and violent killer are rather more porous than Jeebleh and, by extension, we as readers might like to imagine. The ambiguous area occupied by the central protagonist of *Links*, confusing, as it does, a series of rigid binaries and moral absolutes, corresponds with those moments of moral ambivalence that pepper earlier texts, such as *Sweet and Sour Milk* and *Sardines*. Transpose this to a macrological level, concerning the chaos induced by civil conflict, and the political implications are as stark as they were in the *Variations* cycle. Once again, we are confronted with a situation where power, and the propensity to abuse that power, is relational. With this in mind, it is multiply revealing that, when tasked with disposing of sadistic warlord Caloosha, Jeebleh employs others to do his dirty work. The cathartic killing done, he imagines passing through the departure gate as if it were a figurative cleansing. As I have argued throughout, this resonates with those issues of detachment, participation and engagement that inform every aspect of *Links*. Jeebleh's final exit, therefore, is only assured by his material position, metonymically captured by his wallet and even more valuable passport. With an all-too-ominous insight into the slipperiness of moral distinctions, as well as the threat that he may be consumed by the kind of contagion afflicting the collective body politic and conscience, it becomes imperative that he put some distance between himself and a place once called home.

Once again, Farah invokes the betraying body to represent his most pressing meditations:

> [Jeebleh] was having difficulty breathing, not because the smells were new to him – they weren't – but because they had become even more overpowering. People living in such vile conditions were bound to lose touch with their own humanity, he thought; you couldn't expect an iota of human kindness from a community coexisting daily with so much putrefaction. Maybe this was why people were so cruel to one another, why they showed little or no kindness to one another. (*L*: 200–201)

It is multiply revealing that the familiar politics of privilege are reconfigured at an embodied level here. Indeed, the idea of losing touch seems to encompass *Links'* underlying concerns with the physical and the metaphysical, the political and the symbolic. The comprador protagonist surveys the scene on the ground, only to find his body has left him exposed and vulnerable. As above, such fictive episodes appear intimately connected with Farah's own accounts, as well as those of his professional interviewees, in *Yesterday, Tomorrow*. This interpretation aside, however, Farah also reworks Deeriye-esque metaphors of moral asphyxiation to interrogate the profoundly un-Islamic activities he has elsewhere critiqued. The above incident refers to the brutal beating of a pregnant dog. When Jeebleh chases the culprits away so that he can attend to the wounded creature, he is viewed with incredulity for breaking taboos regarding human and animal conduct. As I have argued throughout this study, it has been one of Farah's primary objectives to disrupt such taboo politics, from his first novel *From a Crooked Rib*, through *Secrets* to *Links* and beyond. Ultimately, Jeebleh returns to America to resume his struggle with the phantoms of detached affiliation: 'after all, he was not prepared to dwell in pronominal confusion, which was where he had been headed. He had to find out which pronoun might bring his story to a profitable end' (*L*: 332). As with the supposedly definitive revelation in *Secrets* and Askar's interrogation in *Maps*, this end is no ending at all. Whilst Farah may appear to paper over these indeterminacies with the final plane ride home, he typically urges his reader to wrestle with these open-ended questions and areas of confusion.

As I have maintained, *Links* is informed by some of the most urgent geo-political debates of our time, shaped as they are by those Foucauldian concerns I have referred to here and elsewhere. In anticipation of my final chapter, I suggest *Links* asks supplementary questions of both individual and collective body politics, in a manner at once in keeping with and distinctive from the corporeal underpinnings of Farah's oeuvre. As with the shadowy figure of Ahmed-Wellie in *Variations*, Af-Laawe's status as impartial guide is compromised by the wider power games being played out on Mogadiscio streets. Shanta, the mother of kidnapped Raasta, delivers the following indictment:

'Terrible things are done to the bodies between the time they are collected in Af-Laawe's van and the time they are taken to the cemetery. A detour is made to a safe house, where surgeons on retainer are on twenty-four hour call. These surgeons remove the kidneys and hearts of the recently dead. Once these internal organs are tested and found to be in good working order, they are flown to hospitals in the Middle East, where they are sold and transplanted.' (*L*: 208–209)

Whilst this may seem mere sensationalism, I maintain it serves a more critical function. As Nancy Scheper-Hughes, amongst others, suggests, a truly transnational economy in the body-as-commodity exists along all-too-familiar trade routes. It is truly postmodern in its blurring of early modern and post-human/post-nation discourses: 'at one level … the commodification of the body is a new discourse linked … [to] the spread of global capitalism … But on another level [it] is continuous with earlier discourses on the desire, need and scarcity of human bodies and body parts for religious edification, healing, dissection, recreation and sports, and for medical experimentation and practice' (Scheper-Hughes 2002: 3–5). As such, debates clustered around the global phenomena of postmodern forms of human sacrifice intersect with similarly pressing concerns being probed in the name of post-national/post-human fallouts. These issues are all too pertinent within a Somali context: 'the flow of organs follows the modern routes of capital: from South to North, from Third World to First World, from poor to rich, from black to brown to white, and from female to male' (Scheper-Hughes 2005: 209). It is the forging of such links, over space and time, that remains vital, and it is once again significant that much of the most compelling work being produced in these fields continues to wrestle with Foucault's legacy.[8] When it comes to speculating on the possible directions Farah's work might take beyond the *Past Imperfect* trilogy, Zizek's comments on the spectre of bio-terrorism also demand our attention. Here, the body not only becomes a potential incubator for contagions that exist off the radar; it also threatens the porous borders of all seemingly sovereign states: 'a superpower bombing a desolate desert country and, at the same time, hostage to invisible bacteria – this, not the WTC explosions, is the first image of twenty-first-century warfare' (Zizek 2002: 37). In the analysis that follows, I consider some of the ways in which this bio-political exploration of disorder, at the level of individual bodies and that of a haemorrhaging body politic, is intensified in *Knots*.

References

Agamben, G. 1998. *Homo Sacer – Sovereign Power and Bare Life*. (D. Heller-Roazen, Trans.). California: Stanford University Press.

Ahmed, S., Castaneda, C., Fortier, A-M. & Sheller, M. (Eds). 2003. 'Introduction: Uprootings/Regroundings: Questions of Home and Migration'. In S. Ahmed, C. Castaneda, A-M Fortier & M. Sheller (Eds). *Uprootings/ Regroundings – Questions of Home and Migration*. Oxford: Berg.

Allen, T. 1999. 'Countering Myths of Ethnic Violence'. In T. Allen & J. Seaton (Eds). *The Media of Conflict – War Reporting and Representations of Ethnic Violence*. London: Zed Books.

Anzaldúa, G. 1999. *Borderlands/La Frontera – The New Mestiza*. (2nd ed.). San Francisco: Aunt Lute Books.

Bigo, D. 2006. 'Security, Exception, Ban and Surveillance'. In D. Lyon (Ed.). *Theorizing Surveillance: The Panopticon and Beyond*. Devon: Willan Publishing.

Binebine, M. 2003. *Welcome to Paradise*. (L. Norman, Trans.). London: Granta Books.

Butler, J. 2006. *Precarious Life – The Power of Mourning and Violence*. London: Verso.

Chow, R. 1993. *Writing Diaspora – Tactics of Intervention in Contemporary Cultural Studies*. Bloomington and Indianapolis: Indiana University Press.

Clifford, J. 1997. *Routes – Travel and Translation in the Late Twentieth Century*. Cambridge, Mass.: Harvard University Press.

Coetzee, J.M. 1982. *Dusklands*. London: Secker and Warburg.

Davidson, B. 1992. *The Black Man's Burden – Africa and the Curse of the Nation-State*. New York: Times Books.

De Waal, A. 2010. 'An Emancipatory Imperium?: Power and Principle in the Humanitarian International'. In D. Fassin & M. Pandolfi (Eds). *Contemporary States of Emergency: The Politics of Military and Humanitarian Interventions*. New York: Zone Books.

Eagleton, T. 2005. *Holy Terror*. Oxford: Oxford University Press.

Ewen, D.R. 1984. 'Nuruddin Farah'. In G.D. Killam (Ed.). *The Writing of East and Central Africa*. London: Heinemann.

Feldman, A. 1991. *Formations of Violence – The Narrative of the Body and Political Terror in Northern Ireland*. Chicago: University of Chicago Press.

Foucault, M. 2006. *Psychiatric Power: Lectures at the Collège de France, 1973–1974*. Lagrange, J. (Ed.). (A. Davidson, Trans.). Hampshire: Palgrave MacMillan.

Fumagalli, M.C. 2001. *The Flight of the Vernacular: Seamus Heaney, Derek Walcott and the Impress of Dante*. Amsterdam: Rodopi.

Graham, S. 2006. 'Surveillance, Urbanization, and the US "Revolution in Military Affairs"'. In D. Lyon (Ed.). *Theorizing Surveillance: The Panopticon and Beyond*. Devon: Willan Publishing.

Gray, C.H. 1997. *Postmodern War: The New Politics of Conflict*. London: Routledge.

Gregory, D. 2004. *The Colonial Present: Afghanistan, Palestine, Iraq*. Oxford: Blackwell.

Hashim, A.B. 1997. *The Fallen State – Dissonance, Dictatorship and Death in Somalia*. Maryland: University Press of America.

Hoskins, A. 2004. *Televising War – From Vietnam to Iraq*. London: Continuum International Publishing Group.

Ignatieff, M. 2000. *Virtual War – Kosovo and Beyond*. London: Chatto and Windus.

Jameson, F. 2001. 'Postmodernism and Consumer Society'. In V. Leitch (Ed.). *The Norton Anthology of Theory and Criticism*. New York: W.W. Norton and Company.

Kaplan, C. 1996. *Questions of Travel – Postmodern Discourses of Displacement*. Durham: Duke University Press.

Lewis, I.M. & Mayall, J. 2007. 'Somalia'. In M. Berdal & S. Economides (Eds). *United Nations Interventionism: 1991–2004*. Cambridge University Press, Cambridge.

Montag, W. 2006. 'The Immanence of Law in Power'. In A. Beaulieu & D. Gabbard (Eds). *Michel Foucault and Power Today – International Multidisciplinary Studies in the History of the Present*. Oxford: Lexington Books.

Moynihan, DP. 1993. *Pandaemonium – Ethnicity in International Politics*. Oxford: Oxford University Press.

Ohls, G.J. 2009. *Somalia … From the Sea*. Newport: Naval War College Press.

Ondaatje, M. 2000. *Anil's Ghost*. London: Picador.

Peterson, S. 2001. *Me Against My Brother – At War in Somalia, Sudan, and Rwanda*. New York: Routledge.

Polman, L. 2003. *We Did Nothing – The Untold Story of the Modern Battle for Peace.* (R. Bland, Trans.). London: Viking.

Robinson, P. 2002. *The CNN Effect – The Myth of News, Foreign Policy and Foreign Intervention.* London: Routledge.

Roy, A. 2002. *The Algebra of Infinite Justice.* London: Flamingo.

Sayad, A. 2004. *The Suffering of the Immigrant.* (D. Macey, Trans.). Cambridge: Polity Press.

Scheper-Hughes, N. 2002. 'Bodies for Sale – Whole or in Parts'. In N. Scheper-Hughes & L. Wacquant (Eds). *Commodifying Bodies.* London: Sage Publications.

Scheper-Hughes, N. 2005. 'The Global Traffic in Human Organs'. In M. Fraser & M. Greco (Eds). *The Body – A Reader.* London: Routledge.

Sontag, S. 2004. *Regarding the Pain of Others.* London: Penguin.

Sontag, S. 2007. *At the Same Time – Essays and Speeches.* London: Penguin.

Torpey, J. 2000. *The Invention of the Passport – Surveillance, Citizenship and the State.* Cambridge: Cambridge University Press.

Zizek, S. 2002. *Welcome to the Desert of the Real! Five Essays on September 11 and Related Dates.* London: Verso.

Endnotes

1   See Orwell, G. 1949. *Down and Out in Paris and London.* London: Secker and Warburg, where Orwell undertakes a journey through the subaltern strata. Food and rituals play a similarly crucial role and his travails/travels ultimately tell him as much about himself as his subjects.

2   See Krishnaswamy, R. 1995. 'Mythologies of Migrancy: Postcolonialism, Postmodernism and the Politics of (Dis)location.' *Ariel*, 26:1, pp. 125–146.

3   Lavie, S & Swedenburg, T. (Eds.). 1996. 'Introduction' to *Displacement, Diaspora, and Geographies of Identity.* London: Duke University Press, p. 17. See also Grewal, I. & Kaplan, C. (Eds.). 2002. *Scattered Hegemonies – Postmodernity and Transnational Feminist Practices.* Minneapolis: University of Minnesota Press.

4   For an effective juxtaposition of the first Gulf War and Operation Restore Hope, see Robinson, P. 2002. *The CNN Effect – The Myth of News, Foreign Policy and Foreign Intervention.* London: Routledge, p. 46.

5   See Somerville, K. 'Africa after the Cold War: Frozen Out or Frozen in Time'. In Fawcett, L. & Sayigh, Y. (Eds.). 1999. *The Third World beyond the Cold War: Continuity and Change.* Oxford: Oxford University Press, pp. 134–169.

6   Moynihan names *Pandaemonium* after Milton's conception of hell, p. 24. See Moynihan, DP. 1993. *Pandaemonium – Ethnicity in International Politics.* Oxford: Oxford University Press, 'Order in the Age of Chaos,' pp. 143–174. Typically, Moynihan depicts Somalia as an apocalyptic backwater, pp. 15–16.

7   See 'Media Culture, Politics and Ideology: From Reagan to Rambo'. In Kellner, D. 1995. *Media Cultures – Cultural Studies, Identity and Politics Between the Modern and the Postmodern.* London: Routledge, pp. 57–92. Also consider Wimmer, A. 'Rambo: American Adam, Anarchist and Archetypal American Frontier Hero'. In Walsh, J. & Aulich, J. (Eds.) 1989. *Vietnam Images: War and Representation.* London: MacMillan Press, pp. 184–195.

8   Wilkinson, S. 2003. *Bodies for Sale – Ethics and Exploitation in the Human Body Trade.* London: Routledge.

A Woman Apart: Entanglements of Power, Disintegration and Restoration in *Knots*

It was common enough for people to leave their doors open night and day when [Cambara] lived in Mogadiscio and you could take peace for granted. Later, with kickbacks and other forms of corruption creating overnight millionaires, the city became flooded with the unemployed, the poor, and the migrants from the starving hinterland, and fences went up faster than you could tally the changing death and birth statistics. Sometime later, residents upgraded the fences, putting broken glass, razor blades, and electric wire on top to deter robbers. Imagine: an open gate. What can it mean?

(Knots: 112–113)

[While] much current opinion, stretching from libertarian to Foucauldian, might minimize the importance of the state, there is plentiful evidence in popular fantasy of a nostalgia for authoritative, even authoritarian government ... in their *imaginaire*, a metaphysics of *disorder* – the hyperreal conviction, rooted in everyday experience, that society hovers on the brink of dissolution – comes to legitimize a physics of social order, to be accomplished through effective law enforcement.

(Jean Comaroff & John L. Comaroff – 'Criminal Obsessions, after Foucault: Postcoloniality, Policing and the Metaphysics of Disorder', 2006: 293–294)

I BEGAN WRITING *THE DISORDER OF THINGS* IN THE UNITED KINGDOM, BUT it really only came to life following my relocation to South Africa in 2010. If this book has considered how and why a discursive marriage between aspects of Foucauldian thought might enliven a reading of Farah's work, I, unlike Patricia Duncker's protagonist in *Hallucinating Foucault*, have been fortunate enough to encounter the subject of my academic interest. Having met Farah in Cape Town in 2011, I found myself reflecting on the ways in which *The Disorder of Things* might be re-energised by taking into account the process of adapting to life in a republic where certain Foucauldian concerns impact the everyday. Trying to come to terms with the disjuncture between life in a quiet English village and that within Johannesburg's gated communities, protected by twenty-four hour surveillance systems and security services, has certainly been educative. In this concluding analysis, I build on my personal reflections about life in a postcolonial African city to consider how and why *Knots* brings together many of the major preoccupations of Farah's oeuvre. It serves as a prelude to my brief consideration of *Crossbones*, a novel that both draws the *Past Imperfect* trilogy to a close whilst also offering tantalising clues as to where Farah's work might go next.

The epigraphs to this chapter resonate with my own experience of shifting away from a fairly abstract engagement with Foucault to one in which, in both local and global contexts, the practical implications of his thought inscribe themselves with greater visibility. The first citation problematises the archetypal, anarchic image of Mogadiscio by situating it within a much longer, more entangled genealogy, spanning colonial, postcolonial and neo-colonial epochs. Whilst the present instability is writ large in the form of increased security measures, Farah suggests that the city's fate cannot be comprehended outside historical processes. As such, his commitment to de-familiarising the hegemonic notion that Somalia has always been, and thus will always be, an incubator of disorder is as resolute in *Knots* as at any other point in his career. If this corresponds with the didactic strain that runs throughout Farah's writing, it is the Foucauldian inflection that appears most striking in this instance. He simultaneously renders Mogadiscio's changing face as well as inviting the reader to frame it within a South African context. References to the rate at which old orders, both individual and societal, are inverted are critical, once again exposing a world in flux. The spatial gesture is similarly crucial, highlighting how the post-Barre period, and its associated civil conflicts, were experienced differently in crumbling metropole or famine-stricken hinterland. Bio-political allusions to the collection of birth and death statistics, therefore, are as crucial in *Knots* as they are in *Gifts*. If the

Foucauldian maxim relating to the shift away from sovereign to bio-political power, centred around the notion of who is allowed to live and who must be made to die, carries peculiar burdens of significance in both conflict and famine contexts, the collection of data itself gestures towards those intertwined relations between discourse and normalisation referred to previously. Alongside this, Farah concludes with an exclusive, fortified image, pertinent to life in South Africa and beyond. As I argue below, preoccupations with the politics of space, surveillance and security are presented in alternative guises throughout *Knots*.

If the first epigraph aims to defamiliarise, the second is an all-too-familiar depiction of how negotiations of various orders/disorders impact upon a certain reality in the South Africa that Farah has, with due qualifications, called home since 1999. In *Law and Disorder in the Postcolony*, editors Jean and John Comaroff state their commitment to interrogating the dominant representations of 'the schizophrenic landscapes of many postcolonies' (Comaroff & Comaroff 2006: 20). Whilst schizophrenic tropes are mainstays for various commentators on Somalia, it is the Comaroffs' 'Metaphysics of Disorder' chapter that provides another potential connection between Farah and Foucault. In part, it focuses on the dialectical relationship between a seemingly insatiable appetite for popular culture, be it television series, films and/or music concerned with crime and criminality, and the fear, symbolised by each razor-wire fence and security-guarded compound, that South African society teeters on the brink. Whilst Farah writes out of this context about a homeland which, for many, has atrophied in hugely different ways, I consider how and why attending to that axiomatic relationship between fear and/as nostalgia, as foregrounded in the Comaroffs' chapter, can open *Knots* up in provocative ways. As such, whilst the differences between Somali and South African geo-political realities are vast, I am intrigued by how and why an entangled fascination with nostalgia/order and fear/disorder figures so prominently throughout the novel. As Farah has stated, the rules of the game, however repressive, were certainly clearer in the old days: '[t]he Siyad Barre dictatorship was easy to find as a theme, whereas it was very difficult nowadays, you couldn't actually tell' (Farah 2002: 43). Building on an argument presented earlier, therefore, I consider the ways in which this post-Barre confusion, compelling as it invariably is for the reader, is channelled by the author into his characters. To an extent arguably unparalleled in any Farah novel to date, *Knots* appears to yearn for a time when it was easier to distinguish between friend and foe and where, for all the manifest abuses of power as well as the inequities of gender, class and status, a clearer sense of order prevailed. As in *Links*, therefore, the decision to employ a returnee protagonist only amplifies these tensions, compelling the reader to think in alternative, oftentimes discomfiting ways about how old orders and new disorders are to be negotiated.

Since *From a Crooked Rib*, rigorous debates have taken place concerning the degree to which Farah's work shores up and/or destabilises oftentimes sensationalist archetypes of the African continent and Somalia in particular. As Jean and John Comaroff state in their introduction, exploring the processes by which these dominant discourses emerge and embed themselves in the popular imagination remains vital:

> Lawlessness and criminal violence have become integral to depictions of postcolonial societies, adding a brutal edge to older stereotypes of underdevelopment, abjection, and sectarian strife ... Mounting images – of Colombian druglords and Somali warlords, Caribbean pirates and Nigerian gangsters, Afghani poppies and Sierra Leonean blood diamonds – add up to a vision of global enterprise run amok: a Hobbesian nightmare of dissipated government, suspended law, and the routine resort to violence as a means of production ... Why has a preoccupation with legalities, and with the legal subject, come to be so salient a dimension of post-colonial dis/order and its mass-mediated representation? (Comaroff & Comaroff 2006: 6 & 21)

If the *Past Imperfect* trilogy focuses on the kind of Somali warlords referred to here, more nuanced engagements can only come about by taking account of the spirit of critical ambivalence in which it is written. From Koschin in *A Naked Needle* to Medina in *Sardines* to Askar in *Maps* and now Cambara in *Knots*: Farah's most memorable protagonists exasperate as much as they enthral the reader. This chapter explores the dialectical qualities of Cambara as a character who, in essence, distils the author's own divided feelings about the subject and subjects of his fiction. As in previous chapters, I seek to show how and why Farah exposes us to an imagined world defined by its very knottiness. It is a notion that applies to individual characters and their fraught relations with others as well as the fraying nation itself. It also captures the entangled nature of the political complicities and complexities these various characters attempt to negotiate. As such, a concept that has become increasingly central in the context of post-apartheid cultural studies within South Africa informs much of what follows.

In *Entanglement: Literary and Cultural Reflections on Post-Apartheid*, Sarah Nuttall defines entanglement as 'a condition of being twisted together or entwined, involved with; it speaks of intimacy gained, even if it was resisted, or ignored or uninvited. It is a term which may gesture towards the relationship or set of social relationships that is complicated, ensnaring, in a tangle, but which also implies a human foldedness' (Nuttall 2009: 1). My reading of *Knots* exists in the discursive shadow of such twists, tangles and foldedness. Similarly, to borrow from the novel itself, Farah's finest writing is 'winsome, circuitous, challenging, original' (*K*: 254). The interpretative challenge it poses is not so much one that calls upon the reader to unpick the knottedness of its thematic preoccupations and stylistic peculiarities. Rather, it is one that bids us speculate on how and why certain threads are woven together to produce a tangle of original thoughts that remain long after the text has been returned to the shelf. When thinking about the formal qualities of Farah's work, engaging with another of the terms above offers an interpretative entry point into *Knots*.

As with many Farah novels, *Knots* operates in a circuitous fashion, presenting a narrative that invariably loops back on itself. This invites the kind of analytical approach I took in relation to *Gifts*. With its at times overdetermined reliance on motifs of entanglement and entrapment, *Knots* amplifies those familiar Farah preoccupations with spatiality and power, ontologies of state and self, as well as individual body politics and the wider body politic. Returnee Cambara arrives in Somalia following the tragic death-by-drowning of her son Dalmar. Her purported mission is to reclaim her family's property from a Mogadiscian warlord. The association between reclaiming and reordering domestic space can be seen as a reconfiguration of Medina's various challenges in *Sardines*. Fittingly, it also corresponds with the theme of laying claim to a broader geo-political terrain, be it wresting Mogadiscio from the hands of armed youths or attempting to address some of the schisms that have wounded the national body politic. Farah therefore invites the reader to explore how and why Cambara's efforts to achieve some sort of post-traumatic stability intertwine with her negotiations of a space and place once called home.

Typically, Farah relies on motifs concerning journeys that are invariably confused. Again, these are metonymically captured in the figure of a labyrinth. The spectre of the maze haunts the structure of *Knots*, as illustrated in both its opening and closing sections. Another chronotope, allowing Farah to intensify his concerns with the dialectics of order/disorder as well as individual and collective spaces, is that of the theatre. He uses it to reflect on the processes by which the cultural superstructure invariably cracks when the economic, political and civil base is riddled with fault lines: '[t]he National

Theatre is in the hands of a warlord whose militiamen have used the stage and props, as well as the desks, doors, ceiling boards, and every piece of timber, as firewood. The roof has collapsed, and everything else ... all has been removed, vandalized, or sold off' (*K*: 8). This early privileging of the symbolically laden spaces of both labyrinth and theatre suggests their importance, in terms of charting the degree of disorientation and disrepair experienced at broader geo-political levels, will only intensify. As the novel evolves, Cambara takes it upon herself to defend the primacy of performance as a mode of both defiance and instruction. Harnessing the energies of those around her, including two youths who morph into surrogate sons as well as the activist Women's Network, she stages a performance, not in the theatre itself, but within her newly reclaimed, newly repaired house.

If the blurring of domestic and performance arenas corresponds with a critique of Cambara that simmers throughout the novel (to what extent, it seems to ask, is her life such a performance that her real identity and motivations are hard to fathom?), of greatest significance is the manner in which *Knots* closes. With the successful staging of her adaptation of a West African folktale, chosen for its resonance with Somalia's peculiar dynamics, and the prospect of a burgeoning love with Bile, the reader seems set for a *Gifts*-like, comparatively uplifting ending. Staying true to his defamiliarising impulses, however, Farah implies that the restoration of order, both personal and political, will take much longer and will be more labyrinthine than first anticipated:

> [Cambara] loses touch with everything that matters: She has no idea who or where she is anymore, what she is supposed to do where, and when she looks at the faces of the women and men sitting in the hall and watching her play, she finds she cannot name them. Nor can she put a name to her mother's or Raxma's faces, which look familiar but no more than that. (*K*: 418)

This corresponds with those intertwined themes and tropes of connection and disconnection, order and disorder, orientation and disorientation that haunt *Knots*. From its opening lines, the reader is presented with a protagonist who, like Jeebleh in *Links*, has lost touch, finding herself reliant on a series of guides to navigate the complexities of both urban and political spaces. In the early stages of the narrative, however, Cambara depends on those, invariably men, with vested interests in adding to rather than easing her various insecurities. As such, it is enabling to compare and contrast Cambara with the two other female protagonists who dominate the central instalments of both preceding trilogies: Medina in *Variations* and Duniya in *Blood in the*

Sun. Farah's decision to place three women at the heart of all his trilogies to date carries particular burdens of significance. I suggest, therefore, that Cambara can be read as an amalgam of Medina and Duniya. She is portrayed as a stoical, autonomous woman who, whilst initially reliant on Zaak, is driven to find a room of her own. Kiin's hotel provides temporary sanctuary before she reclaims the family property. As with Medina, however, Farah is careful to qualify his celebration of these women apart, implying that their unswerving natures often endanger themselves as well as those around them. If distinct from invariably patriarchal autocrats, whether dictators or *qaat*-chewing militiamen, these figures reveal themselves, through the microphysics of their actions and most typically within domestic spaces, as having the propensity to abuse power, often manipulating others to their own advantage. Once again, this corresponds with what I argue to be Farah's Foucauldian fascination with the interstices and negotiations of relational power.

Tying *Knots* in Farah's Oeuvre

Comparisons across the respective trilogies become even more provocative when considering how and why Farah offers variations on the theme of dependance in *Knots*. As discussed in relation to *Gifts*, this operates at both micro and macro levels. Whilst Cambara repeatedly expresses her disdain for the culturally compelled nature of her dependence on a series of men (something that is particularly debilitating given the responsibility Wardi, her recently estranged husband, has for the death of their son), Farah once again makes the essential point that the concept of reliance is, by its very nature, knotty. If Cambara determines and follows her own path at key points, she can only do so as a result of others' generosity: of spirit, pocket and, indeed, forbearance. *Knots* therefore reiterates the point that dependency is inherently dialectical; the conditions through which Cambara can enjoy the fruits of her autonomy, in a way denied to subaltern others in the novel, are guaranteed by those around her. As has been the case throughout Farah's fiction, therefore, the reader is called upon to judge his respective protagonists in terms of their capacity, or otherwise, to develop a more refined sense of self. This involves a process of acknowledging and ultimately accepting that, for good and ill, relationships, whether within families, other networks or in terms of the body politic itself, are, to borrow from Nuttall, defined by their 'human foldedness'. As the titles of his three most recent novels suggest (*Links*, *Knots* and *Crossbones*), Farah's preoccupation with such mutually implicating and imbricating relations has only intensified as his project has developed.

If this gestures towards some of the ways in which *Knots* might be read in relation to earlier Farah novels, it is also vital to consider how and why it exists in the discursive shadow of *Yesterday, Tomorrow*. The first, perhaps overdetermined connection between both journalistic and novelistic texts is Farah's decision to present Cambara as a former reporter, working for Canadian television and responsible for interviewing those Somalis suffering war-related trauma. Of arguably greater interest, however, are questions concerning the audience for and thus the consumption of these mass-mediated discourses, explored in terms of the complex, at times fraught relationship between returnee interviewer and stayee interviewee. As in *Yesterday, Tomorrow*, Farah's decision to foreground rather than evade these defining tensions demonstrates his commitment, whether as essayist, journalist, novelist or academic, to sketching a much-needed, more-nuanced portrait of certain aspects of Somali reality. The following, for instance, captures the undulating representation of time in *Knots*, where often uncanny memories disrupt both the linearity of narrative and the stability of self:

> Many point out how lucky she has been not to have experienced it firsthand. She has read enough about these men and women and met a sufficient number of these veterans to know that some of them tell the tales of their woes as though they were medals they wear to a gathering of fellow sufferers; they revel in excluding those, like her, who have not endured the physical and mental pain of strife. (*K*: 297–298)

Invert the gendered pronoun and this section could conceivably come from *Yesterday, Tomorrow*, with Cambara's lack of firsthand experience considered to be both blessing and curse. As for Farah at key moments in his diaspora study, Cambara is locked out of the pained memories and realities of those on the ground. This in turn gestures towards much broader debates within and beyond trauma studies and ethnography. Who has the right to write? What can be revealed and/or concealed, and by whom? (Luckhurst 2008: 5). The true impact of Cambara's hyphenated identity (Somali-Canadian) is suggested by the detail that her expert knowledge, about events, victims and perpetrators, is taken from other written accounts. From flesh-and-blood to paper-and-ink, the experiential chasm is vast. Similarly significant is the critique, again a feature of *Yesterday, Tomorrow*, of the monopolisation of pain by certain victims to the exclusion of others. Whilst leading to a failure in imaginative empathy, it also shows how trauma can be used to evade certain existential responsibilities.

In light of the above, perhaps the most striking aspect of such sections is the haunting obsession with and resultant commitment to posing a series of searching questions (of Cambara, the veterans and, by extension, the reader) defined as they are by their very knottiness. What underpins the *Past Imperfect* trilogy, therefore, building on foundations established by the *Blood in the Sun* series, is the extent to which those realities, for stayees and returnees alike, have been profoundly affected by a globalised, entangled reality. The citation that follows, for instance, offers a vignette framed by the bio-political realities of international migration. As such, the comparative reader can detect discursive echoes stretching back through *Yesterday, Tomorrow* and *Secrets* to *Maps*. If Askar's warring sense of self was somewhat appeased by the questionable gift of the identity card, a similar order of things pertains in relation to immigration and asylum:

> ... planeloads of Somalis were arriving illegally at major ports and airports everywhere in the world, including Toronto, nearly all of them declaring themselves as stateless, and no one was turning any one of them back, not from Canada, anyhow. But Arda did not want her nephew to board an aircraft from Nairobi, where he ended up fleeing after the fighting in Mogadiscio, like tens of thousands of other Somalis, as a refugee ... She felt protective toward him, solicitously making sure that he was not vulnerable to harassment at the hands of the Kenyan immigration authorities, who were given to extracting exorbitant corruption money from Somalis relocating to Europe or North America. (*K*: 21)

Such passages once more demonstrate the material, fleshy and uncompromising political commitments that have and continue to inform Farah's writing. In *Knots*, as in *Yesterday, Tomorrow* and *Links*, this manifests itself through an attendance to, rather than an airbrushing of, differential class politics. They characterise a world in which the fluidity of transnational capital exists alongside the evermore rigorous policing of bio-political borders.

Another instance where the presentation of class taxonomies hits home with peculiar force comes halfway through the novel. Cambara has left Zaak's fetid environs for the comfort of Kiin's hotel. As in *Yesterday, Tomorrow*, Farah's privileging of certain spaces invites the reader to consider how and why they are laden with much broader, figurative significance:

Cambara's display of marked, positive attitude toward Kiin's generosity is short lived when she starts to sorrow over the general state of decay in the compound opposite the hotels. The unsightly scene before her pulls her up for further grief. She stands directly behind the window, looking out and surveying a wasteland of heartbreaking ugliness: trees that have not grown to their natural height, scraps of wood and metal thrown any which way, children rifling in the arid waste all around, as though in search of something precious they can sell. The fact that she sees adult men squatting and defecating in full view of the road, which is about fifty meters to their back, troubles her no end. Then her wandering gaze dwells for a few moments on a man wielding an ax and turning a huge metal pipe of industrial size into fragments, chopping it into cartable portions. She reckons that men giving themselves in to insatiable greed employed similar destructive methods first to dismantle the national monuments and then to break them up into bits before selling them off dirt-cheap in one of the Gulf States.

It is when she turns away from the desolation outside and reenters the bathroom that she is impressed with how clean its floor is. She even forgets all about other disconsolate impressions for a minute, and her eyes shine forth with radiance. (*K*: 188)

If dialogue in *Knots* is intermittently clunky and/or its similes a little forced, the novel's significance, in terms of those concerns that have endured and deepened as Farah's oeuvre has evolved, is suggested by passages such as this. Most immediately, the reader is struck by the proximity, rather than the mere presence of two opposed spaces. In many ways, the coterminous relationship between the hotel's ordered, sanitised environment and the disorderly compound, housing suitably anonymous bare life, figuratively captures Farah's vision of Somalia in his latest novels. As discussed above, it again suggests a provocative comparison between protagonist and author as it recalls the strikingly similar juxtaposition with which *Yesterday, Tomorrow* closes. In the above passage, however, Farah recasts those dialectical connection/disconnection relationships that have fascinated him throughout his work. Whilst the 'unsightly' compound remains within Cambara's view, the respective bodies are separated by a chasm of difference. If she experiences a certain grief, this quickly gives way to revulsion at what lies before her. Crucially, therefore, Farah relies on the optical repository that has always served him so well. Cambara assumes an elevated position at once literal and figurative, her hotel suite serving as a panopticon from which she can observe, if not touch or smell, this abject spectacle. The inclusion of 'surveying', therefore, is key.

The scene is spectacular in its grotesque fecundity, allowing her 'wandering gaze' to switch from one diarama of disorder to another, secure in the knowledge that this 'desolation' will not infect her. It thus gestures towards one of the most pivotal preoccupations in *Knots*: the establishment and policing of various boundaries which, from a Foucauldian perspective, are inherently bio-political. In both metaphorical and experiential terms, there is little possibility of the dividing window between Cambara and these voiceless, faceless individuals being broken. As above, it places her hyphenated identity on trial. If Cambara's quest is figured in terms of her desire to negotiate the complexities of her Somali-Canadian self, the moments at which her profound disconnection from an alternative, often apocalyptic order of things are brought into focus assume added importance.

In the passage, it is the bathroom's cleanliness, metonymic of that which is ordered and thus opposite to what is living, breathing and defecating beyond her window, that is prized above all else. Because Cambara can turn away from this scene, she can cling to certain normative standards. In filtering this episode through her eyes, Farah portrays a protagonist at war, both within and against the terms of the world beyond. As Cambara is drawn in by this environment, she is simultaneously disgusted to the point of disconnection. Building on this, her reaction to this scene might therefore represent a suitably schizophrenic response to the bifurcating realities of civil war. This is something provocatively discussed by Mariella Pandolfi in her contribution to *Contemporary States of Emergency: The Politics of Military and Humanitarian Intervention*. Whilst she focuses on the post-Communist Balkans, I suggest that her Foucauldian critique can be usefully appropriated in relation to both a post-Barre and a post-Operation Restore Hope Somalia. 'In postconflict laboratories of biopolitics, where military and humanitarian intervention has paved the way to institution building ... the analytical utility of Foucault's concept of neoliberal governmentality can be clearly observed in all its fundamental ambiguity' (Pandolfi 2010: 165). Throughout *Knots*, Farah is concerned with exploring Somalia as just such a 'postconflict laboratory of biopolitics'. The decision to consign the subalterns beyond the hotel to silence is therefore critical, given the internecine backdrop against which the novel takes place. Viewed within both national and transnational contexts, they constitute those rendered mute during and after conflict. This is also suggestive when considering the rationale behind Farah's choice of protagonist. It is only through the eyes and experiences of returnee Cambara that certain normalising, multimedia discourses of apocalypse can be probed. Her own sense of what civil war Somalia might be is thus profoundly defamiliarised in the act of bearing witness. Scratch the surface of what appears to be absolute anarchy, Farah seems to suggest, and a certain order, however precarious, will reveal itself. This is illustrated in the following, where the local market plays host to an unlikely array of actors:

> This being the second time she has been to a civil war Mogadiscio market, she finds it curious that the money changers, the armed youths, the women running the vegetable stalls, and those selling bundles of *qaat* all mix freely, as if amicably. One may be lulled into believing that everything is normal. (*K*: 123)

Once more, Farah calls upon his readers to forge their own links between the most innocuous, quotidian occurrence and reflections pregnant with broader signification. Again and again, we are asked to consider discourses of visibility: what do we want and/or what are we allowed to see? The citation that follows, for instance, passes a *Gifts*-like, if somewhat clunky comment on the representational strategies of global media providers. Bemoaning a 'nothing-good-comes-out-of-Africa litany', Bile maintains:

> 'The news, *sui generis*, is about politicians and their doings ... isn't it? Not about the ordinary person in the Midwest in the United States; in a small village in Darfur, surviving the daily horrors; a fisherman in Sri Lanka; or a mother raising her children under difficult circumstances in Baghdad.'
>
> Cambara, confirming this and agreeing with the drift, adds that she knows that you can have a good day and a bad day in civil war Mogadiscio as you might in a small farming village anywhere. (*K*: 381)

When viewed alongside the earlier, Cambara-as-surveyor passage, several provocative connections emerge. The 'ordinary person', surviving their own version of hardship, is consigned to anonymity and silence once more. Whilst the concluding association between civil war Mogadiscio and any 'small farming village' jars at first, Farah uses Cambara to make a more searching point about the principles and practices of the global media, recalling his privileging of Duniya and Bosaaso's love story in *Gifts*. The arguably Foucauldian sense is that, if the narrative cannot be accommodated within hegemonic binary frameworks (good/bad, apocalyptic/acceptable), the microphysics of daily struggle and survival are sidelined. This corresponds with what, building on *Yesterday, Tomorrow*, is an increasingly prominent concern in Farah's latest novels: the political primacy of storytelling. Before turning to this in greater detail, I consider the significance of *Knots'* self-reflexive concern with contingent notions of normal and abnormal.

Normal and Abnormal Body Politics

At strategic points, Cambara weighs the true significance of Kiin's various acts of kindness in relation to the peculiarities of the Somali situation. That Kiin has done everything to assist her, despite their different clan origins, defamiliarises a hegemonic (dis)order of things: 'Cambara thinks that this goes to prove that not every Somali is obsessed with the idea of clan affiliation and that many people behave normally even if the conditions in which they operate are themselves abnormal' (*K*: 188). If Farah's tribute to the female capacity to enact alternative ways of being and seeing recalls *Yesterday, Tomorrow*, the frequency with which *Knots* refers to notions of, as well as discourses surrounding the normal and abnormal is striking. In disavowing the idea that they are value-neutral, Farah shows how and why their particular burdens of significance shift according to the contexts in which they are used. Kiin's rejection of absolutist clan paradigms, for instance, is a blessed normality when viewed against what, from a non-Somali perspective, may appear to be the abnormalities of the lineage system as well as the bloodier backdrop of civil disorder. Yet, seen from the perspective of those with vested interests in a patriarchal ordering of society, and all it entails, Kiin's decision is supremely transgressive. In a Foucauldian manner, readers are reminded that normal and abnormal are discursively produced, the result of complex ideological and other entanglements. In peeling away the layers of their apparent universality, their contingent epistemic and semiotic functions are exposed, as is the slipperiness of their practical applications. It is, therefore, no coincidence that many of Cambara's struggles to reconnect with a place once called home as well as to achieve some form of existential stability are presented in terms of her often tenuous conceptions of what is normal and abnormal. A comparison between two of the most significant men in her life, ex-husband Zaak and partner-in-waiting Bile, is revealing in this regard. Cambara's relationships with and perceptions of them buttress the novel.

Early on, Farah establishes those senses of alienation and disorientation that will define Cambara's struggle throughout *Knots*. That he aligns this with a jolt to her conceptual and, arguably, ethical coordinates is key: '[i]t is no easy matter to be in a city with which she is no longer familiar, what with the civil war still unfolding after more than a decade and her long absence from the metropolis ... Maybe it is the norm for the likes of Zaak to behave abnormally in atypical circumstances' (*K*: 41). Moments such as these reiterate *Knots'* intertwined concerns with the extent to which individual behaviour exists in relation to that of the collective order of things (and therefore, to some degree at least, remaining contingent upon it), whilst also suggesting the nature of Cambara's disconnection, both literally and figuratively. When all that once seemed solid threatens to melt into air, the text asks, who determines the criteria by which normal and abnormal are judged? This is brought home even more painfully later in the text where, following another fraught encounter with Zaak, Cambara is left in no doubt as to his view of her: 'when we Somalis are hemorrhaging one another, it is best that we sort out our differences without outside interference' (*K*: 158). This half sentence showcases many of the dominant tropes of Farah's work that I have explored above. Inevitably, collective pronouns are politically charged, determining who can, and cannot, be included in designations such as 'we Somalis'. Similarly, allusions to haemorrhaging draw from the corporeal repository Farah has relied upon throughout his work. Arguably, however, it is the provocative conflation of internal and external spaces of disorder that gives some indication of the imagistic continuity that underpins *Knots*. When framed in this way, the following citation is even more provocative:

> [Cambara] seems most herself when she thinks that she can adequately describe her current mental state as turbulent, because she is at a crossroads where anything may happen: She could lose almost every major gain she has made at one single go or just as easily hold on to what she has won and procure more. This is the arbitrary character of civil war: wanton in its injustice, casual in the randomness of its violence. No law protects you; everything is in disorder ... She is reflecting on the nature of her agitation and whether she can do something about the inopportunity of Bile's and her affections ... when she not only loses her way in the labyrinth of her conflicting emotions but also follows the wrong fork in the footway leading down. (*K*: 333)

'Turbulent', 'arbitrary', 'wanton', 'injustice', 'randomness', 'violence', 'disorder': all have and continue to litter discourses concerned with Somalia and its unravelling. Once more, however, Farah's reliance on the labyrinth image is crucial. Whilst Cambara convinces herself that her journey is a linear one, with clear achievable goals, the unsettling realities of her personal grief, set against the backdrop of the 'arbitrary character of civil war', condemns her to a maze holding little or no hope of a simple exit. In the aftermath of infrastructural, political and civil atrophy, a return to and reaffirmation of a set of personal, moral coordinates assumes particular importance. Farah again privileges the microphysics of struggle as the precursor to more systemic change.

A crucial element of *Knots*, therefore, reminiscent of *Sardines* and *Gifts*, is those gestures towards a certain internal development within Cambara. If her attempts to walk an ethical tightrope are under constant threat, they are emboldened by her realisation that alternative relationships and cooperative efforts can bring about a new order of being. 'Cambara will agree, if asked, that it is virtually impossible to live up to one's high ideals in these adverse conditions, but she prays that her effort will not falter or ultimately come to naught. For she plans to construct a counterlife dependant on a few individuals, namely Kiin, maybe Bile and Dajaal, whom she has cast in the likeness of reliable allies' (*K*: p.201). In this instance, disjunctures between idealism and pragmatism are acknowledged and accepted. Rather than leading to resignation and/or the abandonment of deeply held principles, however, it results in renewed appreciation of the ways in which, given the right circumstances, certain dependencies are more productive than parasitic. The familiar reliance on architectural motifs, therefore, remains significant. If orders, discourses and practices are constructed then, like houses, they can be deconstructed and reconstructed anew. In the remainder of this chapter, I consider the primacy of intertwined relationships between bodies, spaces and stories in *Knots*. For Farah, they symbolically anchor his sense that Somalia's national narrative can be reinvented. He explores how, under certain conditions, wounded bodies heal, domestic and other spaces in states of profound disrepair are re-ordered and restored, and stories, however traumatic, can and should be told. A closer consideration of the representation of Zaak and Bile's respective bodies is enabling in this regard.

Whilst the extent of, as well as the reasons behind Cambara and Zaak's fractious relationship only become apparent as the narrative builds, many of their early exchanges recall preoccupations that have haunted Farah's work from *Blood in the Sun* onwards. In the following, for instance, the body is once more figured as a text bearing the multiple inscriptions of pain:

> [Cambara] joined [Zaak] in the kitchenette and right away noticed the telltale disfigurements in body and soul, which she would see more of when she met other Somalis who had just come from Mogadiscio: trauma born of desolation. She could not put her finger on why she felt uncomfortable in his company, maybe because she sensed that he was transmitting to her a flow

of detrimental vibes, possibly without being aware of them. She held back and wouldn't get any closer to him, afraid that he might have transported some kind of contagion from the fighting that he had fled. (*K*: 26)

Assuming the role of reader, Cambara seeks to decipher the 'disfigurements' on and below the surface of the skin. Whilst touching on 'knotty' questions concerning empathy and its limitations, the sense that Zaak represents a broader community branded by a 'trauma born of desolation' is telling. Of arguably greater interest, however, is Farah's decision to shift focus away from the 'stayee' body to the reactions of his 'returnee' protagonist, as well as his reliance on 'contagion'. The figurative rendering of grief and pain as a form of infection, threatening to spill over increasingly susceptible borders, is markedly similar, both to *Yesterday, Tomorrow* and *Links*. As in the above Cambara-as-surveyor passage, ever more rigorous self-policing of certain dividing lines is needed if the fallout is to be contained. Whilst saturated in bio-political suggestiveness, Farah is more concerned with the processes by which these diseases incubate, spread and, ultimately, might be treated. When read in the shadow of his personal reflections in *Yesterday, Tomorrow*, such interventions also prompt the reader to reflect on complicity as a form of 'contagion'. Many of the struggles experienced by Farah's returnee protagonists throughout his *Past Imperfect* cycle hinge on the troubling sense that, whilst a home thousands of miles away separates them from the Somali (dis) order of things, it is this very disconnection that rubber-stamps their culpability in terms of the nation's fate and/or dissolution. If Zaak's diseases are trauma and desolation, perhaps it is an indication of Cambara's own struggles with an abiding sense of complicity, if not guilt, that she seeks to place such bulwarks between them. As Cambara reflects at a crucial point in *Knots*, 'in a civil war no one is innocent' (*K*: 200). The novel has a dogged fascination with a series of binary oppositions (stayee/returnee, guilty/innocent, retrograde/progressive, compound/hotel *et al.*), which exist in dialectical relation to one another. In significant ways, therefore, *Knots* sparks into life as a result of the reaction between Cambara's desire to maintain certain, clearly defined lines and her realisation that, by their very definition, they are knotted.

Accordingly, it is perhaps inevitable that Farah calls upon a motif that has dominated his fictional landscape: 'Cambara thinks that maybe [Zaak's] current physical and mental conditions are symptomatic of the country's collapse, a metaphor for it' (*K*: 76–77). From Ebla's infibulated body in *From a Crooked Rib*, through Deeriye's asthma attacks in *Close Sesame* and on to Askar's psychosomatic capitulations in *Maps*: the invariably wounded bodies of Farah's protagonists are invoked to pass comment on the wider body politic. *Knots* supplements this list, placing greater emphasis not just on the fact of deterioration, be it in terms of individual bodies or Mogadiscio's general disrepair, but also the processes by which it takes place and the rate at which it sets in. The correlative, of course, concerns how reinvention and eventual recovery might take place. Prior to Cambara's reflection that Zaak's faltering body and plummeting personal standards serve as a metonym for Somalia's disorder, the reader is given an insight into the nature and extent of her investment in individual and, perhaps ultimately, collective regeneration: '[Cambara] hoped that [Zaak] would be desperate for a sense of self-recovery in the same way she was trying to channel her grief into a positive outlook, which is what prompted her to come to Mogadiscio in the first place' (*K*: 40). If this foreshadows the sense that people become projects, problems and/or puppets for Cambara, it also calls for a differentiation between individual and collective mourning and melancholia.

From Mourning to Melancholia

Seen through the prism of *Yesterday, Tomorrow*, women, who in Farah's fiction consistently experience the most intense personal and political traumas, have deeper resources to draw upon and thus a greater capacity to endure, if not flourish, than men. Accordingly, this prevents them overstepping the border between mourning and the kind of paralysing melancholia to which Zaak has both been condemned and, the narrative suggests, to which he has condemned himself. If the protofeminist dimensions of *Knots* become more overt as the novel progresses, this early instance warrants more substantial engagement. Whilst we are invited to share a sense of revulsion at Zaak's deterioration as well as the living conditions now passing for normal, this is accompanied by an implicit invitation to turn the critical spotlight on Cambara. In effect, she has run from one trauma (her son's death) to confront a series of others, attempting in the process to negotiate profound disconnections. Seeking to find her own answers, Cambara faces the potentially unsettling realisation that her prescriptions might not be universally applicable. This, in turn, leads to a greater appreciation of the extent and complexity of the struggles of those around her. Fittingly, her incremental appreciation of the (dis)order of things hinges on an acknowledgement of normal and abnormal as contingent notions. In the Foucauldian sense discussed above, when grand narratives fail and universal prescriptions no longer hold, the roots of recovery embed themselves at local and individual levels. Zaak's impact, therefore, on both Cambara and reader alike, is deliberately discomfiting. Responding to Cambara's outrage at the need to pay armed youths to accompany them on a journey through Mogadiscio, Zaak states:

> Our lives are less precious than a handgun or the vehicle we are driving ... If we hire armed escort, it is because we do not want to die at the hand of other armed gangs more interested in the four-wheel-drive truck than they are in who we are, what our clan affiliations are. To those whose services we hire, pay salaries to, humor, bribe, we are worth more alive than dead, but to all armed thugs, we are worth more dead than alive. Tell me what is so perverse about this line of reasoning? (*K*: 86–87)

If, at first glance, Farah conjures dystopian archetypes to satisfy a predominantly Western readership, I argue that such interventions, plentiful as they are throughout *Knots*, demonstrate a commitment to peeling away layers of discursive mysticism. Here, robberies and murders are not motivated by clan-stoked blood lust incubated in the Somali heart of darkness. They spring from the same economic base upon which the global superstructures of today rest. It is crucial, therefore, that this point is reiterated later in the narrative:

> [Cambara] has known of other Somalis who have come out of Mogadiscio following the disintegration and whose moods are high one moment, full of jovial talk and amity, and then in the next instant, when you think that all is going well with their world, something goes out of sync, and all of a sudden they behave out of character ... An individual under so much civil war pressure is bound to succumb to the strain of madness that passes for clan politics, even though most Somalis tell you that what keeps the fire of the strife going is the economic base on which the civil war rests. (*K*: 298)

Alongside familiar references to disintegration and 'the strain of madness that passes for clan politics', the key observation comes from those on the ground. The 'strife' continues because it is in the vested, invariably economic interests of significant numbers of people that it does so. Again, the imagistic richness of motifs of entanglement in *Knots* bids the reader to connect the micrological and macrological pictures and, in these instances, enfold the local, Somali order of things into that of the global and transnational. Both passages speak of Farah's ideological commitment to problematising the distance separating 'us' from 'them'. The truly unsettling implication in the former, for instance, is that the apotheosis of this grab-at-all-costs system lies here, where the value of human bodies and lives has fallen below that of guns and vehicles. As Zaak suggests, in purely economic terms, 'we are worth more dead than alive' (*K*: 87). Moments such as these amplify the bio-political undertones of Farah's post-*Maps* fiction, asking the engaged reader to imagine much wider, and invariably more troubling, connections between seemingly alien worlds and their own. Zaak's final question, therefore, is designed to hit home with the same force felt by Cambara. In this situation, where a deathly, materialistic logic holds sway, what is the true irrationality behind this perceived disorder of things?

If Zaak performs a necessarily unsettling role, Bile provides a striking counterpoint. Whereas Zaak dominates *Knots'* opening sections, embodying everything Cambara seeks release from, Bile assumes greater significance towards the close of the narrative. If Zaak presents a melancholic conundrum for Cambara, the process by which Bile comes to terms with his mourning over the collective narrative leaves both protagonist and reader with the sense that recovery and reinvention might yet be possible. Before this can take place, however, Cambara confronts a figure in the throes of unravelling. Having lost control and self-respect, Bile's is a dysfunctional body operating in unsanitary surroundings. In relation to the above analysis, Farah's reliance on a word that recurs at strategic moments throughout *Knots* is key:

> Cambara decides she is bearing witness to the birth of a terrible ugliness, the start of a gradual falling apart of a giant man who is otherwise famous, from what she has heard, for his inner strength ... She thinks Bile is caving in, his nihilistic self-assessments confronting the evil manifestations of the darker side of the Somali character in these troubled times. Now silent, he gives the impression of being self-contained, a noble man refusing to share his internal torments with a woman barely known to him. Why pretend to be the willing host of this wretchedness? ... There are huge lacks in both of them, she decides. (*K*: 316)

Whilst we come to understand that this shared sense of lack provides the basis for Cambara and Bile's relationship, it is the reference to 'ugliness' that is most significant. When she looks from her hotel window onto the 'general state of decay in the compound', it strikes Cambara as 'a wasteland of heartbreaking ugliness' (*K*: 188). Beyond the repetition, with its suggestion that Bile's crumbling body (like Zaak's) holds up a corporeal mirror to the deteriorating nation, is the initially jarring idea of birthing ugliness. What the generative image allows, however, is a series of more searching reflections on the very process by which decay sets in. If, to pursue the metaphor, it is not the result of some ethereal conception, it suggests it can either develop into something or be terminated.

If Bile's condition is not preordained and/or terminal, the same holds true for the national narrative. Should this seem a little forced, the association between self-cleansing, self-restoring individual and collective bodies is only gestured towards here. Before the process can begin, an oftentimes painfully honest diagnosis must take place. Whilst Cambara can assist, it remains Bile's ultimate responsibility. Again, therefore, it is the nihilism of his self-assessment that invites critique. If references to the 'darker side of the Somali character' are designed to provoke, it is so that a rigorous self-evaluation will factor in context ('these troubled times'), with a view to moving beyond, rather than remaining entangled within and by it. Central to this is the process by which stories, however traumatic, are shared. It is therefore the suggestion that micrological and macrological bodies play 'willing' host to certain forms of 'wretchedness' that is as compelling as it is unsettling. Strikingly, therefore, the passage concludes by focusing on the impact these meditations have on Cambara. Whilst a marked lack of self-reflexivity defines many of her exchanges with Zaak in the text's fraught opening, her development as a protagonist might be seen in terms of how far the contagion of Bile's situation gets under her skin, literally and figuratively. If Cambara is characterised by her dogged defence of various borders early in *Knots*, a greater willingness to confront what she describes as Bile's 'bodily aberrations' might provide the catalyst for reimagining her relationship with the wider body politic (*K*: 320). In both pragmatic and symbolic senses, the following illustrates the extent to which the often discomfitingly material, messy, ugly reality of events has to be faced if anything like meaningful change is to take place: '[Bile's] stench is so pervasive that not only has it stuck to her body, escorting her everywhere, but it has also started to reside in her nostrils, as if permanently glued to the hair growing there' (*K*: 321). This resonates with Farah's own sense of the writer as diagnostician. Alongside references to 'wretchedness', the above also seems inspired by those Fanonian interventions that have proved enabling throughout this study. Farah's enduring preoccupation with the relationship between the physical and psychological impact of conflict-related trauma corresponds with the hauntingly prescient final chapters of *The Wretched of the Earth*. Once again, therefore, the following Fanonian statement is particularly apt: 'individual experience, because it is national and because it is a link in the chain of national existence, ceases to be individual, limited and shrunken and is enabled to open out into the truth of the nation and of the world' (Fanon 2001: 161).

If Bile's situation can be read in this Fanonian light, the connection between his warring sense of self and that of wider Somalia invites further exploration. *Knots* shuttles the reader between a series of different locations (most prominently Canada and the Horn of Africa). In addition, it is also built around a series of temporal negotiations, with Cambara comparing and contrasting, in the nostalgic spirit invoked by the Comaroffs, the order and harmony of previous times with the certain uncertainty of the present: '[Cambara] pays a return visit to her young days in Mogadiscio, when Somalis were at peace with their identities, happy with the shape of their world as it was then. The problem now is how to navigate the perilous paths, with mindless militiamen making everywhere unsafe; occupying other people's homes ...' (*K*: 143). Whilst this conveniently airbrushes the complexities of Somalia's colonial experience, the here and now of *Knots* is characterised by a disorder that manifests itself on the streets and through the appropriation of homes. Typically, the motif of thwarted navigation is invoked, suggesting a symbiotic relationship between the ontological struggles of individuals and collectives alike. Whilst far from innovative, it is Farah's decision to place such reflections alongside those concerning cleanliness that is most revealing in light of the above argument:

> [Cambara] has never imagined she will see the day when she will appreciate the very thing she has always taken for granted – a clean washroom, the toilet system functioning, the bathroom floor immaculate, towels on the rails. She is comforted at the thought of being in an impeccable one for the first time since her arrival, and she is flushed with joy. It goes to show that only a corrupt society tolerates living in such filth, especially the men who put up with the muck they have made, as if dirt makes itself, reproduces itself. No woman with the means to do something about it will endure so much grunge. Her mother always said that you are as clean as you make yourself. (*K*: 143)

Once more, the hotel provides a functional oasis from the dirty disorder beyond, making the entrenched structures and taxonomies of class all too visible. Likewise, Cambara once more adopts a panoptical position, looking down at the society from which she has been disconnected to pass judgements upon it. References to 'dirt' and 'grunge', therefore, are particularly significant, associated, as they are, with the waste products of a patriarchal system. As with contagion, however, dirt comes from somewhere; it can be cleaned and certain orders restored. If the reader questions the extent to which Cambara gets her hands dirty, be it in terms of restoring her own home or assisting the wider community, this section captures Farah's enduring concern with the potential for female autonomy and agency.

In a revealing aside towards the novel's close, with Cambara seemingly getting her house in order, she recalls a time when Somalia was not seen as schizophrenic. That her vision of peace and order depends on the entrenchment of class hierarchies is intriguing in some of the ways gestured towards by the Comaroffs above:

> Cambara remembers a long time ago when there was peace in this country, when everyone knew their place in it and their responsibility for maintaining it. In the order and nature of things, you heard these forms of address ['sir'], because Somali society was at peace with its collective conscience, comfortable in itself and proud of its station, perceived as being unique in Africa and the world at large. It's curious that she hasn't given much thought to any of this before now or hasn't associated these terms with an orderly way of living since moving into the hotel. Of course, it isn't that she has a wistful desire to return to a hierarchical, male-run taxonomy in which women occupied the lowest rung of the ladder. God forbid, no. It is just that she is nostalgic for a past in which your house was yours and you did not involve armed escorts to get it back or to get to it in the first place. (*K*: 361–362)

To fully appreciate this section, it should be read as an amplification of a similar memory, presented much earlier in the narrative: '[Cambara] remembers how – when she was young in Mogadiscio ... Somalis were then at peace with their own ideas about themselves and proud of their uniqueness as a nation' (*K*: 111–112). As I have maintained throughout, the knotty issue of Somali exceptionalism occupies a prominent place in Farah's fiction. *Knots*, however, pays greater attention to its conceptual ambivalence. Read together, both memories dramatise a tension, however implicit, between the ideal of Somali exceptionalism and rather more entangled realities. Farah thus uses Cambara to reiterate one of his most searching political questions: what distinguishes the proud, peaceful, positive connotations that accompany a sense of national and global uniqueness from the more discomfiting associations with hubris, isolationism and potentially abusive power? Typically, Farah is content to dramatise these tensions, initiating debate rather than offering easy prescriptions. It is, therefore, the symbiosis between Cambara's youthful sense of self and that of the peaceful, secure nation-space that is most intriguing. In the face of disorientating developments, in her life and homeland, in terms of what the Comaroffs call 'the metaphysics of disorder', wistful nostalgia has particular appeal. As in his treatment of Somali exceptionalism, however, Farah's engagement with the allure of nostalgia, here and elsewhere, is qualified. Before her memories go into saccharine overdrive, Cambara acknowledges the inequities of this old order. If she is to negotiate a way through the labyrinth of disorder, the most pressing of restorative tasks concerns her family property. This in turn provides a literal and figurative space in which the sovereignty of both Cambara's body and story can be reclaimed and reasserted.

The Possibilities, Poetics and Politics of (Re)Invention

Cambara flirts with all-consuming despair when the disrepair of domestic space presents itself as a stark metonym of the nation:

> [Cambara] calculates the enormity of the ruin all around her and at a guess assumes that it will require a great deal of funds to repair the damage done to the property. She reckons that to make it rentable or habitable, nothing short of destroying everything and rebuilding it from scratch will do. She sees iredeemable wreck everywhere she looks: the walls scaling in large segments; the wood in the ceiling decomposing; the toilet facing her with its door gaping open emitting rank evidence of misuse; the windows emptied of glass panes; the carpets rolled up and stood against the outside wall, in a corner. Cambara retches at the sight of so much callousness; she places her hand in front of her mouth, as if needing to vomit into it. (*K*: 115)

Given the body politics preoccupations of Farah's novels, it is hardly surprising that Cambara suffers such a visceral reaction to the disrepair surrounding her. Seen figuratively, these and other such passages correspond with those political debates that have defined the post-Barre order of things in Somalia. The peculiarly intense secession struggles of Puntland and Somaliland, for instance, can be traced back to both the complexities of colonial cartography as well as the disputed paradigm of the nation-state. Cambara's conundrum, therefore (whether to raze the house and start again), is analogous with those concerns that echo in the chambers of Somali domestic power as well as the United Nations, the World Bank and the Central Intelligence Agency. In suitably knotty ways, all have vested interests in the architecture of power that governs the Horn of Africa. Were it to be allowed to collapse completely, the consensus suggests, the ensuing decomposition would be much more devastating.

Farah's figurative suggestion is that, whilst traces of 'callousness' can be washed from the floors and painted over on the walls, they cannot be completely erased. The remnants of such 'irredeemable wreck' only become redeemable when their discomfiting visibility has been confronted. The sense is that, as it is with the house, so it is with the nation. Later in *Knots*, the reader is given some idea as to how far Cambara has come. Alongside an acknowledgement that her quest for a room of one's own can only be achieved with the help of others, there is also a sense that her manifest travails have necessarily led to more searchingly self-reflexive critiques: '[l]ying in the courtyard that is open to the sky, there are a couple of cisterns, both new, if a little dusty, and other bathroom and toilet wares waiting to be installed. In short, a world, to the construction of which she has contributed little, is now being reinvented, thanks to those charitable souls' (*K*: 301). When it comes to considering how *Knots* operates in terms of Farah's literary-critical vision as a whole, this foregrounding of reinvention is key. Whilst Cambara accepts that, in various ways and for various reasons, her disconnection has left her feeling that she has taken more than she has given back, the profound pessimism of the earlier passage has been replaced by a realisation that, with the genuine gifts of others, change on both individual and collective levels is possible.

For every depiction of a bullet-ridden Mogadiscio, in which anarchy reigns, there are contrapuntal moments where human agency, and its capacity for ingenuity and reinvention, is heralded. As argued above, it is the manner in which this balance is carefully maintained that suggests Farah's ongoing commitment to offering different narratives about one of the most mythologised, demonised spaces in the geo-political imaginary today. That the most significant, counter-hegemonic sentiments are expressed by women in *Knots* corresponds with a set of ideological tenets that have held firm since *From a Crooked Rib*. In the following, for instance, the reader is shown how and why an alternative order of things emerges from the voids created by infrastructural disorders:

> Kiin explains that given the absence of a central government and the lack of a functioning school system in the country, many middle-class families residing in the city have organized themselves into schooling neighborhoods, pooling their financial resources and running home-schooling facilities for their children, with manageably smaller classes. (*K*: 192)

In order to survive, stayees have had to improvise. By foregrounding the microphysics of their struggles to endure, Farah celebrates the agency of both individuals and cooperatives, in turn challenging preconceived notions about the enigma that is Somalia.

Immediately after this account, Kiin reflects on Cambara's disconnection from her homeland, whilst also offering trenchant meditations on the present state of the nation. It is an intervention which, in terms of its form and content, captures Farah's critically ambivalent treatment of the Somali national narrative. Drawing solace and sustenance from her work with the Women's Network, Kiin relies on familiar images of disintegration and fragmentation: '[r]ight now, Somali society is at its most disintegrated. There are so many fault lines that no two Somalis think alike, or are even likely to share a common concern for the nation's well-being. The men prefer starting wars to talking things over' (K: 193–194). This is the prelude to a typically gendered critique, with men identified as being too quick to reach for the gun and women being 'for peace at all costs'. Whilst somewhat reductive, it does reiterate a concern that has animated Farah from the outset: the differential causes and effects of the use and abuse of power within patriarchal society. It thus falls to Kiin to launch the most strident of critiques: '[i]t is times like these and stories like yours and the many tragedies of other women that are disheartening to listen to, the terrible things men have always done to women and gotten away with ... Men are a dead loss to us, and they father wars, our miseries' (K: 194). If Kiin seeks to associate the loss of Cambara's son as well as the ill-treatment she has suffered at the hands of men with the fate of the nation, it is a manoeuvre representative of what Farah has done throughout his career. If the 'many tragedies ... are disheartening to listen to', they are at least being told and heard. Hope for wider, systemic change is invested in the belief that such narratives will find a larger audience, above and beyond particular networks. As with Farah's journalistic study, therefore, the experiences of yesterday can only inform and potentially alter those of tomorrow if certain voices are amplified.

If the final part of this discussion has gestured towards those debates concerning subalternity, visibility and representation so central to postcolonial studies, it is fitting to close with a consideration of Jiijo. Carrying Gudcur's child, the warlord responsible for occupying Cambara's family property, Jiijo is a character whose narrative and life is framed by abuse, both physical and mental, and one who is without middle-class privilege. As bonds of trust slowly develop between her and Cambara, Jiijo slips the shackles of subaltern silence to make her painful story heard. Cambara's response to it is particularly striking:

> It is the way Jiijo talks, the way she lets go of her words with a baffling ease, telling as she does a tale, her own and the nation's. No doubt, the woman's life has been difficult. However, from the way she narrates her story, it is as though Jiijo is laying herself bare to Cambara, in the expansive attitude of one victim to another ... There is order too to Jiijo's narration of her story ... It occurs to Cambara that Jiijo, her countenance grim, is revelling in the telling of her tale; she is enthralling as she continues to improvise, letting go of a sentence at a time, an idea at a time. Captivated, she watches Jiijo reinvent herself right there and then. Cambara, through a combination of circumstances, senses that she has a glimpse of Jiijo's strong sense of personhood, striving hard and desisting from showing how startled she is when she hears Jiijo say, 'What help is there for our doomed nation?' (*K*: 179)

If the nation/narration association is a tired one by now, it is the dialectic between the pain and pleasure of telling that is most important. The improvisatory and thus liberating capacity to '[lay] herself bare' through storytelling emboldens Jiijo. The implication is that this may be one of the few elements of her life she can claim in such a way. As such, the inclusion of 'order' and 'reinvent', entangled as they are, suggests why this section is so central within the interpretative context of this analysis. Set against the experiential indeterminacy of a life defined by abuse and alienation, telling provides sanctuary for Jiijo, allowing her to shape a story, both for an audience and, most importantly, for herself. The role reversal from victim to agent/author as well as narrative's ordering power provides the inspiration, perhaps even the catalyst for self-refashioning.

If Farah invites us to transpose elements of Jiijo's gradual reinvention onto that of the Somali national narrative, he inserts some critical caveats. Describing the relationship between narrative and catharsis, *Knots'* third person narrator reminds us that '[t]alking about her miserable past and touching on the terrible things that had befallen her seem to provide ... a provisional easing of [Jiijo's] agonies' (*K*: 178). The key term, both in relation to Jiijo's own story and how it might be mapped on to that of the nation, is 'provisional'. Whilst Somalia will not be spared a 'doomed' future simply by telling different stories about itself, Farah implies that, when thinking about the entangled relationships between discourse, knowledge and power, the process of opening up spaces, individually and collectively, in which alternative narratives and visions can emerge offers one way to begin the essential project of 'thinking differently'. As Paul Veyne maintains in *Foucault: His Thought, His Character*, a commitment to the notion that 'different kinds of thinking are possible' underpinned the philosopher's life and legacy (Veyne 2010: 141). Similarly, for Farah, it seems that the process by which conceptions and discourses of self, nation and the international body politic are altered remain critical as we attempt to get to grips with the defining, knotty confusions of our time. These encompass everything from the global credit crunch to the spectre of international terrorism. In its own, distinctive ways, *Knots* suggests one of the few certainties in this age of profound uncertainty is that the ties that bind are only destined to become more entangled.

References

Comaroff, J. & Comaroff, J. 2006. 'Criminal Obsessions, after Foucault: Postcoloniality, Policing and the Metaphysics of Disorder'. In J. Comaroff & J. Comaroff (Eds). *Law and Disorder in the Postcolony*. The University of Chicago Press, Chicago.

Comaroff, J. & Comaroff, J. 2006. 'Law and Disorder in the Postcolony: An Introduction'. In J. Comaroff & J. Comaroff (Eds). *Law and Disorder in the Postcolony*. The University of Chicago Press, Chicago.

Fanon, F. 2001. *The Wretched of the Earth*. (C. Farrington, Trans.). London: Penguin Classics.

Farah, N. 2002. 'How Can we Talk of Democracy? An Interview with Nuruddin Farah by Patricia Alden and Louis Tremaine'. In D. Wright (Ed.). *Emerging Perspectives on Nuruddin Farah*. New Jersey: Africa World Press.

Luckhurst, R. 2008. *The Trauma Question*. London: Routledge.

Nuttall, S. 2009. *Entanglement: Literary and Cultural Reflections on Post-Apartheid*. Johannesburg: Wits University Press.

Pandolfi, M. 2010. 'The Permanent State of Emergency in the Balkans'. In D. Fassin & M. Pandolfi (Eds). *Contemporary States of Emergency: The Politics of Military and Humanitarian Interventions*. New York: Zone Books.

Veyne, P. 2010. *Foucault: His Thought, His Character*. (J. Lloyd, Trans.). Polity Press, Cambridge.

10

Pirates of the Apocalypse:
Where Next?

On a clear day, the beauty of [Mogadishu] is visible from various vantage points, its landscape breathtaking. Even so, I am aware of its unparalleled war-torn decrepitude: almost every structure is pockmarked by bullets, and many homes are on their sides, falling in on themselves.

From the roof of any tall building you can see the Bakara market, the epicentre of resistance during the recent Ethiopian occupation; its labyrinthine redoubts remain the operations center of the militant Islamist group Shabab. Down the hill are the partly destroyed turrets of the five-star Uruba Hotal, no longer open. Now you are within a stroll of Hamar Weyne and Shangani, two of the city's most ancient neighbourhoods, where there used to be markets for gold and tamarind in the days when Mogadishu boasted a cosmopolitan community unlike any other in this part of Africa.

So what do I see when I am in Mogadishu? I see the city of old, where I lived as a young man. Then I superimpose the city's peaceful past on the present crass realities, in which the city has become unrecognizable.

(Nuruddin Farah – 'The City in My Mind')

Foucault is fallible … A thinker, *a fortiori* Michel Foucault, is not there to tell you what to think. He is there to provoke you into thinking. Thinking which is both with and against the thinker. Reading a thinker like Foucault you therefore owe a responsibility to your own thought as well as to that of the thinker. Fallibility therefore allows you to derive something additional from

Foucault, something more than being confined to some canonisation of his thought. For one thing, it compels you to think a little more for yourself.

(Michael Dillon and Andrew W. Neal – Foucault on Politics, Security and War, 2008: 1)

IN 'THE CITY IN MY MIND', FARAH RELIES ON MANY OF THE TROPES THAT characterise his writing, both fictional and non-fictional, and that I have sought to explore throughout this book. The first epigraph, for instance, draws on that optical repository that features so heavily throughout his novels. Mogadiscio's beauty reveals itself from many angles, becoming available to those who are willing and able to see it. Perhaps most striking, however, is Farah's sense that the city he once called home is a compelling, complex palimpsest. His roving eye surveys a scene in which its ornate architecture bears the traces of contemporary, invariably violent disorder. From an elevated position, the skilled reader is invited to decipher Mogadiscio as a suitably labyrinthine metonym for Somalia in the twenty-first century. The peculiarity of its historical present is captured in the juxtaposition of bullet-ridden hotels and ancient marketplaces. In keeping with what I have argued to be those defamiliarising imperatives that run throughout Farah's work, it is crucial that these historically saturated sites are celebrated for their cosmopolitanism, a concept that has become something of a buzzword in contemporary postcolonial studies. In effect, 'The City in my Mind' captures what Farah has been doing throughout his more than forty-year career: bidding us to go beyond a series of hegemonic, stultifying images of the Somalia we think we know by presenting much more 'unrecognizable' narratives and voices. It therefore works in the interrogative spirit of Foucault, as identified by Dillon and Neal in the second epigraph.

As I write, so too does Nuruddin Farah. With their unerring tendency to produce new material, living writers can provide real headaches for the critical commentator. As this book was being prepared for publication, Farah released *Crossbones* in the United States and the United Kingdom. Appearing in the same month that marked the tenth anniversary of the 9/11 attacks, the novel completes the *Past Imperfect* trilogy. Offering initial thoughts on *Crossbones* allows me to suggest how and why I have attempted to superimpose a Foucauldian framework onto Farah's oeuvre as well as speculate about the directions future work might take. As its title suggests, *Crossbones* is centrally concerned with the practice by which Somalia is invariably identified in the global media today: piracy. As Farah's author's note demonstrates, a good deal of contemporary research has gone into the novel. More than just an attempt to lend his latest fictional project the aura of topicality, these supplementary investigations provide *Crossbones* with a solid discursive backbone. In addition, these notes also correspond with one of the central features of Farah's most recent writing. From *Links* through *Knots* and now on to *Crossbones*, a greater awareness of and interest in the mediatisation of Somalia in relation to the global (dis)order of things informs the *Past Imperfect* trilogy. In an age where the discursive imaginary around piracy encompasses everything from Disney's 'Pirates of the Caribbean' franchise to CNN reports on oceanic African bandits, Farah once again employs his fiction for the kind of Foucauldian, challenging purposes outlined above. What emerges is a portrait of a suitably entangled set of practices that rely upon, as they also serve, a host of intertwined parties and their strategic interests. Farah is therefore at pains to situate piracy itself as well as the discourse that has grown up around it within a much more expansive genealogy. The result, as with similar such instances throughout *Links* and *Knots*, is that piracy comes to be viewed as an enterprise, determined by an economic base, that bridges certain temporal and epistemological chasms between epochs ancient, modern, and, dare we say it, postmodern.

At the risk of making Foucault walk a discursive gangplank, I maintain that many of the debates that have arisen around the vexed question of piracy are centrally concerned with those issues of space, discipline, power, legality and transgression that have featured so prominently throughout this study. One of the most essential, if complex issues probed by *Crossbones*, therefore, pertains to sovereignty and the sea. The cartographer's ability to delineate and apportion territory is undermined by the literal as well as the figurative fluidity of the realities they are left to contend with. So too, questions of jurisdiction, surveillance and punishment are complicated on the high seas. One implication in *Crossbones* is that the very practice of piracy, disordering as it so profoundly does the discourse and praxis of landed norms, can be seen as a variation of the nomadic and/or diasporic realities that have and continue to define the lived experience for significant numbers of Somalis.

In terms of the directions that Farah's work might take in future, I suggest it is safe to assume that he will continue to anchor his narratives at the level, however precarious, of his native Somalia and its expanding diaspora. The prospect of a follow-up to *Yesterday, Tomorrow*, for instance, is an intriguing one. It would once more allow Farah to explore and pass comment on various national and transnational (dis)orders, considering the extent to which the policing, bio-political or otherwise, of global borders has intensified in the wake of the events of 2001. As suggested above, there is no shortage of Foucauldian-inspired material to draw from in relation to these pervasive and omnipertinent issues. A collection such as *Discipline and Punishment in Global Politics: Illusions of Control* (2008) is an exemplary case in point. Similarly, at the time of writing, the official opening of Somalia's newly refurbished National Theatre in Mogadiscio was marred by an al-Shabab attack that claimed the lives of eight people. Whilst I have not touched on Farah's work as a playwright in this book, it is important to acknowledge the pivotal role played by the theatre in his life. It is entirely conceivable that he might use these dispiriting events as the catalyst for further writing on a homeland that continues to haunt him. Whichever direction this takes him, be it as essayist, dramatist, cultural commentator, journalist or novelist, I believe that the ethical and political values that have defined Farah's oeuvre up to this point will continue to inform his literary vision in the interests of provoking his readers to think for themselves. I can only imagine that Foucault would have approved.

From the claustrophobic, carceral society of the *Variations* series, through the conflict, famine and global trafficking of the *Blood in the Sun* cycle and on to the Black Hawk Down, civil war dystopia and piracy preoccupations of the *Past Imperfect* trilogy, Farah's work has mapped onto Somalia's national narrative in always committed, invariably provocative ways. It has been my aim in this book to suggest how some of the most enervating aspects of Michel Foucault's thought and legacy might be creatively employed to enliven a more sustained, comparative engagement with Farah's oeuvre. To return to a Foucauldian motif referred to in the Introduction, I continue to be inspired by the spirit of his methodological toolbox:

> A book is made to serve ends not defined by the one who wrote it … All my books … are, if you like, little tool boxes. If people want to open them, use a particular sentence, idea or analysis like a screwdriver or wrench in order to short-circuit, disqualify or break up systems of power, including the very ones from which my books have issued… well, all the better! (Foucault 1996: 149).

Rather than take an interpretative hammer to Farah's writing, I hope to have explored the possibilities of the screwdriver approach, as set out by Foucault here. It has allowed me to open up Farah's work, suggesting the benefits of looking at some of its inner workings in a defamiliarising light.

References

Dillon, M. & Neal, A.W. 2008. 'Introduction'. In M. Dillon & A.W. Neal (Eds). *Foucault on Politics, Security and War*. Basingstoke, Palgrave Macmillan.

Farah, N. & Pericoli, M. 2011. 'The City in my Mind'. Published in *The Sunday Review, Opinion Pages* in *The New York Times*, 7 July.

Foucault, M. 1996. 'From Torture to Cellblock'. In S. Lotringer (Ed.). (L Hochroth & J. Johnston, Trans.) *Foucault Live – Michel Foucault, Collected Interviews, 1961–1984*. New York: Semiotext(e).

Index

Printed and bound by CPI Group (UK) Ltd, Croydon, CR0 4YY

10/06/2025

14686734-0001